Commodity Futures as a Business Management Tool

Commodity Futures
as a Business Management Tool

HENRY B. ARTHUR
George M. Moffett Professor of Agriculture and Business,
Emeritus

DIVISION OF RESEARCH
GRADUATE SCHOOL OF BUSINESS ADMINISTRATION
HARVARD UNIVERSITY
Boston · 1971

Library of Congress Catalog Card No. 71–162634
ISBN 0–87584–092–2

Printed in the United States of America

Preface

THIS BOOK is another in the series coming out of the Program in Agriculture and Business at the Harvard Business School. The broad purposes of the Program have been stated as being to "conduct studies of agricultural and industrial relationships through analyses of technical, economic, and human factors which govern these relationships, particularly the decision-making points, and stimulate sound action in the light of these studies so that industry and agriculture may contribute most efficiently toward meeting their responsibilities in our growing economy." The first book, *A Concept of Agribusiness* by John H. Davis and Ray A. Goldberg, was published in 1957, followed by several reports on individual sectors of agribusiness. Subsequently, Professor Goldberg's *Agribusiness Coordination — A Systems Approach to the Wheat, Soybean, and Florida Orange Economies* appeared in 1968 and my book, *Tropical Agribusiness Structures and Adjustments — Bananas,* written with the assistance of James P. Houck and George L. Beckford, was published in the same year.

It is impossible to express adequately my obligations to the many firms, commodity exchanges, government agencies, and individuals whose contributions made the present study possible. However, extremely helpful insights as well as comments and friendly criticisms were provided by such people as Paul H. Cootner, Roger W. Gray, Allen B. Paul, C. S. Rowley, Jr., and Holbrook Working. Other individuals with broad experience in actual trading operations have been most generous and patient in communicating some of the mysteries and understandings of futures markets from the practitioner's viewpoint. These include Dr. Ted Rice of Continental

Grain Company and Johann J. Scheu of The Nestle Company, Inc., as well as Julius Hendel, former Senior Vice President of Cargill, Inc., Oscar B. Jesness, former Head of the Department of Economics, University of Minnesota, and Allan Q. Moore, former Vice President of The Pillsbury Company. The latter three are presently associated with Experience, Inc., consultants to management, Minneapolis.

Even more direct assistance was rendered by my associates at the Harvard Business School. Ray A. Goldberg, George M. Moffett Professor of Agriculture and Business, provided continuing comments and innumerable discussions as the study was progressing. Rowen C. Vogel served as research fellow and was responsible for a major part in the field work and interviews with business firms, as well as participating in the planning and development of major portions of the analysis. Daniel C. Goodman was my research assistant during the later stages of analysis and manuscript development, particularly as related to the cocoa and frozen concentrated orange juice discussions in Chapters VIII and IX. A diligent inquiry by Vernon A. Bacher, then an MBA student, and Mrs. Glennis A. Bacher, CPA, into the tax regulations, decisions, and interpretations discussed in Chapter II provided valuable assistance in exploring this complicated subject.

Anne M. Quintal added much more than secretarial services, holding together the records and programs, notes and data, as well as patiently incorporating the various changes and revisions as the manuscript progressed. My profound thanks also go to Ruth Norton, Editor and Executive Secretary of the Harvard Business School's Division of Research, who designed, edited, and carried the book from manuscript to publication, and to my wife, Charlotte B. Arthur, whose constant encouragement and forbearance were topped off by her devotion in offering to prepare the index.

Financial support was provided by an allocation of funds from the generous gifts of The Associates of the Harvard Business School. Much of the background for the present study was made possible by the endowment from the George M. Moffett Professorship in Agriculture and Business and from contributions from the Whitehall Foundation, whose continuing support for our agribusiness program is greatly appreciated.

I must affirm that all of the positions taken and views expressed in this report are my own responsibility and that even though some conclusions will not be concurred in by all of those whose names are mentioned above, their views were taken into account and my indebtedness to all of them cannot be adequately expressed.

HENRY B. ARTHUR

Soldiers Field
Boston, Massachusetts
June 1971

Table of Contents

List of Exhibits

ABSTRACT

Commodity Futures as a Business Management Tool

This study focuses on an area of business management that has been neglected or has received only superficial treatment by most analysts and students of economics and business. Where do commodity futures fit into the business management picture? How does the business executive view them as a contributor to his primary business objectives? How does his firm organize the responsibilities and authority for carrying out decisions involving commodity futures? What profit centers within the firm are affected by futures trading activity? How valuable are futures contracts as compared with alternative tools for managing price risks? These are some of the business management questions to which this study is addressed.

The author, Henry B. Arthur, is George M. Moffett Professor of Agriculture and Business, Emeritus, at the Harvard Business School.

At the outset of this study the author undertook to find out the nature of the uses which business firms make of commodity futures in connection with their commercial operations, the types of policies that are employed, and the variations in accounting and procedural controls that exist. It soon became clear that it would be necessary to examine not just "futures" and "hedging" but the entire field of price risks and the impact of commodity price changes upon the business involved. There are many questions as to the degree to which price risks relating to the time and nature of business commitments can and should be transferred from one party to another. The commodity futures contract, of course, is used by many businesses to segregate one aspect (price changes) of the risks involved in their operations and to shift a major portion of that risk to others through a sale or a purchase on a futures market.

In the course of the research it was also demonstrated that commodity futures serve many other purposes than simply the transference of a kind of price risk. This made it necessary to broaden the scope of the study and to re-examine both the basic nature of business functions involved and the legal and economic characteristics of commodity futures contracts as a useful instrument.

The study consists of four parts, the first two of which are conceptual and analytical in nature; the third reviews the actual applications and practices in five important agribusiness industries; and the fourth undertakes to summarize the findings and to suggest important policy applications.

The groundwork for later analysis is laid in the first chapter which discusses the nature of the so-called "net position" which involves both physical ownership of inventories and commitments of various kinds. The defining of a total exposure to the impacts of changing prices is not a simple matter. However, the businessman seeking to use commodity futures for hedging purposes must have a reasonably precise estimate if he is to attain successful results. A number of definitions and guidelines are therefore spelled out for the purpose of making it easier to set the commodity futures contract into the scheme of business operations with a better appraisal of the risk-management function.

The second step in conceptual analysis is a careful examination of the nature of commodity futures contracts and the markets in which they are traded. An examination is made of the basic nature of the contract and of the kinds of income or loss that are generated in commodity futures markets, as well as the accounting questions involved. Moreover, tax implications lead to a critical discussion of the present tax regulations and decisions as applied to futures and hedging.

The author introduces a so-called "theory of analogous parts." Given the clear-cut set of specifications which are spelled out in the commodity futures contract, it is proposed that a counterpart of the futures commitment be segregated out by defining one portion of the corresponding commercial commodity commitment as that which is precisely covered in the futures transaction. It is then proposed to describe in detail the residual factors which represent a retained exposure so far as changing prices, rates, yields, and so forth are involved. This makes it possible to distinguish sharply between the risks that are "matched" or "hedged" and those that are still retained, the residuals.

The conceptual analysis proceeds to relate the basic principles spelled out in the first two chapters to the actual operating functions and control problems of the individual firm. This discussion is designed to assist the manager, who must appraise the nature of his price-risk exposure, to pick out the significant variables that affect this exposure, and to weigh the alternative courses of action available to him. Commodity futures are not the only business management tool available to him; other devices may be more appropriate than hedging in the futures market. At the same time there are many other uses of commodity futures than the simple matching or hedging process which has long been regarded as the only thing a conservative businessman would consider in using commodity futures as a business tool.

Specific uses of commodity futures in five major industrial complexes are discussed in detail in Part Three of the study. Separate chapters are devoted to the wheat and flour milling complex, the soybean complex, the cattle and beef industries, cocoa, and frozen concentrated orange juice. The nature of the problems of price-risk management which arise in each of these industries is examined, and the appropriate uses of commodity futures at various stages are explored. The results of intensive inquiries into business practices in each industry are presented along with the organizational and administrative structure which the leading firms employ for carrying out their commodity futures activities. A number of peculiarities which have been identified in the industries discussed in detail have been found to apply to other businesses so that the value of the findings is not limited to these five industries.

A summary chapter, titled "Conclusions and Policy Applications," brings together the highlights of the findings of the study and a comparison between the industries studied. The purpose here is to assist the business manager to assess the possible uses of futures in his total management decision process and to employ the tool in a way that will contribute to more dependable and systematic results.

Certain economic aspects of futures contracts and hedging are examined in detail. It is pointed out that a commodity futures contract is indeed not one but two separate contracts with interlocking consequences. Furthermore, the discussion of the "analogous part" of the hedged commercial commitment, and the consequent need to spell out all of the individual nonmatching residuals, departs from some long-held views about the subjects of "hedging," "carrying charges," "basis trading," and the like.

(Published by Division of Research, Harvard Business School, Soldiers Field, Boston, Mass. 02163. 392 pp. $10.00. 1971)

INTRODUCTION

INTRODUCTION

THE PRESENT STUDY focuses upon an area of business management that has been neglected or received only superficial treatment by most analysts and students of economics and business.

Where do commodity futures fit into the business management picture? How does the business executive view them as a contributor to his primary business objectives? How does his firm organize the responsibilities and authority for carrying out decisions involving commodity futures? What profit centers within the firm are affected by futures trading activity? How valuable are futures contracts as compared with alternative tools for managing price risks? These are some of the business management questions to which the present study has been addressed.

It should be emphasized that the present study is *not* intended to provide instructions to speculators or to explain how to "beat" the futures market. We are interested here in the problems of managing companies whose commercial business involves commodities for which there are organized futures markets which are to be used entirely as a business management tool. This is not to deny that many speculators fulfill a useful purpose but merely to insist that their operations have not been the subject of the present research effort — except, of course, that the speculator must be interested in the activities of others who may affect his market, and vice versa.

In carrying out the study, an analysis is made in Chapter I of the total industry functions that are affected by the impact of price changes for commodities of the kind traded on futures markets. It was also necessary to examine, in Chapter II, the anatomy of commodity futures contracts and of the market in which they are traded. These analyses deal in detail with the conceptual elements underlying "hedging," a term which most businessmen use to cover a wide variety of uses for futures contracts. Chapters III and IV complete the conceptual background by exploring the functions and the risks involved in the management of price-change impacts from the viewpoint of the individual firm.

The experience of five agribusiness complexes is discussed in the several chapters of Part Three. The purposes and policies as well as the organizational arrangements and procedures of selected firms in these industries are covered in some detail. However, it was not the purpose of the study to go into matters of individual trading strategies, or of forecasting methods which are usually regarded as competitively confidential. Instead, an in-depth study of the nature of commodity futures and of the management problems in which they have helped provide solutions should enable more businessmen to develop programs appropriate to their own unique situations.

There are organized commodity futures markets for a considerable number of commodities not of agricultural origin. These include such products as major nonferrous metals, propane, and such products as plywood, hides, or fishmeal which are somewhat indirectly related to agriculture. (See Exhibit I-1.) Except for the precious metals, especially silver, the use of commodity futures by other business firms is very similar to the uses made by handlers of products related to agriculture. Hence, the findings in this study are applicable to nearly every kind of firm dealing in tradable commodities, even though the particular analysis relates to agribusiness products.

The factors that are considered here bring out very clearly the necessity for regarding vertical agribusiness commodity complexes as being comprised of a series of closely interrelated units or stages. Indeed, one of the major thrusts of the present study relates to the usefulness of commodity futures markets as critical coordinating elements in the multistage complex they serve. It is only by examining the coordinating functions performed by commodity futures that one can comprehend their true value in the agribusiness economy. They are certainly much more than simple devices for transferring risks or for speculating in commodity price movements.

Many firms which were interviewed provided valuable information even though they are not included in the individual situations selected for discussion in Part Three. Their contribution to the study has nevertheless been extremely important, and they are included in the list presented in Appendix E.

PART ONE

The Total Industry Position
and Futures as a Management Instrument

CHAPTER I

Of Products, Prices, and Time

Most of the past studies of commodity futures markets[1] have dealt primarily with the operation of the futures markets themselves and with various characteristics of price behavior on these markets. The present study examines the uses of commodity futures markets by the businesses which produce, handle, process, and market those important agribusiness commodities for which there are organized futures exchanges. The first four chapters present some of the problems, methods, and instruments involved in futures trading by businessmen, without going into detail regarding individual commodities. Thereafter, applications in five commodity areas are discussed in order to explore some of the specific aspects that distinguish one commodity situation from another, one production stage from another, and one business function from another in actual practice. The selected areas are wheat and flour milling, the soybean complex, live cattle, oranges (frozen concentrated orange juice), and cocoa. It is a reasonable assumption that the situations that emerge in discussing these five commodity complexes will reveal most of the critical factors that apply in other industries.

Historically, commodity futures trading developed out of commercial trading, not out of the hedging or the speculative needs which are commonly used today to explain the organized futures

---

[1] See Bibliography.

markets.[2] This underlying concept of serving commercial needs has conditioned the approach employed in the present study. This chapter outlines in very broad terms the economic aspects of the total vertical agribusiness complex in which futures trading may play an important part. This provides a conceptual base for the later discussion of the individual business firm and its use of futures as a management tool.

INVENTORIES AND THE PRODUCTION PROCESS

Modern industry is characterized as "production over time." This concept, however, goes all the way back to the beginning of civilization, when "agriculture" replaced the earlier hunting and gathering cultures which preceded it. Men found they could provide more abundantly and with greater certainty if they had ways to subsist while the next crop was in process; meanwhile, nature, given time, responded plentifully to the systematic application of human effort.

The elaborations of technology down through the industrial and the technological revolutions of modern times have served to multiply the importance of the "roundabout production process" and the tying up of resources within the production system.

Today business managers are spending much of their effort in coping with the many problems of looking ahead, scheduling, planning, and providing for requirements and contingencies which reflect the importance of "time" in management. Indeed, economists have long since identified the production and marketing processes in terms of the creation of utilities of time, place, and form. This is an important and basic concept, but bringing it off in the modern industrial world has called into being an almost infinitely complex system.[3]

----

[2] See *Commodity Trading Manual*, pp. 1–13, and Gold, *Modern Commodity Futures Trading*, Chapter I.

[3] For a discussion of a systems approach to agribusiness complexes, see Arthur, Houck, and Beckford, *Tropical Agribusiness Structures and Adjustments — Bananas,* Chapter VII.

It is the purpose in this study to deal with only a small segment of this system, namely, the ways in which business managements can handle the impacts of changing prices of important basic agricultural commodities in carrying out their decision processes and in attaining and measuring their results. The focus is specifically on those agricultural commodities which can be traded on organized futures markets, although the same problems are encountered, with some modifications, in nonagricultural commodities having futures trading.

THE IMPACT OF PRICE CHANGE

Prices are almost always acknowledged to be a key element in the environment within which the business manager must operate. In some industries it is appropriate to speak of pricing policy, which implies considerable discretion in the setting of individual prices. In others, the manager is depicted as having to cope with market prices entirely beyond his own control. The present study undertakes to examine management problems and opportunities in those business situations where price changes are not matters that can be controlled by business policy decisions. In such cases prices are frequently volatile and to a considerable degree unpredictable.

More specifically the study is concerned with commodities which can be traded on commodity futures exchanges. While the list of such commodities is not a long one (see Exhibit I-1) their importance in both domestic and international trade is substantial.[4] Moreover, the potential impact of their price changes upon their own vertical industry complexes is often critical.

There are two characteristics of commodities which are traded in the futures markets that clearly relate to the problem at hand:

---

[4] Gunnelson estimates that in 1968 the commodities of agricultural origin, for which there is an organized futures market, represented 60% of total U.S. farm production. See *A Study of the Impact of Organizational Changes in Agricultural Commodity Markets on Futures Markets*, p. 1.

EXHIBIT I-1. WHERE COMMODITY FUTURES ARE TRADED

Exchange	Barley	Broilers Iced	Boneless Beef	Cattle (Live)	Citrus	Cocoa	Coffee	Copper	Corn	Cotton	Cottonseed Oil	Eggs	Fishmeal	Flaxseed	Grain Sorghums	Hides	Hogs (Live)	Lead	Mercury	Oats	Palladium and Platinum	Plywood	Pork Bellies (Frozen)	Potatoes	Propane	Rapeseed	Rubber	Rye	Silver	Soybeans	Soybean Oil	Soybean Meal	Sugar	Tin	Wheat	Wool & Tops	Zinc
Chicago Board of Trade		•							X											X		•						X		X	X	X			X		
Chicago Mercantile Exchange			X	X								X					X						X	X													
Citrus Assoc. of N.Y. Cotton Exchange					X																																
Commodity Exchange Inc., N.Y.								•								•		•	•								•		•					•			•
Kansas City Board of Trade									X						X																				X		
London Cocoa Terminal Market Assoc.						•																															
London Coffee Terminal Market							•																														
London Commodity Exchange																																					
London Corn Trade Assn.																														•							
London Metal Exchange								•										•											•					•			•
London Sugar Terminal Market Ass'n																																	•				
London Wool Terminal Market Ass'n																																				•	
Minneapolis Grain Exchange														X																					X		
N.Y. Cocoa Exchange						•																															
N.Y. Coffee & Sugar Exchange							•																										•				
N.Y. Cotton Exchange										X															•												
N.Y. Mercantile Exchange																					•	•		X													
N.Y. Produce Exchange											X		•																								
Paris Commodity Exchange																															•	•	•				
Rubber Trade Ass'n, London																											•										
Sydney Greasy Wool Futures Market																																				•	
Winnipeg Grain Exchange	•													•						•						•		•							•		
Wool Assoc. of the N.Y. Cotton Exchange																																				X	

X = Under CEA Supervision • = Trading supervised by rules of the Exchange only.

NOTE: This list is subject to frequent changes. For instance, plywood trading began in late 1969 at both the Chicago Board of Trade and the New York Mercantile Exchange.

1. First, these are commodities (including even frozen citrus concentrate or ice-packed broilers) which are subject to important price fluctuations; otherwise they would not be likely to be the subject of organized futures trading. This does not mean that all commodities with volatile prices are so traded. Many products (lettuce is an example) have extremely volatile prices but are not traded in organized exchanges, either because of the difficulty of establishing specifications, the thinness of the market, the nature of the ownership patterns involved, or for many other reasons.

2. Second, the nature of the industries to be dealt with inescapably requires a substantial pipeline of inventories, reaching from basic resource inputs where the initial raw material is created throughout the various stages of processing, down to the emergence of consumable finished products. It is the existence of this pipeline and the fact that transport, conversion and storage extend over considerable periods of time that gives us the rational basis for affirming that someone *must* exercise management and carry ownership of this pipeline of goods. It may or may not be a relatively constant quantity; however, most generally inventories have significant — often nondiscretionary — variations in volume. This is particularly true of agricultural crops which have an annual cycle where a growing period of several months precedes a brief period in which the total output is harvested. This annual yield has to be large enough to serve processing and consumption requirements until the next harvest becomes available. Ordinarily, consumption is spread through the year on a more or less even basis so that inventories are drawn down to a point usually designated as "carryover." At any given moment all the inputs, including even the pre-harvest accumulation of crops-in-process, can be expressed in appropriate units and thought of as goods-in-being that are subject to evaluation in the commodity markets.

Because of the fragmentation of vertical commodity complexes into many individual firms at each stage and many exchanges from one stage to another in the product flow, there is a wide dispersion of ownership exposures and of shifting impacts of price variations within the total commodity complex. Many commitments are much less tangible than actual ownership. They may not be identifiably associated with any physical supply of the commodity, as, for example, in the case of firm-price purchase orders for goods not yet received. Moreover, intrafirm transfers and departmental positions may become quite involved, sometimes offsetting each other, sometimes not. Orders[5] and requisitions, when enforceable, are as real a commitment as physical ownership. The requirements of intrafirm management will introduce an additional problem of definition before we can begin relating commodity futures to the management problems of individual business firms. These will be discussed further in Chapter III.

TOTAL INDUSTRY POSITION

In order to examine the nature of the phenomena with which this study is dealing, the several elements that make up the total industry position will be scrutinized. First, it is assumed that all ownership and contractual commitments can be expressed in terms of quantity units of the basic commodity under consideration. This may imply conversions and estimates of various sorts. Second, the assumption is made that actual ownership or a firm-price purchase commitment constitutes a positive exposure, while a firm-price sale commitment (whether in the cash or the futures market) is a negative exposure or an offset to positive exposures. Since the discussion at the moment deals only with quantity units of exposure, it is not necessary to be concerned here with the characteristics of prices for the commodity in its various forms, or whether the prices concerned are simultaneous spot prices, deferred commitments, season's average price or some other. These are matters to be taken up later. For the present our concern is with *who* is exposed to price-change impacts and *what kinds* of commitments comprise the exposure.

Aggregate "Long" Position of the Total Industry Complex — The Actual Goods Pipeline

To illustrate in a schematic diagram, the contents of an industry pipeline may be visualized in which the basic commodity is the

---

[5] The term "order" will be used herein to mean contractual bilateral trade commitments. They are assumed to represent a confirmed obligation with price and delivery terms defined. This contrasts with buy or sell orders to an agent or broker, or other unexecuted offers.

major element. At the early stages, the commodity may not be actually present; only the committed input resources actually exist. As the product is harvested, it reaches a second stage. Until recent years it had been assumed that storability would be a critical consideration if the commodity were to be tradable in a futures market. However, this requirement has been found not to be inescapable, as in the case of live cattle or ice-packed broilers. In some cases such as frozen orange concentrate the need for storability (or more specifically, of uniformity and deliverability) has been met by trading the product not as raw oranges, but at a semiprocessed stage. The same could no doubt be said for refined metals which are traded in futures markets.

At the end of the pipeline, it can be assumed that the basic commodity is disposed of either when it is consumed or when it takes a form that makes it largely insensitive or unresponsive to the price fluctuations of the basic commodity.

The aggregate net long position of the industry system as respects a particular commodity can be represented by the physical pipeline supply as outlined in Exhibit I-2 (below the broken line).

EXHIBIT I-2. ILLUSTRATIVE DIAGRAM OF THE ACTUAL GOODS
PIPELINE FOR A FUTURES-TRADED COMMODITY

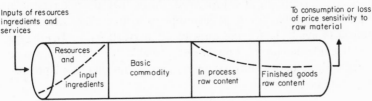

For any particular tradable commodity there is a unit of quantity, such as bushels or tons, in terms of which the total industry commitment can be identified simply by adding up the appropriate physical units of that commodity in the pipeline. The adding sounds simple enough. The total supply, however, as will be seen below, calls for special units of measurement which for the moment can be classified into units of (a) the commodity itself, (b) the product in its emergent forms such as growing crops, and (c)

the product in combination with other inputs which make it a part of a composite (e.g., wheat in bread) in which our primary product has a diminished price influence. Thus, a growing crop might be equated to a number of bushels representing that fraction of expected harvest yield that is justified by the growth to date, or by the share of total expected inputs that have already been applied. For example, a half-grown crop might be covered by selling futures contracts equal to half of the conservatively estimated yield; or an estimate of dollars invested to date in the growing crop might be used as a guide for selling futures up to an equivalent value. Farther along toward the consumer end of the pipeline, there may be an erosion of the sensitiveness of product values to raw material price fluctuations. In such a case the appropriate quantity of raw material considered to be still in the pipeline could be expressed as a lower number of units than actually entered the goods in question. (In effect, a portion of the raw material has emerged from this commodity's price-sensitive pipeline and entered another inventory category which responds to other evaluation factors.)

Often, the industry's statistical reports will include only the basic material itself, classified according to the category of the holder or the location. Such statistics seldom include the raw content of goods further processed. Also, they do not record an incremental value for growing crops, although there are usually forecasts available for the anticipated harvest. These figures can provide the managers who are responsible for the supply pipelines with valuable information regarding "in-sight" and prospective supplies.

Contractual Commitments Other Than Inventory Ownership

Beyond the physical property aspects of the pipeline, the manager must take account of bilateral contractual commitments, which are clearly a part of his exposure to the impacts of price change. By far the most common of these are firm trade understandings or contracts representing undelivered purchase or sale commitments.[6] Also included in this category of bilateral commitments are the contracts on commodity futures exchanges, in which the "trading partner" may be a speculator entirely outside the commercial operations of the industry.

The total commodity "position" for the industry is shown in the schematic diagram, Exhibit I-3, with bars representing the

EXHIBIT I-3. DIAGRAM OF TOTAL COMMODITY POSITION

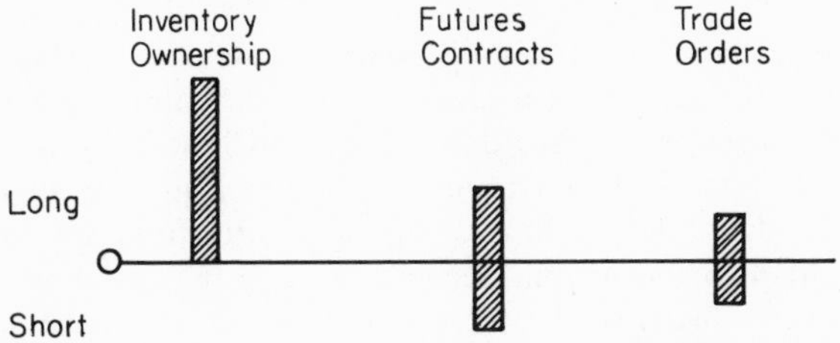

physical volume units in each category. (The height of the bars is intended to approximate roughly the relative magnitudes of these components in a typical post-harvest grain situation.)

The physical commodity pipeline ownership in the first bar represents goods which exist and can be thought of as inventories in someone's business accounting records.

The futures contracts bar represents the aggregate of all futures purchase contracts (above the zero line), and the corresponding futures sales contracts (below the line) which comprise the total open interest on the futures exchange. These can be expressed in the same quantity units as the inventory figures.

The third bar represents trade commitments contracted for at

---

[6] Orders to buy or sell are distinct from tangible property or evidence of title to such property (as in warehouse receipts or bills of lading). The buy-sell contract is bilateral. It may be fully documented in legal terms, or it may be a firm understanding between two parties often confirmed in writing. Less formal orders or sales have to be treated pragmatically, according to trade practices or even case by case. In practice the transaction may be fully as valid as a title deed, or it may be a most tenuous understanding of intent by either or both parties.

a firm price but not yet delivered, unfilled purchase contracts being represented above the line and undelivered sales below.

A few comments are in order regarding certain relationships between the bars.

First, the typical commercial firm would have commitments in several or all of the five categories represented in the three bars. Its net position would be the algebraic sum of its various ownership or commitment contracts above and below the zero line.

Second, the three types of commitments are handled quite differently in the books of account. The inventory is obviously a current asset on the record books (although accounting records are unlikely to show conversions to common quantity units, discussed above). The futures contract is ordinarily not a book asset, although the margin account or deposit does show up on the balance sheet as a current asset or as an adjustment of another asset item. The trade commitments, in contrast, need not show up in the official balance sheet records at all[7] (unless, of course, deposits or advances are called for).

Third, for the total industry (including commodity futures speculators) the total *long* position in both bar 2 and bar 3 must equal the total *short* position in the same bar. It is important to recognize that firm bilateral commitments (since in the total market there is a compensating buyer for every seller) leave the industry's "net long position" at the level that is defined by the physical pipeline alone.

There is a special kind of implicit unilateral commitment that is not covered either by the pipeline inventory or by the formal bilateral contracts or orders. This type is illustrated by understandings such as published catalog prices, offers, or options that are still subject to formal acceptance, and policies or promises which impose constraints upon the terms of product procurement or sale. The mail-order catalog, the dime candy bar, and the fixed-price-line garment are examples. Access to a nonrecourse government

---

[7] It will be seen in Chapter III, however, that price variances for unfilled trade contracts may be entered as an inventory adjustment under certain accounting methods.

loan is another instance.[8] These price commitments are not in the inventory as property, nor are they considered a part of the "net commodity position," but nevertheless they are often matters of great concern to the manager of price risks. Generally they are ignored so far as the total industry position is concerned, even though, theoretically (and in a judgmental way) they are a part of the total industry price-risk position and sometimes quite an important one. At least it can be said that these conditional exposures often compensate for each other within the total industry complex — i.e., a potential penalty to one firm conveys an optional benefit to another, and there may be ways of self-insuring against unfavorable outcomes the same as for many other business contingencies or warranties. No attempt has been made to show these exposures on Exhibit I-3.

Therefore the outline of the "Total Industry Position" can be summarized to cover:

1. *Tangible property* (inventory), converted to the appropriate quantity units of the tradable commodity.
2. Bilateral *commercial commitments* excluding physical inventories owned and excluding contracts on organized futures exchanges. These may involve commitments at a firm price or at formula prices of certain kinds, but they exclude transactions in which the price has not been defined and offers that are subject to acceptance by the other party. For every buyer committing himself to assume the price risk, there is a corresponding trading partner on the other side of the transaction which created the commitment.
3. The *futures contracts* on organized commodity exchanges which are matching within the operations of the exchange itself. This category of commitments (long and short) must represent a cumulative net position of zero within this segment of the commitment market.
4. In considering the measurement of commitments on an industry-wide basis it is necessary to *exclude* that broad *shadowland of special arrangements carrying implied or one-way commitments* which are so varied as to defy measurement and classification and

---

[8] In this case, of course, the government (i.e., the taxpayer) carries the risk, not the firm.

which seldom appear in any statistical reports. The magnitude of these obligations (floor-stock protection, nonrecourse loans, price catalogs or highly advertised prices, cooperative pooling of seasonal returns, open options, and even escalation and profit-or-loss-sharing deals) is surely huge and their implications in relation to price change are very important. Some of them are designed to provide protection to buyers, some to sellers — occasionally to both. They must be regarded as "special situations" to be discussed in the context of the problems of an individual firm or industry. It should be added that they represent an area where the application of commodity futures as a management tool is often difficult or inappropriate, but sometimes they represent very special applications of great importance.

In the area of quasi-commitments and special arrangements, there is almost no statistical information to help judge either the nature or the magnitude of such exposures in realistic terms.

The Gross (*as distinguished from Net*) *Long or Short "Commitments"*

These commitments are very incompletely known for the industry as a whole except for holdings represented by physical inventory ownership and totals on commodity futures exchanges.

1. The portion represented by commitments on organized commodity exchanges are regularly reported (as "open interest").[9] However, such commitments are not regularly included in financial reports of businesses, except as an adjustment or a similar account.
2. Those firm trade commitments represented by unfilled "cash" or commercial transactions are reported in only fragmentary statistics. For some commodities they appear in the form of reported "backlogs," "unfilled orders," "forward purchase contracts," "to-arrive purchases," and so on. Sometimes they are specific as to price but may not specify definite quantities, as in the case of "requirements contracts." Within the firm, trade commitments are, of course, a matter of record, since they are essential to the operation of the

---

[9] This is a reported statistic, but it must be recognized that this gross open interest figure may include many matching transactions within a single firm, as in the case of "straddles."

business; but they are not required as a part of the books of account since they represent claims rather than legal title to goods. Hence, despite the known zero *net* position for the industry as a whole, the gross volume of firm trade commitments in the industry and the position of individual firms are essentially unknown.

3. Any effort to put a gross figure on the "exposures" inherent in open-ended or implied commitments would be pointless, unless one were able to make a careful analysis of all the attendant conditions in each particular situation.

Some of the types of individual commitments underlying Exhibit I-3 can be classified graphically by filling in the details on the same schematic bar diagram. These are shown in Exhibit I-4. The relative height of the bars is only roughly indicative of actual magnitudes, since these differ from one commodity to another and from one season to another. (The height of the third bar representing trade commitments is largely conjectural since almost no data are available.)

The specific offsets in the diagram are identified by the symbols in parentheses. The other segments of the bars (not designated with parentheses) represent trades or positions in which there is an uncovered price exposure for one or both parties involved.

For instance, A-1 represents actual inventories not matched by a trade sale commitment or a futures hedge. Similarly, the segments of the second bar designated F_L-1 and F_S-4 represent speculative positions not offset by other ownership or commitments. The two extreme segments of the second bar, F_L-4 and F_S-5, are also speculative in the sense that (a) they do not offset each other (since in that case they would be classed as spreads) and (b) they are not matched against either actual ownership or by a formal sale or purchase contract in a commercial transaction.

In the third bar there are two commitment categories that represent specific price exposure. These are O_B-1 and O_S-4. The indefinite extension of this bar shown in dashes represents the mixed situation implied by semicommitments that do not represent firm contractual transactions. This area can be thought of as including those expected transactions against which the anticipatory long and short futures hedges have been placed. However, since these intentions, offers, and expectations are not firm bilateral

EXHIBIT I-4. SCHEMATIC DIAGRAM OF TOTAL OWNERSHIP AND COMMITMENTS
FOR A TYPICAL TRADABLE COMMODITY

(Bars indicate volume. Shaded areas are exposed to price impact.)

Actual (A) Inventory Pipeline

Hedged in Futures	A-3 $(=F_S\text{-}1)$
Undelivered Trade Sales	A-2 $(=O_S\text{-}1)$
Owned Unhedged	A-1

Long ← → Short

Futures (F) (open interests)

Anticipatory Long Hedge	$F_L\text{-}4$ $(=O_S\text{-}2)$
Long Hedge against Sales to Trade	$F_S\text{-}3$
Spread, Long Side	$F_S\text{-}2$ $(=F_S\text{-}3)$
Speculative Long	$F_L\text{-}1$ $(=A\text{-}3)$
Inventory Hedge	$F_S\text{-}1$
Hedged Purchase Orders	$F_S\text{-}2$ $(=O_B\text{-}3)$
Spread in Futures	$F_S\text{-}3$ $(=F_L\text{-}2)$
Speculative Short	$F_S\text{-}4$
Anticipatory Short Hedge	$F_S\text{-}5$

Firm Trade Orders (O) and Intentions (I)

(Purchase Intentions, Offers, Options, Budgets)* I_B

Purchase Commitments, Hedged	$O_B\text{-}3$ $(=F_S\text{-}2)$
Purchases against Trade Sales	$O_B\text{-}2$ $(=O_S\text{-}3)$
Purchase Orders Unhedged	$O_B\text{-}1$
Sales against Inventory	$O_S\text{-}1$ $(=A\text{-}2)$
Sales covered with Long Futures	$O_S\text{-}2$ $(=F_L\text{-}3)$
Sales Covered by Purchase Orders	$O_S\text{-}3$ $(=O_B\text{-}2)$
Sales Booked, No Cover	$O_S\text{-}4$

(Sales Intentions, Price Lists, Open Bids to Sell, etc.)** I_S

* may be covered in part by anticipatory futures sales $(F_S\text{-}5)$.

** may be covered in part by anticipatory futures bought $(F_L\text{-}4)$

commitments accepted by both parties, they must be considered to represent, at least for the moment, a speculative exposure.

All the categories shown as shaded segments on the diagram are comprised of ownership or contractual commitments for which the individual holder has no specific commitment that is matching and expected to have offsetting impacts from price changes. Incidentally, the algebraic sum (net, not gross) of these "firm-price exposures" is theoretically equivalent to the NET industry position as represented by the physical pipeline inventory alone. This version of the firm-price exposure picture shows the categories of commitments where the overall price risk is carried.

It is not possible to secure aggregate statistical quantities for some of the categories shown on this diagram. This is especially true in the third bar where data are not generally published. However, the individual firm and the individual management decision maker is theoretically well able to compile this kind of information regarding his own operations. These are the data that the sophisticated hedger lives with. They are the primary components of his "position statement," which will be discussed later.

COMMERCIAL AND FUTURES TRANSACTIONS NOT INTERCHANGEABLE

The inventory position as described above is a useful concept for measuring where one stands at a particular time in respect to exposure to price impacts. It is still incomplete so far as the operational needs of a commercial trader or purchasing officer are concerned. If a trader is to take advantage of the best of a number of alternative courses of action in a volatile market, he can conduct his transactions in the several categories — spot ownership and availability, commodity futures trading, and the conducting of contractual purchases and sales with commercial suppliers and customers — but this requires many skills that go far beyond simply planning or balancing a "net position."

The number of variables which the commercial trader must understand and follow is much greater than those with which the futures market speculator is primarily concerned. The latter has a

narrowly defined set of specifications with interchangeable contracts to deal with, while in the commercial market each transaction has to be specific as to all qualities and terms of delivery and
payment. To match up commercial requirements with availabilities
and other opportunities is an extremely complex assignment. To
fulfill commercial needs without a futures market would at times
almost certainly require trades to be made with customers or suppliers even though the commitment could not be matched with
an offsetting commitment with another customer or supplier. One
of the great advantages of the futures market is its ready accessi-
bility on short notice with a well-publicized price.

The solution of the problem of managing a net position is much
easier when the alternatives available include a futures market
with its great fluidity for absorbing sudden changes in the volume
of business, its assortment of delivery months and the opportunity
it offers to reverse a position at any time. The futures market
thus offers a "time dimension" which means much more than just
reaching out into the future; it means a time flexibility and
maneuverability that is almost never available in similar degree
in the cash or commercial market.

As the discussion in the following chapters unfolds, it will be
seen that futures and hedging involve much more than merely the
management of a net position. The net position is a valuable summary measure and guideline as to total primary exposure to price
impacts, but the management of price risks involves many additional considerations.

SUMMARY

The purpose of the present chapter has been to identify the
primary reasons why business managers have been concerned with
problems imposed by the changing prices of major commodities.
Attention has been focused upon the total industry position; that
of the individual business will be taken up in Chapter III. It has
also been seen that:

1. The concept of a *net* position for the industry as a whole can be
   represented in volume units by the physical inventory pipeline

alone, even though there are important *gross* price-exposure risks in the form of futures contracts and trade orders.

2. In a multistage industry, operating at many locations, involving many firms, there is a crucial need for planning and likewise for commitments that reach far beyond the services that could be provided by spot transactions which require instant transfer of possession from one hand or from one individual stage to another. Hence, trade commitments and futures contracts become valuable tools, not just for managing an inventory position but also for planning all aspects of buying, selling, and other commercial activities.

3. There are several categories of commitments that fix the points at which price changes will have their impact. Some of these are inventory ownership titles, some are contracts in the futures market, and some are firm trade orders to purchase or deliver. Both the futures commitments and the firm trade commitments involve a buyer and a matching seller in each case. Hence, for the total industry (including speculators as well as commercial operators) every transaction on the long side has a counterpart on the short side. The several categories of commitments do, however, permit extensive transfers of risk from party to party, and from inventory owners to those holding other commitments.

4. There are, of course, many unilateral or conditional and nonmatching commitments, guarantees, and assurances; also, many so called "soft" orders to buy or sell. These must be treated as special cases so far as the incidence of price changes is concerned. This study will give its primary emphasis to the more conventional hedging situations, but there will be recurrent instances where commodity futures contracts can be used effectively in dealing with the special price risks that are less precisely "matching" in nature.

5. The consideration of price impacts upon individual buyers and sellers of a commodity becomes much more involved than the impacts upon the vertical industry complex as a whole. This will be discussed in Chapter III, after considering in Chapter II the nature of the commodity futures contract as a commercial tool.

CHAPTER II

The Commodity Futures Contract
as a Business Instrument

THE ENTERING, maintaining, or terminating of commodity futures contracts falls entirely in the "commitment" not in the "ownership" realm. What has been said about Product, Prices, and Time in Chapter I supplies a background for one further step in defining our primary area of concern — that of the commodity futures contract as a management tool. Tools are usually thought of as tangible instruments. As such, they are often difficult to explain without including a description of the tangible instrument, the methods and purposes for which it is designed, and the entity upon which it is to be employed. An instrument such as a wrench or drill can be described in some detail, together with instructions as to how to make it work. Beyond this, however, it does not become really meaningful until the user is informed about the peculiar characteristics of the machine or structure to which the tool is to be applied. In this case, a description of the salient attributes of the commodity futures contract as an instrument and of the market where it is created, traded, and validated, will be given, followed by a description in general terms of the types of problems and situations to which this tool can be applied commercially. One feature of this part of the analysis is the development of a "theory of analogous parts."

During the early stages of the research it became apparent that certain ambiguities arise as to how profits or losses are generated by futures transactions. The difficulty involved the question of whether gains or losses from open futures contracts are realized from day to day or whether such gains or losses can accumulate in unrealized capital accounts.

Before attempting to shed some light on these issues, it is necessary to make a distinction between the two primary users of the futures markets as different tax rulings and income problems apply to each. One user is the business entity which uses the futures market as an adjunct to its normal commercial operations. Such a user is often conveniently classified as a hedger.[1] The other user is one who engages in futures transactions with the sole purpose of profiting from price fluctuations. This user is the speculator. The common bond between the hedger and the speculator is their use of futures contracts, so let us now turn to an examination of the nature of such a contract.

THE NATURE OF THE COMMODITY FUTURES CONTRACT AND THE INCOME IT GENERATES

In general terms the commodity futures contract consists of a firm, legal agreement between a buyer (or seller) and an established commodity exchange or its clearing house whereby the trader agrees to accept (or deliver) between designated dates, a carefully specified "lot" of a commodity meeting the quality and delivery conditions prescribed by the commodity exchange, with cash settlement on delivery date at a settlement price[2] to be prescribed; provided further — and this is most important — that:

1. The trader agrees to an arrangement with a qualified broker (or the clearing house) to provide him with a margin deposit as required, and
2. The trader agrees to reimburse him or accept credit for all interim gains or losses in value of that futures contract resulting from day-

---

[1] See Appendix A and the Glossary for a discussion of the definition of hedging.

[2] See footnote 6, p. 30.

to-day changes in its price on the floor of the established commodity exchange.[3] Also,

3. The trader has an option which permits him to close out his contract at any time (at the market) simply by notifying his broker of his desire; and, on the other side, it permits the broker to close out the commitment if the margin is impaired by disposing of the contract at the market.

---

[3] The following example of a margin calculation is taken from a Chicago Board of Trade training course manual (mimeographed):

Calculation of Margins

When calculating the requirements for individual accounts two elements are always considered — Exchange requirements or firm margins, whichever is higher, and the open trade profit or loss of the trade. The calculation of these elements gives the net equity in the trade.

To illustrate these concepts let's assume the following:

a. Speculative Customer A has a $1,000 credit balance in his commodity account at Firm X
b. Two days ago Customer A bought 10 December Wheat at $1.60 and the market closed at that price on that day
c. Yesterday December Wheat closed at $1.58-½
d. Today December Wheat closed at $1.57-½
e. Both the Exchange and Firm X's minimum speculative margins on wheat are:
1. Initial — 10¢ per bushel
2. Maintenance — 8¢ per bushel

Two days ago Customer A's account was fully margined since the initial margin (10¢ times 10,000 bushels equal $1,000) was on deposit and there was no open trade profit or loss (trade price of $1.60 equalled closing price of $1.60). Therefore, A had a net equity of 10¢ in this trade.

Yesterday A had only 8-½¢ net equity in the account because he had an open trade loss of 1-½¢ against his 10¢ margin deposit. The margin clerk would take no action since the account was still above the maintenance level.

Today, however, the margin clerk would put a call on the account for $250 to bring the net equity back to the prescribed 10¢. This would be necessary since the net equity had gone below the maintenance level of 8¢ which automatically requires calling the account back to initial requirements. At the closing price today the net equity would be only 7-½¢ since the open trade loss is 2-½¢ against the initial requirement of 10¢.

If a customer fails to respond to a margin call and his equity is close to being exhausted then the management of the firm may liquidate the account.

As a corollary to the above definition, it is necessary to recognize a number of other attributes of this basic commitment:

1. The contract defines a so-called "par-delivery" specification which is the basic unit being traded on the exchange. This specification includes a precise set of terms relating to the quantity, the quality, the location, and the services that must be met in making delivery.
2. In addition to the par-delivery specifications there are usually alternatives available to the seller who chooses to make delivery of a commodity not precisely conforming to the par-delivery specifications. Thus a scale of premiums or discounts is established for those deviations from the par delivery which are still permissible or "deliverable" under the terms of the contract. For instance, multiple locations of delivery may be permitted; variations in unit weights or tolerances in total quantity making up the delivery; grade deviations or penalties for imperfections; and similar premiums or penalties for other variations that are acceptable to the exchange. (These may not be refused by the person receiving delivery against a long contract.)
3. Delivery for most commodities is permitted to take the form of a warehouse receipt or, at times, a shipping certificate or a bill of lading, which is construed as an actual transfer of title.
4. As implied above, the individual entering a contract may be dealing directly with the commodity exchange clearing house (if he is a clearing member), or he may be dealing through a broker (or commission firm), in which case the exchange clearing house holds the commission firm responsible for the transaction.
5. In national emergencies or other extreme situations commodity trading has on rare occasions been stopped. In such cases there are usually arrangements for arbitration of outstanding commitments prior to recourse to the courts.
6. The operations of the exchanges are subject to various published trading rules, legal provisions and regulations which may restrict individual trading in various ways. These rules may originate from the exchange or from the government.
7. While the exchange undertakes to maintain open public trading in the various contracts, it sets its own hours and rules of trading and may suspend trading or set limits beyond which prices may not move in a single day.[4]

---

[4] When prices on the exchange for a particular contract reach the limit of permitted daily movement, trading is halted since only bids or offers within

Such are the chief attributes of the commodity futures contract.[5] The act of using it consists of entering a commitment (to buy or sell), of closing out an open commitment, or of making or receiving delivery in accordance with the terms of an open commitment. Meantime, the required margin deposit is maintained at a prescribed level at all times, as prices go up or down. Trading is open to anyone who can meet the margin and other requirements as specified by a qualified broker.

It is important to re-emphasize the two major dimensions of the commitment undertaken in the purchase or sale of a commodity futures contract. Indeed it is well to consider it a dual contract or at least a contract which stands on two equally important legs. The first is the commitment on the part of a "short" to deliver a commodity meeting the exchange specifications at a designated future date (and a matching commitment by someone taking a long position). This part of the contract merely promises delivery of the goods; the price at which the delivery occurs will be dependent not upon the price at which the commitment was entered but upon the settlement price[6] at the time of delivery. The second leg of the con-

---

this limit can be executed. If the market closes at the limit, then this point becomes the base for measuring the limit on the following day. When trading encounters these limits, there may be a few orders "at the market" (either to buy or sell) which can be executed at the limit. For example, when the market is down to the limit, it can be assumed that would-be sellers are numerous and buyers scarce. The few buy orders that come into the market have to be distributed to sellers by some form of allocation, pooling arrangement or lottery.

In cases of severe and extended price movements in which a trader can neither maintain his margin nor liquidate because trading is halted by the daily limit, the clearing member is still responsible to the clearing house for the completion of his own or his clients' outstanding commitments for daily settlements.

[5] Appendix B outlines the specifications, trading rules, limits, etc. applicable to futures contracts for some of the commodities discussed in the several chapters of Part Three.

[6] There is a "settlement price" declared at the end of each trading session and all accounts are brought to this level. For transactions within the day, such as a new contract bought, that trade is moved from the transaction price to the day's settlement price, which ordinarily reflects the closing quotation or quotations on the trading floor. This is the same settlement price that is used in making deliveries.

tract involves a promise to keep up with daily price adjustments as quoted on the exchange through payment or receipt of cash at the clearing house window. This daily settlement process has the effect of maintaining the validity of the delivery promise so that any cancellation of the delivery commitment can be accomplished without further transfer of funds. A transaction in commodity futures (unless and until settled by delivery) does not involve an exchange of any substantive value since only the process of daily adjustment generates income or loss. Nothing is borrowed in order to finance a purchase or sale of commodity futures, although a good-faith margin deposit is required of both buyer and seller. There are no debit balances in the entire futures operation other than the daily payment requirements which have to be made in cash; all net balances of traders are on the credit side. The trader is never allowed to be in debt.[7]

Most commodity futures contracts are terminated without actual delivery of the commodity. Such termination can be accomplished at the request of the trader simply by notifying his broker of his desire to terminate at a price in line with current quotations in the futures market. It can also be terminated by the broker if the customer fails to make prompt payment of any amounts due the broker as a result of day-to-day price changes. If actual delivery of the commodity is made, the final daily settlement price adjustment is applied to the contract, and then the seller, in order to meet his contract obligation, supplies the commodity and receives a price for it based upon the same settlement quotation determined on the exchange. The delivery process is officially initiated by the holder of a short contract who files a notice of intention to deliver through the clearing house. There is always a corresponding holder of a long position who must accept this deliverable commodity and pay the prescribed current settlement price subject, of course, to any quality discounts or premiums that may apply.

---

[7] This statement may be subject to qualification for certain commodities not under Commodity Exchange Authority regulation, like cocoa.

The Clearing House Records

The essence of the commodity futures contract can be illustrated by tracing a single transaction. Assume that a trader instructs his broker to buy one contract — representing 5,000 bushels — in December Wheat at $1.50 at Chicago. The broker (being assured that his customer has a sufficient uncommitted credit balance, or is satisfied that a cash deposit will be made promptly to cover the initial margin) instructs his floor trader to make the purchase at that price. The trade will be made only if a seller is available and willing to trade at $1.50 or under. (The seller may be entering a new short contract position or surrendering a previously held long contract. In either event, the transaction will only take place when two traders, a buyer and a seller, get together.) Up to this point the clearing house is not involved.

However, once the trade is consummated on the exchange floor, the clearing house takes over as intermediary.[8] It enters on its books the obligations — one long and one short — of the two brokers who made the trade. (If the brokers are not clearing members, each must have a clearing member[9] who acts on his behalf.)

It is important to note that, once the clearing house has confirmed the trade and the specific price at which it was entered, the individual transaction loses its identity so far as the clearing house itself is concerned. Several things happen henceforth:

1. No one cares who was the seller who paired up with this particular buyer; instead, each party is directly obligated to the clearing house.
2. Each party (through his clearing member) is held responsible for maintaining an unimpaired credit balance sufficient to cover the required deposit against all open commitments.
3. This deposit (which, for regulated commodities at least, must be

---

[8] See Board of Trade of the City of Chicago, *Commodity Trading Manual*, pp. 113–132; Gold, *Modern Commodity Futures Trading*, pp. 37–40; and *Party to Every Trade*, booklet issued by the Board of Trade Clearing Corporation, Chicago.

[9] A "clearing member" may handle accounts of other (nonclearing) members as well as its own, thus reducing the number of accounts carried by the clearing house.

maintained in segregated funds by all parties) is charged each day with the amount by which prices changed that day.

4. The clearing house has records for each clearing member to show all aggregate positions, long and short, for which that member is responsible. It does not care at what prices these contracts were initially entered, because each one has been brought up to last night's settlement price and the accounts are charged and credited daily. Since there is a short for every long contract, the clearing house is always in balance with a zero net position, as respects both number of contracts and dollars.

5. The clearing house can thus operate without having any record to identify the original price at which a particular contract was entered. This is a matter for the broker and the trader, not the clearing house.

6. By virtue of the process of making cash settlements each day to reflect the daily price changes on the exchange floor, all profits and losses are settled at once — all losses are paid and profits are credited. Any two positions, one short and one long, in a particular contract can be paired up and closed out simply by a "close-out" transaction without any additional cash changing hands (except for commission charges and any price differences since the previous night's settlement quotations). In fact the close-out operation releases back to the traders the cash they had deposited as their required margin.

7. If the buyer who entered a long commitment in December Wheat at $1.50 decides to take delivery, he will receive through the clearing house a notice of intention to deliver from a seller which in effect does two things. First, it closes out the buyer's contract account with the clearing house on the specified settlement date and at the settlement price set on that date. This cancels the buyer's obligation to make further daily settlements at the clearing house. (Matching this action, a short contract was canceled when the wheat delivery tender was presented.) The second part of the delivery process is the actual change of title of the wheat delivered and the payment of cash to the party making the delivery. This is accomplished by use of the same settlement price as that which closed out the futures contracts, namely the current price on the exchange for a "par delivery" quality and location of wheat deliverable under the rules of the exchange, adjusted for whatever prescribed premiums and discounts apply to the grain actually delivered.

EXHIBIT II-1. WEEKLY FUTURES TRADING POSITION STATEMENT

NAME _____
WEEK ENDING _____
EXCHANGE _____
NAME OF COMMODITY _____

UNITS (BU., LB., ETC.)
PER CONTRACT _____
MIN. FLUCT. = _____ PTS.
MIN. FLUCT. = $ _____ PER CONTRACT

1	2	3	4	5	6	7	8	9	10
			Profit or (Loss) on Open Contracts					Results to Date	
Delivery Month	No. of C's	Total Margin $'s	Long or Short (L or S)	Bought or Sold at (price)	Price at Fri. Close	No. Min. Fluct. Units Gained or Lost Per Contract	Min. Fluct. Units X No. Cont.	Gain	(Loss)
Totals									

Net Dollar Gain or (Loss) on All Open Contracts

Profit or (Loss) on Contracts Closed During the Week

1	2	3	4	5	6	7	8	9 10
Delivery Month	No. of C's	Total Commission $'s	Long or Short (L or S)	Orig. B or S Price	Price at Close Date	No. Min. Fluct. Units Gained or Lost Per Contract	Min. Fluct. Units X No. Cont.	Gain (Loss)
Totals								

Net Dollar Gain or (Loss) on All Contracts Closed During the Week

SUMMARY OF FUTURES TRADING ACCOUNT

Last Week's NET CAPITAL POSITION ON ALL
  COMPLETED BUSINESS _____
Gain or (Loss) on Contracts Closed during week _____
Less Commissions incurred during week _____
Cash transferred to (+) or received from (−) broker _____
NET CAPITAL POSITION ON ALL COMPLETED BUSINESS _____
Plus Net BOOK gain (loss) on OPEN contracts _____
NET EQUITY (available to margin open contracts) _____
MARGIN requirements on OPEN contracts _____
Net uncommitted credit in margin account _____

It can be seen that the trader who originally went long at $1.50 per bushel may have had to pay a very different cash price when he took delivery — perhaps $1.75 or $1.25 depending upon what happened in the market quotations for December futures up to the time of delivery. However, he would have paid or received interim cash charges or credits which could be balanced out against the cost of his delivery wheat to give him a net cost equivalent to that at which he entered the contract.

The Broker or Commission Firm Records

In contrast to the accounts maintained by the clearing house, the broker has to meet the needs of his individual clients. He therefore carries a record of the individual transactions of each client in each contract classification, and he also maintains a record of the current status of the account including the daily updating of debits and credits resulting from price changes, together with the cash transfers and the net credit balances of the customer. This latter record also shows the number of open contracts in the account as a basis for calculating the credit balance required by minimum margin regulations, to be checked against the actual credit balance. As stated earlier, the broker calls for more cash when margins fall below a prescribed maintenance level (see footnote 3); otherwise he will close out enough contracts to bring the amount of margin required by the rules into line with the available credit balance. Finally, the broker customarily compiles a monthly statement for his clients, recording the summary of transactions and status of the account. This statement can be drawn up to show the results of all contract positions closed out during the month, together with cash transfers, in or out, and the current status of open contracts, together with a summary of end of month credit balances and margin requirements. A simple illustration of a position statement, developed for teaching purposes, is presented in Exhibit II-1.

The broker thus is able to provide a record (1) of all transactions, (2) of daily results, (3) of open commitments, (4) of margin requirements, and (5) of the current equity status of the account. These accounts include data showing the specific outcome of each contract entered and terminated.

Individual Trader Records

So far as the individual trader is concerned, the records he needs for accounting and for decision purposes can vary widely. It all depends upon his purposes and his total situation. If he is a speculator, he is presumably following a plan; and he must have enough information regarding his own situation and the relevant factors operating in the market to enable him to see how he is doing and how well his plans are working. If the trader is one who uses the futures market as a business management tool, he must be able to relate the futures market experience to his commercial transactions and positions, and this calls for additional or different kinds of information.

For our present purposes we will confine ourselves to the actual transactions and adjustments affecting the financial status of the individual trader. If he is a speculator, he certainly may have a number of instructions for his broker — standing orders, stop orders, and the like — which become effective under certain market conditions. Beyond this he undoubtedly maintains a volume of information which will be useful to him in decision making. However, for purposes of measuring income or loss and current position, the information outlined in Exhibit II-1 covers most of what he needs.[10]

The commercial trader needs to have his information in a form that will fit into his total accounting system. For instance, he may use the futures market to hedge his inventory position and will in most cases want to price his inventories of this particular commodity at market and then adjust it price-wise for the net gains or losses on *open* futures contracts. In business uses of this sort it is a common practice to assign the gains and losses from *closed* futures contracts as an adjustment in the calculations of cost of goods sold. (Futures profits would reduce the cost and thus increase earnings, while losses on futures would increase costs, reducing earnings.)

There are a good many other uses of commodity futures in con-

---

[10] This summary position statement would normally enable him to ascertain the length of time which a particular contract commitment has been held so that he can comply with present income tax requirements regarding capital gains and losses. See below, pp. 38–44.

nection with commercial businesses. The futures may be a procurement instrument or a method of earning storage. They may be indirect or cross-hedges, and they may be in the nature of an anticipatory hedge against commercial expectations rather than against firm commitments. A long hedge, for instance, may be used as a device for fixing the cost of a raw material which will be used at a future date without tying up nearly as much capital as would be involved if the physical product were to be acquired and held until needed. Without going into detail, it should be clear that the accountant is confronted with many possible ways of interpreting and accomplishing the accounting requirements. It is sufficient for the present purpose merely to affirm that the results of futures transactions are expected to be entered into current operating results of the business and may not be interpreted as capital gains or losses. It is not entirely clear whether gains or losses from open contracts (as distinct from closed contracts) need to be taken up currently or may be deferred until each contract is closed. Some are handled in each way. Certainly, open contracts are taken into account on a cumulative basis when they are used in the process of adjusting inventory prices, but it is not at all clear that such treatment is necessary in all situations.

Tax Status of Commodity Futures Operations

Operations in commodity futures have been the subject of a number of tax rulings. These have made certain situations clear but have left other operations unclear. A situation which seems quite straight-forward at first glance becomes highly complex upon further scrutiny. The involvement seems to center upon the question of whether a futures contract is "property," and whether income is generated while contracts are still open or whether the income is deferred until the contract interest is terminated.

In ordinary accounting practice, commodity futures contracts themselves are not a balance sheet item to the holder. They are neither an asset nor a liability on the books, but rather a cancelable agreement. In contrast to short sales in the securities market, there has been no borrowing and delivery of a stock certificate to the buyer as evidence of a title transfer. At the same time there is a tangible asset in the form of a margin deposit or "receivable from broker" credit which is usually a current account receivable.

The impacts of price fluctuations upon open futures contracts, however, are clearly a significant factor in financial results.

Certain pragmatic rulings have been affirmed which can be summarized as follows:

1. Speculative futures contracts on the long side apparently are "capital assets." Losses on long speculative positions have been required to be treated as capital losses rather than as current operating expenses.[11] However, no rulings were found to substantiate actual experience with such losses (or gains) as "long term," although according to Internal Revenue Service practice and to "non-court" tax opinions, long speculative positions held over 6 months can receive long-term capital gains treatment.[12]

2. On short-sale, speculative positions (as distinct from hedges), total gain or loss is a short-term gain or loss. Apparently an open short-sale contract is not legally a "capital asset" (i.e., it is not "property") except in very unusual circumstances.[13] Apparently, however, when a long contract is purchased for the purpose of canceling the short position, the long contract is "property" which instantaneously takes on the loss or gain resulting from the prior short commitment. Thus, the net loss or gain from speculative short positions must be treated as short-term in nature.[14]

3. For a firm dealing in futures as a part of its regular commercial operations, both the futures contract and the matching commodity commitment are ordinarily valued at, or adjusted to, current market, so there is no tax liability involved in the paired transactions, assuming the hedge is perfect.[15] The courts have also regarded futures transactions (even though not matched against a trade com-

---

[11] See *Tennessee Egg Company, petitioner,* v. *Commissioner of Internal Revenue,* 47BTA, August 18, 1942, as reaffirmed by *Frank B. Polachek, petitioner,* v. *Commissioner of Internal Revenue,* 22TC 858, July 9, 1954.

[12] See, for instance, Belveal, *Commodity Speculation with Profits in Mind,* p. 136.

[13] See U.S. Internal Revenue Code 1. 1233-1(b) and 1. 1233-1(d.2).

[14] See Briloff, "Income Tax Aspects of Commodity Futures Transactions."

[15] In some cases the accounting adjustment of both the inventory price and the matching futures contracts are deferred until the goods are sold and the hedge is closed. The income effects are still substantially the same since the two sides of the hedge compensate each other.

40   *Commodity Futures*

mitment) as producing only current operating profits or losses if
the commodity is intimately involved in the day-to-day dealings of
the business.[16]

While accounting practices vary from one situation to another,
Exhibit II-2 describes, as nearly as we could ascertain, the major
categories of tax treatment that prevail today in the United States.

The categories outlined in Exhibit II-2 reveal distinct contrasts
in the method of treating — for tax purposes at least — the income
or losses generated by commodity futures operations. In the case
of speculative accounts, the results may not be taken up as taxable
income or loss until the contract is closed out whereas most commercial users take them up on a current basis. This is the official
position, even though cash may change hands on a daily basis and
no one who is involved in the operation acknowledges an accrual
of values due him except in the form of a credit balance with the
broker. This balance may be drawn down on demand with no strings
attached, so long as it does not drop below the level of the good-
faith margin requirement which is a constant amount per contract
set up when the contract is opened and released when it is closed.

On long speculative contracts the final results are treated tax-wise
as long-term or short-term capital gains or losses, depending on
how long the particular contract position remained open. This
situation seems anomalous in view of the fact that profits may have
been realized and spent from day to day and no additional settlement is made (other than release of the required margin) when
the position is terminated.

In view of these facts relating to long contracts, it appears to the
author that the long contract, even though it may be defined as
"property" or "capital asset," [17] must *a fortiori* be regarded as having a zero value at any given time. All accruals become cash values
divorced from the contract, while the contract itself can be liquidated at any time without any cash settlement (other than release
of the required reserve or margin).

---

[16] See *Corn Products Refining Co.* v. *Commissioner of Internal Revenue*,
1958, U.S. Supreme Court decision.

[17] It should be remembered that a short-sale contract is denied the status
of "property" or "capital asset," since it is apparently interpreted as selling something you do not have.

EXHIBIT II-2. TAX TREATMENT OF COMMODITY FUTURES CONTRACT RESULTS

Open Contracts	Closed Contracts
I	
Speculator Gains on Long Positions	
Results are capital gains; they must be deferred till contract is closed. They may not be accrued to reflect current market, even though cash in margin account is withdrawn and spent.	Results may qualify as long-term capital gains if the particular contract is held for the prescribed length of time. Certain switching operations are permitted without breaking continuity of holding.
II	
Speculator Losses on Long Positions	
These are capital losses; they must be deferred, even though cash must be paid out as prices fall.	Must be regarded as capital losses, not as current operating expense.

NOTE ON I AND II: Long contracts are legally regarded as "property," or "capital assets." However, see comment in text.

III	
Speculator Gains or Losses on Short Positions	
Outcome must be deferred till contract is disposed of.	Must be regarded as short-term (nonproperty) income or loss — like gambling — realized at date of closing a contract commitment. It may not be accrued on a current basis.

NOTE ON III: Short futures contracts are not legally regarded as "property," but the cancellation of the speculative short position is interpreted as requiring the acquisition momentarily of a long contract which *is* "property," and hence can generate only an instantaneous (short-term) capital gain or loss.

IV	
Gains and Losses from Futures Contracts Qualified as Hedging	
Contract results normally kept on current market basis. Many methods of handling the books, including (a) variance accounts, (b) reserve adjustments, (c) posting to raw material costs, or (d) entering as cost of goods sold.	Must be taken up on closed contracts, if not already covered earlier.

NOTE ON IV: Hedging is regarded as an adjustment to inventory or cost of goods sold. It is thus a current operating expense or credit.

Moreover, in cases where the contract is terminated in actual delivery, it is settled by a cash transaction at the current futures market settlement price (assuming par-delivery specifications are met) rather than at the original contracted price, whether the market is higher or lower. All interim price changes will already have been absorbed in the transfers of clearing house and brokers' balances. The clearing house (as distinct from the broker or clearing member) need not know or care at what price the futures commitment was entered.

This interpretation would imply that speculative capital gains or losses from the price impacts upon long commodity futures contracts should be regarded as realized on a current day-to-day basis, not as deferred capital gains or losses. At the same time no attempt is made here to define the tax status of the margin account itself, the "receivable from broker" item. If this is a capital asset account in which capital gains and losses accumulate over long periods before a "realization" occurs, there may still be a basis for claiming long-term capital gains treatment, but it would appear difficult to associate such "realizations" with the specific entering or liquidating of a particular commodity futures contract.

A futures contract differs from a stock or bond in that no evidence of title is passed, and no specific value inheres to the contract beyond the daily settlement adjustments. No security is borrowed to effect a delivery as in a short sale of a stock. A futures contract, long or short, is not a pledgeable asset; a deficiency in the broker's or clearing account has to be settled at once in cash, while a favorable accrual is available as cash, not merely as a trial-balance credit.[18]

In contrast to the long position, the short speculative contract

---

[18] "One of the most important concepts of the Clearing Corporation system is daily settlement in cash for all price variations in every commodity traded on the Board of Trade. The Clearing Corporation pays out cash daily to those Clearing Members having a net gain due to favorable price movements during the previous trading day. At the same time, the Clearing Corporation requires immediate payment from those Members having a net loss as the result of the same price movements." See booklet entitled *Party to Every Trade*, issued by the Board of Trade Clearing Corporation, Chicago.

enjoys only short-term capital gains treatment, no matter how long the short-sale commitment has been in effect. However, the fact that gains or losses from such transactions (under present tax rules) are deferred until the contract is closed or repurchased has the effect of permitting the deferral of incomes or losses, pending liquidation, despite the actual practice of daily settlements.[19]

The net outcome of our examination suggests that commodity futures contracts are current items which are in fact maintained at a net value of zero through a continuous cash settlement process. They are not the same thing as buying and holding a tangible asset[20] which ties up resources over a period of time and can yield a gain or loss only when it is liquidated.

What would be involved if the interpretation that is being explored were to be adopted? Essentially the "capital asset" or "property" classification of the long contract itself might or might not be retained, but if so, all gains or losses would be considered as realized on a current day-to-day basis, which is what actually happens. Similarly the short contract, assuming it continues to be denied the status of "capital asset" or "property," would be regarded as generating day-to-day (not deferrable) ordinary income or losses. In either long or short speculative operations, of course, these daily income adjustments could readily be accumulated between account-

---

[19] A speculator with capital gains from other sources may use this deferral provision to shift such income from one year to the next on a relatively riskless basis. In October he may open a "spread" transaction (e.g., long April and short June). Then, whichever direction the futures price swings he can, before his tax year ends, liquidate the side which shows a loss, replacing it with a different delivery month. See Goldfein and Hochberg, "Use of Commodity Straddles Can Effect Impressive Tax Savings."

[20] One of the leading commodity brokerage houses (Hayden Stone) in its "Commodity Commentary" for February 2, 1970, included the following statement in citing some of the advantages of speculating in commodities as compared with stocks: "There is no interest charged on debit balances used to buy or sell commodity futures. This is true because commodity futures don't yet exist and the margin put up is simply a performance deposit, not a partial payment against a purchase or sale total price."

The Board of Trade Clearing Corporation booklet, *Party to Every Trade*, affirms the same position in its statement: "Commodity margins do not represent 'down payments' for goods received and should not be confused with margins required of buyers of securities."

ing or fiscal closing dates without detailing each daily increment.

For the commercial use of commodity futures in conjunction with a business, the treatment of all results as ordinary income or loss would require no change except that the logic of the present interpretation would make it mandatory without exception to record all price changes affecting open contracts on a current accrual basis, rather than to permit the (apparently occasional) practice of not taking up results until the contracts are closed.

It should be recognized that the questions and suggestions presented here would have the effect of moving the essential focus of commodity futures operations in the direction of current adjustments to current market factors and less toward the use of the futures markets for securing favored tax treatment. Nevertheless, the extremely high leverage that is characteristic of futures trading should cause little doubt that commodity markets would remain a highly attractive vehicle for speculators.

This discussion has centered on the nature of income and losses generated by the operating of the commodity futures market. These gains and losses can be thought of as self-contained results so far as speculators are concerned. For the commercial business, however, the futures contracts are, almost by definition, an instrument used in conjunction with other business activities including buying, selling, inventory, and other trade commitments. Once the immediate nature of the outcome of commodity futures operations has been defined, the more involved problems of incorporating these results into the commercial accounting system of the firm must still be resolved. As with many other accounting procedures the answer must be found in light of the unique needs of the industry or the individual firm, and a considerable variety of specific applications can be expected.

THE COMMODITY FUTURES MARKET

An understanding of the commodity futures contract as a business management tool requires that commodity futures be recognized as more than simply a contract instrument. They are also important because they provide access to a market.

Liquidity of the Market

The market assures liquidity. The contract can be closed out in a forum where many buyers and sellers stand ready to trade on instant notice. It is especially in this respect that valuable services are rendered by speculators.[21]

The volume of trading rises to huge figures in the course of a year (see Exhibits II-3 and II-4). Trading on U.S. futures exchanges rose from 3.8 million contracts[22] in 1959–60 to 12.3 million contracts in 1969–70.

Time Flexibility

The market provides for time flexibility. It enables traders to select from an assortment of delivery months and thus allocate the time factor involved in the price risks which are transferred.

---

[21] For further discussion of this point see Chapter III, pp. 102–103, and Chapter IV, pp. 119–120.

[22] The size of a contract varies widely according to the bulkiness and value of the commodity. (See, for instance, the items in Appendix B.) A very rough idea for agricultural commodities would be gained by thinking in terms of a truckload or carload — more for some products, less for others. In terms of dollars, the value represented by the commodities traded might run from $5,000 to $15,000 or more per contract. The gross dollar figure representing the value of commodities on which futures transactions were entered (not the margin money or deposit) came to $135.6 billion in the 1969–70 year. In terms of gross values involved, the figure is comparable with the estimated total volume of trading ($124.4 billion) on the New York Stock Exchange in the same period. However, actual deliveries against commodity futures normally represent 2% or less of the transactions recorded on the commodity exchanges as against 100% in the securities markets. The gross dollar figure for commodities is still a valid aggregate to represent market liquidity for the purpose of transfer of price change impacts.

EXHIBIT II-3. ESTIMATED VOLUME OF TRADING ON U.S.
COMMODITY EXCHANGES, ANNUALLY 1959–60 TO 1969–70

July 1 Fiscal Year	Total Contracts Traded[1]	Value[2] of Commodities Contracted	
		CEA Regulated	Total
	(million contracts)	(billion dollars)	
1959–60	3.8	$26.4	$ 29.3
1960–61	5.6	52.3	54.7
1961–62	5.0	36.7	38.9
1962–63	5.8	45.3	49.8
1963–64	6.9	60.4	68.6
1964–65	7.9	73.5	83.3
1965–66	9.0	71.8	88.8
1966–67	10.6	74.7	94.0
1967–68	8.8	59.4	71.1
1968–69	10.3	67.4	81.3
1969–70	12.3	92.8	135.6

[1] Contracts are counted once, not twice for each transaction.

[2] Dollar figures represent contracts entered rather than deliveries made or margin deposits required.

SOURCE: Association of Commodity Exchange Firms, Inc.

Uses of Futures Quotations

The futures quotations (quite apart from actually trading in them) provide a number of valuable services:

1. They provide a good indicator of the variations from moment to moment, or day to day, in the price of a typical specification.
2. They evaluate the difference in the unit value of that specific commodity removed from present availability by different delivery or time intervals. These differences are often referred to as "spreads" or "carrying charges."
3. They provide a benchmark or bellwether quotation to serve as a basing point for measuring in price units the relationship between the variety of specific terms that apply to a particular commercial commodity transaction and the "market" for the standard contract specification. These "deviations from benchmark" are typically referred to as "basis," [23] expressed in units of price difference.

[23] For further discussion of "basis," see below, pp. 64–69.

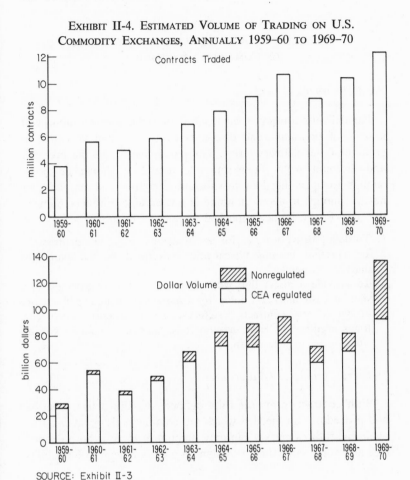

EXHIBIT II-4. ESTIMATED VOLUME OF TRADING ON U.S. COMMODITY EXCHANGES, ANNUALLY 1959–60 TO 1969–70

SOURCE: Exhibit II-3

Cost of Using Futures

There is a cost for the services rendered in the use of this tool. This is the commission charged the trader and whatever cost may be associated with tying up funds in a margin deposit.

Operational Requirements and Practices
on Commodity Exchanges

Par-Delivery Contracts

Par-delivery contract specifications must be adopted along with a scale of premiums and discounts for permissible variations in grade or other delivery terms. The par delivery plus the premium and discount scale for permissible deliveries should be broad enough to open the door to substantial commercial supplies, but narrow enough to avoid dumping of undesirable products. Some of the purposes to be accomplished are the following:

1. To define delivery terms for actual completing of the contracts.
2. To represent the most typical price movements for the commodity market represented.
3. To provide a direct link with the cash market by having a substantial cash market volume for transactions matching the terms of par-delivery contracts. (Actual deliveries against futures contracts need not be large or numerous, but they should be possible when buyers or sellers wish.)

Delivery Periods and Procedures

With contract terms carefully defined, definite delivery periods and procedures are needed which are commercially practical. Here again the futures market can only function if there is both definiteness and at the same time provision for a certain degree of flexibility.

Inspection and Arbitration

Provision for impartial inspections and arbitration is regarded as necessary for most commodities.

The Commodity Exchange as an Institution

1. Legally it is usually a corporation, mutually owned and controlled by its members, whose title is normally vested in their membership rather than in stock ownership.

2. Eligibility for membership is open to financially qualified traders, commission brokers, commercial operators in cash markets and others who subscribe to the rules of the exchange.
3. The exchange establishes its own rules subject in certain cases to governmental regulation and supervision.
4. The exchange (or, rather, its clearing house) acts as intermediary in all trades between its members but takes no net position on its own account. It holds each member responsible for maintaining a required cash balance with the exchange, including the adjustments to reflect changes in the daily level of prices for all open contracts.
5. The exchange provides a trading place, trading and recording procedures, reporting services, auditing and other facilities to assist in the conduct of its business. In some cases there is trading in cash commodities on the exchange floor as well as the trading in futures contracts.
6. For most commodities, exchange rules provide that there will be four to eight delivery months (each representing a separate contract) open for trading at a given time, ranged over a period of twelve to eighteen future months.
7. The commodity futures exchange prices apply to a highly standardized commodity commitment. Each transaction in the cash commodity market is a complex event involving many elements unique to that particular deal; each futures contract transaction for a particular delivery month carries identical terms with every other transaction in that contract except for the price and the time the trade occurs. Hence, time and price (or price changes over time) are isolated, as all other variables are held constant by the standard contract terms. A person acquiring a long contract position thus assumes consequences of price changes over time as the market continuously reappraises that set of contract specifications. By the same token a person taking a short position assumes, in inverse form, the consequences of the same price changes continuously updated.

Government Regulations

The Commodity Exchange Act of 1936, as amended, establishes a Commodity Exchange Authority which is responsible for administering various rules and regulations relating to the trading in designated commodity futures on boards of trade or commodity

exchanges. The CEA regulates those commodities specifically designated in the Act, which include wheat, cotton, rice, corn, oats,
barley, rye, flaxseed, grain sorghums, mill feeds, butter, eggs,
onions, Solanum tuberosum (Irish potatoes), wool, wool tops, fats
and oils (including lard, tallow, cottonseed oil, peanut oil, soybean
oil, and all other fats and oils), cottonseed meal, cottonseed, peanuts, soybeans, soybean meal, livestock, livestock products and frozen concentrated orange juice.[24] CEA does not regulate a number
of others such as cocoa, coffee, sugar, fresh and frozen broilers and
turkeys. The nonagricultural commodities are not under CEA
regulation. (See Exhibit I-1.) Certain of the subject commodities
(like onions, cottonseed, or peanuts) are not actively traded on
commodity futures markets.

The Commodity Exchange Authority licenses the exchanges and
registers all floor traders. It issues regulations and requires numerous reports regarding commodity futures operations, and it has
the power to perform surprise audits of the records and books of
commission agents. The CEA reports upon such matters as trading
volumes, open interest, price, and various special topics such as
weekly stocks of grain in deliverable positions or reports of special
studies and investigations.

The regulation of trading practices is of importance to business
managers both as an assurance against abuse and fraud and as an
aid in assuring reliable performance. While both the regulated and
nonregulated commodities are subject to strict rules of conduct
administered by their respective exchanges, the pattern of government controls provides extra assurance and serves as a guideline
for trading in commodities for which CEA is not directly responsible.

The manager in a commercial business must adhere to certain
regulations. His firm is not permitted to carry an unbalanced open

---

[24] See Section II-A, Commodity Exchange Act, As Amended, July 23,
1968, p. (1). The Commodity Exchange Authority Regulations are more
specific regarding certain of these items, carrying the following parenthetic
explanations: eggs (including shell eggs, frozen whole eggs, frozen plain
egg whites, and frozen plain egg yolks), livestock (including live cattle and
live hogs), and livestock products (including frozen pork bellies, frozen
skinned hams, steer carcass beef, and hides).

futures position in excess of specified limits (a position which must include such transactions as anticipatory hedging, but must exclude certain parts of cross-hedges involving products not regarded as "substantially identical"). Such constraints, designed primarily to protect against certain speculative practices, may present problems in the development of commercial hedging policies, but on the whole they are designed to improve rather than penalize the orderly conduct of market operations. The CEA has the power to suspend trading or to deny trading privileges to individual commission merchants, brokers or floor traders. It may hold hearings or prosecute violators of its regulations in the courts.

Now that the futures contract as well as some of the pertinent mechanisms relating to its operation and control have been described, the next step is to define a conceptual scheme whereby a business manager can employ commodity futures contracts as an effective contributor to the attaining of management objectives. Instead of describing the total business activities involved, a "theory of analogous parts" will first be proposed. In this theory, a segment of a commercial position involving actual ownership or a purchase or sale contract in the trade may be defined as an exact counterpart of the futures contract just described. This "analogous part" is first identified; then the remaining parts of the commercial operation are treated separately. (Sophisticated grain dealers will immediately identify this residual as their "basis.")

HEDGING — THE THEORY OF ANALOGOUS PARTS

Hedging in Its Simplest Form — Matching of Identical Parts

Hedging can be regarded as a matching or pairing of two commitments which are expected to have offsetting effects. The offsetting commitments may take the form of (a) actual title to goods, (b) unfilled purchase or sale contracts in the cash market (at defined prices), or (c) long or short positions in the commodity futures market. They may also include, in certain cases, (d) anticipated or implied ownership (as in the case of growing crops, for instance) or anticipated product requirements (as in the case of budgets or plans involving expected sales at published catalog prices or ingredient purchases needed in the production of products whose prices are deemed to be unresponsive to short-run raw material costs). The word "hedge" is usually used by the trade to refer to cases where commodity futures contracts on an organized exchange are employed, and the futures contract is correspondingly spoken of as the hedging instrument. We think of hedging as being appropriate in commodity transactions in which:

1. Price fluctuations are expected.
2. They will be of significant magnitude (to the hedger).
3. They are unpredictable as to direction or amplitude, or are expected to be adverse to the hedger.
4. There is a "tradable" market which can be expected to have a reasonably predictable degree of price parallelism.[25]

The Typical Case — Imperfect Matching

In hedging, the offset is never perfect, for many reasons, among which are the following:

1. Precisely parallel price movements seldom occur.
2. A commission charge has to be paid on hedge transactions in commodity futures.
3. The specified qualities and terms of delivery and payment applicable to commodity futures can depart appreciably from those applicable to the specific commodity commitment being hedged.
4. The commodity futures commitment can be liquidated at any time on a public exchange, whereas liquidating the matching or cash commitment may be much more expensive or cumbersome.

The Matching Portion or Analogous Part

One way to understand and analyze a hedging operation is to define the commitment to be hedged in such terms as to make it pos-

---

[25] For the moment the precise definition of parallelism can be deferred, so long as it is understood that there will be a substantial correlation between the quotations in the cash market and the futures market from day to day or from the commitment date until the delivery date for the futures contract involved.

sible to split off that segment of the cash commitment which can be described as the exact counterpart of the standard (par delivery) futures contract in which the hedge is made. This becomes the "analogous part" or analogue of the futures specification. It is understood that a *long* cash[26] commodity position will correspond to an equivalent *short* position on the futures market, or vice versa.

The Residuals

The actual specifications and terms of sale or ownership in the cash commodity commitment can be restated to show two separate parts. The first is the cash counterpart or analogous part described above. This set of specifications will merely state explicitly the specifications that the cash commitment would have if it were a "perfect hedge." (This includes, for instance, prepaid delivery and carrying costs that would match those that are assumed to be prepaid in the par delivery terms of the futures market.)

The second part is a carefully itemized set of specifications to be called the "residuals," which are either present in the actual cash commitment or would be required to make delivery at par on the exchange. Each of these can be evaluated in terms of expected costs or expected premiums that will be realized if the hedge is to be liquidated by actually making or taking delivery of cash product.

The Analogous Part and Hedging Profits

In the above, the analogous part has been discussed in terms of specifications, rather than of dollars. It remains to relate the analogous part and the residuals to the prices inherent in (a) the actual cash market commitment, and (b) the futures contract price with which it is matched.

The first step in this process is to secure a realistic quotation for the analogous part. Such a figure can sometimes be secured easily, especially for a storable staple commodity, simply by getting the

---

[26] The term "cash" commodity, or commitment in the cash market, refers to an actual commercial lot and stands in contrast to a "futures contract" on an established commodity exchange. (A "spot" quotation refers to a cash commodity available for immediate delivery.)

spot market quotation for the par delivery quality and adding estimated added cost for carrying and delivery. In other cases the analogous part will have to be priced by building up the pro-forma components (as, for instance, spot feeder cattle plus current estimated cost of grain at standard conversion rates).[27] In other words, the pricing of the analogous part is nothing more than the pro-forma costing out of a physical delivery on the exchange.

A very simple illustration of the "analogous part" phenomenon is seen in the case of a situation where a dealer can buy a cash commodity which qualifies for par delivery and is located in an acceptable warehouse. He has merely to add to his actual purchase cost the cost of storage and financing until the delivery date of the futures contract he has used to hedge this purchase. Thus, his analogous part would represent a pro-forma cost for completed delivery of his commodity on the exchange. By comparing this cost figure with the price at which he entered his short sale on the exchange, he can tell whether he is earning something over storage costs or falling short of the amount. (Since everything in the transaction is of par delivery quality and location, there are no "residuals" of the sort discussed above.) The outcome of the whole operation is, therefore, summarized in this margin between the pricing out of the analogous part and the amount to be realized from holding the short sale position and then delivering against it.

This calculation differs from the usual definition employed in discussions of "basis" and "carrying charge markets." The "analogous part" calculation provides an estimated net realization and is directly related to a specific delivery month in which the transaction is hedged. The "basis" calculation uses the gross spread between the futures quotation and the spot cost and leaves it to the trader to work out the added costs implicit in the storage factor.[28]

---

[27] It is not possible to use already finished cattle for pricing purposes, since these cannot be held over for later delivery.

[28] One of the confusions in the trade jargon is the use of the term "carrying charge market," and its opposite, an "inverted market." To many people, the "carrying charge market" represents a futures market in which the differentials between one delivery month and the next one are sufficient to cover *full* carrying costs. It is not clear how the markets would be described if the quotations provided some premiums but not enough to cover full

The second step is the most significant reason for applying the "theory of analogous parts." The residuals are the detailed descriptions of that which is retained by the hedger, both premiums or discounts to be realized for quality, and obligations or services to be fulfilled. By placing a realistic value upon each of these residual elements, the trader has a benchmark from which he is able to spell out just how far he expects to do better than going the Exchange delivery route. A "short hedger" is thus "long the residuals." Anything he can do to enhance his realizations or reduce his actual costs compared with his benchmark estimates for these residuals will turn him a profit on the residuals.

A third aspect has to be incorporated in this conceptual model before the pieces all fit together. Since the *specifications* of the actual cash commitment equal the combination of the specifications for the analogous parts together with the specifications implicit in the residuals, it is possible to add the values attached to these items (plus or minus) to arrive at a pro-forma value for the cash side of the hedged commitment, assuming fulfillment on the Exchange. This figure can be compared with the actual dollars per unit in the cash commitment. If the actual commitment price differs from the figure that assumes delivery via the Exchange, then the difference can be said to represent a "good" or "poor" buy or a "good" or "poor" sale vis-à-vis using the Exchange as the outlet where a return could actually be "locked in" today.

The final step for the commercial operator is to compare the margin representing a "good" or "bad" buy just discussed with the amount by which he thinks he can enhance his realizations compared with the pro-forma Exchange-delivery option.

The idea of the analogous part lends itself to applications of futures trading where the concept of basis or carrying charge would be very difficult to apply. The case of the cattle feedlot operator who is considering whether to buy unfinished steers and feed them out against a pre-sold future position is a good example. In this case the pro-forma detailed compilation of feeding

---

carrying costs. An inverted market is almost always one in which the more remote delivery months are quoted lower than the nearby ones. In this case there is zero or less than zero available for so-called carrying charges.

costs, assuming that the animals will actually be delivered on the
Exchange, provides the evaluation of the "analogous part." If
the feeder actually makes such delivery, his realization will be a
reflection of the margins between the futures market and those
shown in his cost estimates, including the adjustment for any variance of actual costs from the figures in his estimate.

On the other hand, the feeder may have little or no intention
of delivering his cattle on the Exchange and will have a number
of "residuals" to take into account in deciding between various alternative feeding and marketing strategies. In such a case he is in
a position to appraise all of his various alternatives by estimating
the costs and adjustments involved in moving his cattle through
other channels, accepting any premiums or discounts which the
market may offer and measuring the total costs of these alternatives against the opportunity he has to close out his hedge by re-
purchase on the market.[29]

*   *   *

The theory of analogous parts is also applicable in the case of
the "long hedge" situation, where a long position in futures is
taken in connection with an actual or anticipated sales commitment on the cash market. For example, we can assume that a
Chicago grain dealer books a sale of wheat to a flour miller in
Amsterdam at a firm price in guilders, payment to be made upon
arrival of the grain shipment three months later. The grain dealer
may not yet own the wheat called for by this order, so he buys
the required number of long futures contracts on the Chicago
Board of Trade.

His commercial commitment has a number of elements: (a)
wheat of the customer's type and quality must be bought in the
cash market (we assume it will not be taken as delivery on the
Exchange); (b) shipping facilities must be secured and scheduled;
(c) possible foreign exchange fluctuations could make the guilders
convertible into fewer dollars than expected.

The portion of this commercial commitment that has been

---

[29] The total results of the lifted hedge must include all the debits and
credits resulting from interim price changes in the futures market, and
these results are naturally to be included in the gain or loss from the
completed transaction.

hedged — the analogous part — is simply an assurance of control over a quantity of deliverable wheat needed at a price fixed by the long futures contract purchased.

The residuals are obviously crucial considerations in such an operation. These were all taken into account when the sale was booked, representing answers to the following questions: (a) Can I acquire the type and quality of wheat the customer wants at a more favorable price basis compared with futures than was envisioned in my sales price? (I am "short" this differential; I want to buy wheat cheaper.) (b) Can I engage transportation more favorably than my allowance? (I am "short" the transportation until this item is covered.) (c) Should I take special steps to guarantee the conversion rate for guilders into dollars? (I am "long" in guilders and "short" in dollars. Should I have a guarantee or is it a good risk to carry on my own?)

Depending upon the skill with which these (and other) residuals are appraised in making the sale offer, the transaction may turn out to be successful or catastrophic. In any event, however, the seller is protected against major changes in the absolute market for wheat by virtue of this hedge. Moreover, he has the time and opportunity to seek out the most suitable supply source without having to have the wheat in hand before he makes the sale offer.

By consciously lining up the analogous part (that actually protected by his hedge) and each of the residual factors, the trader attains flexibility and analytical tools for appraising and managing his retained risks.[30]

By carefully defining and identifying the individual specifications making up our set of residuals, we have available a tool for helping the commercial manager to appraise his retained risks in a much more specific way than as though a single differential between a cash and a future price was his primary guide. The trade, nevertheless, has learned to use such summary figures — often referred to as their basis — with great skill and effectiveness.

It would be futile to suggest that as complicated a concept as

---

[30] For similar illustrations of trades of this sort see Raclin, "Futures Market in Soybeans and Their Products."

we are discussing in the theory of analogous parts should be applied in each individual commercial decision. Instead, we should regard this discussion as underpinning the considerations which traders do — either intuitively or consciously — employ when they deal in terms of "basis" or "differentials." Thus, the term "basis" has been used throughout the present study and will undoubtedly continue to be the common terminology of traders, even though there are many who recognize that it is a summary figure which may well obscure critical factors and result in confusion.

In addition to the problems connected with basis on the score of its obscuring significant details, there is also a serious problem of communication for the uninitiated student. Therefore, a note entitled "What is BASIS?" is presented at the end of this chapter to help clarify some of the implications of the term as well as to illustrate some important problems of terminology that seem to pervade the whole discussion of hedging.

The Residuals — The Vehicle for Earning Basis Profits

Conceptually we can think of every departure of the cash commitment from the par-delivery specifications of the futures contract as being one of the components or ingredients making up MY BASIS. These ingredients include departures from par-delivery specifications because of transportation cost to the par-delivery point; grade and selection differences; condition of the product; packaging; special warehousing and handling costs (to match those included in the commodity futures contract). The process of reducing each of these definable deviations to an estimate expressed in dollars, plus *or* minus, is the daily practice in the trade. It is for this that "basis traders" sharpen their pencils. In fact, it is the regular practice to add up the values of these specific plus or minus residuals, expressed in money terms, and to compare this total with the market difference (MY BASIS) arrived at by subtracting the futures contract price from the cash transaction price, in order to identify a good buy or a poor one.

Thus, it is possible to take a cash commodity commitment of the sort considered hedgeable and break it down into two segments: (1) the analogous part which is directly complementary to the futures contract used as a hedge, and (2) the residual just described.[31]

The significance of the hedge can thus be stated quite simply. The commodity futures market provides a measure of the value which large numbers of traders place upon a typical specification of a commodity to be delivered in a particular future month. The hedger can segregate that portion of his total risk that will result from price changes in this bellwether specification and transfer that portion (the analogous part) to others by entering a futures contract (long or short). He then retains all other aspects of the commercial and business risks he has undertaken, and he naturally expects to manage them in such a way as to attain a profitable outcome.

The residuals (basis) or differentials within the price pattern for a commodity (i.e., cash vs. futures, one quality vs. another, one location as against another, or one delivery month vs. another) are all-important to the business that operates from a fully hedged or zero net position. At the opposite extreme, the primary or absolute price swings in the market, which the out-and-out hedger can almost ignore, are all-important for the straight speculator (i.e., the one who takes outright positions rather than spreads or straddles between delivery months). The speculator needs to forecast absolute price swings; the hedger focuses upon the factors affecting his differentials. Mr. Allan Q. Moore, Senior Vice-President of Experience, Incorporated, with wide experience in commodity hedging, illustrated the importance of both kinds of forecasting in a paper he delivered at the International Commodities Conference held in New York City September 30, 1970. More than half of his list of "important factors influencing the price of cash commodities" have their major thrust not so much in causing the total market level to change as in causing changes between

---

[31] The "analogous part" plus the "residual" is a pro forma breakdown of the cash market values; the futures price can then be matched (i.e., hedged) against the cash market equivalent ("analogous part" of the cash transaction) while the "residuals" represent the entirely unhedged portion of the operation. In contrast the term "basis" is applied to the crude differential of actual cash price minus the futures quotation. For further discussion of basis, see p. 64 below—Note: What is BASIS?

the prices of nearby vs. deferred deliveries, between one quality
and another, or between easy vs. difficult availabilities. The list
of factors presented by Mr. Moore was as follows:

1. General economic conditions influence the size of inventories.
2. Whether storage space is available to take care of the movement.
3. The availability of transportation facilities to fulfill contracts and
   facilitate the movement.
4. The weather influences the quality as well as the quantity of production.
5. Availability of deliverable qualities in the market makes trading
   more liquid.
6. Availability of commodities or qualities that can be substituted,
   at home and abroad.
7. Government regulations, such as support prices, subsidies, export
   taxes, and allocation of funds to finance concessionary sales, as
   well as international commodity agreements, levies, import quotas,
   and other restrictive measures.
8. Monetary conditions at home and abroad tend to affect the accumulation of inventories.
9. Prices of nearby futures versus the deferred (carrying charges
   versus inverse), and their influence on current inventories.

It can be seen from the variety of factors discussed above that
the concept of price parallelism requires careful scrutiny. What
are the entities that are supposed to be parallel? Even more important, what degree of parallelism is presumed to be a prerequisite for hedging operations?

To answer these questions in order, it seems best to state arbi-
trarily that the prices quoted in the futures market for a specified
contract will be used as the reference point. Then the question
becomes one of defining the commitment in the cash market
(actual or implicit) which the manager can assume will have a
high degree of price correlation over time with this commodity
futures contract. (The relationship need not be on a one-to-one
basis. In fact, a regression coefficient other than one-to-one is
quite feasible. Theoretically, it would even be possible to hedge
an inverse coefficient. Hence, the term parallelism is not used in
a strict mathematical sense. Moreover, the correspondence need

not be perfect, since one almost invariably expects a residual in actual practice.)

The actual commitment in the cash market, we have suggested, can be broken down into the analogous part (which has specifications and terms identical with those incorporated in the futures contract) and the residuals. Assuming that the analogous part can be priced in the cash or "to-arrive" market, it should have a very high degree of correlation price-wise with the futures quotations, while the residuals are subject to variations of their own.

The farmer provides a complex but revealing example of the need for this kind of analysis. He may find his residuals very large indeed if they include all the uncertainties of yield, grade and special harvest and delivery problems. In effect, if he makes a short futures sale of 5,000 bushels of December Wheat as a hedge against his growing crop, he can then calculate an analogous part and a set of residuals. To do this he must construe his actual ownership as consisting of 5,000 bushels of wheat of a quality and in a location that will be ready for delivery on the exchange in December (for this is what he has contracted to deliver) including the expected cost of all of the services, interest, transport, storage, and an insurance allowance to cover uncertainties of yield, quality, etc., required to move him from "wheat in the field" to "wheat of par-delivery quality in deliverable position." He has made a commitment to meet all these residual charges for he has "sold" his wheat on these terms in the futures market. His hedge assures him the price that will be paid for the analogous part, and he is protected against increases or declines in this price, but not in the residuals.

Looked at in this way, the residuals appear impressive, but two things should be recognized: (a) Most of the costs reflect merely the familiar procedures that have to be performed in any event. (b) The differentials implied in the obligation to deliver wheat according to exchange specifications are seldom actually incurred, since actual delivery on these terms is rare. Instead, the sale of the farmer's wheat in local markets, when it is ready, can be effected more advantageously costwise. This normally results in the incurring of lower outlays than exchange delivery would have required. But at the same time, local delivery would usually be expected to bring a lower price than that quoted for the exchange contract. Hence, the "usual" discount (or, in some instances, premium) of the farmer's local cash market relative to futures at delivery time can be taken into account as a way of "saving" some of the residual expenses that would have been required in making exchange delivery.

In summary, the farmer who has hedged in the wheat market and then later bought back his hedge at a lower price and sold his wheat locally will have received an amount reflecting the decline in the futures market price during the time he was hedged. He continued to carry the residual risks on the cost side of uncertain yield, of uncertain quality, of any unexpected harvesting, storing or delivering experiences; and — in addition — the risks on the price side, during the period he was hedged, resulting from factors that would alter the margin between local and exchange delivery prices. The farmer might think of the latter as "his basis" risks, the former as his "production" risks.

The commodity futures hedge, then, serves its dual role by (1) transferring to others the impact of price changes in the par-delivery specification as it is traded continuously upon the commodity exchange, and (2) releasing or isolating a residual in the form of a bundle of quality, time and service factors, from which the skilled hedger expects to gain a trading or merchandising profit. In the first role, the hedge (assuming it matches a similar transaction on the cash market) acts as an immunizer or insulator, not as a direct source of gain or loss. It is its second role, the opening up of residual or basis positions, that enables the hedger to profit from his hedging operations.

Futures contracts, of course, have numerous other business uses besides those involving a specific pairing or matching of a similar cash commitment. These uses imply a "net position" other than zero and are most commonly employed when futures represent an added procurement tool, a more flexible sales channel, or, in general, a market extender for commercial trades that could not have been executed as advantageously in the cash markets. Sometimes hedging is appropriate, sometimes inappropriate; sometimes it is more costly than the prospective benefit could justify; often it provides a degree of flexibility in commercial strategy that would be unattainable otherwise. These and other considerations require an examination of the broader management and commercial decision problems of the individual firm, which will be taken up in the discussions to follow.

Note: What is BASIS?

On August 10 two members of the Minneapolis Grain Exchange (one representing a country shipper, the other a flour manufacturer) were discussing the market. Actual cash prices were not mentioned, although the September Future (the basis future) was $1.60⅞ a bushel.

"What's the Minneapolis cash basis today?"

"It's going up. I just saw the market close at two under for ordinary protein compared with four under a week ago."

"That means that basis country track it's around 22 under at Fargo. Can we do some business?"

"My basis on those ten Fargo cars I offered you last week is 18 under, but the protein is 15 per cent and it's 12 per cent moisture; that should carry a good premium."

"All right I can take ten cars of 15 protein at 16 under. Is it a deal?"

"Yeah. We can start loading tomorrow. It's a deal."

To himself: ("That's a profit of two cents — pretty good when you consider the market fell off a dime since I bought.")

*   *   *

In view of the promiscuous use of the word "basis," as illustrated in this conversation, it seems essential that at least a few of the *key* meanings of the term be clarified. The following discussion will, it is hoped, help the novice to take a few first steps with greater understanding. In order to be explicit, certain symbols are used to designate the various cash and futures transactions involved.

   c — Prices for specific commercial product transactions: including locations, grades, delivery terms, etc.

   C — Spot price quotation for a cash commodity meeting all the specifications and terms for par delivery against futures contracts.

   F — Price quotation for nearest future contract.

   f — Price of futures contract for specified more distant delivery month.

The noun "basis" is one of the very common trade terms used by futures market operators, but one which is misunderstood by practically anyone outside the trade. Trying to get traders to give a sharp definition of the term is a frustrating experience. Every one of them can use the word to describe an exacting set of specifications, and another trader can understand this meaning without any trouble; still, the next sentence may use basis in an entirely new sense. (The confusion over the word basis requires special care when the word pops up as an adjective or preposition, as in the cases of basis grade, basis f.o.b., basis Chicago, basis No. 2 Yellow corn, or even in its more usual dictionary meaning, as when we speak of quotations on a firm basis.)

In order to help pin down the special uses of the word basis as it relates specifically to futures trading, the word can be defined in four stages. First, we can attempt a general statement to cover the essential aspects of its meaning *whenever* the word is used as a noun in connection with futures trading:

1. BASIS (general definition)

Whenever the word BASIS *is used in connection with futures trading, it is a spread or difference (premium or discount) of the price relating to actual (c) grain (or other product), above or below the price (f) or (F) of a futures contract for such product.*

Usually the price of the futures contract for the nearest delivery month (F) is regarded as one side of this spread (for instance C − F, or c − F); however, a more remote delivery (f) may be specifically designated in certain cases.

2. THE BASIS (in market reporting) sometimes called "the cash basis."

The second stage, a more specialized meaning, is one that may not relate to a specific transaction, but rather applies to the state of the market, future versus spot. It is a sort of bellwether guide or statistic. In order to distinguish it without trying to coin a lot of new words, we can call it "*the* basis."

This is a *statistical statement reflecting* (*as of any given time*) *the premium or discount of the cash price for a deliverable product of contract grade* (*C*) *over or under the nearby future* (*F*). The cash product is assumed to be available on a spot basis, ordinarily at the same delivery point as applies to the futures contract (i.e., C − F).

The basis is primarily important as a market reporting device. It ties the futures market to the spot market and shows how the relationship between the two changes over time. The premium or discount reported as of any given time is a valuable point of reference for traders.

3. MY BASIS (a specific trade position). Where appropriate, refer to YOUR BASIS, HIS BASIS, etc.

This use of the word basis expresses *the premium or discount of a specific commitment* (*c*) *in actual grain* (*or other product*) *over or under a specific futures quotation* (*F or f*).

If no delivery month is specified, the nearby future (F) is assumed to be the one employed; otherwise a particular delivery month is stated. The transaction in actual product refers to a particular grade, quality, location, delivery point, and all considerations that identify some specific commitment (c) I have made. Hence c − F, or c − f expresses MY BASIS. MY BASIS would refer to a purchase transaction or commitment in actual product, expressed as a price premium or discount from the specified futures quotation in which I have made a corresponding hedge sale. In other words, a sale of futures against a long position in the cash commodity results in my being long the basis (or, if I have a commitment to deliver specific actual product and have covered this by purchasing a futures contract I am short the basis).[1]

MY BASIS represents the cost relationship I have established by a pair of specific trades or ownership positions (one in cash and one in futures). When used in this sense MY BASIS remains unchanged as long as these remain in effect, regardless of what may happen in the vertical price fluctuations on the market in the interim. I may, of course, switch my basis from one delivery month to another, in which case I revise my basis from, say, two cents under March to, perhaps, three cents under May. In any case my basis represents the price difference between a pair of firm commitments, and the size of the premium or discount represents a cost bench mark, against which I hope to profit by a favorable change in price relationships.[2]

4. MY OPPORTUNITY BASIS or MY CLOSE-OUT BASIS

Another aspect of MY BASIS has to be carefully distinguished. This may be referred to as my *"close-out" or "opportunity" basis.* This *calls for the quotations at which I either do close out my position on both sides or have the opportunity to close out my positions.* To the extent that the spread has moved from MY BASIS (initial commitment) to a more favorable close-out basis, my transactions have been successful. This "opportunity" basis then represents a trial balance that may be taken at *any given time.*

*   *   *

Returning to the illustrative conversation at the beginning of this note, the references to basis that appear there can now be explained:

---

[1] The truth is that I am long MY BASIS, not long THE BASIS, in this case. An important portion of the risk I retain depends on what happens to THE BASIS $(C - F)$, but I also have at risk, in addition, whatever spread exists between the quoted spot market —C— for the product meeting par delivery requirements and the unit price realizable for the particular grade and specifications of the actual product I am committed for —c.

[2] In daily operation of the market, the terminal elevator operator located at an authorized delivery point frequently hedges actual grain which meets the contract specifications in all respects. For such trades, MY BASIS can be considered practically identical with THE BASIS as of the time the trade was instituted.

(a) The "Minneapolis cash basis today" refers simply to the difference between the current quotation on the nearby delivery, September, and the price at which wheat that meets all the requirements under the contract is trading in the cash market at the
same moment. Note that the nearby future is the bench mark
while the basis is usually stated in terms of cents under or over
this future delivery quotation. Hence, in the illustration the
market closed at two under, meaning that the September future
or bench mark was selling for $1.60⅞ while cash grain was
moving at $1.58⅞. This cash grain represents that which could
be delivered under the futures contract with no premiums or discounts. (The actual cash grain on the floor of the exchange is
normally based on samples, and may include variations in quality from lot to lot. Hence, the price for cash grain which is
equivalent to the grain quoted in the futures contract may have
to be a judgment figure, interpolated from the specific transactions actually taking place. On some exchanges there is a committee responsible for reporting this price.)

It is to be noted that this quotation of the dollar value of THE
BASIS can change from minute to minute, since its components,
the nearby future and the cash grain transactions, are continually
in the process of change.

(b) The phrase "basis country track" here refers to the point of
delivery for grain to be loaded at Fargo. In this case the word
"basis" is simply a descriptive adjective. However, the next phrase
"it's around 22 under at Fargo" does relate to an adjustment of
the cash basis to take into account the freight cost of 20 cents
for moving grain from Fargo to the official delivery point of the
grain exchange. In other words, if cash grain was trading at two
under in Minneapolis, then a corresponding figure of 22 under at
Fargo would be primarily a reflection of the inbound freight cost
of 20 cents plus the two-cent-under of THE BASIS.

(c) "My basis on those 10 Fargo cars" represents a historical cost
figure, namely, the difference between the actual cost of the wheat
acquired at Fargo and the price of the corresponding futures contract in which those 10 cars were hedged at Minneapolis when
they were purchased. Thus, MY BASIS is minus 18 cents or 18
under Minneapolis futures. The rest of the sentence states that
this wheat is of a quality that is better than the par-delivery
specifications for wheat deliverable on the Minneapolis Exchange.

(d) The offer to take 10 cars "at 16 under" refers to a current

OPPORTUNITY or CLOSE-OUT BASIS. In other words, regardless of what the price is in dollars and cents, the two parties are willing to enter a transaction by using the immediate quotation on the September futures contract as a bench mark, and invoice the actual grain at Fargo at a price 16 cents lower. Note that this refers to the opportunity or close-out basis and implicitly assumes that the seller will buy back his hedge at the same time that he prices the actual grain to his customer. (The customer who bought the grain can now say that "MY BASIS is 16 cents under"; this is his cost, which he will presumably modify if he pays the freight to move the wheat to a different point. In other words, he may ship the wheat to Minneapolis. He will then own it at 4 cents over the Minneapolis future after he pays the 20 cents freight to get it to Minneapolis.)

(e) Finally, the "profit of two cents" refers to the net outcome of the hedged transaction, which was entered into at 18 cents under and closed out at 16 cents under. Figuring the profit in this way, it is possible to ignore what may have happened to the actual level of wheat prices since the operator was in fact trading on the differential, so long as he had a fully compensating position in the cash and the future.

PART TWO

The Policies, Functions, and
Risk Management Problems of the Individual Firm

CHAPTER III

The Individual Firm: Management Information Needs and Functions Affected

THE FIRST chapter dealt almost entirely with the industry or the vertical commodity complex as a whole, while the second chapter dealt with an important institution — the commodity futures exchange — and the nature of the primary tool or instrument which it makes available, the commodity futures contract. Attention can now be turned to the problems and opportunities of the individual business in which commodity futures can serve a useful purpose. To do this a number of dimensions of commercial activities must be considered in order to provide a realistic view of the alternatives and interrelationships involved. What kinds of variables are involved in management's exposure to price risks and how can they be measured under a variety of situations? Chapter IV will then take up the problems of deciding between alternative risks and alternative courses of action.

The primary phenomenon with which this entire study is concerned is that of changing prices. If prices never moved up or down, the businessman would have little need for a futures market (and the speculators would probably have no interest at all). However, there are few agribusiness industries that are not plagued with major price fluctuations, often with climactic effects upon the earnings or incomes of the firms making up the industry. While everyone is familiar with the dramatic price swings that have occurred since pre-World War I, or even since World War II, the user of commodity futures must consider price movements that occur within a shorter time span. Typically, the futures contract permits the anticipation of prices from 12 to 18 months in the future, rather than for several years ahead. The range from low to high in a single year is therefore of more immediate interest, but it may still be very wide, with levels frequently showing a high 33% to 50% above the low, and sometimes over 100%. Exhibit III-1 presents these figures for July 1969 to June 1970 for CEA commodities.

To some businesses such as commodity dealers, price change is the crucial element in earnings; to other businesses such as custom processors it may be almost a matter of indifference. Most businesses fall between these extremes.

The needs of a typical commercial firm might be outlined under three headings:

1. The *physical commodity requirements* of the business call for (a) assurance that there will be an available supply of raw materials, (b) a pipeline of goods in process to permit efficient operations, (c) a supply of finished goods which will be available when they are needed for making deliveries, and (d) some form of assurance to enable the firm to accept orders with a confident expectation that delivery can be made.
2. The firm also has *financial requirements* which include the need (a) to finance goods that are owned in connection with the business and (b) for financial and security arrangements, insurance against fire, spoilage, loss, or destruction. The latter represents a financial cost which will not be incurred if the physical property is not actually required to be on hand in the business.
3. Every business must conduct its *operations with a time dimension*. Every purchase and every sale transaction (whether a trade commitment or a futures exchange contract) defines a date or moment at which the price involved becomes firm. Usually this is the quoted price on the date the trade is booked, although there are exceptions such as "market on date of delivery," "season's average price," or a formula price based on current quoted prices on a date to be chosen by the buyer (or seller). The manager responsible for planning, the making of contracts, and the management of product flows must have enough flexibility to take advantage of the environment and the opportunities that arise. It is almost axiomatic that business should be conducted without being limited to

EXHIBIT III-1. HIGHEST AND LOWEST PRICES OF FUTURES ON PRINCIPAL MARKETS,
BY DATE AND FUTURE, DURING THE YEAR, JULY 1969 TO JUNE 1970

Commodity	Market	Unit	Highest Futures Price			Lowest Futures Price		
			Price	Date	Future	Price	Date	Future
Wheat	Chicago Board of Trade	Cents per bushel	154 3/4	June 29, 1970	1971 Mar.	119 1/2	July 28, 1969	1969 Sept.
	Minneapolis Grain Exchange	do.	179 1/2	Jan. 21, 1970	1970 Mar.	149	July 29, 1969	1969 Dec.
	Kansas City Board of Trade	do.	144 1/2	June 29, 1970	1971 Mar.	119 1/4	July 28, 1969	1969 Sept.
Corn	Chicago Board of Trade	do.	144 7/8	June 29, 1970	1970 May	114 1/2	Aug. 20 & 21, 1969	1969 Dec.
Oats	Chicago Board of Trade	do.	72 1/4	June 29, 1970	1971 May	56 1/2	Dec. 1, 1969	1969 Dec.
Rye	Chicago Board of Trade	do.	127	July 7 & 9, 1969	1970 May	100	June 26, 1970	1970 July
Soybeans	Chicago Board of Trade	do.	308 1/8	June 29, 1970	1971 May	233 1/8	July 29, 1969	1969 Nov.
Cotton	New York Cotton Exchange Contract No. 2	Cents per pound	28.78	Nov. 10, 1969	1970 July	24.08	Mar. 9, 1970	1970 Mar.
Wool	Wool Associates of the New York Cotton Exchange	do.	119.0	Aug. 19 & 21, 1969	1969 Oct.	93.0	June 30, 1970	1970 July (old)
Eggs (Shell)	Chicago Mercantile Exchange	Cents per dozen	65.25	Dec. 5, 1969	1969 Dec.	30.50	Apr. 2, 1970	1970 Apr.
Potatoes	New York Mercantile Exchange Maine Grown	Dollars per cwt.	4.80	Mar. 5, 1970	1970 May	2.09	Oct. 10, 1969	1969 Nov.
Soybean oil	Chicago Board of Trade	Cents per pound	13.56	Mar. 3, 1970	1970 Mar.	7.13	July 14 & 25, 1969	1969 Dec.
Soybean meal	Chicago Board of Trade	Dollars per ton	98.50	Jan. 20, 1970	1970 Jan.	66.30	Nov. 12, 1969	1970 Jan.
Live beef cattle	Chicago Mercantile Exchange	Dollars per cwt.	32.82	Mar. 12, 1970	1970 June	26.00	Aug. 21, 1969	1970 Dec.
Choice steers	Chicago Board of Trade	do.	33.25	Mar. 12, 1970	1970 Apr.	26.95	July 25, 1969	1969 Dec.
Live hogs	Chicago Mercantile Exchange	do.	30.05	Feb. 19, 1970	1970 Feb.	18.25	June 25, 1970	1971 Apr.
Frozen pork bellies	Chicago Mercantile Exchange	Cents per pound	48.87	Feb. 2, 1970	1970 Feb.	30.30	June 26, 1970	{ 1971 Feb. 1971 Mar.
Frozen concentrated orange juice	Citrus Associates of the New York Cotton Exchange	do.	58.90	Jan. 19, 1970	1970 Sept.	34.00	June 22, 1970	1970 July

SOURCE: "Commodity Futures Statistics, July 1969–June 1970," Statistical Bulletin No. 464, USDA, Commodity Exchange Authority, March 1971, p. 44.

the goods actually in hand. This involves lead times which in many cases require some kind of assumption about price changes.

The businessman can seldom accept, as a measure of his concern, a simple direct impact of X cents per unit of price change times Y units of inventory. But the measurement of the price change and the degree of its impact can be extremely complex when pricing policies and price parallelism between raw material and finished goods are considered, or between various qualities, locations, and other specifications. The valuation methods used by accountants may also be critical.

The units or quantities of commodities involved likewise have to include, in addition to the physical inventory ownership, many of the kinds of commitments discussed briefly in the preceding chapters. Some of these are assets or liabilities on the official books of account; some are not, as in the case of unfilled orders.

The following sections are a survey of the major dimensions of exposures to risk of price change which have to be measured or estimated and taken into account by the business manager. Some bring up problems that involve contractual arrangements; some relate to accounting methods; some fall in the area of planning, budgeting and forecasting; still others call for the identification and analysis of special commercial situations and opportunities. In examining such a diverse field of information sections have been devoted first to measuring the (1) net at-risk position in volume terms, then (2) in price terms. While the concept of "net position" is a primary overall measure, it is vital to the manager to have further detailed information, to cover (3) some important differences between the major types of ownership and commitment components of the net position, (4) the particular requirements of managers handling different business functions that expose them to special price-risk management problems, and finally (5) some of the data that are needed to record the mass of diverse transactions in a form that will serve day-to-day management decision needs and also enable accountants to compile reliable interim and annual accounting results. The next section (6) brings together in outline form the information needs implied in the previous five sections.

The balance of the chapter moves on to consider (7) some of the types of price patterns and impacts, and (8) some of the variations in hedging methods employed.

Throughout these considerations it will be helpful for the reader to keep in mind what has been said in Chapter II about the concepts of "analogous parts" and "residuals" or "differentials", even though trade vernacular makes it necessary to continue to use the term "basis." [1]

THE NET AT-RISK POSITION OF THE INDIVIDUAL FIRM IN VOLUME TERMS

In order to secure a measurement of the magnitude of price risks for the individual firm, it is essential that for any particular commodity there be a definition in volume terms of the "net position" or net exposure to price impacts. (For the moment this determination can be thought of without including commodity futures contracts, since these will be brought into the picture later.) The primary categories making up the net position for a firm have already been discussed in industry terms in Chapter I.

1. The first ingredient will ordinarily be the book inventories of the specific commodity in question. These should be stated in volume units for the present purpose.
2. Second, there may also be inventories on hand representing the product in modified form, cruder or more processed than the basic item itself, but still considered subject to about the same

---

[1] As the study progressed, it became evident that the term "basis" could not adequately denote all of the considerations that had to be taken into account. While "basis" is precisely the same as "residuals" or "differentials" in some commodities for some situations, it is a single summary figure which often lacks the precision required for careful analysis and decision making. At the same time there are many situations where it is not a comprehensive enough term to embrace all of the variables to be dealt with. Moreover, the idea of splitting the commercial or cash commitments into two parts, one part specifically analogous to all the specifications contained in the commodity futures contract and the other comprised of all the residuals, tends to call for an explicit treatment of each residual component, as well as the single net residual called basis.

price risks. These items will be converted if necessary to "equivalent" units[2] and expressed in the same volume terms as the commodity in question on the books (for instance, estimated cottonseed oil content of seed on hand, or the wheat content in flour inventories, or corn equivalent in mixed feeds).

3. The business may well have firm trade commitments — contracts to buy, or bookings to be delivered — at a firm price. These are inescapably factors in the firm's price exposure, and a fully hedged position will normally have to cover these commitments (which will be plus for commitments to buy and minus for undelivered sales), as well as the physical holdings. Most businesses do have good information at this point, comprised of goods on hand plus purchase contracts, less undelivered sales, which is characterized as the net cash inventory position before hedging.

4. Beyond the physical holdings and the firm-price contractual commitments are the many quasi- or one-way commitments, such as options, purchases or sales not fully confirmed, open offers, guaranteed floor stock protection, or published price lists. These are important, but they should not ordinarily be combined in the previous compilation. Price changes will have a very different impact in these cases which can seldom be covered by a compensatory or offsetting transaction such as matched hedging in commodity futures. They represent a separate category of exposures, however, which cannot be ignored, and which can be considered separately. These are represented in Exhibit I-4 as segments I_B and I_S. They cannot logically be included in the hedging program; nevertheless, some of them might be covered (imperfectly, however) by an "anticipatory hedge."

These anticipated or implied exposures are in many cases an important factor in hedging considerations. Since they are not firmly defined commitments, the amount of exposure they represent is usually a matter of judgment. This is no reason, however, why the manager should not try to pin down an estimate in quantitative terms, and to consider how this particular exposure might be expressed if it is to be regarded as the analogous part of a hedging operation. The residuals in such a case may then show the elements of risk that are retained or covered by other strategies, actions, escape clauses, or similar devices.

---

[2] For further comments on equivalent units, see Chapter I, pp. 14–16, and below, pp. 87–91.

EVALUATION OF THE NET AT-RISK POSITION IN PRICE TERMS

Assume that the categories outlined in items 1 through 3 give a record of a "net position" expressed in physical units. It is still unsafe to assume that price impacts can be measured simply by entering into the profit and loss column a single dollar figure showing the market price change times the number of units of "net exposure." This would be possible if (a) all units experienced identical or strictly parallel changes in market value and (b) the books of account reflected immediately all such changes in valuation for inventory on the books, while (c) the commitments not on the books of account were likewise reassessed to take up as profit or loss the "paper gain or loss" inferred from the price change. It is never as simple or precise as this. Any experienced manager of hedging operations will agree that such strict conditions are at best only roughly approximated in real life, and even these approximations are subject to judgment factors.

Nevertheless, it is clear from what has been said in Chapter II that a practice of hedging the entire open or net at-risk position in the commodity futures market presumes something like the formulation just suggested. It is equally clear that even after expressing the at-risk information in the form suggested, then hedging by using commodity futures contracts can only cover what has been defined as the analogous part of the commercial exposure, leaving significant residuals. (See the discussion of analogous parts and basis in Chapter II.)

Therefore, the simple concept of price-risk exposure as being represented by the fluctuations of a single "market price" or a family of market prices moving in parallel courses is unrealistic. It is the limiting case which does reflect an important underlying current in the price flow, but the real-life situations practically always have to deal with a wide variety of inequalities and differentials. The simple textbook illustration of matched price movements has therefore been amended to take into account the changing differentials between components of the price complex.

Holbrook Working was one of the first to give a clear exposition of the theme of "hedging for profit" as contrasted with hedging for the sole purpose of avoiding the risk of price swings.[3]

The fact that significant differences do exist between price movements of various cash and futures components means that these differences must be a part of the management information record, to be used both for decision making and for evaluation purposes.

The analysis of factors which underlie or explain price interrelationships and the expounding of how commercial advantages can emerge from making proper use of their variations are taken up in later chapters. For the present purpose, it is sufficient to characterize price differentials as factors of crucial importance to the business manager; and he must therefore look at the several price components, not just one market price.

A Word About Commitments as Distinct from Inventories on Hand

Commodity futures contracts are like other trade commitments in many respects. Both types of commitment are given a similar role in adjusting the "net" position. Also, they are a part of the paraphernalia whereby the commercial operator who would otherwise be limited to spot or physical availabilities of goods can carry out his transactions and manage his net ownership or price-exposure responsibilities without this limitation. He can plan ahead much more flexibly, and he can pin down certain costs and realizations without the handicaps of having to own and store that which he buys or of having to sell only that which he has in hand.

Another of the well-known aspects of the commitment device is its value in facilitating the transition from "plans" to "action." Scheduling of processes and product flows is made more smooth and certain and the vertical coordination from one stage to the next in the commodity complex is made efficiently without having

---

[3] Working, "Hedging Reconsidered," and "New Concepts Concerning Futures Markets and Prices," esp. pp. 436–437.

to resort to vertical mergers and ownership integration. In other words, a firm can compete[4] in the vertical industry complex even though it is not a vertically integrated firm.

A still further advantage, which applies particularly within the firm using a commodity futures market, is the possibility it offers for delegation of commercial authority to subordinates without loss of central control of the overall price risk. Managers, buyers or salesmen at various plants or locations can be authorized to buy or sell locally, thus committing the firm to a price risk, while the net exposure of all such commitments or holdings can be balanced out by a single headquarters desk trading in commodity futures hedges.

An entirely different factor affecting commercial operations is the contrast between the typical commercial commitment, the commodity exchange futures contract, and the owned inventory, as respects cash flows. The distinctions can be summarized as follows:

1. Commercial commitments require no cash (unless there is a good-faith deposit) and no cash is required if prices change while the commitment is still open.
2. Commodity exchange contracts of course require a minimum cash margin deposit at all times. They also require additional cash if prices move against the holder or they may release cash if prices change in his favor.
3. Owned inventories require cash to finance them initially. Such goods on hand do not yield or require additional cash (except for such costs as storage), no matter how prices change, until the goods are turned over.

PRICE FLUCTUATIONS AS RELATED TO THE FUNCTIONAL
ORGANIZATION OF INDIVIDUAL FIRMS

In order to identify the price impacts in a particular business firm, it is helpful to look at certain major business functions. The

---

[4] A firm having access to a futures market is even more secure in that it cannot be denied or frozen out from the current flows of goods to meet its need.

ones that have been selected for the present purpose are those of (a) procurement, (b) processing, (c) marketing, and (d) stewardship or custody of assets. Each of these will be considered briefly in order to establish the management problems resulting from fluctuating commodity values as they affect these functions. These are commonplace categories, frequently used to define the nature of the entire business operation, although the final category which is referred to as "custody" or "stewardship" is included primarily because it is regarded in many firms as a distinct responsibility which may be assigned to a particular individual, sometimes even designated as a separate profit center. In this context it might be thought of as the "commodity policy" responsibility, whether or not there is a specific individual assigned to carry it out.

Procurement

Practically every business is confronted with a procurement problem. The businesses that will be of particular interest in the present study comprise either firms which create and sell one of the tradable commodities (farmers, for instance) or those which are buyers of the commodity itself or of commodities derived from or closely related to the tradable item. In the simplest form of business organization, the procurement function may not be a separately organized department or be treated as a separate profit center; procurement might be one of a combination of responsibilities with no separate accountability for this particular function. In other firms procurement may be regarded as a service function in which the purchasing officer acts as a buying agent for another part of the firm; in organizational terms this is still not considered a profit center. By contrast, we have found instances where the procurement does have guidelines, budgets, or targets which establish a profit base that is expected to be met or bettered in the actual carrying out of the function.

Naturally, the person responsible for procurement is expected to assure the firm of a dependable supply of goods required in the business, and in so doing to minimize costs. He can attain this by his commercial astuteness, by selective buying, or by effective planning which may entail the authority to reach out into the future with purchase commitments beyond the minimum that might be required to assure a dependable supply. He may also avoid price exposure by engaging in special price commitments through various devices to be discussed later. These can include contracts containing formula prices, complex futures arbitrage and the like, as well as conventional hedging.

Processing

In the ordinary business, the processing or conversion operations are structured in a way that emphasizes engineering considerations. These ordinarily call for optimum use of production facilities and minimum delays or tie-up of materials. Inescapably a certain volume of pipeline inventories is required, but at the same time the manager of plant operations is unlikely to be the best situated official to assume management of the price risks involved.[5]

In contrast to the general case just outlined, the processing function may also include storage or warehousing services wherein a number of specialized storage facilities are employed. The optimum use of warehouse space may become a matter of planning the proper capacity and then attaining high occupancy to reduce per unit overhead costs. Moreover, many processing requirements call for quality assortments and product availability needed for the best planning of production runs and product mixes. All these situations mean that careful attention has to be given to the inventory problem. Thus, those responsible for capacity utilization must consider the impact of price changes and the management of risks resulting from these assorted requirements. While this is not often the production man's direct responsibility, he cannot escape some of the effects.

Marketing

In the marketing function is included not only the traditional problems of finished goods inventories, but we have found it realis-

---

[5] He can still be charged for the working capital employed as an incentive to avoid carrying excessive supplies.

tic to embrace herein the entire question of commercial strategy, including selling ahead, built-in customer price protection, and the like. The reason for handling the marketing function in this broad manner is that it has been found to be consistent with the way many firms actually organized their functional assignments. Moreover, the interplay of cash and futures prices is often extremely important in developing marketing strategy. Since the marketing job differs so much from one firm to another, more detailed discussions of this assignment will be deferred until particular commodity situations have been taken up. It is clear, however, that the marketing man is nearly always involved in price risk decisions.

Custody

The concept of custody or stewardship as a business function may seem at first glance to be a duplication of categories. It is certainly true that most business managers who are responsible for a profit center are responsible for the management of certain assets assigned to them. However, it is also true that any or all of the procurement, processing and marketing functions can be so organized as to operate on something resembling an intracompany agency or custom conversion basis without having each functional department or each plant manager assume ownership and price responsibility for the goods being handled (in some cases they become cost centers rather than profit centers). In addition, there are frequent instances in the analysis where the overall management of commodity ownership and price responsibility is a head-office responsibility with limited discretion allocated to individual departments. This responsibility may be retained by the top executive alone, or it may be assigned to a financial or planning staff officer or a commodity mangement group which acts to integrate the total corporate exposure and capital allocation in this field. In any event commodity policy is an important aspect of the management of working capital which might be overlooked if the procurement, processing, and marketing objectives were examined separately without a central point of coordination.

The approach that has been taken in the present study has been structured in an important degree around the management problems of executives charged with the four major functional responsibilities just discussed. These in brief are the ongoing activities which the businessman expects commodity futures contracts to serve.

ACCOUNTING FOR PRICE CHANGES AND EXPOSURE

Two primary components of any accounting system are the balance sheet and the income statement. Owned inventories carry a value in the balance sheet but neither unfilled trade sales and purchases nor commodity futures contracts are regularly regarded as balance sheet items. Hence, these important components of the "net position" are not required or available in the balance sheet computation. In this sense they are recorded in memorandum or side-account form.

What this says is that the balance sheet is designed to record inventory titles, not commodity price exposures.

While the net exposure or net impact of price change does not show explicitly[6] on the balance sheet, the price-change impacts clearly do affect the operating statement. Normally, the results of *closed* hedges are entered as a part of cost of goods sold. When futures results are in favor of the firm, they are applied to reduce the cost of goods sold; when they represent a loss, they add to these costs. Theoretically, these gains or losses have offset a corresponding loss or gain from the effect of price changes upon transactions in the cash commodities, as embodied in the figures for sales revenues and procurement costs.

The results of *open* futures contracts are essentially matched up with inventories on hand or uncompleted cash transactions. There are a variety of methods for handling these items, all of which seem to have the common purpose of seeing that the effects of price changes on one side are in fact offset by appropriate handling of price changes on the other; i.e., they are either included on both

---

[6] In some instances the valuation method is explained in notes to the financial statement. For examples, see Appendix C.

sides, or excluded.[7] The problems involved in the application of these methods are extremely complex, and a simplified statement about them has to be treated with great reservation. However, three observations may be in order.

1. The area being considered — open futures contracts (not closed), inventories on hand, and unfulfilled trade commitments — is relatively limited, since closing inventories for a typical raw material usually represent a relatively small fraction of the total year's turnover. Thus the price exposure reflected in open accounts and goods on hand is likely to be a moderate part of the total impact of price changes over a full year.

2. The two principal methods of entering the necessary adjustments do not produce significant differences in results. One method consists of pricing inventories at current market and then adjusting them to allow for up-to-date pricing of open futures and trade commitments. These adjustments (up or down) bring inventory values back to approximate the cost at which the goods went on the books (assuming a fully hedged or zero net position). The second method is one which is designed to defer the price impact by carrying inventories at cost of acquisition, and leaving all price adjustments in the futures and unfilled trade commitments in a deferred status. In this situation the results of both sets of price changes are taken up at the time deliveries are made and contracts closed out. The first method would appear to be most appropriate under certain conditions (such as 100% full hedging) while the second might fit better in other situations (for example, seasonal accumulations, or less closely parallel price movements).

3. The particular modifications of these methods are numerous. Most often they represent an adaption to the situation of the particular firm or industry and to the question of whether or not the firm has a policy of being fully hedged. In most cases the accounting procedures are designed with the objective of tying in with detailed information for management decisions and delegations of profit responsibility. This may account for considerable differences in detail from firm to firm.

Returning to the broader impacts of price change under fully

---

[7] For further information on accounting treatment of commodity futures transactions see references to Logue, Rowley, and Geiger in the Bibliography.

hedged conditions, two further observations are of significance. First, operating results are roughly equivalent to replacement cost operations so far as the hedged commodities are concerned. Net price exposure is zero, thus, results reflect an outcome approximately equal to the use of simultaneous replacement cost for goods sold. Second, the "cost" value of inventories on the books, *despite a fully hedged policy,* will still move up and down with the longer swings of prices. Correspondingly, cash will move down or up to the extent that payments to the broker (or receipts from him) reflect the fact that someone else (e.g., the speculator) is realizing financial gains or losses for carrying the price exposure from which the hedger's income statement is insulated. Hence, over a period of rising prices a hedger will see his inventory values rise (cost basis) and his cash fall off, while during a period of price decline, cash will be augmented but inventory values diminished.[8]

SUMMARY OF INFORMATION NEEDS

Before proceeding further it may be well to review some of the classification problems presented so far.

Commensurable Volume Units

It has been indicated that there are three "commensurable" elements in the net hedgeable position so far as volume of a particular tradeable commodity is concerned. These are:

1. Units of the commodity itself in inventory.
2. Equivalent units of the commodity in other forms (unextracted, in process or incorporated as part of finished goods).
3. Firm trade commitments to buy or sell the commodity.

If the net summation of these elements is fully matched by a futures contract position on the opposite side, the net position can be defined as zero or "fully hedged."

---

[8] For further details regarding this phenomenon, see below, Chapter IV, "The Impact of Inventory Changes — An Elementary Case."

Noncontractual Commitments and Implicit Exposures

In addition to these conventional "hedgeable position" factors are the nonfirm or noncontractual commitments and implicit exposures. These have to be handled as special types of risk, seldom amenable to the simple matched transaction type of hedge. In most industries, for instance, the use of futures as a procurement tool is unlikely to be matched against a confirmed sales contract. Nevertheless, commodity futures can be a valuable tool to use in management decisions for handling some situations in this category, to be discussed in the following two sections.

Price Relationship Information

The price dimension of the risk exposure requires an awareness and appraisal of similarities and disparities of price movements, both past and prospective, between the "offsetting" transactions. These disparities, or hedging residuals, are of many sorts, varying from one industry or one firm to another. In some commodities, especially the grains, the residuals are all combined and become known as "basis"; in others the traders refer to the same phenomena as "differentials," which may be plus or minus, large or small, increasing or diminishing, related to a specific trade or to the overall market. Sometimes certain disparities can be lumped together and assumed to compensate or average out over a period of time in the give and take of trading;[9] however, an alert manage-

---

[9] To illustrate this situation a particular spot cash purchase in December is assumed to be matched against a short futures contract for May delivery. This produces a specific residual or "my basis." (See Chapter II, pp. 66–67.) Normally, it is my hope that there is a disparity between "my basis" as thus defined and the close-out basis on which the paired commitments will be terminated. The disparity may be "built in" at the outset by virtue of my having made a good buy or a good trade (in either the cash or the futures, or both). Or, it may develop later out of market imperfections, bad storing quality, bad yield estimates, or the like. These erratic variances in my close-out basis are very real, and a wise trader tries to make them bring a profit in his favor. Most statistical studies of hedging, because of the nature of available data, are likely to treat them as disparities that average out over a period of time, thus often losing sight of them altogether.

ment will intend and expect to make basis profits as a part of its hedging operations.

One of the major premises of the present study, however, is that for tradable commodities there will be fluctuations in the level of prices which (1) will be reflected in both cash and futures contracts and which (2) will have a direct impact of major importance in the results of the individual firm if left unhedged.

Intrafirm Responsibilities and Functional Specialization

The intrafirm specialization of functions must be recognized in trying to isolate the nature of price impacts and the ways of dealing with them. The basic decision areas affected are those of procurement, processing, marketing, and the one which is called "custody." The latter can be regarded as one which can coordinate, if it does not take over, the price impact interests of the other three. Business functions have been presented as a guide to help identify where price-risk responsibility exists within the typical business.

Hedging Accounting Procedures

The traditional business accounting records do not for most firms bring together the elements needed for price-risk administration and appraisal. New accounting procedures have been developed in a few industries, notably grain dealing, flour milling, oilseed processing, and animal feeds,[10] in an attempt to provide decision guidelines as well as accurate accounting records. This is not a simple task, but it has been proved possible; a number of firms have developed effective programs for gearing price-risk measures to operating results.

---

[10] See Grain and Feed Dealers National Association, *Management Accounting Manual,* Washington, 1968; also, American Institute of Certified Public Accountants, *Case Studies in Auditing Procedure — A Grain Company,* New York, 1949; and Rowley, *Inventory Pricing in the Grain Industry.*

A Management Information System

A management information system for use in handling price risks should be tailored to the needs of each particular commodity situation. What follows is an illustrative list of categories of information which is more complete than is needed for the simplest cases and insufficient for the more complicated ones. These are in addition to the usual book accounts.

1. At the highest level (price-risk or hedging policy for the firm) it is highly desirable to have a written statement of objectives and responsibilities, together with explicit details regarding delegated functions and authority. In the selected interviews for this study relatively few cases were found where such a policy and procedure statement existed, and an appreciable number were encountered where different officials of the same firm had conflicting ideas as to how the decision responsibility was allocated.

2. For the firm as a whole a net position statement, kept current on a daily or weekly basis, would appear to be essential both to the top management and to the major functional managers (those responsible for procurement, processing, marketing, and custody). This statement would present at least the following items, stated in volume terms:

   (a) Inventory on hand (expressed in standard quantity units).
   (b) Unfilled orders (purchases to be received).
   (c) Unfilled orders (sales on the books).
   (d) Futures contracts long.
   (e) Futures contracts short.
   (f) Net trade position combining (a), (b), and (c).
   (g) Net futures position combining (d) and (e).

   In many instances a greater amount of detail is desirable for top management use. Some firms make detailed hedging strategy decisions at a high level. In these cases a statement of each specific program, together with frequent progress reports is in order. In other firms the detailed information (which has to be compiled in any case — see below) is not specifically reviewed so long as operations remain within authorized ranges.

   Such a simple net position statement as the one just described will show the net exposure at a given time, but it will not show the exposure in monetary units, nor will it show the financial results of price change impacts, except by inference from the net exposure information. At the very minimum, an appraisal of financial results of the price impacts requires that prices be applied to the position statement items. This would give at least a crude estimate, by multiplying the average net position volumes, (f) and (g) above, by the change in market price per unit.

3. The records required by the people making detailed decisions are of course much more voluminous than the figures entering the summary reports. Full detailed specifications are needed by buyers and sellers, including quality, location, delivery dates and the like. These records go beyond those required for the usual financial accounting procedures, but they should be classified in such a way that they can be reconciled with the official books. Some of the problems encountered in this connection are discussed in later chapters and in Appendix C, as well as in the remaining sections of this chapter.

Some, but seldom all, of the following reports and analytical statements are available in the management information systems of firms which make active use of commodity futures for hedging.

(a) Total company policy, delegations, and procedures.

(b) Company or divisional position statement.

(c) Futures position (by deliveries, products, spreads, etc.) trading record.

(d) Futures results (opportunity basis).[11]

(e) Trading positions and basis (in detail).

(f) Inventory management positions and results, with and without hedging.

(g) Outlook for commodity prices and availabilities.

(h) Strategy on specific project expectations.

A TENTATIVE CLASSIFICATION OF TYPES OF PRICE PATTERNS AND IMPACTS

The basic functional classification of procurement, processing, selling, and custody correspond in general to the intrafirm organ-

---

[11] This means an evaluation of the accrued profit or loss including open commitments which could be closed out at the current market. See discussion of "What is BASIS?" at the end of Chapter II.

izational units which are likely to be affected by price changes. In addition it is important to distinguish between the various price patterns that characterize the performance of these functions.

1. If the firm's buying and selling prices are likely to move parallel to each other and both of them follow the same price patterns as the futures quotations, we have the theoretically[12] ideal situation for a conventional, fully hedged operation, involving both the procurement and selling functions. This kind of business lends itself to operating "on the basis." It is typified by grain dealers, millers, feed dealers, and others who can be broadly characterized as "dealers" and "converters." [13]

2. A second category might be referred to as "producers." These firms produce and sell the tradable commodity, but they buy or apply an assortment of inputs whose costs may bear little resemblance to the price pattern of the tradable commodity. Farmers are a prime example of this category. Theirs is a problem of selling their product at the most advantageous time and terms. For them the futures market offers an opportunity to select the advantageous time to sell, free from the restraints of harvest dates, storage facilities or other limitations that would apply if only cash trades were possible.[14] The systematic use of futures by this group is usually defined as hedging, even though the "matching" process may be, at best, a rough estimate.

3. A third category is the "processor" or "manufacturer" who buys the tradable commodity to be used as an ingredient for processing into end products whose prices are subject to diverse influences other than the raw material price. The candy company which buys sugar and chocolate or the bakery which buys wheat flour are examples. Here the interest is primarily that of procurement on the most advantageous terms.

It is rather unusual to find a policy of keeping the raw material position fully hedged in situations of this sort. It is not unusual,

---

[12] This statement should not be understood to imply such perfect parallelism of price movements as to eliminate the opportunity to make a profit from trading on the basis.

[13] The categories used here are a modification of those suggested by Johann Scheu, Director of Purchasing, The Nestle Company, in a talk at Seminar/'69 held at New York Coffee and Sugar Exchange, October 6, 1969.

[14] Hieronymus, *Uses of Grain Futures Markets in the Farm Business.*

however, to use commodity futures to keep the net exposure or position at a planned level, often expressed in terms of so many weeks' requirements or so many bushels or tons.

4. Other businessmen have special situations of their own. For instance, a broker may find that he can organize a trade which will bring a buyer and seller together only if he, the broker, provides a bridge by taking a spreading or other position in commodity futures so that he can accommodate the delivery conditions each party desires. Here we have what may be called a "trade-making hedge," which is similar in a way to the arrangements bankers sometimes make in setting up foreign exchange cover to facilitate trades by their customers. The middlemen, by undertaking a futures hedge may be able to accommodate a seller wanting to make an immediate sale on which the buyer does not want to take delivery until a later date.

5. In addition to the types just discussed are the wide assortment of speculator transactions which take the form of arbitrages, spreads, straddles and the like. These are not strictly within the purview of this study of commodity futures contracts as a management tool, since this is not a treatise on the speculator. However, there is an "offset" of one futures contract against another, and the devices referred to are very widely used by commercial operators as well as speculators.

It is obvious that the price changes of tradable commodities will have a different impact on earnings in the various situations just outlined. In the first case, for the dealer or converter, if buying and selling transactions are simultaneous, and if prices move together, the margin between purchase and sale might be said to consist of a replacement cost basis. However, any lags between purchase and sale (which is another way of saying a variable net exposed position) can have very serious effects. Without a hedging program using the futures market, it would be practically impossible to match each purchase with a sale (or vice versa) so that it would be extremely difficult for management to control the exposed position.

In the case of the producer, his objectives and his alternatives may be of several sorts, quite different from the dealer or converter. He may want to borrow money on his growing crop and to assure his banker of the viability of the loan by the sale of futures contracts. Or, he may decide to keep his farm storage facilities occupied longer even though he thinks the best price levels for selling his crop have already been reached.

In the various other categories referred to above, the price exposures and their management offer a rich variety of uses for the commodity futures contract as a management tool. The possibilities in these areas can be inferred from what has already been said and from the accounts of specific business practices that will be discussed in subsequent chapters. Each situation, it will be seen, requires a careful study of objectives and of price behavior before suitable policies and plans can be developed. One thing becomes very clear; there are many situations where any futures hedging at all is inappropriate, and very few where hedging is a simple matter which can ignore the complex problems of residuals. The latter is only possible where the commercial commitment involves little more than the "analogous part," as in the so-called "perfect hedge" of economic theory. Where other factors (residuals) are significant, the residual factors may well offer very important marketing and profit opportunities, as will be seen later.

HEDGING PATTERNS IN VARIOUS COMMERCIAL SITUATIONS

Handlers, Dealers, and Converters

The fully hedgeable "basis" operations of handlers, dealers, converters, etc., represent the oldest and most highly developed of the hedging patterns to be considered. As stated earlier, this type of operation reaches a high degree of refinement in the normal dealing within the grain, the feedstuffs and the milling industries. It is also common among other raw material dealers and international traders, embracing a number of commodities such as cocoa, sugar, coffee and fats and oils as well as grains and soybean products.

Typically the participants in these categories of trade deal in large volumes, with volatile prices and narrow profit margins. They operate on both the long and the short side of commodity futures markets. The special services of the participants in this type of trade have to do with *time* availability (storage or holding), *place* availability (transport and locations), *form* availability (selection, grading, standard conversions, refining, etc.), and the bringing together of buyers and sellers who have many diverse interests and needs.

For this group most of the cash transactions required can be readily split into the "analogous part" (i.e., that corresponding to the par-delivery contract specification) and the residual or basis.

The purchasing, converting, and marketing functions in such businesses are closely allied, with two or three of these functions involved in almost every commercial transaction, every commodity selection, every movement, every storage decision. Obviously, a central communication system is needed and actions of all individuals must be closely coordinated.

Organizationally there must be a central control point for the total risk-management function, usually reporting to the top executive officer in charge of the business in that commodity.

Delegations of authority to make buying and selling decisions in day-to-day trading operations must provide enough leeway to conduct commercial transactions, but normally these delegations are made with the proviso that price-change risks are to be managed by the firm through hedging, thus leaving the commercial decision maker responsible for current replacement margins and other terms making up his basis. The margin or basis figure is a byword in trading negotiations; it is a natural reflection of the fact that the critical trading factors can be reflected in this type of residual margin. A purchase or sale is likely to be consummated at so many cents over or under the specified future on the exchange, rather than at a specified price.

Each firm usually has a total "position statement" which is designed to show the categories of holdings and commitments, including futures contracts as well as other exposures, and a net position, long or short. Backing up such a summary statement are many detailed records showing each futures account, locations and specifications of commodity holdings, open trade commitments, delivery dates, and the like. These are needed for trading purposes. In addition, the accounting records of the firm tie this information in with operating statements, margin deposit positions, cash flows, and the official balance sheet.

There are many degrees of complexity, especially in businesses classified as converters. In cases such as soybean processors there are futures markets in beans and also in soybean oil and meal. The net positions may be expressed in either the raw material or the products, and special procedures are employed to handle the various possible situations that develop. The access to oil and meal markets for futures contracts opens numerous choices for the commercial firm dealing in all these commodities.[15] Such situations are so varied that their diverse nature will have to be inferred from the examples presented in later chapters.

The Producer

The producer of a tradable raw material has to think of his exposure primarily from the viewpoint of his marketing function.[16] He has to decide at what point he is exposed to price risks. Once he has made irreversible commitments of his land resources and other inputs to the production of a particular commodity, his only way of recovering these outlays is through the sale of the finished commodity. With access to a futures market the grower has several advantages. (1) He has the benefit of a price estimate for the product before he decides to commit his resources to that commodity. (2) He can actually make a hedge contract to deliver his output at a known price (assuming the location and quality of his crop makes this feasible). (3) He can hedge in futures with the intent to repurchase the short hedge and book his crop to a cash buyer when he considers the spread of the cash offer against the futures closeout price is most favorable to him. (4) He can usually find a local buyer who will offer to buy his crop for later delivery, since the

---

[15] These include "putting on a paper crush" by selling oil and meal futures against soybeans owned, or even against long soybean futures contracts. Even further, one can put on a "reverse crush" by buying oil and meal futures and selling soybean futures to balance these sales. In the last instance, the firm might take delivery against these oil and meal contracts to take care of customer requirements, and deliver its beans to the exchange if cash margins are so narrow as to make crushing the beans unprofitable.

[16] For a discussion of some applications to farm producers, see Hieronymus, op. cit.

buyer can cover the price exposure he incurs by a commodity exchange hedge.

In short, the commodity futures market affords the agricultural producer with an escape from being "at the mercy of the market" if he wishes to cover his production commitments with an assurance of price protection before he buys his seed. He still carries the risks of yield and quality,[17] but price assurance can be a great advantage. He can cover his price risk all at once or gradually according to his judgment and his desire to transfer price risks to others than himself.

The method of recording his net position sounds very simple compared with the dealer or converter. An estimate of expected crop output is a ready measure of ultimate exposure. The problem comes if the expected crop does not turn out. In any event, the exposure begins when inputs of resources are committed. The producer will judge whether to hedge all at once a value corresponding to his total expected output, or whether to take out price insurance progressively on the resources and costs he feels he has sunk during the growing season. Another guideline, which is perhaps more realistic, is to make a short sale in futures at the time he feels selling prices are favorable to him (or more favorable than they are likely to be at a later date).

In any event the net position expressed in terms of prospective crop, minus contracted sales, gives a guide to indicate the net price-risk exposure. These are figures for his own guidance in management decisions; ordinarily neither factor enters his books of account until deliveries are made and contracts closed out.

It should be remembered that an adverse price swing in futures contracts will require cash to maintain required margins; but if a bank lends money on growing crops, it should be ready to augment any such loan if the addition is reflected in an increase in the value of the collateral (i.e., the prospective harvest).

In the case of the producer, as with the converter, the principle of the "analogous part" can assist the user of the commodity futures

---

[17] The yield uncertainty presents a special hazard since a widespread crop failure would be partly compensated by higher prices, to the double disadvantage of the grower who is hedged.

contract. What has been hedged is precisely the prospective fluctuations of value of a par delivery specification applied to the quantity hedged. The futures market will reimburse or expect payments corresponding to these fluctuations and nothing more. Risks of yield, quality, and changes in his basis are still retained by the producer. If he concludes that such risks are acceptable or even in his favor, so much the better. The hedge served to pin down the price level at which his crop could be sold if the local cash prices bear their usual relationship to the futures, and he still stands to gain the benefits of favorable productivity.

The Processor or Ingredient Buyer

The processor or ingredient buyer will be distinguished from the so-called "converter" discussed earlier. The converter is characterized by the fact that his purchases and his sales are subject to substantially parallel price movements, both dominated by market fluctuations of a tradable commodity. The processor on the other hand usually buys the tradable commodity as raw material, but incorporates it into a product which does not have predominantly parallel price movements. There is of course some degree of price relationship, but there is likely to be a delayed or diluted effect or even a complete absorption of many of the short-term changes. The degree of price impact is thus subject to estimate or judgment, although the cost of an important input expense is fully and directly affected.

1. This type of situation is often viewed as one in which the revenues of the ongoing business are more or less predetermined because of selling price insensitivity, but raw material costs can wipe out expected earnings if their prices move upward. The manager therefore has to decide the extent to which he should protect his raw material requirements.
2. There are at least three apparent ways to attain the desired degree of price protection. Actually owning goods in inventory is the first and most apparent. The business must have the physical goods needed to keep its operations going. But beyond that necessary for operating requirements, the holding of goods may be costly and unwieldy. Firm forward orders from suppliers is a second

possibility, but this is often difficult; the seller may be reluctant to commit himself ahead and the buyer may be tied to a fixed set of specifications when he would prefer to remain flexible. The third alternative, the futures market, can provide a substantial measure of cost protection at a minimum of cash outlay and with maximum flexibility.

3. The processor is usually a buyer of futures contracts, although he may use futures to reduce his raw material price exposure below the amount represented by goods he actually has on hand or on order. His management guideline is basically a matter of maintaining a planned net position, although unlike the dealer or converter, he is seldom justified in maintaining a policy of a fully hedged or zero net position. One reason for not having a fixed policy of this sort is the difficulty of defining such a zero exposure position. Another, and more logical, reason is that the selling price of finished products is generally more subject to independent management decision and adjustment than is the case where raw material and product prices are both determined by factors beyond the manager's control.

4. As in the other cases just discussed, it is necessary to recognize that the futures contract provides price protection for that "analogous part" of the price exposure which parallels the par-delivery specifications on the futures exchange. The residual risks are still left with the firm, and they can often provide a real source of gain or earnings to the astute procurement strategist.

5. In the case of the processor or ingredient buyer, the internal responsibility for hedging operations rests altogether with the purchasing official, once general policy lines have been established at the higher level.

6. In some cases the purchasing department turns over the raw material for processing at the net cost (including results of hedging and risk management decisions) while in others the purchasing function is a profit center, delivering raw material at a current or average market value and reporting separately the results of the special buying strategies employed.

7. In some cases there have been questions in this group of users as to whether the definition of hedging applies and to what extent. The conventional grain dealer is permitted by the CEA to buy or sell futures so long as his net speculative position does not exceed an amount specified by CEA regulations. In effect, for the bona fide hedger, this net speculative position rule applies

only to the net futures contracts not matched against opposite cash positions (inventories or trade commitments) in the commodity in question. For some processors (bakers, for instance) the rules have been interpreted to prevent counting ownership or contracts for sale of baked goods against procurement hedges in the form of grain futures.[18] Flour millers are, however, permitted to make such an offset in respect to flour sales.

Nonmatched or Contingency Hedging

The fourth category of commerical situations employing commodity futures contracts for risk management has no commonly used name. It involves an assortment of transactions or risks which do not qualify under some of the official CEA regulations as "hedges" even though the intent may be in many cases to match specific risks of price-change impacts. In other cases the purpose is to take advantage of the time flexibility which futures contracts offer in carrying out legitimate business plans.

1. For the most part the exchange rules that apply to such not-strictly-matched futures contracts will regard them as "speculative." However, the accounting and management information required to handle them is an integral part of the commercial operation and deserves to be treated as such within the firm. This means that the manager can appropriately pinpoint the risk or exposure he has in his "cash" or "commercial" operations and identify the elements in this exposure which comprise the "analogous part" (that is, the part which corresponds to the commodity specifications for par delivery of the futures contract). The residual risks may be then recognized and dealt with separately after transferring to others through the futures exchange, the portion of price risk that can be covered in futures.
2. Some of the businesses within this group regard their futures con-

---

[18] This is a good illustration of the necessity of drawing a distinction between hedging and speculation, presumably turning upon the phrase "substantially similar commodities." Whatever the intent of the commercial manager in using the commodity futures, he may be subject to one ruling which defines his operation as "speculative" and thus subject to the speculative trading limits even though he is not in the speculative category for capital gains purposes. (See Appendix A.)

tract operations as an adjunct to procurement, some to processing, and some to marketing, or to general policy combining these. Hence the location of responsibility can differ from case to case. The essential consideration is that the function to be served must be rationalized in terms of the objectives and commercial activities of the business if we are to regard management decisions as anything but outright speculation (i.e., hoping for a profit based upon futures operations alone).

3. Examples of uses of this technique include the following:

   (a) A cattle feeder may deliver his fed cattle but may still feel that he wants to keep his interest in the commodity since he will be buying feeders in a few months for his next cycle of operations. By purchasing live cattle futures contracts, he expects that these contracts, plus the revenue realized from his previous marketings, will afford him funds for replacing his feeders even if prices rise in the interim; if the futures should decline, he expects that the feeders will cost less, too.

   (b) A mail-order house may want an assured supply of textile items to meet the implied "short sale" of its catalog price, but its supplier is anxious to be protected against possible increases in cotton costs. Such protection can be offered by giving the supplier a formula price geared to the cotton market, then purchasing cotton futures contracts to cover the estimated exposure.

   (c) Candy makers may be similarly bound by custom to hold finished product prices more stable than their sugar or cocoa costs which can fluctuate widely. With appropriate study they may find a suitable formula for establishing an appropriate offset in the futures market.

   (d) Innumerable opportunities for cross-hedging exist where parallelism in price movements exist, even though the commodities may not be classified as "substantially similar" to qualify under conventional hedging regulations. This would apply, for instance, to the hedging of coconut oil in soybean oil futures.

4. It is our understanding that such operations as those just described would be considered under the *tax* laws to comprise "normal business operations" rather than speculative gains or losses, provided a record of the intent and relation to commercial activities is clear. Thus, accounting methods would presumably take results into the current account, even if the operation is defined

as "speculative" under the "speculative limits" set for the open futures position.

Arbitrage or Spreading

Four general categories of operations have been discussed which we as laymen can regard as hedges. The *definition of a hedge* which is being used is that based upon the idea of *a deliberate offset provided by a futures transaction to balance the price impacts which the hedger considers he is exposed to in the conduct of his commercial business.*

Another type of hedge which is equally logical is one undertaken in any of the numerous arbitrage operations within the futures markets themselves. These include spreading between delivery months, cross-hedging between markets which conduct trading in the same or very similar commodities, or a matching of purchases in one commodity with a sale in an entirely separate commodity which the trader believes will experience a relative decline compared to the one he bought.

Transactions of this sort are very useful adjuncts to the types of hedging described earlier, and they do not involve a net exposed position so far as the trading policy is concerned. The use of such trading, however, is usually regarded as speculative so far as CEA limits on holdings of contracts are concerned.

So far as the present study is concerned, techniques such as arbitrage, spreading, and cross-hedging are added tools for the business manager, and at the same time this type of operation provides a useful service to the market mechanism by helping correct price distortions and disparities within the component elements of the futures markets themselves.

Hedging as Related to "Speculation"

It is unfair to lump all trading situations not specifically outlined above as "speculation." In the context of commodity trading, speculation has been defined as the buying or selling of futures contracts for the purpose of making a profit from the price moves of the futures alone, without respect to commitments in the cash commodity. It is not unusual for the prudent businessman to "take a view of the market" in connection with his many commercial transactions. In a sense he can use the futures market to make a good buy or a good sale just as he would use the cash market if the futures were not available. The time flexibility offered by the continuous trading in futures may be a dimension of the market which the commercial manager cannot afford to ignore, even though it is not used with a specific view toward the matching or offsetting of other commitments.

The present study does not cover the many patterns, purposes, strategies, and practices of the pure speculator as defined above. Nonetheless, it is important to acknowledge the critical importance of the speculator in providing the assurance of an active open market and the availability of people willing to accept the risks of price change, which the commercial hedger wishes to transfer to others. Thus, the speculator is an important adjunct to the commercial uses of the futures market; without him, the hedgers would have only each other to deal with.

CHAPTER IV

Price-Risk Insurance, Price-Risk Avoidance, Hedging, and Profit Opportunities

CHAPTER IV introduces the action and decision processes by which a manager, equipped with the tools and measurements discussed in Chapter III, can appraise the nature of his price-risk exposure in broad perspective, pick out the significant variables that affect this exposure and weigh the alternative courses of action available to him. Since the scope of the present study is confined to industries whose businesses involve tradable commodities, it follows that commodity futures contracts are among the tools he can use.

In Chapters I and II the inevitability of inventory pipelines in modern industry and the useful device of firm contractual purchase and sales commitments (whether in commercial or futures markets) as a business tool were discussed. These contracts can serve two very major purposes, even though within the overall position for the entire industry they add up to a zero net exposure; (a) they permit planning of operations with assurance that goods will be available even though not presently in hand through actual ownership or vertical integration, and (b) they permit buyers and sellers to operate with much more precise knowledge and control of cost-price relationships. Chapter III discussed the individual business and its situation at a single stage of the vertical industry system of which it is a part, including the functional organization and allocations of responsibility for inventory and price risks within the firm.

THE IMPACT OF INVENTORY CHANGES —
AN ELEMENTARY CASE

In order to examine the next phase of the problem, it is well to take another look at the nature of the business risks and business decisions that are being dealt with. For simplification of this task we will return temporarily to the elementary concepts of price risks as they affect inventories and inventory accounting. In all cases it is well to remember that price change impacts can act in either direction; they may increase or reduce profits. They are not like destructive catastrophes which have only damaging effects.

To illustrate the accounting impacts of inventory price changes in as simple terms as possible, it seemed easiest to visualize a retail shoe store which has an opening inventory of 50,000 pairs of shoes valued at a cost of $10 per pair or $500,000. Assume further that annual sales represent one complete turnover of the inventory or 50,000 pairs and that the gross markup is, for simplicity, $10 per pair or a retail price of $20 per pair resulting in sales of $1,000,000. Costs and prices have been constant up to the present year. What will happen if shoe prices at wholesale are increased by $2 per pair and the store owner (not wishing to add to inflationary pressures) marks up his shoes at retail by only the $2 increase per pair ?

He will in effect be taking a $2 per pair additional markup on each pair of shoes as he sells it out of his inventory, and this will increase the sales on his books by $100,000 and the same amount will be added to gross profit.[1] At the same time the replacement of each pair of shoes sold will add its extra cost ($2 per pair) to the cost value of his inventory. This will absorb all the added cash generated by greater dollar sales. Thus the gross profit on the books will show a $100,000 increment; there will be no extra cash to show for that profit (or to pay taxes on it) because the entire amount was used just to maintain the same shelf stock of inventory needed to run the business.

---

[1] The assumption that sales volume will not suffer with the higher shoe prices is realistic if these prices reflect a situation where prices generally are rising.

By the time income taxes are paid on this phantom income, the business has less cash than as though prices, sales, and profits had not changed.

The starting point for this illustration was the assumption that the conventional first-in, first-out (Fifo) inventory accounting method would be applied. Exhibit IV-1 presents the illustration in terms of the major bookkeeping entries using three methods in the accounts: first the Fifo method, then running through the same basic transactions using two other devices — last-in, first-out (Lifo) inventory accounting and (by assuming that a commodity futures market was available) a fully Hedged inventory operation. Some striking contrasts result.

The following are the specific assumptions that apply to these cases:

1. The inventory of shoes is held constant at 50,000 pairs.
2. Sales in one year equal 50,000 pairs, a complete inventory turnover.
3. Wholesale cost of shoes had been $10 per pair for an extended period prior to the opening of the year in question. Hence opening inventory values can be set at $10 per pair whether figured at cost or at market.
4. Normal markup is $10 per pair, including $8 operating costs and $2 profit (before taxes). This is held constant throughout the illustration.
5. Shoe prices at wholesale are assumed to increase by $2 per pair, to $12, on January 2 of the year in question. The merchant decides to retain his $10 per pair markup, making the retail price $22 per pair. Each pair sold is replaced at the price of $12.
6. No further price changes occur during the ensuing year.
7. It is assumed that the merchant can treat his inventory valuation in either of three ways, Fifo, Lifo, or Hedging in a perfectly operating futures market. Under the Hedging alternative it is assumed that all Hedges reflecting the price change have been closed out and replaced by open futures which show no accrued price change.

Under these assumptions, the asset accounts representing inventories, cash, and margin account with broker are shown, along with the appropriate operating statement.

EXHIBIT IV-1. FINANCIAL IMPACT OF FIFO, LIFO, AND HEDGING

A. *Fifo Accounting*

Inventory

Beginning inv.	$500,000	To cost of goods sold	$500,000
Purchases	600,000	(Ending inventory)	600,000
	1,100,000		1,100,000
(Beginning inv. next year) =	600,000		(up $100,000)

Cash

Sales	$1,100,000	Purchases	$600,000
		Operating exp.	400,000
	1,100,000		1,000,000
(Bal. for'd.)	100,000		(up $100,000)

Operating Statement:

Sales		$1,100,000
Cost of goods sold		
Beginning inv.	$500,000	
Plus purchases	600,000	
	1,100,000	
Less ending inv.	600,000	500,000
Gross Margin		600,000
Operating Expenses		400,000
Net Operating Profit (per books)		$200,000
Net Cash Flow		+$100,000

It becomes apparent in this exhibit that under A. Fifo the year shows a book profit of $200,000 which takes the form of $100,000 of added cash and $100,000 paper profit on inventory.

Under B. Lifo, the book profit is $100,000 and there is added cash of $100,000, but inventory is priced below the market by $100,000.

With C. Hedging the outcome is a book profit of $100,000 (just as under Lifo), but cash has been required to pay the broker

EXHIBIT IV-1 (CONTINUED)

B. *Lifo Accounting*

Inventory

Beginning inv.	$500,000	To cost of goods sold	$600,000
Purchases	600,000	(Ending inventory)	500,000
	1,100,000		1,100,000
(Beginning inv. next			
year) =	500,000		(No Change)

Cash

Sales	$1,100,000	Purchases	$600,000
		Operating exp.	400,000
	1,100,000		1,000,000
(Bal. for'd.)	100,000		(up $100,000)

Operating Statement:

Sales		$1,100,000	
Cost of goods sold			
Beginning inv.	$500,000		
Plus purchases	600,000		
	1,100,000		
Less ending inv.	500,000	600,000	
Gross Margin		500,000	
Operating Expenses		400,000	
Net Operating Profit		$100,000	
Net Cash Flow		+$100,000	

$100,000 to cover the Hedging loss, while the only place the $100,000 of book profit can be found is in the appreciated inventory value, not in cash.

Such illustrations can give very misleading impressions unless they recognize that prices can go down as well as up. In such a case (assuming next year reverses the price movement in the earlier illustration) it would be seen that Fifo results would show no profits at all. Lifo results would be unchanged but there would be

EXHIBIT IV-1 (CONTINUED)

C. *Hedged Operations*

Inventory

Beginning inv.	$500,000	To cost of goods sold	$500,000
Purchases	600,000	(Ending inventory)	600,000
	1,100,000		1,100,000
(Beginning inv. next year) =	600,000		(up $100,000)

Hedge Account Margin

Maintenance Margin deposit	X	Paid to cover losses on short sales (to cost of goods sold)	$100,000
From cash	$100,000		
(Bal. on deposit)	X		(No Change)

Cash

Sales	$1,100,000	Goods purchased	$600,000
		Operating expense	400,000
		To margin acct.	100,000
	1,100,000		1,100,000
			(No Change)

Operating Statement:

Sales		$1,100,000
Cost of goods sold		
Beginning inv.	$500,000	
Plus purchases	600,000	
Plus hedge losses	100,000	
	1,200,000	
Less ending inv.	600,000	600,000
Gross Margin		500,000
Operating Expenses		400,000
Net Operating Profit		$100,000
Net Cash Flow		0

no cushion under inventory values. The Hedge option would in fact show a book profit of $100,000 but an enhancement of cash availability by $200,000, since the broker would pay cash on the futures transaction profit.

What we are saying in effect is that if all these assumptions of constant quantities and rigid parallelism of sales prices and cost of goods purchased were to apply, a dealer will reflect his paper profits in earnings under Fifo, whereas he will avoid paper profits and losses by the Lifo method, and his profits will be reflected in the cash account. The Hedging method states profits on a "replace-ment cost" basis as does Lifo, but since cash is paid or received on the futures transaction, the firm in effect uses cash to finance the inventory appreciation and receives cash when inventory prices decline. The real life situation, of course, involves a much more complicated set of conditions, and the great flexibility available to a Hedger becomes a very important consideration.

One thing is clear in the simplified illustration. The Lifo method and Hedging cannot be used on the same inventory quantities with-out being redundant. This does not mean that the two methods cannot be used in conjunction with each other[2] even on the same commodities (e.g., Lifo to apply to basic or carryover pipeline, while Hedging is used to cover the temporary or seasonal increases in exposure). The limitation applies when the same inventory is protected from price impact through Lifo accounting, and then is protected again by a short sale in the futures market. This situa-tion would be equivalent to a "Texas Hedge" (see Glossary).

These are some of the barest essentials of the long-familiar[3] phe-

---

[2] For example, the notes to financial statements for several firms, e.g., Archer Daniels Midland, A. E. Staley, Swift & Company, Hershey Foods, Monfort of Colorado, and Wilson & Company, all of whom are active in hedging, cite Lifo inventory valuation methods. See Appendix C.

[3] For some early articles, see:

Arthur, "Inventory Profits in the Business Cycle."

Arthur, "Something Business Can Do About Depressions."

Nickerson, "Inventory Valuation — The Use of Price Adjustment Ac-counts to Segregate Inventory Losses and Gains."

Peloubet, "Problems of Present-Day Inventory Valuation."

Putnam, "The Role of Paper Profits in Industry."

Walker, "The Base-Stock Principle in Income Accounting."

nomenon so frequently referred to as "inventory profits" or "paper
profits." In one of his early articles, the author suggested that the
relative importance of inventory profits in a business operation
might be measured by "comparing the average value of inventories
with the average earnings of a company, then examining how
widely the prices of the goods it handles typically fluctuate." [4] This
suggests a rough formula:

$$\text{Impact on the business} = \frac{\left(\substack{\text{Volume of inventory} \\ \text{in units}}\right) \times \left(\substack{\text{Typical price change} \\ \text{in \$ per unit}}\right)}{\text{Profits before taxes}}$$

OR

$$= \frac{\left(\substack{\text{Value of} \\ \text{inventory}}\right) \times \left(\substack{\text{Typical \% change in} \\ \text{value per unit}}\right)}{\text{Profits before taxes}}$$

This formula may be applied to individual commodities in the
inventory as well as to the broader total (for which a price composite or index would be required). The inventory involved can
be an average of several years or periods; the price change figures,
however, must relate to the same time period as the earnings figures. The formula is designed to employ figures drawn from conventional lower-of-cost-or-market and first-in, first-out accounting
procedures.[5] It will give a reasonable basis for judging the order of

---

[4] Arthur, "Something Business Can Do About Depressions."

[5] To apply this formula to the shoe store example it may be assumed that
average profits before taxes had been running at $100,000 per year or 10%
on sales. A price increase of $2 per pair for inventory replacement would
thus work out as follows:

$$\text{Impact of price increase} = \frac{50,000 \text{ pairs} \times \$2 \text{ per pair}}{\$100,000 \text{ average profit}}$$

$$= 1.00, \text{ or a 1 to 1 ratio with profits from other sources.}$$

This is a high figure, but not unrealistic for industries with high inventory
requirements, volatile prices and narrow profit margins. In the shoe business, of course, one does not expect a 20% wholesale price increase every
year.

The practical application of this measure in an individual firm requires
much more detailed information than is typically available in annual reports. The data presented in Appendix C, for instance, show sales and
inventories for a number of the firms that are included in the present study,

magnitude of this phenomenon between two accounting period closings. (It would of course be a more refined figure if it included the effect of trade commitments other than actual goods on hand. Moreover, it may not be easy to isolate the portion of the inventory to which a particular price change measure should be applied. For a manager contemplating a hedging policy a problem also comes up when he tries to define the appropriate units to employ in establishing a guideline for determining the amount to be hedged, especially in such cases as growing crops or raw material content of goods in partly processed or finished form.)

We know, moreover, that changing prices affect the decisions of buyers and sellers, each of whom takes his price anticipations into account whenever he is negotiating a transaction. Hence it is not just an inventory valuation problem we are dealing with. It can be a factor in decisions to trade or not to trade. In some cases price is only one of the very complex set of factors entering into a commercial decision. In such a situation, the businessman may be able to isolate the factor of possible market price swings from other considerations in his transaction and weigh the consequences separately. Then, if the risk from price swings can be broken away and transferred to others through hedging, many opportunities for advantageous trades and services may become apparent which would otherwise be obscured by the inescapable uncertainties relating to price changes. This is a further complication but it must be included if we are to be realistic. Price impacts are indeed a combination made up of a number of segments, and the manager who can treat these segments separately and skillfully will enjoy a considerable advantage in the market.

PRICE CHANGE PROTECTION METHODS —
SOME ADVANTAGES AND LIMITATIONS

The elementary illustration of price impacts presented in the imaginary shoe store has innumerable ramifications, some of

but these do not usually reveal information for particular products, nor do they show any price change data.

which will be discussed in connection with specific industry experience and practices presented in later chapters. Before proceeding to these it is necessary to consider several inventory valuation procedures which have a bearing upon this problem.

What kind of price change protection do business managers need or want? Should they try to escape price-risk exposure, even if price changes can help their business as well as harm it? The answer to this last question appears to be that some managers feel that they can apply their resources and skills to better advantage if they are spared the exposure to major price-change catastrophes even if there may sometimes be gains, sometimes losses. This is not just a matter of seeking stability or security. Rather, it reflects a desire to do those things they know they can do well, and a conviction that those things can be better done and on a larger scale if exposure to major price impacts can be minimized. For other managers, market price fluctuations are not to be buffered with matching hedges, but to be turned to profitable account by proper anticipation and position taking.

Whichever view the manager may take, we will assume that he regards his job as one of decision making in a business enterprise in which his own time and talents will be employed in directions where they can make the greatest contribution to profits over a period of time.[6] In this context, it is important that each manager have available the tools to manage and control his net inventory position, whether it is held constantly at a fully hedged, or zero, position, or whether it is adjusted according to a pattern which affords wide discretion from one moment to the next. (In the shoe store example, the net position is assumed to be held constant in all three cases, but not at a zero level except in the fully hedged assumption.)

Two other characteristics of actual commercial operations should be kept in mind. First, the commercial manager who chooses to maintain a zero or fully hedged net position will have many profit and loss opportunities in the residual exposures which

---

[6] In this connection the idea of "risk aversion" may be useful; however, it is by no means simple, but highly complex, and very difficult indeed to quantify.

he carries even after matching the "analogous parts" of his commodity ownership and cash market commitments with futures hedges. Second, the manager with a variable net exposure is not going to be a perfect forecaster. At best he will be dealing with probabilities, not with certainties about future price changes.

At least six decidedly different alternative arrangements or "management tools" are worthy of consideration by the manager wishing to be the master rather than the victim of his price risk exposure.

1. The first is the one receiving greatest attention in the present study — that of hedging in commodity futures contracts. This is available only if appropriate tradable commodities exist.
2. A second is the adjusting of trade commitments and orders in such a way as to control the net exposure without using commodity futures. This device, while widely used, is seldom flexible enough to permit the manager to turn orders on and off just to meet his inventory price exposure plans.
3. The third is the complete avoidance of inventory commitments by becoming a broker or warehouseman or a custom processor and leaving the inventory ownership and price risks to others. Most industrial firms are likely to do some contract or custom work, but it should be remembered that *someone* has to own the industry inventories.
4. The fourth alternative is the adoption of Lifo inventory accounting, which in effect holds the per-unit value of the basic (or opening) inventory constant from one year-end to the next. This amounts to treating the basic pipeline inventory almost as though it were a long-term capital asset like a building whose value does not change with market price fluctuations.[7] (New increments of inventories, and open trade commitments are still fully subject to price impacts.)
5. The fifth category is in fact a miscellaneous group which might be characterized as "spreading the risk." Devices of this sort include the use of three-year or five-year average prices for both inventory costs and cost of sales, the establishing by cooperatives

---

[7] Somewhat analogous results are attained by establishing reserves for inventory price fluctuations or by the base stock method of inventory valuation. These are much less used than Lifo since they are not accepted for tax purposes.

of conservatively valued inventory pools or the developing of long-term formula-pricing contracts.

6. A sixth category is that of having an outside authority peg the prices. This is not strictly a "management" tool, since it removes discretionary control from the business manager. However, it is included here for two reasons. First, it is a common situation in controlled economies and in a good many supported industries in the United States;[8] and, second, the price pegging decisions are often participated in by industry members. Moreover, it does in fact provide a route of escape from being "at the mercy of the marketplace" which has been a long-familiar complaint in many businesses, especially farming.

The six categories just outlined can be thought of as ways of modifying the impacts of price change from those which would have resulted under conventional (Fifo) accounting rules for valuation of inventories at the lower of cost or market. This is the base from which we can start.

Hedging offers a high degree of flexibility as one of its greatest advantages.

1. It is a separate transaction which need not affect in any way the carrying out of the commercial transaction or commitment which has been hedged. (If one wishes, it is even possible to keep a separate book record of hedging results and post them directly to profit and loss without entering them elsewhere in the operating statement or inventory accounts.)

2. It is possible to maintain any desired net exposure, whether this is to be constant or variable, high or low, provided the net specu- lative exposure does not exceed the limits prescribed by the com- modity exchange or the CEA.

3. A net position can be changed on very short notice by utilizing the high liquidity offered by an actively traded futures market.

At the same time there are certain limitations or conditions that have to be recognized by the hedger.

1. He is covering only the price fluctuations that match those in the fu- tures contract he is employing (the analogous part). His actual inventory or trade commitment involves residual factors which

---

[8] This topic was discussed in some detail in Arthur, "Impact of Agricul- tural Programs upon Market Structures and Functions."

have not been covered by the hedge. This is usually a distinct advantage to the "basis" trader, but it may be troublesome for other
operations.

2. Hedging requires cash payments (apart from the cash required
   to finance the physical inventories) whenever price changes move
   against the futures position.

3. A hedge transaction involves a decision regarding "time," meaning the choice of delivery month in which to be hedged. What
   has been transferred is the impact of changes *over time* in the price
   at which the market appraises a par delivery at a specified month
   in the future.

The other inventory management alternatives involve an assortment of inventory price impacts which differ from the conventional
unhedged shoe store situation. For instance, the custom processor,
who is most nearly immune, is seldom free from such secondary
impacts as result from volume fluctuations or pressures to adjust
processing methods or formula mixes.

The Lifo method may hold a constant unit value for quantities
present in both opening and closing inventories, but variations in
closing inventory quantities will have substantial repercussions on
results, as will the price impacts upon seasonal accumulations and
liquidations. Frequently managers on Lifo find themselves taking
special measures with their suppliers or customers to make their
closing inventory quantities "come out right."

The other procedures referred to roughly as "spread the risk"
devices work in various ways. Some employ long-term average
prices in valuing inventories, as in the tobacco industry. This
smoothes out price impacts but does not eliminate them. The use
of conservatively priced inventory pools defers inventory profits to
be drawn upon in subsequent periods as the inventory is liquidated.
Most of the price guarantees, price pegs, and otherwise administered prices serve to shift price impact decisions to the regulators,
usually with the objective of holding prices stable at levels designed
to provide a "fair return."

To sum up, a variety of tools are available to managers for
modifying the impact of commodity price changes. In some situations, ownership can be avoided altogether, while in others the

impact of price fluctuations may be transferred to others without forgoing ownership or possession. One advantage of the specialized inventory valuation methods is that they can be applied to inventories where there is no appropriate commodity futures market. Where trading on an organized exchange exists, the commodity futures contract is one of the most flexible and effective tools available since it permits a very wide range of discretion to the user without hampering his commercial operations in the cash market. In fact, most of the other methods, once they have been adopted, offer the business manager little room for discretionary inventory risk decisions except by changing his commercial transactions or policies.

SOME THEORETICAL ASPECTS OF RISK AND UNCERTAINTY: INSURANCE AND AVOIDANCE

Professor Frank H. Knight, in his classic discussion in *Risk, Uncertainty and Profit,* distinguished sharply between economic risk on the one hand and uncertainty on the other:

> Uncertainty must be taken in a sense radically distinct from the familiar notion of Risk, from which it has never been properly separated. The term "risk," as loosely used in everyday speech and in economic discussion, really covers two things. . . . It will appear that a measurable uncertainty, or "risk" proper, as we shall use the term, is so far different from an *unmeasurable* one that it is not in effect an uncertainty at all. We shall accordingly restrict the term "uncertainty" to cases of the non-quantitive [sic] type (pp. 19–20).

For our purposes it will be worthwhile to take a brief look at the full spectrum from certainty to uncertainty: (1) Pure uncertainty is an imaginary situation where nothing is known about anything and where there are no measurable variables, or even an idea as to what factors are relevant to a problem. (2) At the other extreme, complete certainty assumes that outcomes are sure and that all variables are measurable. (3) Between these two extremes there exist various degrees of uncertainty and these can be broken down in terms of certain important characteristics based on the kinds of uncertainty and the importance of the outcomes upon profits.[9]

The definition of risk relates to quantifiable unknowns. In other words, we are dealing with a concept which can be expressed in probabilities and numbers. It is the field in which the actuaries resolve many individual uncertainties into broad but dependable, even certain, outcomes. In effect the process of converting "uncertainties" into "risks" is an important function of business and economic research, even though in each individual case it is not possible to come out with a single certain result.

"Uncertainty" has also been given a working over by the decision theorists in recent years. Uncertainties range from the utter and unclassified chaos of ignorance up to the point where the decision maker can work out an assortment of outcomes associated with his possible decisions, but he still lacks a basis for pinning down a specific outcome for any specific case. It is still a chancy decision but, as in playing bridge, you decide whether to finesse the queen, and which is the best way to finesse her.

Looking again at the spectrum which runs from absolute uncertainty (some people say this implies a state of complete insanity) to the other unattainable extreme of complete certainty, it is easy to see that most business judgments contain elements that are akin to each extreme. The job which the businessman faces in many of his decisions is simply one of lining up his decision-making activities in such a way that he minimizes the amount of what we are calling uncertainty either (a) by getting more information; (b) by better analysis and management of relevant factors; or (c) by making actuarial appraisals of risks in such a way that he is protected by broadening his exposure to avail himself of a less uncertain average result.[10] Or, finally, he can sometimes (d)

---

[9] The concepts discussed here were presented in more detail in Arthur, "Risk, Uncertainty and the Futures Market."

[10] The question of diversification is largely of this nature — a dispersal of uncertainties by extending the exposure over a wide enough field to reduce

accept the uncertainty entailed in an operation and try to match it with a countervailing commitment for the primary purpose of offsetting a segment of that uncertainty, and in effect avoiding it altogether by transferring it to someone else.

On the basis of this simplified framework it may be interesting to reexamine where the futures market can play a part. It seems clear that for many speculators futures contracts represent simply a vehicle whereby they expose themselves to a high degree of uncertainty in hope of realizing a large gain. Such speculators include some who base their activities upon extensive economic and statistical analyses, and others who assume that they are reducing their own uncertainty by leaning on the advice of others. On many occasions the speculator uses no rational technology for advancing his own objective. He falls victim to the fact that even if all the price movements were pure chance, the quantifiable costs which he incurs in the form of commissions will inevitably load the scales so that the net probability is on the side of an adverse outcome in the long run.[11]

---

the *relative* severity of any one adverse outcome. As a general principle, it dilutes rather than enhances *profits,* but, properly planned, it does reduce the over-all degree of uncertainty.

[11] It has been contended by some distinguished scholars (see reference to J. M. Keynes and J. R. Hicks in the Bibliography) that the speculator enjoys the benefit of a kind of insurance premium paid by the hedger, who accepts a downward bias in the price at which he places his forward hedges because of his desire to have the price protection it affords him in carrying out his ongoing business. Other statisticians (e.g., Cootner, Houthakker, Telser, Working) have produced conflicting evidence upon this matter. It is my view that numerous factors exist which make it impossible to expect a consistent relationship between cash and futures quotations which would confirm or disprove this reputed bias, or "normal backwardation," to use Keynes's term. These factors vary from commodity to commodity and from time to time, as for example the relative attractiveness of various penalties and premiums on nonpar delivery specifications, or locations. So far as this factor is concerned, 'it might be expected that the tighter the par-delivery specifications and the more severe the penalties for departures (under existing market preferences) the less likely will be the tendency to discount the future below the expected cash value of the par delivery specification. It is frequently stated by commercial traders that the futures market tends to move toward the price of the least preferred selection of quality

If the futures market is to be thought of as a useful adjunct in the kind of economic system to which we belong, it may be defended in considerable part by the argument that the futures market enables businessmen performing the necessary functions of supplying economic needs and allocating economic resources to make *their* many decisions more efficiently and with assurance that they are operating farther over toward the "certainty" area of our spectrum than would have been the case without the futures market. To illustrate, a farmer may be an expert at producing crops or livestock, but unskilled in undertaking the financial burden entailed in price-risk exposures. He might be able to enlarge his production, using funds he can borrow against a hedged inventory. The flour miller does this; the cattle feeder may do it more and more as cattle futures trading becomes more widely used.

Two or three characteristics of the futures contract are particularly important to this discussion of risk and uncertainty. The first characteristic is that the product specifications in the contract can serve as a *common denominator*. We choose a set of delivery terms — quantities, grades, locations, and agencies — to define the contract. Not all — indeed only a small part — of the wheat covered by futures contracts ever moves physically to Chicago, Kansas City, or Minneapolis. Yet the contract specifications provide a set of standards which the trade can use as a quoting basis. This may or may not represent the largest volume selection or the highest traffic

---

and location specifications which can still be used to make deliveries against futures contracts.

A detailed consideration of this and other issues related to futures price behavior, hedging, and speculation appears in the series of technical papers that make up the "Proceedings of a Symposium on the Price Effects of Speculation in Organized Commodity Futures Markets." See Food Research Institute.

It is interesting to note an observation in one of the studies reviewing various theories of futures trading, a reflection of the preoccupation of economists with the statistical configurations rather than the business application of this tool. Venkataramanan in his book, *The Theory of Futures Trading,* said: "The importance of the study of futures markets, to which we now turn, lies in the fact that they provide us with an abundant data for the study of social behaviour under conditions of uncertainty" (p. 10).

point. Th: best bellwether, not the biggest sheep, is what we're after; on a golf course we use "par" as our common denominator, rather than some score that is more likely to be attained by the average would-be golfer on the so-called average course. We want a basis for translating price risks from one transaction to another, and we want a unit that lends itself to reliable and easy use as a common denominator.

At the same time, we want actual deliveries to be practical for as many traders as want to make such deliveries. It is an aberration of the market when peculiar conditions at the delivery point make the common denominator untypical, as when channels of trade are clogged, when strikes or weather tie up transportation, or when deliverable storage holdings for one reason or another are undesirable in the trade. The futures market has an obligation to minimize the frequency of such incidents. The fact that commodity futures contracts can terminate in the delivery of the tangible commodity is the primary linkage between this contract-trading world and that of physical commodities in the world of commerce.

Finally, as was mentioned in Chapter I, some of the specific characteristics of vertical industry complexes have made futures market contracts a useful device. These are usually (but not always) found where relatively long production cycles, as in agricultural or other extractive industries, make substantial inventory positions necessary, where broad trading in staple articles makes ownership positions reasonably fungible, and where supply or demand variations lead to substantial price fluctuations. Firms in these industries have plenty of other worries as they try to provide the necessary "time, place, and form utilities" without adding or exposing themselves to the hazards of gyrating prices. The managers in these industries have a plentiful bundle of risks to manage, but the impact of price change over time is perhaps the biggest. These are the people who really need the futures market. For others it may be a convenience or an opportunity, but for them it is almost a necessity, if their resources and skills are to be employed most effectively.

What we want to examine now is the place of the futures market in the total complex of risks and uncertainties faced by operators who use futures trading. We are not interested in those transactions which stand alone as speculative commitments not related to any other commercial business of the same firm, but rather in those transactions which are an adjunct to related commercial operations. The speculators do contribute a great deal toward spotting and correcting temporary or illogical disparities within the market. Sometimes they become powerful enough to manipulate the market itself for short periods of time, in which case supervisory authorities are likely to be around with an eagle eye. Many authorities, including John Maynard Keynes and other economists who have studied the matter,[12] concluded that this group of "intra-market" traders makes a major contribution toward giving the market breadth and toward improving the focus of the forces in the market upon the determination of true economic values. Therefore, the flexibility of the speculators and traders tends to provide a demand on whichever side of the market there seems to be a deficiency, whether it be for long or short positions.

It is those who use futures as an adjunct to their commercial activities who interest us here. Of this second group, those participants in the market who are fully hedged — including commodity dealers, growers, processors, etc. — can, once their hedges are placed, carry on their business without much concern over what the "right" level of price may be. The fact that they hedge out their price commitment implicitly assumes that they do not know, or do not care, which direction prices will move, or cannot afford to undertake such an unknown exposure. Most of these people are trying to set up a transaction which will dispose of a part of the exposure entailed in their commercial operations. So long as the net residual of an individual's matched commitment (his "basis") embraces price relationships which these traders are confident will not worsen during the life of their commitment, they need not much care whether prices are at the "right" economic level or not. These are people whose interest is not in appraising and taking on the *risks* of price change. Instead, for the parts of their commercial commitments that are analogous to the par-delivery terms on the

---

[12] See, for instance, the writings of John Maynard Keynes, Holbrook Working, Gerald Gold, Roger Gray, and L. Dee Belveal in the Bibliography.

exchange, they are intent upon *escaping* the *uncertainties* of price change by shifting that responsibility to others, and thus limiting their *risk* to the residual factors. They are, of course, alert to take advantage of any new switching opportunity or any new need that will further enhance their opportunity for profit.

The transactions of growers, dealers, and processors which are not hedged to neutralize the major price risk element would be considered as retained or speculative commitments.[13] These "uncovered" commitments can be large or small in relation to the total trading by the firms involved. The significant point is that with a futures market available, they can represent considered positions based on careful study and analysis. In other words they would fall in the classification of carefully managed risks in most cases, rather than inescapable uncertainties.

POLICY CONSIDERATIONS RELATING TO PLANS FOR USING FUTURES

How do these elements of uncertainty, risk, price levels and price relationships fit together to give the business manager some perspective in dealing with them? The several components of the problem can be summed up as follows:

1. "Uncertainty" has to do with unknown factors and unknown impacts. It is a general term but it is useful to think of it as a spectrum which runs all the way from complete uncertainty at one extreme to complete certainty at the other.
2. "Risk" can be thought of as a particular aspect of the total uncertainty field we have just described. In the case of risk, enough elements are known and can be expressed in quantitative terms so that the businessman can have some confidence as to where his problem is located along the certainty-uncertainty spectrum and can, thus, have a good judgment regarding the future outcomes, at least when a number of similar incidents can be combined into an average.

---

[13] Special cases of other forms of price assurance such as government supports or Lifo accounting would require a modification of this statement. See above, pp. 114–115.

In this case, it has been assumed that the changes in the general level of prices offer a high degree of uncertainty from the commercial manager's viewpoint. At the same time a much smaller degree of uncertainty (indeed, a basis for reasonably confident judgment) exists in respect to the merchandising or trading factors that have been discussed as residuals, differentials, or "basis." These have been thought of as manageable risks, whereas for many managers, general price level fluctuations are regarded as highly uncertain.

3. The third element in the problem is based upon the fact that an organized futures market makes it possible for the manager to transfer and thus avoid the impact of the major uncertainty through hedging. In using the term hedging, reference here is only to those matching transactions wherein the business manager can establish a commitment on the futures market which will compensate for the price impacts resulting from changes in the absolute level of prices. This compensation relates to the "analogous" components of the commercial commitment which embrace the elements that are specifically matched by the par-delivery specifications in futures.

We, therefore, have a situation where the businessman can avoid a major "uncertainty" (price-level changes) and still retain the more manageable "risks" in the form of residuals or basis from which he plans to derive a merchandising profit.

The businessman, thus, has a choice in the way he treats the phenomena just described. He can divest himself of the impact of changes in the level of prices and still retain the risk involved in the residual portions of his commercial commitment by using futures, or he can retain an exposure to both the price level changes and the changing interrelationships within the market by not hedging. If he wants to divest himself of both the primary price exposure and the residuals, one way he may be able to do this is by selling or booking his particular products to cash customers. In actual trading, he has many strategic choices, especially when we include not only the various delivery months in the futures market but also all the special terms and arrangements for forward commitments as well as actual ownership in the cash market.

This division of risk exposure can be illustrated by thinking of a separate certainty-uncertainty spectrum relating to:

1. Absolute price changes (on the par-delivery grade).

Certainty   *Uncertainty*
(predictable |————————————————————| (unpredictable
   prices)   (low) ← Degree of Risk → (high)   prices)

Where the *degree* of risk is high there is a strong incentive to operate with a full hedge — that is, to offset the uncertainty of the cash price change with a complementary uncertainty of a futures hedge.

Where the risk is reduced because the absolute price change is more predictable, the manager may want to take a position other than a fully hedged one. This can be net long or net short, and can be attained by using inventory holdings and forward cash orders or sales, as well as futures contracts.

The second risk spectrum can be designated as that relating to:

2. Changes in the differential between cash and futures prices. This differential can be defined in terms of a particular commercial trade or commitment price and a particular delivery contract on the futures market. (It can also be applied as a special case to intramarket spreads between a simultaneous buy and sell commitment either on the cash or the futures side.)

Certainty   *Uncertainty*
(predictable |————————————————————| (unpredictable
  spreads)   (low) ← Degree of Risk → (high)   spreads)

In this case the tendency would be to use the futures market freely if changes in the spread are considered predictable, but to avoid unnecessary positions in both the cash and futures market if they are not.

Hedging does two things: it transfers the exposure to absolute price changes to another party; and it establishes the nature of the exposure to residual factors that are retained by the hedger. The nonhedger retains both kinds of exposure (assuming that he does not use other means to offset his risks covering categories 1, 2, or both). "Hedging for security" relates to 1; "hedging for profit" relates to 2.

Theory would thus suggest that a business manager in a volatile-price industry might want to be fully hedged (i.e., completely divested of the probable price level impacts as he conceives them) when:

1. It is considered that market price swings are unpredictable and a serious impact on his business can be escaped by use of commodity futures.
2. His business objectives are best attained by applying his energies and resources to making a profit from other factors besides the effects of price swings. These other factors may be changes in intramarket spreads and margins, as distinct from changes in the general market level over time.
3. He recognizes the desirability of being able to plan his operations and strategies with a knowledge that price-level changes will not upset his calculations.

By the same token the manager may want to use a "judgment hedge," i.e., a selective use of futures contracts for risk avoidance, under certain conditions. These might be characterized as special situations which can be isolated and fully or partially hedged apart from any overall or normal hedging policy, as when:

1. He can differentiate or predict probable price occurrences at one time better than at another.
2. His business may be in need of selective or partial insulation from possible price-change effects because of financial considerations, unusual or temporary transaction requirements such as an extra large order or purchase, special seasonal needs for inventory accumulations, and similar situations.
3. He can enter into specific contractual commitments in which a futures contract can be regarded as a built-in part. (A formula price including the futures quotation would be an example.)

Sometimes the manager may forgo the use of futures as a management tool even though the firm deals in tradable commodities in the course of its regular business. In these cases the desire to avoid price uncertainties and risks may be outweighed by other considerations such as the following:

1. Complete lack of parallelism in price movements.
2. Insulation of his books from price-change impacts through Lifo accounting or other special arrangements such as custom processing or price protection through escalation agreements. (Even with Lifo, he may well want to hedge temporary seasonal accumulations or temporary large commitments.)

3. Distrust of the futures market because it is considered too thin and subject to manipulation or erratic influences.
4. Unwillingness to delegate authority for operating in futures.
5. There may be cases where hedging is not engaged in merely because the severity of price impacts on results would be very small even with wide price changes.

While the transference of risk or uncertainty is an important consideration in appraising the usefulness of commodity futures, it is not the whole story. Thus, we find that the avoidance of risk and uncertainty, which has had such a central position in the literature of futures markets, may at times be the number one consideration in developing policies for use of commodity futures, but in other situations the risk-avoidance may be either incidental or even non-applicable. The latter would be the case where net positions are deliberately taken in certain procurement activities. Futures markets are very useful where they serve as an extension of the cash market, giving the buyer or seller an additional outlet or source for actual goods, and most importantly giving a time flexibility which is not available in dealing with cash customers and suppliers. Where the control of a new "exposed" position is involved, one of the great advantages of the futures market lies in the fact that the manager can deal freely in the residuals and differentials without impairing the control of his overall position.

Most of the types of situations suggested above in somewhat general terms are discussed in the chapters on applications which follow.

OTHER BUSINESS POLICY CONSIDERATIONS IN EMPLOYING FUTURES

The previous section has concentrated upon what the manager "escapes" through hedging operations. A more positive statement can be made if we think in terms of what he does with those exposures he retains in the form of residuals, planned net positions, and the like. Many commercial users of commodity futures think of their operations in different ways. These are not mutually exclusive categories; some of them represent merely differences in the psychological viewpoint of the manager, some are accommodations to the particular kind of accounting and control system into which they are fitted. Most of them, however, can be related to the primary functions of the firm, and are tied in with the incentives and profit objectives of the management. In this perspective the user of futures may think of his operation in the following terms.

Hedging in Order to Establish a Basis Position

This basis becomes the actual net commercial commitment in terms of which transactions are conducted. It applies especially in grain dealing, feed and milling industries, international trading and in the case of a few other converters, such as coffee roasters, cocoa bean grinders, sugar refiners, citrus extracters, etc.

Holbrook Working in his article, "Futures Trading and Hedging," expressed the (then unorthodox) view that the primary objective of hedging was to make a profit rather than the avoidance of price risks. What Working referred to was the activities of traders and basis operators who entered commitments in which they expected their basis (or MY BASIS, as defined at the end of Chapter II) to move in their favor between the time the commitment was entered and the time it was to be closed out.

This is indeed one of the major uses of the hedging process and no doubt accounts for a large portion of all the open hedging positions on the exchange, especially in the case of grain merchants. In one case a grain dealer told me that he considered it a great advantage to have a large, open position because it enabled him to offer a wide assortment of grain of different qualities, locations, lot sizes, or kinds of delivery methods in taking care of his customers' needs. As Working has stated, the purpose "to make a profit" should be understood to include "to make a merchandising profit" as well as an exploiting of price swings in the cash versus the futures market.[14] The cash-futures offset is only part of the purpose and often not a critical part. It is still true, nevertheless,

---

[14] "Futures Trading and Hedging," pp. 323–326.

that the act of hedging does have the immediate, if not the "primary," purpose of shifting the risks resulting from the broader swings in price levels.

Hedging to Earn Storage[15]

This is one of the clearest uses of commodity futures as a device to help the economy to carry its inventory pipeline, especially its seasonal accumulations. It enables warehousemen, elevator operators or others with storage facilities at their disposal to "lock in" a return for their services by holding deliverable cash commodities and selling futures against them, thus assuring the earning of carrying charges (which the buyer of the more distant futures contract has agreed to pay) by having the option of actually making deliveries. It assures also that the storage capacity will be utilized, not left vacant awaiting a customer. (In effect, some speculator is making it possible for the economy to carry the inventory.)

In addition to the purpose of "earning" storage, it is also a common practice to take advantage of opportunities to blend, clean, or otherwise upgrade the products to bring them to deliverable quality. Such operations are analogous to some of the activities of "basis" traders, although the practices and trade terminology may be different.

To be sure, the carrying charge margin is not always present. The spot value in the cash market plus expected storage and handling expenses may be greater than the return to be realized by later delivery through the futures exchange. If this margin becomes very narrow or negative (referred to as inverse carrying charges), then there is a dis-incentive to store. The dis-incentive may become very pronounced in years when a new harvest is expected to change the situation from one of relatively short supplies to one of abundance. At such times the futures for new-crop delivery months may drop substantially under the old-crop months. Accordingly, stocks will move out of storage into consumption, thus reducing carryover.

---

[15] Allen B. Paul has made a detailed study of factors involved in the hedging of storage operations in "The Pricing of Binspace — A Contribution to the Theory of Storage."

It should also be noted that the idea of carrying charges may not be applicable in the case of nonstorable commodities like live cattle or ice-packed broilers.

Use of Futures as a Channel for Procurement or Sale

This use is for the procurement or sale of physical products, with the expectation of making or accepting delivery via the exchange.

This broadening of the market for the commercial operator is usually regarded as the exception rather than the rule.[16] However, the futures market derives its viability from its firm connection with a cash market for deliverable commodities and there are many situations where deliveries serve a useful commercial purpose.[17]

Extending the "Time Dimension" of a Market

The family of concepts represented here can be illustrated by a variety of business situations. A person may wish to prepare a definite plan or to make a business bid or proposal involving the acquisition of products he does not own or control and does not need till a considerably later date. He may put himself in a much more secure position by covering certain parts of his requirements in futures. This will at least protect him price-wise, and it may in addition give him assurance of the availability of the goods when he needs them.

Another application of this use is the farmer who feels he can

---

[16] Usually no more than 2% or 3% of the futures exchange transactions are consummated in product deliveries, according to various statements of commodity exchange officials and the Commodity Exchange Authority.

[17] Trade comments have on occasion been heard which questioned whether large firms like Central Soya Co. or Minute Maid Corporation were expecting too much of the exchanges in the way of supplying a source or an outlet for cash products. Such situations may make it necessary for those who want to retain open futures positions as delivery months approach to be more alert to the prospect that actual delivery may be required. It may even be said that if the market cannot meet such requirements, it is not a legitimate market.

choose the most advantageous time for selling his crop without having to await the harvest.

"Leaning into the Wind" or "Going with the Trend"

Businessmen in many industries often feel helplessly committed to their inventory requirements in order to keep their plants running or their shelves stocked. When markets are soft, it is often impossible to interest a customer in placing his normal volume of orders. In a rising market the raw material suppliers may be reluctant to book ahead.

In such cases the amount of price exposure of the firm may be involuntarily changing. The availability of a futures market may enable the manager to attain the desired net position despite the reluctance of suppliers or customers to make commitments.

This may be a practice only employed under unusual conditions, but it falls in the hedging category so long as it provides protection for the accomplishment of regular business functions and is looked upon as an adjunct to these functions rather than as a separate speculative undertaking.

Discretionary or Variable Hedges

Another illustration of "going with the trend" is the fairly common practice of having a discretionary trading range within which the net position is varied around a normal level according to the market judgment of the commodity expert in the firm. In this way advantage can be taken of special analytical skills and familiarity with the industry situation.

The discretionary hedge operation is sometimes extended to include special situations where a one-shot project or opportunity presents itself. This proposition may emerge from careful analysis of market conditions and may involve commercial transactions and futures in various combinations. It is akin to the opportunities which occasionally develop to earn storage revenues by purchase of cash commodities and selling futures. These are ordinary operations for some traders, but may be special (nonrecurring) operations for others.

SUMMARY

What has been discussed in Chapter IV relates to the broader aspects of business policy. The major points may be summarized briefly.

1. The "impact" of commodity price changes in the individual firm must be considered in terms of the way these changes (and the measures for dealing with them) affect the operating results, including the earnings, the balance sheet items, and the cash flow.
2. Many questions of corporate policy, operating strategy and accounting methods are involved. There are a number of alternatives available to management in each of these areas (i.e., policy, strategy, and accounting), and all are interrelated.
3. The alternatives are not merely "protective" measures. Positive contributions to profits, to financial strength, and to cash flows are as important considerations as the mere avoidance of risk or exposure. These considerations call for careful analysis and planning.
4. The risk factor in dealing with hedging and other price-related operations can best be appraised by separating the "absolute" price level changes on the one hand from the price relationships, differences or residuals on the other. A good bench-mark measurement for both purposes, where tradable commodities are involved, is the par-delivery specification for the futures contract. The contract itself is priced on the futures market; the "analogous part" of the actual business commitments can often be priced commercially or estimated for analytical purposes. A hedge in the form of a futures contract serves to transfer to others most of the impacts of absolute price change. It leaves the management of residual factors and their changes to be administered by the businessman, and hopefully to return a commercial profit (i.e., realizations in excess of costs).
5. Since risks have been divided into two broad categories — absolute price level changes in the "analogous part" and changes in the valuation attached to residual or differential factors — it follows that hedges in commodity futures have certain characteristics that differ from those pertaining to other devices and arrangements for risk management. For instance, futures hedging transfers to others only the impacts of absolute price change as the term is used here. The firm retains the risks inherent in the residuals, and this may be good or bad. Forward commercial commitments, on the other hand,

generally encompass specifications which include both the bell-wether price level factors *and* the residuals.

The residuals, it is clear, consist of a multiplicity of elements differing with each type of commitment. Therefore, the skilled operator must appraise each situation and decide what "mix" of commitments (holding of actuals, forward commercial sales or purchases, or futures contracts) will be most advantageous for him. Sometimes hedging will be the very best device, but sometimes it may be quite inappropriate and even "lock in" a loss. Certainly a hedging policy is not something to be undertaken lightly or pursued mechanically.

6. Various types of hedging approaches have been presented in general terms, but these are suggestive of types which almost always exist in combinations which reflect the unique situations or viewpoints of individual firms.

Part Three, which follows, undertakes to present the results of the inquiry into the policies and hedging arrangements of firms at various stages in five major agribusiness industry complexes.

PART THREE

Major Commodity Complexes — Policies and
Programs in the Use of Futures

INTRODUCTION TO PART THREE

THE preceding chapters have been concerned primarily with concepts and tools which are related to the problems of inventories, price risks, and commodity futures. We are ready now to turn to problems of specific industries and firms which make use of these tools in the handling of business problems.

Profits and return on investment are universal guides in appraising business performance, whether the business be a corporation, an individual businessman, or a cooperative organization. (In the latter case the word savings may have to be used in the place of the word profits but for the present purpose it amounts to the same thing.) Our immediate task will be to relate some of the concepts that were presented in the first four chapters to the profit objectives of the businessman and then proceed to a consideration of the variations from commodity to commodity and from firm to firm based on a selective sampling of actual business uses of commodity futures.

Most businessmen think of hedging as a part of their inventory policy. It is a very special part of that policy which can be designated as inventory price-risk management. For businesses which do not deal in commodities having organized futures markets, the manager may not even think of price-risk management as the primary focus of his inventory policy. Instead, the term inventory management is likely to suggest to him an entirely different field of business tools and techniques than it does to the hedger. We refer to the rich body of management skills and methods that have been developed to minimize the cost of moving goods through the production and handling process by use of computerized analysis dealing with optimum lot sizes, reorder procedures, lead times, and trigger points for stock control. They have resulted in great savings in the working capital and other costs required to carry physical inventories. Although their importance is undeniable and they do impose dimensions which must be recognized in the study of price-risk exposures of the sort we are dealing with, our present purpose does not require us to be concerned about these particular procedures for managing inventory flows.

The inventory policies for which commodity futures come into play relate to the handling of price exposures which are still present after the computer and the inventory control specialist have minimized the amount of working capital that must be tied up at any given time in physical inventories. Thanks to the existence of futures contracts (and of the institution of forward ordering and forward sales in the cash market), it is possible for managers to deal with the impacts of price change on the basis of positive controls far beyond the reach of similar managers in industries not favored by the existence of futures markets or practices of contracting ahead. Through inventory risk management it is possible not only to control and even to avoid the exposure to impacts from the changes in the general level of prices for the tradable commodity but also to open up numerous profit possibilities based on the intra-market differentials that are present between segments and selections within the market apart from the overall level of prices.

The use of futures as a hedging medium was originally thought of as a way of avoiding risk rather than contributing to profits, but it has been seen that hedging has a dual role. What is avoided is the effect of changes in the overall level of prices, but concurrently, there are profit opportunities to be gained from merchandising services and astute trading in which the futures transaction plays an important part. For a firm with volatile prices, large turnover and narrow margins, the avoidance of the risk from changes in price levels may mean the difference between the prospect of consistent profits over the next 10 years as against the probability of a series of sensationally fat years mixed with disastrously lean ones. In such businesses, most managers would favor the greater stability of a hedged operation. This preference is reinforced when it is realized that new profit opportunities based on intelligent trading patterns are opened up to the hedger who thinks in terms of differentials and basis.

We are therefore dealing with a profitable instrument at the same time that the means for avoiding the primary risks resulting from price volatility are being examined.

The scheme of analysis of actual experience in using commodity futures contracts as a business management tool will present the experience and practice of firms in several commodity areas. It was decided to concentrate upon the more sophisticated users of commodity futures rather than to seek out a representative cross section of the industries concerned. We were looking for evidence as to how this tool is used rather than to measure the degree to which its use has become a common practice in the industries concerned.

We have gone into some detail regarding the techniques employed by selected firms in each of five major agribusiness industries, supplemented by observations regarding an assortment of special situations in other industries. The industries discussed in some depth are wheat and flour milling, soybeans and their products, cattle and beef, cocoa, and frozen concentrated orange juice. These five industries present an assortment of situations which extend from the old-established users of commodity futures like grain and flour milling, where hedging is a highly developed practice, to the much newer and less widely used hedging practices in the livestock industry. Cocoa is an international product and has unique characteristics of its own, while soybeans presents one of the few commodities where active futures markets exist for both the raw material and the derived products. The frozen concentrated orange juice futures were introduced at a time of skepticism on the part of various industry groups as to whether the necessary conditions for successful futures trading would be met by this commodity, and the market is still characterized by mixed industry participation.

Specific information was secured for a number of firms handling each of the commodity categories mentioned above.[1] Extended interviews were carried on with a portion of these firms and an effort was made to seek out unusual or novel policies and procedures that would be important to note. The information concerning the individual commodity complexes follows an analytical outline

---

[1] See Appendix E for list of firms interviewed.

which is similar in each case. An effort is made to point out some
of the distinctive features of the industry and its markets as they
relate to the use of futures trading. Then, a few companies have
been selected to illustrate the assortment of policies and practices
that exist at several levels in the commodity complex.

In what follows, major emphasis is placed upon business policies
and objectives or purposes; the internal organizational arrangements, delegations and assignments; and the accounting and control procedures for carrying out hedging programs. It was not the
purpose of the present study to explore the specific statistical and
research methods used by the firms interviewed, nor to appraise
the trading strategies or hedging results attained. However, such
information as became incidentally available suggested an appreciable contribution to earnings in nearly all cases of regular hedgers.
While a few executives viewed futures as an instrument of the devil,
many more looked upon them as a godsend.

CHAPTER V

Wheat and Flour Milling

THE WHEAT[1] and flour milling complex represents one of the oldest industries in the world, dating back to the earliest days of civilization. It is not only the staff of life, the primary source of food energy, in most of the economically developed countries, but it is also the number one cereal in international trade. The principal exporters are the United States, Canada, Argentina, and Australia. Most of the other producing countries, in Europe for example, consume the bulk of their own production.

World production of wheat has been estimated at 10.5 billion bushels for 1969, and the total volume moving in world trade was 1.75 billion bushels. United States production amounted to 1,459 million bushels in the 1969 crop year, while U.S. exports in calendar 1969 came to approximately half that amount.

Most of the world's wheat (except that reserved for seed) is milled into flour and consumed in baked goods. Some of it is used for livestock and poultry feed, but this is usually a secondary outlet or a result of efforts to balance out national farm support or supply control programs.

The formidable task of growing, storing, handling, shipping and processing the huge volumes of wheat and other food and feed grains has resulted in (a) a highly organized industry and market structure, (b) an impressive commitment of working capital for growing crops and inventories (much of which is committed on a seasonal basis), (c) a number of very important governmental

---

[1] See Chicago Board of Trade wheat contract information in Appendix B.

programs in the United States and elsewhere to provide both direct services and regulatory constraints. These structural or institutional elements have been expounded in many published sources, both governmental and other. It will be assumed that the reader is familiar with much of this background.[2]

The primary interest for our purpose is found in the industry's experience with changing prices. It is from this point of view that certain aspects of the industry are selected for special comment.

There are five basic types of wheat. These are hard winter wheat, hard spring wheat, soft red wheat, white wheat, and durum wheat. These types are not easily interchangeable in their uses because of their processing characteristics and other unique properties. For this reason each type of wheat-based consumer product is made from a flour derived from a specific wheat type or combination of types. Similarly within a basic type of wheat there are many varieties of wheat which also vary to a lesser extent in their characteristic baking properties. It is the skill of the flour miller in mixing wheats to obtain a flour which will meet the baker's specifications that differentiates one miller from another. Not only must wheat be procured at the lowest possible cost, both by careful purchasing and by the maintenance of adequate inventories, but also in the right variety proportions to meet the requirements of the baker.

Many of the variables in the wheat business find their expression in price patterns and intramarket differentials as well as general market swings. Because the different varieties of wheat are to a large extent grown in separate areas or regions, the harvest of one type compared with another may be relatively abundant in one year and very short the next, depending on such factors as weather, disease, and pests. Local shortages of storage facilities

---

[2] Useful outlines of the wheat industry, especially as background for the present discussion, can be found in the following sources:

USDA, ERS, *Agricultural Markets in Change.*

Schonberg, *The Grain Trade: How It Works.*

Goldberg, *Agribusiness Coordination: A Systems Approach to the Wheat, Soybean, and Florida Orange Economies.*

National Commission on Food Marketing, *Organization and Competition in the Milling and Baking Industries.*

USDA, ERS, *Wheat Situation.*

can produce temporary geographical distortions of price. Export requirements are particularly variable from one period to the next. Foreign assistance programs have played an important part in causing changes in the world market situation; so have droughts or crop failures in various parts of the world, even to the extent of substituting wheat for other grains, such as rice. As between wheat varieties, some farmers can switch from one type to another, but such adjustments are not readily made unless the prospect of economic gain from doing so is stronger than the average farmer can usually predict.

Somehow the industry must find ways to balance out the pressures that exist in this complex set of market factors. There is at any given time a "world market price" for wheat, but this is an extremely nebulous concept. It can usually be interpreted through quotations at an important trading market for a representative set of specifications. However, any single quotation may become unrepresentative if particular varieties either become scarce or become a glut on the market. Internal prices in most countries are influenced by governmental control programs; and bilateral trade arrangements, changing duties, or embargoes are not uncommon.

In domestic markets the problems are, of course, simpler than in international markets. The export and import process is usually subject to all the complications of two different domestic wheat systems, plus a whole additional set of problems relating to currency and exchange, to shipping and clearances, to distance and communication, to mention only a few.

At the heart of the wheat trade complex in the United States are the great international grain trading firms such as Cargill Incorporated, Continental Grain Company, Bunge, and Dreyfus. These and similar firms, because of their world-wide operations, provide a close set of linkages between internal and international factors that makes the flexible fabric of the wheat market amazingly responsive and resilient. And among the backbone elements that give this structure viability and efficient performance are the large organized markets which trade in wheat futures on a contract basis. Nowhere does one find the interrelatedness of markets better exemplified than in such places as the Board of Trade of the City of Chicago, the Minneapolis Grain Exchange, the Kansas City

Board of Trade, and similar exchanges for other world commodities. As sensitive as radar, these markets reflect almost instantly the impulses from next door or from anywhere in the world that may affect the commodities traded there.

The pipelines through which United States wheat moves are well illustrated in a U.S. Department of Agriculture diagram for the 1963–64 crop year, reproduced here as Exhibit V-1. This complex of alternative channels reveals the directions and relative volumes of the physical flow of wheat and its products. It also suggests the assortment of points (e.g., on the farm, in country or terminal elevators, in transit, or in the hands of processors or exporters) at which exposures to price risks occur. The same points imply the presence of business managers who have the responsibility for decisions relating to financing, planning, scheduling, merchandising, and, above all, risk taking. All these are functions that embrace a time consideration.

If the only markets available to these decision makers were spot transaction markets, without provision for forward commitments, it is certain that instability of prices and of product flows would be immeasurably greater than we see today. If there were forward commitments, but these were limited to trade bookings with specific customers, the dependability of market flows and product availability would be of a low order compared with what is possible with an active, highly liquid futures market where commitments can be entered and canceled at a moment's notice and at a price level determined by wide participation and active bidding.

The product changes form as it moves from stage to stage, but until it is incorporated into bread or other preparations, its value and its price movements are never very far removed from the basic wheat. The farm, of course, is a major exception if we think of the farm inputs of labor, fertilizer, and acres of land. However, the farmer does in effect "own" prospective wheat from the time he plants the seed. Beyond the farmer, the elevators — country, subterminal, and terminal — not only store the wheat, but they also arrange in many cases for financing it, as well as for cleaning and blending it. Such services may upgrade the product or bring it closer to a quality that could be delivered on a futures market. Once it is milled into flour the wheat has passed beyond the stage

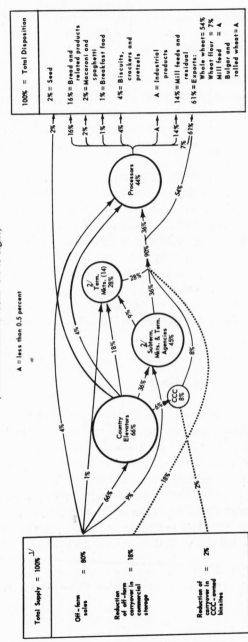

EXHIBIT VI-1. MAJOR U.S. MARKETING CHANNELS FOR WHEAT, 1963–64

(All movement is from left to right)

[1] Total supply for the 1963–64 marketing year was 1,387 million bushels. Off-farm sales (97% of total production) totaled 1,103 million bushels, or 80% of the total supply. Reduction of off-farm carryover in commercial storage totaled 249 million bushels, or 18% of the total supply, and entered the marketing channels from the terminal and subterminal elevators. Reduction of carryover in CCC-owned binsites totaled 26 million bushels, or 2% of the total supply, and entered the marketing channels from CCC storage sites. [2] Terminal receipts are based on the volume of inspected receipts. Fourteen terminal markets include Chicago, Duluth, Hutchinson, Indianapolis, Kansas City, Milwaukee, Minneapolis, Omaha, Peoria, Sioux City, St. Joseph, St. Louis, Toledo, and Wichita.

SOURCE: *Agricultural Markets in Change*, Agricultural Economic Report No. 95, USDA, Economic Research Service, July 1966, p. 233.

of deliverability on the exchange, but its price is highly correlated with the wheat market, and the miller is an active handler of wheat as well as flour. It is not difficult for him to make or accept delivery of wheat against futures contracts. Therefore, in the vertical wheat complex the degree of price parallelism is high over a wide span, even though the diversity of wheat varieties, grades, locations, and other factors provide many differentials and discrepancies compared with a more strictly homogeneous product such as some of the nonagricultural futures commodities like silver, copper, or propane gas.

Only three-quarters of the weight of wheat is actually turned out as flour. The remaining one-quarter consists of the outside hull and other "leftovers" or the so-called offals of the wheat milling process. Known also as bran and middlings or millfeeds, these by-products are incorporated into animal feed mixtures. There is no millfeeds futures market for reducing the price risk of ownership of millfeeds.[3] A number of millers have integrated into the production of mixed animal feeds, and in some cases, even into various types of livestock feeding enterprises, but a more common practice is to dispose of the offals in the cash market as they are produced.

The Market

The futures markets for wheat which are located at Chicago, Kansas City, and Minneapolis conduct their trading in a similar manner, but the delivery terms are not the same. They differ as to the types of wheat that are the basis grade for quoting purposes, the varieties that are acceptable, and the geographic points at which delivery can be made. These differences account for most of the price differentials that exist between the markets; most of the time, price changes are likely to be approximately parallel, one market with another, but the skilled trader is quick to seek out

---

[3] Millfeed prices tend to move in the same direction as corn. They can, to a degree, be hedged in corn, oats, or even wheat when wheat's marginal use is feed.

opportunities to take advantage of any disparities or special situations that develop.

The Commodity Exchange Authority has conducted occasional studies of the trading in wheat futures.[4] These studies are in addition to the regular daily, monthly, and annual reports on futures market statistics. The special reports classify trading positions by numbers and size of accounts and by the occupations of traders, providing valuable insights regarding the users of commodity futures. Two tables from the March 1967 report on the Chicago market are presented as Exhibit V-2 and Exhibit V-3, showing the occupational classification data.

The problems of interpreting such reports are numerous, but certain highlights are worth pointing out, even though many of the figures may not be typical. September 29, 1967, was selected as the survey date partly to examine unusual factors present at that time, such as a record crop, low government stocks, and emphasis upon export programs. In any event, the types of participants and their relative positions are of interest. At that time, 1,097 accounts were classified as hedgers and 8,558 as speculators. Naturally most of the hedgers fell in categories clearly associated with the cash grain trade. As shown at the bottom of Exhibit V-3, six such categories, including farmers, covered all but 30 of the hedger accounts. A notable point, however, is that farmers classed as speculators in the top section of the table numbered 1,722 as against the 357 designated as hedgers. Exhibit V-2 shows that both the speculators and the so-called hedgers in the "Farmers and farm managers" group were predominantly holders of long positions, the totals running 24,500,000 bushels long against 7,960,000 bushels short.

Furthermore the speculative positions of almost every category in Exhibit V-2 showed long holdings in excess of short (the exceptions were those classed as "Bank officials and employees, financiers, and capitalists" and "Manufacturers (other than wheat), wholesale trade proprietors, managers, food brokers." The hedgers held 60,565,000 bushels in long contracts against 122,390,000

---

[4] See USDA, CEA, *Trading in Wheat Futures, May–November 1967.*

EXHIBIT V-2. WHEAT FUTURES: OCCUPATIONAL DISTRIBUTION OF ACCOUNTS, BY NUMBER AND CLASS OF ACCOUNT, CHICAGO BOARD OF TRADE, SEPTEMBER 29, 1967

(Positions in thousands of bushels)

Occupational Group[1]	Speculators			Hedgers			Total		
	Number of Accounts	Long	Short	Number of Accounts	Long	Short	Number of Accounts	Long	Short
Grain merchandisers, exporters, and elevator operators	270	6,570	3,545	597	44,005	101,120	867	50,575	104,665
Wheat millers	37	1,096	245	59	8,430	11,605	96	9,525	11,850
Feed manufacturers	7	190	110	21	515	6,310	28	705	6,420
Cash grain brokers	0	0	.	3	50	40	3	50	40
Feed and seed dealers	45	460	160	21	250	140	66	710	300
Livestock feeders and dealers	87	955	600	12	310	90	99	1,265	690
Subtotal	446	9,270	4,660	713	53,560	119,305	1,159	62,830	123,965
Processors and refiners of grains other than wheat	7	150	10	5	215	625	12	365	635
Dealers in agricultural commodities other than grain or livestock	53	760	275	2	90	15	55	850	290
Farmers and farm managers	1,722	19,060	6,810	357	5,440	1,150	2,079	24,500	7,960
Employees of grain merchants, elevators, and processors	63	820	230	7	570	615	70	1,390	845
Brokerage houses and employees	314	33,465	29,635	9	155	20	323	33,620	29,655
Floor traders	146	33,735	30,890	1	25	310	147	33,760	31,200
Professional speculators	74	9,655	4,580	0	0	0	74	9,655	4,580
Commodity and investment counselors	70	1,865	995	0	0	0	70	1,865	995
Doctors, dentists, trained nurses, pharmacists, etc.	365	3,870	2,245	0	0	0	365	3,870	2,245
Lawyers	171	5,305	3,825	0	0	0	171	5,305	3,825
Accountants and auditors	146	2,090	1,015	0	0	0	146	2,090	1,015
Chemists and engineers	458	4,590	2,195	0	0	0	458	4,590	2,195
Teachers	139	1,385	600	0	0	0	139	1,385	600
Other professional occupations, such as architects, contractors, social workers	289	5,210	3,235	0	0	0	289	5,210	3,235

Semiprofessional occupations, such as aviators, draftsmen, radio and television operators	59	630	245	0	0	0	59	630	245
Bank officials and employees, financiers, and capitalists	127	3,775	6,985	0	0	0	127	3,775	6,985
Manufacturers (other than wheat), wholesale trade proprietors, managers, food brokers	140	2,565	3,835	3	510	350	143	3,075	4,185
Retail proprietors and managers: grocery, food, apparel, furniture, automobile sales and services, etc.	399	5,215	2,585	0	0	0	399	5,215	2,585
Other proprietors, managers, and officials (excluding farm)	886	13,840	6,870	0	0	0	886	13,840	6,870
Salesmen and purchasing agents	238	3,360	1,910	0	0	0	238	3,360	1,910
Insurance and real estate persons	326	4,760	2,505	0	0	0	326	4,760	2,505
Clerical, sales and kindred non-manual workers, such as bookkeepers, cashier stenographers, office-machine operators	92	1,300	540	0	0	0	92	1,300	540
Craftsmen, foremen, electricians, machinists, and kindred skilled workers in plants and factories	144	1,155	455	0	0	0	144	1,155	455
Service occupations, unskilled workers, and laborers	288	3,855	1,885	0	0	0	288	3,855	1,885
Transportation, communication, and utility workers	61	830	295	0	0	0	61	830	295
Housewives	273	4,625	3,110	0	0	0	273	4,625	3,110
Students	42	380	200	0	0	0	42	380	200
Retired persons	812	9,785	3,700	0	0	0	812	9,785	3,700
Miscellaneous	208	1,795	1,065	0	0	0	208	1,795	1,065
Subtotal	8,112	179,830	122,725	384	7,005	3,085	8,496	186,835	125,810
Unclassified	—	—	—	—	—	—	1	100	0
Grand total	8,558	189,100	127,385	1,097	60,565	122,390	9,656	249,765	249,775

[1] Occupations have been grouped from specific descriptions as reported by futures commission merchants.
SOURCE: *Trading in Wheat Futures, May–November 1967*, USDA, Commodity Exchange Authority, March 1968, p. 16.

EXHIBIT V-3. WHEAT FUTURES: SIZE DISTRIBUTION OF ACCOUNTS, SELECTED OCCUPATIONS, CHICAGO BOARD OF TRADE, SEPTEMBER 29, 1967

(In thousands of bushels)

Occupational Group[1]		Number of Accounts by Size of Long or Short Position[2]						
	Total	5	10–15	20–45	50–95	100–195	200–495	500 and over
		SPECULATORS						
Grain merchandisers, exporters, and elevator operators	270	77	100	63	17	9	3	1
Farmers and farm managers	1,722	893	533	212	52	27	5	0
Brokerage houses and employees	314	48	95	66	36	34	12	23
Floor traders	146	17	10	26	26	25	21	21
Professional speculators	74	12	24	18	5	5	4	6
Doctors, dentists, trained nurses, pharmacists, etc.	365	181	114	55	11	2	2	0
Lawyers	171	58	57	40	9	4	1	2
Accountants and auditors	146	68	48	20	5	4	1	0
Chemists and engineers	458	254	139	49	8	8	0	0
Other professional occupations, such as architects, contractors, social workers, teachers	428	205	136	55	19	9	3	1
Bank officials and employees, financiers, and capitalists	127	38	43	23	12	5	2	4
Manufacturers (other than wheat), wholesale trade proprietors, managers, food brokers	140	51	41	34	8	0	3	3
Retail proprietors and managers: grocery, food, apparel, furniture, automobile sales and services, etc.	399	169	130	68	22	9	1	0

Other proprietors, managers, and officials (excluding farms)	886	340	295	179	40	25	6	1
Salesmen and purchasing agents	238	126	69	29	8	4	1	1
Insurance and real estate persons	326	144	97	61	11	9	4	0
Craftsmen, foremen, electricians, machinists, and kindred skilled workers in plants and factories	144	91	38	14	1	0	0	0
Service occupations, unskilled workers, and laborers	288	145	92	30	15	4	2	0
Housewives	273	139	71	41	8	13	0	1
Retired persons	812	392	257	119	30	9	5	0
Other	831	362	279	137	38	9	6	0
Total	8,558	3,810	2,668	1,339	381	214	82	64

HEDGERS

Grain merchandisers, exporters, and elevator operators	597	111	161	154	72	46	23	30
Wheat millers	59	2	3	14	9	9	13	9
Feed manufacturers	21	4	6	4	2	2	1	2
Feed and seed dealers	21	7	5	8	1	0	0	0
Livestock feeders and dealers	12	3	5	1	2	1	0	0
Farmers and farm managers	357	136	119	69	25	7	1	0
Other	30	5	9	4	5	2	3	2
Total	1,097	268	308	254	116	67	41	43
Grand total	9,655	4,078	2,976	1,593	497	281	123	107

[1] Occupations have been grouped from specific descriptions as reported by futures commission merchants.

[2] In allocating an account's position to a size group, the largest total long or short position in all futures is used; not the "net" of such long and short positions.

SOURCE: *Trading in Wheat Futures, May–November 1967*, USDA, Commodity Exchange Authority, March 1968, p. 17.

bushels short. These figures can be compared with a total U.S. supply (new crop plus carryover) of around two billion bushels. Kansas City and Minneapolis futures would have added roughly 50 million to the 250 million bushels open interest at Chicago. This would leave well over three-fourths of the wheat in the country on which the futures market could not have been involved as a price-risk management tool. The general magnitudes represented earlier in Exhibit I-4 is intended to reflect a similar situation.

The actual considerations involved in management decisions regarding the use of futures are discussed below, where the problems of firms operating at various stages in the wheat and milling industry are considered.

THE FARM MANAGER

The farm manager[5] can utilize the futures market to hedge his crop either before he plants it, while the crop is growing, or after harvest. The farmer theoretically has a long position in cash wheat so he may enter the futures market selling wheat contracts in some relationship to the anticipated size of his crop.[6] While this is not a common practice among farmers, it offers the farmer an opportunity to lock in a minimum price for his crop and, assuming that he knows his costs of production, he can pin down a known profit. The farm manager can also use the futures market to fix the price of wheat he holds in storage. Further, he can use the futures market by purchasing wheat contracts after he has sold his own wheat crop where he does not have adequate storage facilities of his own but, if he did, would have held his wheat for later delivery.

It was reported by dealers that farm managers in general are becoming more sophisticated in their use of this coordinating de-

---

[5] For further discussion see Hieronymus, *Use of Grain Futures in the Farm Business,* p. 53.

[6] The Commodity Exchange Authority explicitly recognizes the operation as a "hedge" even though the farmer does not yet have the wheat actually in his possession. See Appendix A.

vice. However, it is still common for farm managers, when they desire to set a fixed price for their wheat production, to enter into a direct fixed price contract with an elevator operator, who in turn sells futures against this purchase commitment. Such a contract serves as the farm manager's hedge, thus limiting the price risk on his crop. The elevator operator or his correspondent commission firm is more readily able to do the futures trading and is more closely in touch with the market machinery than the farmer himself. Moreover, by booking his crop on terms that specify how his particular wheat will be handled, delivered and graded, the farmer can be given a definite price in dollars and cents. He is often allowed a tolerance as to the number of bushels to be delivered in order to allow for uncertainties as to his yield per acre. If the farmer sold in the futures market himself, he would still have to make a firm commitment as to quantity and then estimate all the differentials between the country price he is likely to receive at delivery time and the prices on the exchange at which he will buy back his hedge in futures. (Actual delivery of his own wheat on the exchange by a grower, even a very large operator, is most unlikely except as a test shipment of some sort.)

The CEA special analysis of trading in grain futures in 1967 gives an indication of the extent of farmer participation in wheat trading. (See Exhibit V-2.) The Chicago Board of Trade is the only market shown in this study, but it embraces around 80% of all wheat futures activity. As of September 29, 1967 the total accounts with open futures positions in wheat came to 9,656 of which 2,079 were classified as "Farmers and farm managers." Adding to this a rough guess for the Kansas City and Minneapolis markets, a total number for farmer traders in futures would be in the range of 2,500 accounts. This is a tiny portion of the million farmers who are reported as wheat growers by the USDA. Also, these farmers traded mostly on the long side of the market — 24.5 million bushels long as against 8.0 million on the short side — and 1,722 of the farmer accounts were classified as speculators against 357 listed as hedgers. The short sales by these farmer-hedgers came to only 1.15 million bushels, as compared with the total crop estimated at 1.5 billion bushels.

It appears obvious from the above facts that an insignificant number of farmers use the futures market, and that those who used it in September 1967 were mostly adding to the speculative risk exposures they take as wheat growers. If they were large sellers, it was in the cash and "to be delivered" market, not the futures. So far as farmers are concerned they do have a "floor" under prices when they qualify for the government loan program.

A more detailed discussion of possible procedures for an individual large farmer is presented in Chapter VI where problems of the soybean complex are examined. The alternatives available to producers of either of these two commodities are essentially similar.

ELEVATOR OPERATORS AND GRAIN DEALERS

The group designated as "Grain merchandisers, exporters, and elevator operators" have by far the largest positions in wheat futures. As shown in Exhibit V-2, this is the group which accounts for most of the hedging, their volume running far ahead of the millers and feed manufacturers.

Since most of the wheat purchased by smaller country elevators moves to subterminal or terminal elevators, it is not uncommon for the country elevator to book the wheat he controls for later delivery in the cash rather than in the futures market. Subterminal or terminal elevators, however, are large dealers and almost universally use the futures market in a carefully planned way. One example of these operations is described below, that of the Continental Grain Company.

The large grain dealers are masters of the art of basis operations. For the most part they conduct their commercial operations under a policy of being fully hedged at all times. Their net unhedged position is maintained at the zero point. A sale is booked for every purchase that is made, and vice versa. The sale or purchase is likely to have its origin in the cash grain market where an offer of wheat or a sale to a customer is negotiated. As soon as there is a firm price on this transaction it is immediately balanced by a matching transaction in the futures market. (There may be occasions when a simultaneous purchase and sale can be matched up in the cash market without using the futures market, but this is not usual.)

By having all cash grain positions matched with corresponding positions on the opposite side of the market, the dealer uses the futures market quotations as benchmarks and concerns himself almost altogether with his basis relationships or residuals. He can for practical purposes almost ignore what direction the actual price is moving in the wheat market. What he must watch most alertly are the relationships that exist between the cash and futures commitments with which he can make trades. Sometimes he may offer firm prices to his customers, knowing that it will be a profitable turnover when he buys back his short hedge on the futures market. At another time he may offer to sell wheat at so much over or under a future, say July, the price becoming fixed at a specified date or at a time to be selected by the buyer. The dealer would continue to hold his short July futures position until the date arrives to fix the price of the cash sale, at which time the futures hedge is lifted. Such transactions are referred to as "price to be fixed" or "buyers call." Many variations exist in the uses of this type of trade arrangement.

The types of transactions and the flexibility offered by access to a commodity futures market is only one aspect of the problems that confront business managers in their handling of hedging and inventory policies. The establishing of objectives and organizational arrangements for attaining a coordinated performance within the firm are matters of crucial importance, as are the procedures for control and appraisal of results. These are matters that can best be discussed in terms of the actual experience of firms in the industry. This has been done in the present study by carefully selecting from among the many firms that were interviewed a few in each product area which could best illustrate the assortment of practices and problems that have arisen. To be exhaustively complete in each instance would be uselessly repetitive; hence it should be recognized that each instance is rounding out a part of a more general pattern while the special focus may emphasize only certain functions in an individual case.

The Continental Grain Company

This business had its origins in Arlon, Belgium, in 1813. It is a U.S. company, incorporated in Delaware with subsidiaries and affiliates overseas. The executive offices of the company are located in New York City. Other prominent international grain firms include Cargill, Incorporated, with its home offices in Minneapolis, Minnesota, and an associated company in Switzerland; Bunge with its home offices in Buenos Aires, Argentina; Dreyfus with its home offices in Paris, France; Garnac Grain Company, Inc., with home offices in Lausanne, Switzerland; and several other companies, such as Archer Daniels Midland, Inc. at Decatur, Illinois, and Peavey Grain Company with home offices in Minneapolis.

Continental is primarily a grain merchandiser. It does buy some grain direct from farmers; however, this is basically the job of country elevators (including independent elevators, "line" elevators which are members of multi-unit elevator groups, and cooperative elevators). Continental buys most of its grain from second and third hands — that is, country elevators and grain merchants. Roughly two-thirds of the company's sales are for export, although the relationship of domestic and export business varies according to the kind of grain and the location.

As a merchandiser, Continental's primary functions can be characterized as those of providing (a) place utility, (b) time utility, and (c) the management of price risks associated with these functions. A third kind of utility — form utility — is primarily provided by processors, although Continental Grain does make a contribution in the sense that drying, cleaning, and blending grain (primarily for grade) is a part of this function. It is clear that these functions are essential to the grain economy inasmuch as grain is generally produced and consumed in different locations and there are great distances to be bridged between the areas of production and consumption. Similarly, time utility is another way of characterizing the fact that the rate at which grain is used or consumed during the year is very different from the rate at which grain is produced and harvested. The adjusting of rates of movement when put in a world perspective, including carryover and reserve requirements, is a formidable task, especially when one contemplates the number of agencies involved and the political and other decisions that are in the picture.

In order to perform its major functions Continental has several categories of grain handling facilities in the United States which can be grouped as follows:

1. Export elevators, e.g., Beaumont; Houston; New Orleans; Longview, Washington; Norfolk.
2. Dual purpose export-domestic terminals at Lake points, e.g., Superior, Milwaukee, Chicago.
3. Interior terminals and subterminals, e.g., Hutchinson, Kansas City, Columbus.
4. Subterminals and terminals on the inland waterway *primarily* (but not exclusively) devoted to originating grain for the export elevators, e.g., East St. Louis; Savage, Minnesota; 8 Illinois River subterminals; Mt. Vernon and Evansville, Indiana, on the Ohio River.

The company also operates leased rail cars; it owns and operates barges, and it owns and charters ocean vessels. Continental has increased its U.S. grain storage capacity from 40 million bushels in the early 1950s to over 100 million bushels in 1970.[7]

The company deals primarily in those grains which move in bulk in great quantity, such as wheat, corn, oats, rye, barley, sorghum, soybeans, and rice. Because of its large storage facilities, Continental typically maintains large stocks of these grains. These inventories will vary in product mix and in size at different locations and seasons of the year. Thus, inventory management is one of Continental's major concerns.

The success of a grain merchandising firm depends, of course, upon efficient handling of the grain and competitive pricing. To an even greater extent, however, it depends on having the kind and

---

[7] In addition, Continental Grain is associated with Continental Companies which owns a majority of the stock in Allied Mills, Inc., a large, diversified company in the grain, feeds, poultry and processed foods industries. Allied operates as an autonomous unit. Moreover, an independently operated commodities brokerage division, with the name ContiCommodity Services, has been set up in Chicago to act as a commission broker in commodity futures markets. Many of ContiCommodity Services' customers are among Continental's cash grain clients who have occasion to use the futures markets.

grade of grain that customers need at a given time and place, and on proper use of futures markets in merchandising operations. The large firm "stands ready at any time to buy or sell any given quantity of merchantable grain at a fair price."

Use of commodity futures markets is a major operating tool in most of Continental Grain's activities. If we regard the company's primary turnover in terms of cash or actual grain bought or cash or actual grain sold, the futures can be thought of as a bridge which enables the company to operate effectively without having to have a customer at hand every time a purchase is made or a supplier at hand every time that a sale is booked. The holding of inventories provides a reservoir which helps to smooth the flow of transactions, but with access to effective futures markets the company has the advantage of a much greater degree of flexibility. When Continental books a sale, it can readily enter a long hedge (i.e., buy futures contracts) which can be held until cash grain is acquired to fill this order. Similarly, a grain purchase (either for immediate delivery or for later arrival) can be covered by a short hedge through a sale of futures contracts. Where large inventories are held one would expect the short hedge to predominate, especially when there are "carrying charge markets," i.e., the more distant futures contracts are selling at a sufficient premium over spot grain to assure that storage costs will be recovered even if the grain is delivered on the exchange.

For the most part futures are employed as a "temporary substitute" [8] for a cash transaction and are in fact canceled without making physical delivery via the exchange. This, of course, is not the only important aspect or objective in hedging since the futures market can serve as a valuable device for maximizing storage income from Continental's elevator facilities and for other purposes such as spreading or financing.

It has just been noted that a grain merchant like Continental tends to be both a long and a short hedger, the balance differing by season. This is in contrast to grain processors who often are primarily long hedgers and grain storers who tend to be predominantly short hedgers.

---

[8] See Working, "New Concepts Concerning Futures Markets and Prices."

Continental's Hedging Policies. In a business as complex as that of Continental Grain Company, it is not possible to speak of "hedging" in a narrow, sharply defined way. Rather, one might better refer broadly to the "risk management function" and to the use of futures as one of the many tools in carrying out this function. From this viewpoint, the total complex of factors involved has to include the following classes of commitment: (a) actual inventory held, (b) forward purchase and sale commitments in the cash market, and (c) futures contracts on commodity exchanges. But this is far from the whole story, since every exposure to price risks involves relationships between the individual characteristics of each of the commitments. Thus, the risk exposure actually includes all the variables for which there are not precisely matching specifications on the purchase and the sale side of a commercial operation. Such variations usually do exist between the actual commodity specifications that apply to the commitment (this relates to grades, age, condition, and other quality variables); they also include variables related to location (including distances, transportation, transit privileges, type of access to terminals and other facilities); also, the time variable (which includes the uncertainties when the purchase and sale commitments do not relate to simultaneous delivery requirements, or when storage and holding of stocks is involved).

This suggests that risk management involves not just a set of homogeneous arrangements which can be summarized in terms of a single series of price changes. Instead, the management of risk employs not only hedging in futures, but also the use of domestic and international arbitrage, and offsets between different grains as well as different qualities and locations of the same grain. Often, this requires selective or nonconventional rather than standard or orthodox hedging. While the concept of hedging usually implies a process of "matching" one exposure against another, the combined handling of all the elements of risk may require the firm to have short hedges in deferred rather than nearby contracts even though the transaction being hedged calls for a nearby delivery. Similarly, a sale of cash grain which may call for long-deferred delivery may nevertheless be hedged in nearby contracts. Moreover, the company may find that its risk position is better managed if it hedges hard wheat on the Chicago Board of Trade rather than in Kansas City or soft wheat in the Kansas City futures market instead of Chicago.

To summarize, the company's responsibility for risk management is not simply a matter of risk avoidance. The futures contract permits a trader to transfer to others the impact of price changes resulting from the fluctuating price on the futures market itself (or, more accurately, on the portion of the cash commitment which exactly corresponds to the specification traded in the futures market — the analogous part). However, this risk transfer is only a part of the total risk to be managed. The remaining risks are composed of many variables or residuals which can frequently be summarized in terms of "basis." It is obvious, however, that basis includes many elements and its proper management calls for a high degree of skill.

Generally speaking, Continental's policy is to hedge those commodities which may be hedged and this policy covers the vast bulk of the firm's business. However, the application of the hedging policy has to be treated in a very flexible way and to employ all the variables discussed above, not just a ritual application of futures contracts. Any net long or short positions are carefully controlled under policy guidelines set by top management. Sometimes such positions are a result of the anticipation of overnight sales or purchases (often referred to as prehedging). Sometimes a temporary imbalance of the net position results from the time needed to cover a major purchase or sale operation without unduly disturbing the market. Beyond such technical adjustments any deliberate position in the market is restricted with greatest care and has to take into account the kinds of exposure to which the firm is subject in its various commodities and various world market situations.

It should be mentioned parenthetically that in world markets price parallelism is often much less close than it is between the markets of a single country. Many of the transactions have very special conditions, service or transportation arrangements, currency conversions, or accommodations to meet government control and other requirements which may even make it inappropriate to use the U.S. commodity futures market as a hedging vehicle. However, as a general rule all the wheat transactions of the company through its many regional offices and agencies are conducted as a hedged operation which is coordinated in New York and is closely geared to the futures markets in Chicago, Kansas City and Minneapolis.

A hedging strategy has to be developed and continually reviewed, taking into account the questions of balancing one commodity against another (such as a long position in corn and a short one in wheat), the decision as to whether to favor nearby or deferred futures, or one market such as Chicago as against another (Kansas City or Minneapolis). This strategy is typically arrived at through discussions involving the president and senior vice presidents as well as officers in charge of a particular commodity, the company economist, and regional managers who have their own special viewpoints and information.

In a very fast-moving operation a number of traders, including a number in regional offices, have responsibility for hedging as well as a cash buying and selling function. They have authority to do their own hedging (consistent with the corporate hedging strategy) as a matter of day-to-day operations. Such trading is on a fully hedged basis. For example, if a cargo of soybeans is sold overnight, the trader may simply come into the futures market with a purchase of the appropriate amount of futures in the proper contract, for example July, to cover the sale.

As an international firm, a good deal of flexibility is required and in many cases where world trading does not lend itself readily to an orthodox hedging operation, the management is likely to think in terms of arbitrage of one position against another. This may balance a commitment in one country with a roughly compensatory position in another, or in one commodity as against another. Thus, an unbalanced position in the U.S. corn or wheat futures market may be a part of a total operation in which a trade in Argentine maize or Mexican wheat may stand on the other side.

Despite the flexibility, it is the function of the New York headquarters to maintain an orderly implementation of company policy regarding hedging.[9] Most of the regional offices and agencies, how-

---

[9] The communications system in a firm such as Continental is impressive, with cable facilities, telephones, tickers, quote-boards — even closed circuit television — to show an instantaneous view of futures trading pits.

ever, operate as profit centers, and the New York headquarters are
often called upon to supply a balancing function whereby the total
company position is brought into line with established policy.

This detailed comment about hedging policies should not obscure the important fact that the basic business at Continental
Grain is that of merchant and dealer, providing its primary services in the handling, storing, conditioning, and delivering grain
from points of production to points of use. The futures market not
only provides for a flexible management of the exposure to price
fluctuations but also makes possible many intricate commercial
strategies that result in improved services to customers.[10] By having a broad and active futures market, the company can enter very
large sales commitments at a time when the grain may not be in
hand, or large purchase commitments when no customer is instantly available; the futures market also provides a bridge which
enables firms like Continental Grain to handle tremendous volumes
and to work with a gross inventory many times larger than the
firm's resources would permit if all transactions were in the cash
market only.

Other Large Grain Dealers

Other large grain merchandising firms follow an essentially similar scheme to that described for Continental Grain. Operations
throughout the industry employ the futures market as a benchmark
and most of the trading and the thinking of managers is carried
out in terms of their basis or differentials. These represent the risk
retained by the firm after using futures hedges to transfer to others

---

[10] For instance, futures contracts are so much a part of most large grain
transactions that it is a common practice to trade in cash grain at, say, "so
many points over the Chicago July future," and to arrange for the terms
on which the actual price is to be pinned down by transferring the futures
hedge from the seller to the buyer. Such a procedure, frequently referred
to as "crossing against actuals" or "futures to be exchanged," follows a
regular established practice on many futures markets. The transfer of the
futures from one trader's account to the other's is officially carried out on
the exchange and cleared through the Clearing House, but it does not
require a "pit trade" (a trade accomplished through competitive public
outcry in the trading pit). See Glossary: "crossing against actuals."

the primary exposure to price changes. The grain merchant can thus conduct his operations with relatively little concern over the specific level of prices because he is enabled with the help of commodity futures to follow the market up or down and to earn his profit by exercising skill in finding, selecting, storing, and moving grains "on the basis."

For management control purposes it is also possible for a trader to think in basis terms, almost ignoring the actual or flat price of the wheat in which he is dealing, or of the futures in which it is hedged. He may own 100,000 bushels of a particular grade and type of wheat at one of the country elevators at a cost of 20¢ under the March future at Chicago. No matter what happens to the price of wheat, if he can sell this 100,000 bushels at only 10¢ under the Chicago March future, he will have earned a 10¢ per bushel margin which may be more than adequate to cover handling and storing costs for a short period.[11]

In summary, a large grain dealer regularly uses the futures market not merely for transferring risks (i.e., hedging), but also for earning basis profits. Futures enable him to design transactions which will accommodate purchases and sales of cash grain for spot or future execution according to the wishes of individual suppliers and customers, without having to seek out a simultaneous matching of the one against the other. Finally, he can extend the total volume of business the firm can handle to a volume much larger than could be afforded (considering both risks and availability of funds) with the firm's own resources.

MILLERS AND PROCESSORS

The Pillsbury Company

Of all the firms interviewed, Pillsbury is probably the most structured in its use of commodity futures as a management tool, including a systematic program to clearly document such use. More often than not the firms that were interviewed followed unwritten

---

[11] For another example of this kind, see the note, "What is BASIS?" in Chapter II.

procedures and policies which had been developed over a number of years based on experience and the personal responsibility of the executive carrying out the policy. This was one of the difficulties encountered in evaluating the commodity futures trading activities of many individual firms.

Pillsbury makes use of the futures market to serve a considerable number of business needs. The firm conducts a diversified group of food and feedstuffs businesses, most of them having grown directly or indirectly out of the firm's original grain and milling operations. The distinctive character and requirements of each business call for a careful analysis of the separate functions to be performed and the relationships of factors wherein price-risk management can best contribute to dependable earnings performance. This means not one but many "approaches" to hedging.

Moreover, the complexities of commercial operations, with special local supply conditions, changing customer needs, and limitations of the market place, may call for a high degree of specialized planning in order to choose wisely among alternative opportunities. Hedging in commodity futures is considered to be only one of the tools to be used, albeit usually the most flexible. This permits the hedging policy to be adapted to the need of cash market and commercial operations, rather than vice versa.

Pillsbury Company Background. The Pillsbury Company was founded in Minneapolis in 1869 and has become the largest flour miller and the largest exporter of flour in the United States. It ranks among the first three companies in the sale of consumer food mixes, refrigerated dough products, family flour, bakery flour, instant mashed potatoes, as well as prepared mixes for the bakery and institutional (eat-out) market. The company is third or fourth in the integrated broiler production and marketing business. It also has important international marketing activities (11.1% of company sales in fiscal 1970) and a substantial participation (through the Burger King chain) in the franchised fast food industry.

With the diversification of its product line, Pillsbury has necessarily moved away from its overwhelming reliance upon the pri-

mary function of dealing in wheat and processing it into flour, although this is still a very important part of the business. The importance of commodity raw materials is reflected in the fact that
around 75% of the annual sales dollar is represented as going to
"raw materials and purchased services." Inventories as of May 31,
1970, were valued at $71.9 million, of which about 20% were
grains. This date is near the end of the marketing year for grains,
however, and the figure need not represent the average importance
of the grain inventory requirements during the year. Sales in the
1970 fiscal year came to $674.4 million.

Hedging Policies — Pillsbury. An effort to characterize the futures trading activities of Pillsbury is complicated by the large
number of businesses it is involved in, the types of businesses (i.e.,
family flour vs. bulk livestock and poultry feed ingredients), and
the wide variety of commodities procured. Recognizing the difficulties encountered in each business and in each commodity, the
company has employed the principle of managing its commodity
price fluctuation risks by exception rather than by having rigid
rules to apply to all cases.

To be more specific, for each business and each commodity
definite policy guidelines have been adopted. These guidelines spell
out maximum net positions permissible during the year, and some
of the variations to be expected, such as those imposed by seasonal
requirements. The positions authorized by policy statements set
maximum acceptable limits within which operating managers are
expected to make discretionary decisions. Such position authoriza-
tions are set at a point intended to permit smooth operations. They
are not intended to be used for speculative commitments if commercial requirements do not happen to make full use of the maximum net position. In effect, maximum positions are determined on
the basis of limiting risk without putting unnecessary limitations
on the carrying out of commercial strategy.

*Pillsbury's Hedging Practice — Organization, Procedures, and
Decisions.* In general, the guidelines concerning maximum acceptable net positions have been based on extensive management expe-

rience and a careful evaluation to minimize the potential risk to the company. While these guidelines serve as a basic limit within which a manager is permitted to operate, the stated maximum net position can be modified if such an action can be justified; i.e., the management of risks by exceptions. Such exceptions, however, are infrequent and require top management review and approval.

It is the specific responsibility of a group vice president to oversee risk management policies and operations on a company-wide basis. He is also chief corporate procurement officer and is responsible for the direction of a commodity analysis department. The activities of the commodity analysis department include the preparation of price analyses, including seasonal and intramarket price variations, and the development of recommended actions in the light of such anticipated changes. In addition, the specialists in this department serve as consultants to the commercial and operating departments on commodity matters.

Forecasts and recommendations are submitted directly to the business head who typically serves as chairman of the "hedging" committee within the business. The manager of the commodity analysis department usually serves as a member of this committee, along with other members who are expected to develop and carry out the action program. Typically, quite specific guidelines are drawn up as to the maximum net position permitted, delivery months, and commodities in which hedges will be placed, etc. Also covered are those exceptions which may be permitted upon agreement of the hedging committee. Any changes beyond these permitted exceptions have to be submitted by the committees to the group vice president. An example of the form of policy statement employed appears as Exhibit V-4, from which dates and figures have been deleted.

This operating procedure applies both to the regular operating programs of the commercial departments, such as seasonal and budget plans, and to "special situation" activities. The latter might include, for example, opportunities arising from local surplus or shortage conditions, from availability or need for special grades and selections, or from individual projects relating to such things as new business, special customer needs, unusual foreign sales, or bids on large contracts.

EXHIBIT V-4. THE PILLSBURY COMPANY PROCUREMENT POLICY

Policy No.: P5-18
Subject Class: 511
Date:

SUBJECT: MAXIMUM NET POSITIONS THAT CAN BE TAKEN
ON WHEAT AND WHEAT FLOUR

Limited volume of trading in wheat futures at
Kansas City and Minneapolis at certain seasons
of the year makes it difficult to hedge grain
and flour positions in those markets in the same
strict manner that was feasible some years ago.
The wide swings in the spread between prices in
these two markets, where most of our cash wheat
is purchased, and prices in Chicago also make it
impractical to hedge these classes of wheat in
Chicago at certain times of the year.

The difficulties associated with a "close"
hedging policy are increased by the fact that
flour price changes no longer have any close
relationship with wheat price changes.

With these changing situations as a background,
the following policy limits are established.
These limits are not for speculative purposes,
and it will be the responsibility of the Executive Vice President responsible for Procurement
to see that they are not used that way. Rather,
they will be used to minimize the risks inherent
in forward flour sales and in the accumulating
of needed cash wheat positions.

Wherever a net position is mentioned in the following sections, it means all wheat positions
and all wheat equivalents of flour positions
considered together.

(Continued)

Exhibit V-4. (continued)

Policy No.: P5–18
Subject Class: 511
Date:
Page 2

PART I – FLOUR DIVISION:

1. Positions taken by the Flour Division will
   be determined by a Hedging Committee com-
   posed of the following:
   Executive Vice President responsible for
   Procurement, Chairman
   Manager, Flour Division
   Manager of Grain Procurement, Flour
   Division
   Director of Commodity Analysis Department

2. This Committee will operate within the
   following maximum limitations:
   a. May 1 to September 30:
      1) When contract grade wheat is selling
         at or below net loan levels, a net
         position of up to _____ bushels can
         be taken (approximately an __-week
         supply).
      2) When contract grade wheat is selling
         above net loan levels, a net posi-
         tion of up to _____ bushels can be
         taken (approximately a __-week
         supply).
   3) When the Manager of the Flour Division esti-
      mates that an unusually heavy volume
      of flour sales is expected during
      the succeeding 15 market days, a net
      long position of up to 75 percent of
      the anticipated sales, but not in
      excess of _____ bushels, will be

(Continued)

EXHIBIT V-4. (CONTINUED)

Policy No.: P5–18
Subject Class: 511
Date:
Page 3

permitted. If the flour sales do not materialize at the time estimated, any net long position in excess of the limits provided under 1) and 2) above will be liquidated within five market days.

b. October 1 to April 30:

    1) When contract grade wheat is selling at or below net loan levels, a net position of up to _____ bushels can be taken.

    2) When contract grade wheat is selling above net loan levels, a net position of up to _____ bushels can be taken.

    3) When the Manager of the Flour Division estimates that an unusually heavy volume of flour sales is expected during the succeeding 15 market days, a net long position of up to 75 percent of the anticipated sales, but not in excess of _____ bushels, will be permitted. If the flour sales do not materialize at the time estimated, any net long position in excess of the limits provided under 1) and 2) above will be liquidated within five market days.

c. Western Wheat and Flours:

    1) Montana wheats, both winters and

(Continued)

EXHIBIT V-4. (CONTINUED)

Policy No.: P5—18
Subject Class: 511
Date:
PAGE 4

springs, will be included with
Midwest spring and winter wheat
positions at Eastern mills and will
be hedged in the same manner.
2) Other West Coast wheat and Inter-
Mountain wheats will be hedged on an
intermittent basis since prices of
these wheats bear little or no
relationship to prices of futures at
Midwest markets. The Hedging Committee will decide when intermittent
hedges should be used and when the
position should be carried open.

PART II - FAMILY FLOUR AND SPECIALTY FLOURS:

1. Family Flour and Specialty Flours:
   a. The Director of the General Procurement
      Department has authority to cover
      requirements up to __ days' usage at any
      time.
   b. If the Director of General Procurement
      and the Director of Commodity Analysis
      are in agreement that the least risk to
      the Company is in taking greater forward
      coverage, they are authorized to do so
      up to __ days' estimated usage.

Requests to the risk officer for policy exceptions are made in writing stating not only the reasons for the request but also the plans for entering and closing all positions, together with specific provision for progress check points or stop-loss procedures. Similar information is also communicated to the accounting and control manager. One means by which such requests are evaluated is to determine what would happen if the risk were accepted and the reasoning behind taking the risk then proved to be totally wrong. When such a program involves special risks, it is expected that the hedging committee will have determined and evaluated all other means which could guard against unfavorable results. In other words, if a wrong outcome could seriously affect an entire year's profit picture, Pillsbury would do everything possible to avoid exposing itself to such a possibility.

Despite the fact that the hedging policies are very detailed, a continuing review of hedging policy is made possible by the regular and exceptional requests received. Quite obviously, where restrictions created by the policy become unreasonable, complaints from line personnel or requests for exception approvals may indicate the need for a review and change. Such reviews and subsequent alterations to the policies are the responsibility of the risk officer.

The actual procedures followed in carrying out hedging activities are also formally structured. For each commodity business its headquarters does all hedging for the plants which make up that business. As a result, the plants have no responsibility or control over the results of the hedging. For this reason the specific cost of the grain they use is not their direct responsibility. This permits the plants to be evaluated strictly on the basis of the efficiency with which they use the grain allotted to them.

On the other hand, each commodity business as a whole is responsible for the profit or loss generated through procurement activities, including hedging. Each one is also charged with all trading costs as well as its pro-rata share of the costs of maintaining the commodity analysis department. Each business sets a commodity variance goal for itself at the beginning of the year, attempting to do better than this variance goal though advantageous trading.

The procurement and risk officer for the entire firm receives a weekly report from each business indicating the net position of that business in each commodity it deals in. As a result, this officer has the responsibility for determining the net position of the whole firm. Having reviewed the net position for the entire firm it is possible to evaluate and, if necessary, adjust the net position of the firm to avoid undesirable exposures on both a weekly and a cumulative basis. The data he receives also provide a good deal of the information needed to evaluate risk exception requests as they are presented. These reports also go to the company controller.

Perhaps the most distinctive aspect of procurement risk management at Pillsbury is the emphasis upon appraising hedging results. Since each proposal and program have been spelled out in advance, together with the reasons underlying the decisions taken, it is possible to trace the outcomes and compare them with the earlier expectations. The primary purpose of such a review is not a matter of placing blame or credit (since risk and uncertainty are inescapable ingredients in the outcome) but rather one of improving skills and subsequent performance wherever possible. In view of the diversity of situations being dealt with, there are few standardized evaluation techniques. Instead, each instance is treated individually with as much emphasis upon judgment factors and counseling as upon book results.

Accounting Method — Pillsbury. The company values its hedged inventories "on the basis of market prices including adjustment to market of open contracts for purchases and sales." The annual report (see Appendix C) further notes: "The company follows a policy of hedging grain and certain other inventories to the extent considered practicable to minimize risk due to market price fluctuations."

The company sets up its operating records in a way that enters in the ledger accounts all contracts to buy wheat or sell flour at the point in time where a firm contract is signed. In addition, variances are recorded to reflect fluctuations of price in the cash and futures market, as they affect these commitments.

The system for supplying the management with hedging information is fully integrated with the handling of inventory accounting and valuation on the books.[12] In effect, the company can operate on approximately a replacement cost basis at the time sales are made.

Bay State Milling Company

This company provides an excellent example of the handling of accounting and control information in a flour milling operation which has integrated its hedging activities into a coordinated procurement, processing, and marketing system. While few companies are completely similar, the system followed by Bay State provides at least a bench mark against which to compare other systems. Bay State Milling Company is a family-controlled business founded in 1899 when Bernard J. Rothwell I purchased a flour mill in Winona, Minnesota. The company experienced a rapid expansion between 1954 and 1969 with the acquisition of existing flour mills located in Leavenworth, Kansas; Red Wing, Minnesota; Clifton, New Jersey; and Camp Hill, Pennsylvania. The firm ranks among the top 10 in the U.S. flour milling business and sells its products primarily in the commercial baking market, both domestic and export.

Bay State's Hedging and Procurement. Bay State is committed to earning a satisfactory profit on a fully hedged basis. The firm

---

[12] C. S. Rowley, Jr. in his thesis, "Inventory Pricing in the Grain Industry: A Study of Current Practice," pointed out that for several years prior to 1960 Pillsbury had published a footnote to its financial statements in greater detail than that shown in Appendix C, as follows:

"Grain (including wheat for the account of the Canadian Wheat Board) and grain products have been stated on the basis of market prices of grain at May 31, including adjustment to market of open contracts for purchases and sales. The company enters into commitments for the purchase and sale of these and other related commodities as an essential part of its established policy of hedging these inventories to the extent practicable, to minimize the market risk due to price fluctuations. The financial statements reflect the hedged position by taking into account all elements in the hedge (inventories on hand and long and short commitments) at market, so that the market gains and losses substantially compensate or offset one another, subject to the completeness of the hedge and certain other relatively minor elements. This procedure has been applied in a manner which does not result in taking unrealized profit into account."

recognizes, however, that its knowledge of the grain market and grain marketing offers opportunities to take advantage of market positions or spreads in such a way as to earn more profits than might otherwise be earned by an automatic textbook application of a fully hedged policy. Hedging and spreading in commodity futures as well as limited position taking are regular practices and require close management attention to the handling of price exposures and inventory risks.

Flour, which is the company's primary product, is produced under strict quality control procedures. This is particularly important in serving the baking market as baking formulas have narrow tolerances regarding the mix of wheat, blending, and product handling. At the same time, careful controls have to be exercised in order to attain the desired product with the most efficient, lowest cost set of ingredients. Since the selection of grains is a matter of expert judgment and knowledge of quality variations, the procurement function requires an intimate familiarity with local conditions in order to secure raw materials at advantageous locations and at a time when they are available in a constantly changing supply situation. The acquisition of actual grain thus involves many factors which differ from the standard or par-delivery specifications that provide the bellwether for trading in grain in the futures markets. (For example, the nature of the freight or barge billing is almost always an important consideration, as are protein, moisture, and milling characteristics.)

Wheat is the major cost ingredient in finished flour, comprising as much as 80% to 85% of the finished product cost. Thus, the wheat content of finished flour is a familiar unit of measurement in the flour milling industry and substantially all inventories can be converted into equivalent bushels of grain for inventory management purposes. With rapidly changing prices, it is desirable to maintain current records which reflect up-to-date changes in wheat prices. Therefore, flour inventories can be expressed as so much wheat plus standard conversion cost (or betterment) less byproduct credits. Since the wheat content may be hedged, it can be priced at market on the basis of the current price of wheat, against which the hedge results provide an offset.

Flour Operations and Organization at Bay State. The Milling Division includes three major operating groups: the grain department, the milling department, and the sales department. This scheme enables the milling and sales departments to operate on a fully hedged or replacement cost basis, while the grain department carries the responsibility for gains or losses resulting from special procurement skills and position taking.

The grain department purchases most of the company's grain. There are, however, buyers at some mills who have, within prescribed limits, the authority to make local grain purchases under the direction of the grain department manager. All grain purchased, as well as the grain in flour inventories, is the responsibility of the grain department. However, the grain department shares with the individual flour mills the responsibility for maintaining physical inventories at each mill at certain specified minimum levels, these levels being determined principally by needs to blend specific wheat types in response to demand. Aside from the matters relating to grain requirements, grain costing and grain content of inventories, the responsibilities of the grain and milling departments become definitely separated.

The grain department is responsible for managing the company's overall inventory and net positions. The grain department manager is the only individual who can authorize futures transactions. The company has promulgated certain maximum limits on the net position, straddle positions, and the percentage of the open interest in a future which the company can assume. These limits are not rigid; rather, if the grain department manager feels that exceeding these limits is warranted, he can request approval to do so from the Hedge Committee which consists of the firm's vice president in charge of the milling division, the vice president of operations, and the grain department manager. Normally, the limits are such that the grain department has a considerable latitude for making decisions without requiring prior approval.

The milling department is mainly responsible for converting grain into flour as efficiently as possible. For each plant, standard costs are developed for the various operations and yields expected in the milling process, and variance accounts are used to record the differences between actual costs and the standard costs. Each mill is also responsible for storing the grain at its respective location.

Buyers at some mill locations may make local grain purchases. The guideline used is that each mill should take advantage of locally available supplies and have enough actual grain of the appropriate type on hand to meet milling requirements. Each mill operation is concerned only with cash grain and with its physical handling, not with futures operations. It need not worry over risks of changing grain prices, but rather with scheduling, receiving, and storing raw materials, conversion into flour, and delivering the finished products with utmost efficiency.

The sales department has no grain management responsibilities. Salesmen do not function as traders who handle both ends of a transaction. Rather, the sales force operates on the assumption that all sales will be fully hedged — that is, on a strict replacement cost basis. Sales are booked on the basis of up-to-date wheat prices and salesmen are evaluated on sales volume and margins over current material costs plus standard milling expenses.

From the above, it is apparent that the hedging and inventory management responsibilities are coordinated and carried out by the grain department. In order to carry out this function the department requires accounting and control reports that will provide:

1. Information on which to base sound procurement decisions.
2. Information to enable managers to control price exposures and inventory risks.
3. A set of records to enable the sales force to price flour to customers with adequate knowledge of break-even points and profitability.
4. A means for appraising procurement and inventory decisions.
5. Reports on capital employed and financial requirements.

Bay State's Accounting and Control System. Basic to the firm's accounting and control system is the up-to-date pricing of its three types of commitments: (a) undelivered raw material purchases and undelivered sales commitments, (b) inventories on the books (in terms of grain or grain content), and (c) commodity futures contract positions. All these commitments are priced daily using a daily cost card, and appropriate adjustments are made in the form of a series of records showing premiums or variances.

This daily cost card is an important feature of the overall grain management system. It shows, on a daily basis, the net material cost per hundredweight of all flour blends the company markets. As a starting point in computing these costs, the company uses the near-term Minneapolis Grain Exchange, Kansas City Board of Trade, and Chicago Board of Trade closing futures prices for that day. To these prices, the company applies up-to-date premiums for the various wheat types used in its flour blends.[13]

The combination of (a) the market-based price (derived from nearby futures), (b) the premiums and discounts incorporated in all purchase or sale commitments entered or discharged, and (c) the variances reflecting daily price fluctuations as they affect the full set of open cash and futures commitments, makes it possible to provide a clear replacement cost figure for any commitment at any given time. These figures are incorporated into the regular accounting records to provide the operating information discussed above for use of the milling and sales departments. They also provide the basic measure of performance for the grain department.[14] They provide ready records of net at risk positions, as well as all transactions and commitments in futures and cash grain.

The milling department has its own variances (other than grain prices) to enable it to operate on a current basis including departures from standard costs. The sales department in turn has the standard conversion costs and credits plus the current replacement cost figure for ingredients against which to price its sales. These sales can be booked for forward delivery merely by assuring that the grain department is in a position to cover that delivery with an appropriate long commitment in the proper month.

---

[13] These premiums (or discounts) as they are initially entered on the books are analogous to the differentials referred to as "my (or our) basis" in the "Note on BASIS," Chapter II. The daily adjustment of the premium record thus establishes the daily "opportunity basis" of that note. This shows the theoretically possible realizations if all commitments were to be liquidated at the current market.

[14] Since price variations are not the only variance factors reflected in the records, the accounting details are in fact too complicated to spell out fully here. (For instance, the company laboratory analysis of some grain characteristics may differ from the analysis certificate of the state grain inspection report on the basis of which the grain was paid for.)

If the company operated with a zero net position and all futures positions were taken in the future whose price is used to compute the cost card, profitability would largely depend on the grain department's ability to acquire cash grain at or near the cost card prices (that is, cash grain at premiums at or near the premiums used on the cost card) and on the milling department's ability to meet or do better than standard manufacturing costs. However, Bay State's grain department operates in a far more sophisticated manner. The department's goal is to procure its grain requirements at prices below those listed on the cost cards, and numerous alternatives other than astute cash grain purchasing are available. In response to a sales order, the grain department may purchase cash grain (either on an immediate delivery or "to arrive" basis), take a long futures position, or remain short for a period of time. Conversely, a wheat purchase may be made without being tied to a trade sale of flour, but rather in anticipation of later milling requirements, in which case it is likely to be hedged in the futures market. Net positions (i.e., departures from fully hedged or zero exposure) may take the form of actuals or futures, depending upon the market situation. In addition, the grain department may be able to add to the company's profits by intramarket or intermarket spreads (the firm trades on the Chicago and Kansas City grain exchanges as well as at Minneapolis) and by wisely selecting the future and market in which to place hedges or take net positions.

In order to associate the appropriate parts of the grain department results with the different geographic units where milling is carried on, a classification of grain accounts is maintained to make this possible. Premiums and variances relating to grain actually handled at each mill (and the corresponding hedge adjustments) are thus segregated. This leaves corporate (unallocated) results, which reflect discretionary spreading, arbitrage or position taking to be folded directly into the Milling Division's overall earnings.

From the data provided in the daily position and variance accounts it is possible to arrive at an up-to-date balance sheet and operating statement for the fast-moving grain department activities. Inventories are valued at "market" and can readily be adjusted for the effect of price changes upon unfilled trade and futures commitments. Periodic physical inventories and account balances are, of course, taken and reconciled with the cumulative daily records.

SUMMARY

It should be emphasized that the three specific discussions covering Continental Grain, Pillsbury, and Bay State Milling are presented to throw a spotlight upon particular aspects of the operations of firms in the grain and milling business. A total description of these businesses would involve innumerable other factors which are not discussed here since it was felt that they could be adequately covered in connection with the experience and activities of other industries to be covered in subsequent chapters of Part Three. Indeed, an effort has been made to avoid unnecessary duplication as between the three companies discussed above, even though it should be recognized that many of the practices are very similar from one firm to another.

For most readers it is felt that only by examining the problems and procedures of several industries will an adequate picture of the management uses of commodity futures emerge. The industries which are to be discussed below were selected to provide significant bands in a spectrum of distinctive situations. These industries are followed in Part Four with an effort to bring together the high spots and as many generalizations as the wide variety of futures applications has made possible.

CHAPTER VI

The Soybean Complex

THE SOYBEAN industry is unique in having active futures markets in the basic product and the primary derived products — oil and meal. Practically all soybeans, other than those saved for seed, are converted into these two major products as the first stage of processing. Minor by-products such as hulls are relatively insignificant.

Trading in soybeans and soybean products was initiated as follows:

Soybeans	December 8, 1940
Soybean Oil	June 30, 1950
Soybean Meal	August 22, 1951

All three of these contracts are traded in the Chicago Board of Trade (see Appendix C). During the 1960s, soybeans were frequently traded in greater volume than any other CEA-regulated commodity futures — occasionally exceeding in value all the other futures put together. Exhibit VI-1 shows the estimated annual value of trading in the three soybean contracts during the 1960s, compared with other CEA regulated commodities. A similar table, Exhibit VI-2 shows an average of the number of month-end open contracts.

The dramatic expansion of the soybean industry in the United States dates from the World War II period, rising from relative insignificance before 1940 (annual production in 1936–40 averaged 62 million bushels) to a production of 1,116,900,000 bushels in 1969. Exhibit VI-3 provides in perspective the U.S. experience in the production of soybeans for the 1958–70 period.

In recent years the United States has been predominant in world production and trade in soybeans and soybean products. This is revealed in Exhibit VI-4 which shows U.S. production amounting to 1.1 billion bushels out of an estimated world ouput of 1.5 billion bushels. This exhibit also reveals the consistent growth pattern of the industry.

In the soybean industry, futures have been used by participants at all stages from the farmer to the retailer of finished products (margarine, shortening, mayonnaise or salad oil). Naturally, the most frequent use of these three futures contracts as a management tool has been made by handlers and crushers of soybeans since these are the primary coordinators of the throughput and inventories of the industry. Moreover, the crusher is in a position where he can choose between many alternative hedging methods and can thereby make additional uses of the futures market as an adjunct to commitments in the cash market for his sales of meal and oil as well as for protection of procurement or inventory exposure in the form of beans. These alternative uses will be discussed further when we consider hedging activities of crushers.

HEDGING POLICY FOR A LARGE CORPORATE SOYBEAN GROWER

A large grower of soybeans has as his primary objective the realization of the greatest possible return on his crop. He becomes committed to that crop at the time he begins implementing his growing plans for the year and all the outlays made from that point forward can, as a practical matter, be recovered only through the sale of the soybeans to be harvested. The hedging problem involved can be looked upon from two major viewpoints. One of them is the protection of the commitments that represent the growing crop and the outlays that are required during the growing process. The other is to assume a future harvest which will

EXHIBIT VI-1. ESTIMATED VALUE OF FUTURES TRADING IN REGULATED COMMODITIES, ALL CONTRACT MARKETS COMBINED, 1960–61 TO 1969–70

(In millions of dollars)

Commodity	Year beginning July									
	1960–61	1961–62	1962–63	1963–64	1964–65	1965–66	1966–67	1967–68	1968–69	1969–70
Wheat	4,955.0	8,608.8	10,794.9	10,643.3	4,210.7	9,958.9	18,644.3	13,818.5	9,003.3	5,162.7
Corn	2,417.3	5,518.8	4,002.1	4,469.0	4,644.2	6,658.2	18,398.8	8,936.6	10,006.6	7,912.6
Oats	555.7	1,124.6	600.6	415.6	330.5	276.6	430.4	297.8	459.8	336.6
Rye	559.6	1,828.2	937.9	961.4	328.7	512.2	356.5	234.5	160.3	63.5
Barley	0	0	.1	.1	0	.1	0	0	0	0
Flaxseed	53.2	94.0	21.0	2.7	.2	.1	0	0	0	0
Soybeans	34,054.4	12,029.9	21,274.4	37,183.8	56,042.9	46,232.5	28,637.6	12,956.8	12,126.7	16,358.3
Grain sorghums	1.9	.3	.3	1.1	0	0	70.6	13.4	11.5	4.9
Rice	0	0	0	.2	.1	0	0	0	0	0
Cotton	474.9	611.3	486.4	152.2	32.2	7.9	10.7	3,256.1	2,235.6	432.6
Wool	506.3	513.8	249.1	298.5	162.6	367.2	184.2	107.8	55.3	33.0
Wool tops	35.6	12.7	7.4	4.7	1.9	1.4	1.5	1.2	.6	.3
Butter	0	0	0	0	0	7.4	116.8	.2	.3	.1
Eggs (Shell)	2,661.2	1,374.1	1,477.0	695.9	314.9	486.9	423.4	252.5	1,889.4	5,166.9
Eggs (Frozen)	839.6	995.9	443.2	472.7	52.2	158.1	27.2	10.1	19.9	.7
Potatoes	254.2	275.7	194.5	273.3	1,490.6	753.0	1,236.2	580.5	995.5	834.6
Cottonseed oil	750.0	485.0	594.8	694.1	223.6	73.6	34.0	1.4	.1	0

Soybean oil	2,570.9	1,666.5	2,077.0	2,215.8	3,666.4	3,741.1	2,917.7	1,397.1	2,045.5	10,350.4
Lard	72.4	37.4	2.0	—	—	—	—	—	—	—
Millfeeds[1]	—	.4	.8	—	—	—	—	—	—	—
Cottonseed meal	1.0	.1	.3	.2	.2	0	0	0	0	0
Soybean meal	1,563.9	1,537.9	2,136.7	1,881.0	1,996.6	2,614.8	3,343.3	2,470.9	3,061.4	5,342.3
Live beef cattle	—	—	—	—	173.3	711.6	1,618.0	1,873.0	6,141.8	10,313.6
Live feeder cattle	—	—	—	—	—	.6	4.2	.2	—	—
Choice steers	—	—	—	—	—	—	125.2	203.1	383.1	209.7
Frozen boneless beef	—	—	—	—	—	—	—	—	—	22.2
Live hogs	—	—	—	493.4	3,750.5	17.7	41.2	44.7	60.4	709.1
Frozen pork bellies	—	6.7	9.6	—	—	10,475.2	9,731.1	12,998.3	17,310.1	29,034.4
Frozen skinned hams	—	—	—	1.8	2.1	4.5	4.0	3.8	2.5	9.3
Hides	41.4	44.6	23.9	48.7	22.0	85.7	37.4	14.1	3.1	.3
Frozen concentrated orange juice	—	—	—	—	—	—	36.2	607.8	1,514.9	577.5
Total	52,368.5	36,766.7	45,334.0	60,909.5	77,446.4	83,145.2	86,430.5	60,080.4	67,487.7	92,875.6

[1] Estimated value of futures trading for bran, shorts, and middlings is combined. For data on each of these commodities, see Commodity Future Statistics for July 1960–June 1961.

SOURCE: *Commodity Futures Statistics, July 1969–June 1970*, Statistical Bulletin No. 464, USDA, Commodity Exchange Authority, March 1971, p. 19.

Exhibit VI-2. Number of Monthend Open Contracts, in Terms of Contract Units, All Contract Markets Combined, Regulated Commodities, 1960–61 to 1969–70

(Based on average of monthend open contracts)

Commodity	Year beginning July									
	1960–61	1961–62	1962–63	1963–64	1964–65	1965–66	1966–67	1967–68	1968–69	1969–70
Wheat	19,798	33,994	29,984	25,691	24,258	32,043	42,402	48,168	42,986	26,612
Corn	16,604	38,429	24,620	25,334	31,741	33,568	65,142	46,952	49,261	40,364
Oats	7,492	11,756	6,762	5,733	4,589	3,223	5,018	2,814	4,268	5,119
Rye	2,452	6,449	3,132	2,921	1,815	2,155	2,013	1,708	1,014	581
Barley	0	0	2	3	0	0	0	0	0	0
Flaxseed	161	190	101	17	2	1	0	0	0	0
Soybeans	39,449	31,557	34,005	51,109	59,779	47,843	42,927	34,908	33,386	38,331
Grain sorghums	46	11	8	51	0	0	712	184	181	69
Rice	0	0	0	1	1	0	0	0	0	0
Cotton	3,670	4,130	2,820	1,233	384	205	247	5,691	5,812	2,290
Wool	5,737	7,548	3,247	2,675	1,958	4,236	2,727	2,217	1,422	805
Wool tops	636	263	141	58	32	34	25	21	17	19
Butter	0	0	0	0	0	30	228	1	1	2
Eggs (Shell)	8,112	5,832	4,506	2,509	1,369	2,252	1,152	1,208	4,119	6,982
Eggs (Frozen)	1,614	1,991	1,038	968	180	508	132	98	125	5
Potatoes	6,558	9,870	7,462	6,325	13,244	13,429	15,488	14,702	16,771	12,162
Cottonseed oil	4,060	2,667	4,880	3,743	1,357	435	244	27	5	0

Soybean oil	10,041	9,672	15,200	18,424	17,454	17,336	15,135	10,789	16,089	26,923
Lard	544	490	39	—	—	—	—	—	—	—
Millfeeds[1]	—	41	33	—	—	—	—	—	—	—
Cottonseed meal	15	2	4	2	3	0	0	0	0	0
Soybean meal	7,419	8,602	9,181	10,962	12,445	12,037	13,050	11,390	15,012	21,555
Live beef cattle	—	—	—	—	1,945	6,731	16,246	16,460	22,427	21,564
Live feeder cattle	—	—	—	—	—	59	59	15	—	—
Choice steers	—	—	—	—	—	—	1,631	1,859	1,600	646
Frozen boneless beef	—	—	—	—	—	—	—	—	—	285
Live hogs	—	98	73	862	—	689	533	731	732	4,067
Frozen pork bellies	—	—	—	—	6,295	11,100	12,086	15,412	17,754	19,155
Frozen skinned hams	—	—	—	37	16	20	15	23	15	27
Hides	413	335	296	559	321	331	295	310	116	10
Frozen concentrated orange juice	—	—	—	—	—	—	556	3,660	5,619	3,317
Total	134,821	173,927	147,534	159,217	179,188	188,265	238,043	219,348	238,732	230,890

[1] Number of monthend open contracts for bran, shorts, and middlings is combined. For data on each of these commodities, see Commodity Futures Statistics for July 1960–June 1961.

SOURCE: *Commodity Futures Statistics, July 1969–June 1970*, Statistical Bulletin No. 464, USDA, Commodity Exchange Authority, March 1971, p. 20.

EXHIBIT VI-3. SOYBEANS: SUPPLY, DISPOSITION, ACREAGE, AND PRICE, U.S., 1958–70

Item	Year beginning September												
	1958	1959	1960	1961	1962	1963	1964	1965	1966	1967	1968	1969[1]	1970[2]
	Supply and Disposition (Million bushels)												
Supply													
Opening stock, Sept. 1	42.8	87.8	51.8	27.1	78.3	46.0	67.3	29.7	35.6	90.1	166.3	324.4	229
Production	580.2	532.9	555.1	678.6	669.2	699.2	700.9	845.6	928.5	976.1	1,103.1	1,116.9	1,133
Total supply	623.0	620.7	606.9	705.7	747.5	745.2	768.2	875.3	964.1	1,066.2	1,269.4	1,441.3	1,362
Disposition													
Crushings	398.8	394.0	406.1	431.4	472.8	436.8	479.0	537.5	559.4	576.4	605.9	737.5	
Exports	105.0	139.9	134.7	149.4	180.5	187.2	212.2	250.6	261.6	266.6	286.8	428.7	
Seed	27.4	29.3	32.5	33.3	34.6	36.0	40.3	42.9	47.1	47.8	49.4	48.8	
Feed	1.9	1.5	1.3	1.3	1.1	.9	.9	.9	1.0	.9	.9	–.9	
Residual	2.1	4.2	5.2	12.0	12.5	17.0	6.1	7.8	4.9	8.2	2.0	–3.9	
Total disposition	535.2	568.9	579.8	627.4	701.5	677.9	738.5	839.7	874.0	899.9	945.0	1,212.0	1,300
Stocks, August 31	87.8	51.8	27.1	78.3	46.0	67.3	29.7	35.6	90.1	166.3	324.4	229.4	
	Acreage and Yield (Million acres)												
Acreage planted	25.1	23.3	24.4	27.8	28.4	29.5	31.6	35.2	37.3	40.8	42.0	42.1	42.4
Acreage harvested for beans	24.0	22.6	23.7	27.0	27.6	28.6	30.8	34.4	36.5	39.8	41.1	40.9	41.6
Percent harvested (%)	95.6	97.0	97.1	97.1	97.2	96.9	97.2	97.7	97.9	97.5	97.8	97.1	98.1
							(Bushels)						
Yield per acre harvested	24.2	23.5	23.5	25.1	24.2	24.4	22.8	24.5	25.4	24.5	26.8	27.3	27.2
							(Dollars)						
Price per bushel													
Support (U.S. farm basis)	2.09	1.85	1.85	2.30	2.25	2.25	2.25	2.25	2.50	2.50	2.50	[3]2.25	2.25
Received by farmers	2.00	1.96	2.13	2.28	2.34	2.51	2.62	2.54	2.75	2.49	2.43	2.35	[4]2.66
No. 1 yellow, Ill. Pts.	2.12	2.07	2.53	2.41	2.50	2.59	2.81	2.91	2.86	2.61	2.54	2.53	
No. 1 yellow, Chicago	2.22	2.17	2.60	2.49	2.59	2.67	2.88	2.98	2.93	2.69	2.63	2.60	

[1] Preliminary.
[2] September indications.
[3] No. 1 grade soybeans beginning 1969 crop. Prior years No. 2 grade. Differential between No. 1 grade and No. 2 about 5¢ per bushel.
[4] September average.
SOURCE: *Fats and Oils Situation*, FOS 254, USDA, Economic Research Service, September 1970, p. 7.

have to be marketed and disposed of as a matter of completing this year's production cycle. Both approaches are similar — the latter implies that the manager will try to determine the optimum *time* at which to "sell" (that is, fix the sales price of) his product; the former provides some guidance as to the amount that has been committed to the crop and therefore reflects the actual "exposure" as nearly as it can be measured. A combination of these two approaches is outlined in the following discussion which has been prepared in the form of a suggested program for a large farming operation.

I. What could be hedged?
   • Commodity price risks as they will affect the operating results. This means:
   (a) Inventories on the books which are not sold or contracted to sell at firm prices.
   (b) Crops in process which represent a firm commitment at planting time.
   (c) Commitment by decision to plant. This may be a firm decision because of predicted profits (good margins in prospect at hedged prices), or it may be tentative — based on the comparative attractiveness of this or that application of land resources.

II. How to decide how much hedging is needed? This can be answered by stages.
   • (For the purpose of this statement, it will be assumed that hedging will employ futures contracts on the Board of Trade. It should be remembered, however, that a firm-priced forward sale contract booked to a dealer or crusher can serve many of the same purposes and should not be overlooked. The booking to a dealer or crusher is often simpler than a Board hedge. The buyer requires no margin deposit or cash payments in periods when the futures price moves against the hedger. Moreover, the transaction price usually takes into account the local delivery differentials and provides a specific realization price (assuming the delivery comes up to the expected quality). On the other hand, such a contract sale to the trade is irreversible so far as the seller's commitment of his own beans is concerned, whereas a futures hedge can be lifted and re-imposed at will.)
   (a) If a satisfactory margin can be realized at the prospective "uncovering basis" — that is, the normal historical relation-

EXHIBIT VI-4. SOYBEANS: PRODUCTION IN SPECIFIED COUNTRIES
AND THE WORLD, AVERAGE 1962–66, ANNUAL 1967–69[1]
(In thousands of bushels)

Continent and Country	Production			
	Average 1962–66	*1967*	*1968*	*1969*[2]
North America				
Canada	7,126	8,091	9,027	7,664
United States	768,672	976,060	1,103,129	1,116,876
Mexico	1,721	4,446	9,921	9,994
South America				
Argentina	582	753	808	1,168
Brazil	15,367	26,294	24,048	34,906
Colombia	1,429	2,939	3,197	2,756
Paraguay	370	661	514	1,102
Europe				
Romania	228	1,521	1,731	1,764
Yugoslavia	330	326	108	66
U.S.S.R.	16,049	19,731	20,944	21,310
Africa				
Nigeria[3]	673	570	260	300
Rhodesia[4]	11	8	7	10
Tanzania[5]	125	147	147	147
South Africa[4]	113	165	213	298
Asia				
Iran	10[6]	62	93	121
Turkey	178	217	312	331
China				
Mainland	259,600	255,000	238,100	230,000
Taiwan	2,148	2,764	2,682	2,462
Cambodia	312	294	294	331
Indonesia	13,764	13,338	12,236	16,241
Japan	9,718	6,995	6,155	4,986
Korea, South	5,959	7,402	9,012	8,414
Philippines	59	41	46	48
Thailand	1,112	735	808	1,102
Other countries	8,894	10,111	10,431	10,650

EXHIBIT V-4 (CONTINUED)

Continent and Country	Production			
	Average 1962–66	*1967*	*1968*	*1969*[2]
Total excluding Romania, Bulgaria, Hungary, U.S.S.R., Mainland China, North Korea, and North Vietnam[7]	830,397	1,052,960	1,183,790	1,210,131
Estimated world total[7]	1,114,581	1,338,671	1,454,223	1,473,047

[1] Years shown refer to years of harvest. Southern Hemisphere crops which are harvested in the early part of the year are combined with those of the Northern Hemisphere harvested the latter part of the same year.

[2] Preliminary.

[3] Quantities purchased by the Nigerian Marketing Boards for export.

[4] European farms only.

[5] Sales.

[6] Less than 5 years.

[7] Includes estimates for minor producing countries.

SOURCE: Prepared or estimated on the basis of official statistics of foreign governments, other foreign source materials, reports of U.S. Agricultural Attaches and Foreign Service Officers, results of office research, and related information. "Foreign Agriculture Circular," USDA, Foreign Agricultural Service, July 1970, p. 2.

ship between the local cash markets and the futures price at delivery time — then the management should decide how much of this business is desirable. The hedge in this case can be thought of as a step toward *"locking in" a profit.* (NOTE: Hedging is not a protection against variations in yield or quality. It merely protects against price changes in the "par-delivery" specifications.)

This hedge sale in the futures market can be left on until the product is actually sold in the cash market. However, if prices of futures decline to a point where cash crop ownership is regarded as very attractive because an upturn is deemed imminent, the hedge can be lifted (bought back) and the inventory price risk will be again assumed by the management.

(b) It may be decided to hedge only if futures prices get down to a level corresponding to an unsatisfactory margin — below full cost and target earnings. This is a *stop-loss* operation, applying only to crops in process or in inventory. In this operation, any further decline in the hedged price can be thought of as cost reducing in its effect. If price prospects should improve at a later date (especially if the futures market has fallen to lower levels in the meantime) the hedge can be lifted.

When futures prices, translated in terms of the farm's local delivery situation (freight, quality, and handling considered) do not provide a profitable vehicle for hedging, then one has the difficult judgment to make — whether to cut losses right away or to defer action in hope of a market improvement. The answer depends upon such things as: (1) how much loss could be afforded, (2) whether improvement can be confidently predicted, and (3) whether there are other ways out like storing, contracting to others, or putting beans under a CCC loan.

(c) There may be times when prices of futures suggest that the crop will return only a loss. In such a case the best procedure is to switch to another crop if it is not too late. There is *no point of hedging-in a loss if there are other choices.* (In some instances there may be a strong belief that futures prices are too low and will not stay there. In such cases, one can bet on the price improvement by planting anyway. The crop can then be left unhedged. The futures market may still be useful, however, since it permits a hedge sale at any time during the growing or harvest season, without waiting for a cash sale customer. If futures do improve as expected, then the price level may become profitable enough for a hedge sale to be made.)

(d) When the user becomes more sophisticated, the futures market may lend itself to a number of *opportunities to profit by "basis" trading.* This means taking advantage of strategic situations where cash beans are particularly low relative to the future or vice versa. There may be straddle or cross-hedge opportunities, such as hedging sorghums in corn futures, or beans in meal and oil futures, or spreading between delivery months. Operations of this sort ordinarily require the services of a skilled commercial specialist, backed by reasoned analysis and a well laid-out plan of action.

III. Planning the hedging program.

• In studying hedging opportunities, it is desirable for management to have a predetermined "normal" program of inventory or price risk policy, to be followed when (1) the inventory operation is in a normal seasonal pattern and (2) prices are in line with the best estimate that can be made of future expectations, while price volatility is expected to be about normal for the particular commodity. With such a "normal" pattern as a bench mark, it is possible to adopt modifications from this policy rather than start from scratch each time.

(a) The normal hedging policy should be adopted and reviewed annually, or as often as the responsible person feels is desirable. The specific program under this policy should include guidelines expressed in terms of timing, extent of hedging, relation to "net position," etc., with appropriate leeway for the exercise of judgment and maneuverability. There should be specified trigger points (dates or price levels) at which entry or withdrawal of hedges will be reconsidered.

(b) Once a program outline is formulated for general guidance, it is desirable to have a formal specific hedging program for each crop and season, outlined at the same time as tentative planting plans are laid out.

Given a projected production target and production cost estimates, plus a reading of what futures prices and government forecasts show, we can expect an initial hedging strategy to be presented.

Such a plan will show for a given commodity:

A. Internal statistics.

1. Intentions to plant, in acres and expected volume of production.

2. Expected cost per bushel (or bale) for product delivered at farm gate.

3. Normal (historical) spread of the local cash realization price under (or over) the futures quotations at times when crops have normally been sold.

4. The expected cost adjusted to include normal

spread. (This figure will be the one to compare with the current quotation for the futures delivery month in which hedges would be placed.)

B. Market statistics and outlook.

1. Forecast of prices at harvest.
2. Price guarantees, supplemental payments and other costs and credits.
3. Available outlets for cash or contract sale to the trade.
4. "Point-of-no-return" dates such as budget adoption, seed purchase, planting, contract sale commitment, etc.

(c) Hedging authority — procedural decisions needed.

1. Choice of commission firm, based on service, advice, knowledge of trade, etc., after comparing several candidates.
2. Financial arrangements with banks with specific provisions for handling maintenance margins and margin adjustment account payments.
3. Authority and delegations of responsibility: who can trade, what limits, what reports circulated to whom.
4. Bookkeeping and management information system records: for transactions, for monthly result reports, for measuring performance against expectations.

IV. Hedging administration, reports, etc.

(a) A memo explaining the plan should be prepared giving answers for each of the following hedging questions: Why this quantity, why place it now? What are expectations of price movements in the future? How do contract prices compare with costs? At what dates will position be reconsidered? At what price levels?

(b) A simple form for reporting futures contracts and estimating the current unsold position (including currently expected harvest) to show the percentage hedged, should be prepared and examined at least once a month, more often if markets are active.

(c) In a corporate farm, the basic plan and its execution should be the responsibility of the president, subject to approval of the Executive Committee, with review by the Board at its regular meetings.

(d) At the end of the season there should be included in the summary of results, crop by crop, an analysis of the operation both with and without hedging. This can be used in evaluating both the policy and its implementation.

The outline above is far from complete, but it does serve to reveal some of the alternatives and interacting considerations with which a large producer of soybeans has to deal. The suggestions made in the outline are not a substitute for sound market judgment. There is an overall risk to be dealt with and the futures market serves mainly to extend the time flexibility which the grower has available to him in marketing his output. It also gives him a definite bench-mark measure of the market price for the new crop which is still unharvested.

SOYBEAN CRUSHERS AND DEALERS

Those who are primarily dealers and exporters are typically basis operators who carry a fully hedged position and strive to earn a profit by supplying their customers with the services of assortment, location and convenient delivery times and conditions. By being hedged, they can receive a return for their services without exposing themselves to the major risks of swings in the market price, because their exposure is largely confined to the residuals or differentials between the cash and the futures quotations. The operations of dealers and exporters of soybeans differ very little from those handling wheat and other grains. In fact, most of them are the same firms, among them being Cargill, Continental Grain, Archer Daniels Midland, and others.

One of the outstanding characteristics of the soybean complex is the degree to which individual firms carry on, through vertical integration, the functions that are usually designated as several successive stages in the product flow. A number of farmer cooperatives not only handle the marketing of beans but also engage in crushing operations. A number of firms also combine the dealer functions of assembling, storing, transporting, and exporting soybeans with the crushing function. Similarly, crushers may carry their operations forward into the producing of livestock and poultry feeds, many of which, but not all, contain soybean meal as an ingredient. The same firms are likely to operate refineries for converting the crude soybean oil into salad oils, cooking oils and margarine. Some of the firms in this group are also important exporters.

The degree of vertical relationships is sharply illustrated in Exhibit VI-5 which was prepared by Professor Ray A. Goldberg in his study of *Agribusiness Coordination,* published in 1968. The diagram shows that at least 35% (and often over half) of the volume at each stage right down to the retailer was being handled by firms operating at two or more stages in the complex.

The result of the substantial amount of vertical integration makes it almost impossible to characterize the futures operations of a particular firm in terms of a single function. The dealer may be strictly a basis operator. However, the same firm, if it carries forward into feed manufacturing and the production of margarine or shortenings, may have a separate policy and profit center arrangement for managing the use of commodity futures in these operations. Thus, the management decisions involved might be conditioned by an assortment of purposes and objectives within a single firm even though the firm (as is usually the case) has a single trading desk for its futures transactions.

It therefore became necessary to consider the use of commodity futures in the soybean dealing and crushing complex in terms of the several functions performed, since many of the firms engage in an assortment of hedging programs. Just as a number of the major firms in the wheat industry are also active in soybeans, these firms in addition carry soybeans through the crushing process and often process them further into refined or finished products. The larger firms in the industry, roughly in the order of their crushing volume, include Archer Daniels Midland, Cargill, Central Soya, Ralston Purina, Swift, and A. E. Staley, all of which conduct integrated operations and export sales, in several instances going all the way to branded consumer products.

Not only are the firms in the soybean complex engaged in operations at several stages; the three futures markets they use offer an exceptional chance to engage in operations such as spreading between the interrelated products or "putting on a paper

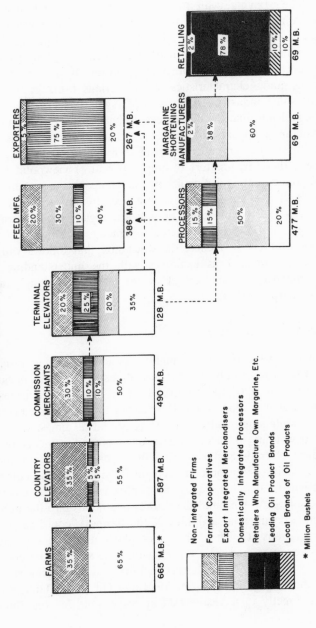

EXHIBIT VI-5. OWNERSHIP PATTERNS IN THE SOYBEAN ECONOMY AS MEASURED BY QUANTITY FLOWS: CROP YEAR 1963

SOURCE: Ray A. Goldberg, *Agribusiness Coordination*, Division of Research, Graduate School of Business Administration, Harvard University, Boston, 1968, p. 116. Reproduced by permission of the author.

crush" (i.e., buying bean futures and selling oil and meal futures). Almost innumerable alternatives are available when spot purchases and sales of beans, oil and meal, forward purchase and sale commitments in the cash market are included, along with the assortment of delivery and other terms to be taken into account.

The common characteristics of the various firms in the soybean crushing industry, so far as hedging is concerned, are far more significant than the differences. Relying in part upon indirect information, it appears that all crushers of soybeans do use the futures markets as an integral part of their commercial operations. However, there are matters of emphasis and of viewpoint which can be pointed out as distinguishing one company's approach from another's. These are not unique practices in any one case, but rather it is the combinations of policies, organizational arrangements and procedures, and actual operating decisions that produce the differences. Hence, the discussion that follows will use individual companies as examples with the understanding that most differences are matters of degree and "fine tuning" rather than of sharp contrasts.

Central Soya Company, Inc.

Central Soya carries on a highly developed hedging program which has been closely woven into all aspects of the business. The basic policy of the company, which has been affirmed in numerous annual reports and in speeches by company officers, is one of maintaining a fully hedged position at all times, with very minor deviations to accommodate overnight adjustments or the avoidance of trading gluts during brief periods of heavy movement of soybeans. In order to remain fully hedged, the company has designed a detailed management information system and trading procedures which build the futures operations into the minute-by-minute commercial activities of the business, coordinating the field operations at each of their nine plants and numerous elevators, warehouses, and sales offices with those at headquarters.

At the company headquarters in Fort Wayne hedging strategy is coordinated by the Soybean Meal and Oil Sales Manager who reports directly to a vice president responsible for the International Division, the Soya Extraction Operation and the Chicago Clearing Operation. A second vice president for grain merchandising and soybean purchasing works closely with these two in seeing that the soybean hedging operations are fully coordinated. Both vice presidents come under one executive vice president of the company.

Central Soya's nine processing plants operate primarily as cost centers, in that they have no control over the prices of their raw material (soybeans) or their end-products (meal and oil). All marketing and purchasing decisions are centralized in the trading room in Fort Wayne, Indiana. Salesmen and buyers are in constant contact with customers and field warehouses, reporting all transactions to the trading room which is connected by phone to traders on the floor of the Chicago Board of Trade. In this way changes in soybean inventories are quickly translated into purchases and sales of future contracts.

Well before farmers start their harvesting in September, Central Soya begins purchasing beans for the coming year. By the end of November it is not unusual for them to have purchased up to one half of their year's requirements. Such a policy was dictated by both the market characteristics and the production economics of the industry.

Price risk is not limited to raw bean inventories. The prices of the meal and oil produced by crushing beans are also subject to wide fluctuations. Such movements could wipe out processing margins, particularly when beans are purchased in large quantities long before the processed products will be sold.

To reduce these risks, the company strives to sell meal and oil for forward delivery at a price that will cover the costs of carrying the soybeans in inventory and processing them, while leaving a reasonable profit. Such an operation, while desirable, is not always possible, particularly when customers foresee general price weakness. In such a case they may order only enough meal and oil to cover one or two weeks' needs, leaving the company in a highly vulnerable position.

In order to illustrate the nature of the risks involved and some of the problems encountered by the manager of the hedging operation, the following paragraphs are taken from a case prepared for teaching purposes at the Harvard Business School depicting a situation that existed in 1968. This, in brief, presents a specific situation in which the problem of choosing between different alternative courses of action is described along with a discussion of some of the underlying factors and considerations.[1]

At the close of the commodity markets at 1:15 p.m. (Chicago time) on April 1, 1968, the Soybean Meal and Oil Sales Manager for Central Soya Company, was considering what strategy he should adopt with regard to near-term operations in the futures markets. He could not afford to wait long before initiating action as Central Soya was committed to delivering 4 million bushels of soybeans in May, having previously sold May futures as part of their normal hedging operation. In April 1968 the company had over 30 million bushels of soybeans in storage.

Central Soya needed the beans for their processing operation, however, and had no desire to liquidate their position by delivering them. Thus, enough May futures would have to be purchased during April to cancel the contracts which had claims on the beans. To do so in an orderly fashion without disrupting the price structure of the May soybean contracts would take the better part of the month, as 4 million bushels (800 contracts) represented about 30% of those currently outstanding (the "open interest").

Aside from this purely technical consideration, the real problem the manager faced was that of having to maintain a fully hedged position in those beans (Central Soya had a firm and long-standing policy of hedging *all* soybean inventories) while retiring the May contracts. Not only did the value of the soybeans need to be hedged until processing began, but also the processing margins (derived by crushing the beans and selling the meal and oil end products) had to be protected against adverse price changes.

Almost all of these soybeans had been purchased, at an average price of $2.54 per bushel (and hedged by sales of May futures at an average price of $2.74 per bushel), at the end of the harvest season the previous November. Since that time they had been kept in storage locations at various of Central Soya's processing plants. At the current rate of production they would be needed

---

[1] See Harvard Business School Case No. AI 268R, Central Soya Company, Inc. See also "Technical Note on Commodity Hedging," ICH 13G 233, AI 269R, Harvard Business School, Boston, 1968.

sometime in the middle of May. Normally, beans intended for May processing would have had their crushing margins already "protected" (by purchasing back soybean futures and selling meal and oil futures) by this time, as Central Soya's management liked to have at least two months' processing volume protected at all times. However, crushing margins between the May bean futures and the corresponding meal and oil futures had been so poor recently that the manager had delayed taking action in the hope that they would improve. Now only about one month's processing volume was protected by having it hedged in the form of meal and oil commitments.

In considering his problem, the manager decided that there were two major courses of action open to him. Both assumed that May soybean futures would be purchased throughout April to liquidate the current position.

1. Roll forward on the bean hedge: July or August bean futures could be sold to protect the value of the soybeans until processing began. Just before processing, this hedge would be translated into a processing hedge by buying back July/August soybean futures, and then selling meal and oil futures.

2. Put on the crush: Alternatively, meal and oil futures could be sold now, rather than performing the extra step of hedging the soybeans separately. This would protect both the value of the soybean inventory and the processing margins in one step.

Selling meal and oil directly to customers now for forward delivery was equivalent to selling meal and oil futures, of course. General price weakness in these products had made customers unwilling to commit themselves more than a week in advance, however, and the manager could not count on making such sales — especially of such magnitude. Thus the burden of margin protection had to come from operations in the futures markets.

The question of which alternative was best was not easily answered. If the manager could be sure that "paper" processing margins would improve over the next month, the two-step process outlined in the first alternative was to be preferred, since one month from now he could protect a higher margin than he could today. Similarly, if margins would become worse for certain, the second alternative guaranteed the best result.

The manager possessed no such certainty, however. He did know that the margins Central Soya had been receiving this year were lower than the previous year's. Furthermore, he realized that margins were usually depressed at this time of the year, as cash soybean prices tended to increase relative to meal and oil prices as a function of storage costs. In the past this effect was usually alleviated in later months as meal and oil prices then generally increased relative to bean prices — due both to shorter supplies of meal and oil as the crushing season tapered off, and to the approach of the new-crop supplies of beans. However, in the face of large supplies of oil and meal so far in 1968, he was not sure this seasonal uptrend would occur. Furthermore, there appeared to be little prospect of an early easing of the bean supply picture; most processors were apparently still able to cover variable costs as they continued to operate at close to capacity.

The situation just presented illustrates the type of problems that exist in the use of futures in a soybean processing company which operates under a policy of complete hedging of its inventory position. Naturally, a detailed and up-to-the-minute analysis of many commercial and industry factors was required in order to select the most advantageous of the alternatives in this one instance. When this simple example is replaced by the almost innumerable choices and special situations that are confronted in a fast-moving, huge-volume operation, it is clear that hedging operations call for a great deal of analytical skill as well as acute commercial judgment.

Central Soya, like other major soybean processors, requires the services of highly sophisticated analytical and communications facilities plus the close attention of well-informed executives. Since the company is primarily engaged in the purchase and processing of soybeans and the selling of oil and meal, hedging is regarded as a temporary intermediate step. Throughout the period in which soybeans are being purchased, various transactions are being entered into, including selling cash contracts for oil, cash contracts for meal, future option contracts for oil, future option contracts for meal, or future option contracts to sell soybeans. Numerous combinations and switches between these commitments make it impossible to follow a flow of any particular lot of soybeans and identify it with particular sales of soybean oil or of soybean meal.

Hence, the company has followed the practice of operating on the "average margin" theory. Under this method a gross margin between all purchase and all sale commitments can be accumulated from period to period. Since the total position is kept fully hedged, there is a sale for every purchase transaction or commitment and vice versa. Hence, it is reasonable to accumulate a combined dollar gross margin from all these purchases and sales and spread this aggregate over the physical volume of delivered sales, and goods still in ending inventories. (The beginning inventories had been subject to a corresponding adjustment, the objective of which was to avoid having inventory values, priced at market, take up an anticipated profit. The two adjustments are in effect balanced against each other so far as reported earnings are concerned.) The resultant earnings statement reflects the hedged position, bringing inventories back approximately to cost,[2] and expressing profits on the equivalent of a replacement cost basis.

This description is presented only as a simplified sketch of an approach, not by any means as a description of the complicated accounting procedures that have to be employed in actual practice. It is a way of looking at the business from the viewpoint of management information requirements, just as a wheat dealer wants to know his basis price on open trades and the basis values he has realized on closed trades.

---

[2] It is of interest in this connection that the Central Soya Annual Reports for August 31, 1967, and August 31, 1968, contained footnotes on inventory valuation, the earlier of which stated:

"Grain, soybeans, soybean oil, and soybean meal valued at *average cost* adjusted for hedges and undelivered contracts."

The following year the same footnote read:

"Grain, soybeans, soybean oil, and soybean meal valued at *market* adjusted for hedges and undelivered contracts."

The apparent change was one of language rather than substance since the accounts had been handled the same in both years; adjusted apparently meant "after adjustment" in the earlier year while in the following year it is assumed that the adjustment process started with the market value which was then adjusted for hedges and undelivered contracts. Such ambiguities, while not infrequent, were seldom spelled out as sharply as in this case.

Archer Daniels Midland Company

This firm has expanded its soybean capacity in recent years, largely by acquisitions, until it has attained the number one volume position in the industry. In mid-1970 it had 10 crushing plants located throughout the Midwest and southern states, enabling it to exercise great flexibility in the managing of locational and transportation factors which are often critical cost considerations.

Archer Daniels Midland follows a policy of fully matched hedging in its regular day-to-day operations and its entire organization is geared to implement this principle. To accomplish this, the headquarters offices, where all hedging activities are coordinated, are responsible for avoiding unhedged positions except for intraday or sometimes overnight intervals to accommodate orderly trading requirements in the market. Moreover, Archer Daniels Midland's President, Lowell Andreas, stated that his firm, like Central Soya, proclaims a policy of staying fully hedged at all times, denying to itself the taking of overall positions which would result in an unhedged net exposure.

One of the distinctive practices of Archer Daniels Midland is the specific relating of futures transactions to product sales and the deferring of gains and losses on closed futures until the month of product delivery.[3] It is the company's belief that this procedure records most accurately the gross margin from crushing operations (which is the prime function of the soybean division).

In computing the month-end inventory and the cost of beans crushed, Archer Daniels Midland's treatment of inventory and product factors can be outlined as follows:

1. Soybeans purchased (cash beans) are identified with and allocated to (a) new short meal and oil futures contracts, or (b) new bean futures contracts sold, or (c) cash meal and oil sold (actual or anticipated). This matching is done on daily trade sheets.

---

[3] In the soybean industry the terms "month of product delivery" or "month of crush" are more than mere descriptions. These are central factors in planning, scheduling, and in the accounting allocations. While they are not always applied in the same way from firm to firm, they are commonly used trade terms.

2. Profits or losses resulting from closing futures are identified with cash beans and, if appropriate, entered in the inventory as a deferred item until the month of the crush. Individual trades are identified by settlement month and number. For example, if during April cash beans are purchased and July meal and oil options are sold, the beans could be entered in the June crush column of the crush book and the futures would be identified as June 1. When the option contracts are closed and replaced with June cash oil sales, the gain or loss will be deferred in the inventory until June. In June the cost of the beans and the deferred gain or loss on the closed futures will be charged to operations.

3. If cash bean purchases are hedged with a bean option contract, a month will not be scheduled until meal and oil are sold and the future lifted at which time it is handled as in point 2 above. Any gains or losses from switching futures are carried with the cash beans (i.e., deferred) until month of crush.

4. For the crushing operations, then, the cost of sales is:
   (a) Cash cost plus or minus futures gain or loss if originally hedged in the futures market and
   (b) Cash cost of beans for any excess deemed hedged in cash products sold.

5. At the end of each month an evaluation is made comparing the inventory cost with the estimated inventory realization. (a) Cost of inventory on hand, (b) unfilled purchases and sales, (c) deferred gain or loss on closed and open option contracts, and (d) market value of any position, are all considered in this evaluation. Conversion cost factors are, of course, taken into account. A reserve is provided to reduce the inventory to realizable value if the evaluation shows the inventory realization to be below the inventory cost.

6. There is a Lifo oil base stock which is priced lower than the current market and generally is excluded from the hedging and evaluation operations.

7. Meal inventory is valued at (a) the average price of unfilled sales or (b) at market, if unsold. This has the effect of selling out all meal inventory in the month it is produced. As a general rule, meal actually is sold prior to or at the time it is produced and there is no unsold meal on hand.

Swift & Company

This company is probably more widely diversified than any other major member of the soybean processing industry. While its largest operations are in the meat field,[4] it also engages in a wide line of foods and nonfoods including animal and vegetable oils, feeds and agricultural chemicals, and includes such diverse activities as petroleum and life and casualty insurance. The soybean operations come under the Swift Edible Oil Company, a division of Swift & Company.

Swift Edible Oil Company is the producer of more than a billion pounds of vegetable shortening and oil products annually, including the nationally distributed Allsweet Margarine, Swift'ning, and Jewel shortening and Jewel salad oil. The Oil Mill Division produces soybean oil, the most important edible vegetable oil used in food processing, and soybean meal, the principal high protein ingredient in feeding of livestock and poultry. The Refinery Division, with six manufacturing units, produces a broad line of industrial and specialty shortening and oil products. Its customers include food processors, bakers, confectioners, the food service industry, and margarine and salad oil manufacturers.

A major emphasis in the operating of this business is the degree to which its planning and decision making is geared to the maximizing of return on assets employed. A special spotlight is thus cast upon the cost of capital as well as the production of maximum gross returns on turnover. The company's four soybean processing plants are located at Champaign, Illinois; Des Moines, Iowa; Fostoria, Ohio; and Frankfort, Indiana. Oil is distributed throughout the United States and Canada; meal, in the United States, Canada, and overseas.

Swift is an important user of the Lifo method of inventory valuation. This means that closing inventories of soybeans and oil carry the same unit prices as opening inventories to the extent that quantities remain unchanged from the opening inventory levels. While this situation modifies substantially the application

---

[4] See discussion of Swift's operations in the Live Beef Cattle Futures market, Chapter VII, pp. 248–255.

of hedging principles, it does not obviate the usefulness of commodity futures or the need to exercise careful management control of commodity positions, particularly as they relate to the intrayear soybean crushing program. This set of circumstances does serve to underline the importance of an operating policy quite apart from the more static concept of price protection for physical inventories owned.

The "month of crush" emphasis, which has already been pointed out, applies to the planning and commercial operations at Swift. While matching positions are taken in the course of managing the company's ownership and commitments, both in the futures market and in the form of unfilled trade orders, these positions are held, so far as the company's accounts are concerned, at the initial transaction prices pending the development of the actual costs for delivery in the "month of crush." In this way, the results of closed futures contracts are entered as costs in the form of appropriate adjustments along with other entries affecting the cost of goods sold. This closely resembles the ADM method of deferred treatment of such items, at least so far as the net outcome is concerned.

A typical comment about factors entering procurement operations at Swift illustrates the number of special commercial considerations that have to be taken into account:

> Cash soybeans are purchased in the area near the location of the processing plants, principally from country elevators.
>
> We purchase cash soybeans for nearby requirements and, occasionally, deferred shipments for requirements later. New crop soybeans are frequently purchased in moderate quantities six months or so in advance of harvest. We must be selective in the procurement of soybeans, obtaining appropriate billing to match meal sales distribution plans; and we must maintain a flexible schedule of billing which requires, depending on the season of the year, an inventory approaching 30 days' ownership. The total capital employed at a given time may be turned over five or six times in an average year.

The company looks at its soybean operation in terms of a basic policy outlined at the beginning of the year subject to seasonal adjustment to make allowance for harvest movement, margin or spreading possibilities, and overall risk. At any given time the total net position — cash and futures — is carefully controlled. Within the policy guidelines, either the vice president or the division manager can handle hedging functions, which are all managed at the headquarters office.

Those responsible for inventory management and hedging policy, as with other leading companies in the industry, are continually in contact with the market and employ very detailed records of positions, price relationships and other market factors. Various market news services and analysts, both on the company staff and outside, are expected to contribute to the formulation of short-time decisions as well as other longer range plans. Flexibility is attained by liberal use of the futures market which provides for rapid adjustments as well as for taking advantage of shifts between the prices of several products and the delivery months.

Futures operations, policies, and decisions are subject to weekly review by the top managers of the soybean operation and specific attention is paid to the basic hedging policy, to special situations regarding price levels and prospects, and to market spreads and relationships.

Mill managers who formerly operated with their own profit centers have recently shifted to operating on the principle of management by objectives, employing standard costs and various yield and performance targets. The mill manager is still commercially involved in the purchase of beans at desirable origins and endeavoring to attain minimum transportation costs in serving customers located at various delivery points. A special analysis is employed to review performance in this respect. It is felt, for instance, that the mill manager may be in the best position to market soybean meal which can be delivered by truck, and one of his primary responsibilities is the making of such sales.

In order to attain assured supplies there are times when it is advantageous to book beans "on the basis" by naming a margin related to the Chicago futures market but without setting the actual price at which the beans will ultimately be purchased. If either party wants to price a transaction, he can do so by a futures trade.

In summary, the various types of purposes and opportunities as well as some limitations involved in using commodity futures as a management tool in a soybean processing business were clearly summarized by Scott E. Cramer, President, Swift Edible Oil Company.[5] He states that the manager can make some or all of the following uses of futures:

1. To lock in a satisfactory margin by selling various combinations of futures or cash products and buying the required equivalent quantity of future or cash soybeans.
2. To transfer to the speculator the risk of inventory price decline or margin deterioration by selling futures soybeans and/or futures products.
3. To obtain adequate and least-cost financing.
4. To minimize credit risk.
5. To concentrate his energy and resources on manufacturing efficiency and merchandising rather than speculation. This works for a high volume, low-cost operation that tends to maximize product consumption.
6. In most years there are periods when it is impossible to operate "back-to-back" and make a satisfactory return on investment. Buying future product hedges or selling future soybean hedges permits deferment of locking in a margin until such time as the margin may be more attractive.
7. A hedged operation, whether in futures or cash, encourages and permits forward planning and its implementation, since operations and marketing are usually unaffected by change in the price level.

Still there are limitations. As Mr. Cramer puts it:

All risks cannot be hedged even under the most favorable marketing conditions. The processor must still speculate on forward product demand, adequacy and availability of raw material, government price support activities that may set a price level above world demand, competition for world demand by other crops, non-tariff barriers preventing access to markets, and over-produc-

---

[5] Letter, S. E. Cramer to H. B. Arthur, September 2, 1970.

tion of products relative to demand. All of these factors influence and set the processing margin which, in the end, is the crucial element that will determine profitability.

FURTHER PROCESSORS, SOYBEAN OIL AND MEAL PRODUCTS

The end products of the versatile soybean are found in many different food items and in a number of industrial and nonfood consumer goods. The food list includes not only the salad and cooking oils, shortening and margarine, plus the many prepared foods and snacks involving these products as ingredients, but also the innumerable meat, dairy, and poultry products made from animals which have been fed soybean meal as an important feed ingredient. The industrial and nonfood articles include paints, fibers, plastics, soap, and kindred products; these, however, are not generally regarded as major outlets for the aggregate soybean production. The same is true of products employing soybean meal as a protein source for human food, interesting and promising though this potential may be.

The big users of soybean products are the edible fats and oils processors for the oil and the animal feed industry for the meal. Both domestic and foreign concerns are included. These major users are confronted with important inventory price risks as well as procurement problems.

The degree of price parallelism between crude soybean oil and its end products (salad oil, margarine, etc.) varies widely from one product to another, but it is safe to say that practically all end products reflect a moderate or high degree of price correlation, at least through the wholesale trade level. One reason for this is that most of the refined oil products (including margarine) are easily processed items with a high raw-material cost element, which makes them susceptible to relatively undifferentiated private label competition. Many refiners and processors sell products which are formula-priced on the basis of crude soybean oil prices. This makes for a straight hedged operation so long as there is a processing margin to be locked in. At the same time there are many users of soybean oil who convert it into further processed products such as baking mixes, potato chips, snacks, specialty salad dressing, or mayonnaise. These products, being more inflexible in price, make the price impact more one of procurement timing than of risk-shifting. The same is true to some degree with high-quality manufacturer brands of margarine, shortening, or cooking oils.

Therefore, among users of soybean oils it was not surprising to find some conventional hedgers who operated on close margins and shifted their inventory price risks through the use of futures, while others sought to use the futures primarily as a flexible instrument for carrying out a procurement policy which involved varying the net position, depending on cost estimates and marketing strategy.

Soybean meal users likewise included those (especially merchant feed mixers) who operated on a generally hedged inventory position, ready to buy ingredients and sell products on a current replacement cost market. Others, e.g., the poultry integrators or feedlot operators who operate their own feed mills, fall in the second category of buyers of input ingredients for an end product having little price parallelism with the product in question. Here futures serve primarily as a procurement tool for assuring availability at an acceptable cost.

Businesses in the soybean meal industry are for the most part thoroughly familiar with grain markets where tradition has made the futures quotation the generally accepted benchmark price in the industry. Soybean meal is somewhat similar, although local situations may result in important departures from any fixed normal pattern.

RETAILERS AND INDUSTRIAL USERS

These two groups are almost universally concerned with procurement problems rather than with shifting inventory price risks to others. Most of them do not use futures in an important way, but there are significant exceptions. Since those using futures for soybean oil experience the same types of problems and opportunities as similar firms using the Frozen Concentrated Orange

Juice futures, to be discussed later, it will avoid repetition simply to refer to that discussion appearing in Chapter IX.

SUMMARY

It is not surprising to find the soybean complex a rich field for the productive use of commodity futures. Both the beans and the primary products, oil and meal, meet most of the traditional criteria for successful futures trading. Moreover, the price volatility tends to be high and the degree of price parallelism is substantial for operators at several industrial stages. One factor which may have been of considerable importance in establishing this industry as a very important user of futures is the newness of the industry and the major part played by businessmen already thoroughly familiar with grain futures. The momentum they provided no doubt helped set the pattern for the very widespread use of futures as an everyday adjunct to business operations.

CHAPTER VII

Cattle and Beef Industries

FUTURES TRADING in live cattle began in November 1964 at the Chicago Mercantile Exchange and a slightly different futures contract was introduced at the Board of Trade of the City of Chicago on October 4, 1966. The Mercantile Exchange contract with its two-year head start has attracted by all odds the largest volume of futures transactions, and in view of its success this contract is taken as the base for most of the discussion which follows.[1]

THE CONTRACT

The Mercantile Exchange Live Cattle contract calls for delivery of 40,000 pounds (prior to the August 1969 future, contract was

---

[1] A futures contract was initiated during the 1960s for feeder cattle at Kansas City and a Chicago Mercantile Exchange contract calling for delivery of fed cattle on the West Coast, as well as a carcass beef contract on the Chicago Board of Trade. None of these contracts succeeded in attracting customers, and trading discontinued. As of early 1970 a Canadian market in cattle futures was getting started in Winnipeg. Also, a contract for Frozen Boneless (manufacturing) Beef was inaugurated at the Chicago Mercantile Exchange on April 15, 1970. The Chicago Choice Steer Futures contract on the Board of Trade was terminated in December 1970, and a new multiple-delivery contract announced for trading beginning in February 1971.

The use of capitals for Live Cattle Futures, or Live Beef Cattle Futures, usually refers to the Chicago Mercantile Exchange contract, although some of the statistical data referred to are drawn from all markets combined.

25,000 pounds) of live beef steers described as "slaughter cattle possessing minimum qualifications for the Choice grade" as defined by the U.S. Department of Agriculture (SRA-AMS 99). Such cattle must be healthy and "shall have an indicated exterior fat covering of not more than 1 inch over the rib-eye at approximately the twelfth rib." (Specifications of this type indicate the degree to which judgment is a factor in acceptability. In order to validate deliveries an arrangement was established whereby graders from the U.S. Department of Agriculture Livestock Division would be employed to identify each lot of cattle qualified for delivery.) Deliveries of Live Beef Cattle were originally made on the basis of approved livestock yards in Chicago for par settlement. However, deliveries were also possible from approved livestock yards at Omaha, Nebraska with an allowance of 75¢ per cwt. and, effective with the February 1967 contract, deliveries were permitted from approved livestock yards at Kansas City, Missouri at $1 per cwt. allowance or discount. Beginning with the August 1971 contract, however, the Chicago market was dropped from the list of delivery points, Omaha becoming the base for par-delivery quotations and the Kansas City allowance was cut to 25¢ per cwt. This was a result of the closing of the Cattle Market at the Chicago Union Stockyards earlier that year.

More specific terms for "par delivery" as well as for substitutions and allowances are specified as follows under the Chicago Mercantile Exchange regulations:

PAR DELIVERY

A par delivery unit is 40,000 lbs. of Choice Grade Live Steers.
(a) Steers averaging within the weight range of 1050–1150 lbs.; estimated yield requirements to be 61%.
(b) Steers averaging within the weight range of 1151–1250 lbs.; estimated yield requirements to be 62%.

Delivery units with estimated yield under par will be acceptable with allowance of ¼¢ per lb. for each ½% or less by which the estimated yield is under par.

A par delivery unit must consist of steers averaging within the weight range of 1050–1150 lbs. or steers averaging within the weight range of 1151–1250 lbs., provided that individual steers shall weigh not more than 100 pounds over or under the average weight of the steers in the delivery unit.

SUBSTITUTIONS AND ALLOWANCES

Steers weighing from 100 to 200 pounds over or under the average weight of the steers in the delivery unit shall be deliverable at an allowance of 2¢ per pound. For purposes of computing such allowance, the weight of such steers weighing over or under the average weight of the load shall be considered the same as the average weight per head of the delivered unit. Steers weighing more than 200 pounds over or under the average weight of the load are not acceptable. The judgment of the grader(s) as to the number of such overweight or underweight cattle in the delivery unit shall be final and shall be so certified on the grading certificate.

Delivery units containing not more than 8 head of the top half of USDA Good Grade steers may be substituted at a 2¢ per pound allowance. For the purpose of computing such allowances, the weight of such Good Grade steers shall be considered the same as the average weight per head of the delivered unit.

Delivery units containing 9 head but not more than 17 head of the top half of USDA Good Grade steers may be substituted at 3¢ per pound allowance. For the purpose of computing such allowances, the weight of such Good Grade steers shall be considered the same as the average weight per head of the delivered unit.

The estimated minimum par yield on Good Grade cattle in the 1000–1150 weight range shall be 58%. The minimum par yield on Good Grade cattle in the 1150–1300 weight range shall be 59%.

USDA Good Grade Steers with an estimated yield under par will be acceptable with an allowance of ¼¢ per pound for each ½% or less by which the estimated yield is under par.

Variations in quantity of a delivery unit not in excess of 5% of 40,000 pounds, shall be permitted at time of delivery.

During the early years of the contract there were experimental deliveries to test the validity of the market since this contract represented a radical innovation in providing for the delivery of a nonstorable commodity and one which had traditionally been accepted by buyers on the basis of their own personal inspection rather than on written specifications. The success of the cattle futures market was thus a technological breakthrough for commodity futures trading. It demonstrated the feasibility of a futures market in a commodity which was not storable, not fungible (as in a homogenous mixture) and, indeed, one which applied to growing cattle which were changing in specifications and quality day by day.[2]

The success of futures trading in cattle, even though the product is not storable, apparently hinged upon the availability of processors willing to accept delivery against the certification of federal graders and the fact that feasible delivery points could be arranged which accommodated those making delivery without handicapping the processor who normally accepted the cattle in fulfillment of futures contracts. Thus validated, it has been possible to meet the very real needs of commercial cattlemen, processors and marketers

---

[2] See Henry H. Bakken, remarks at Live Cattle Futures Study Conference, sponsored by Chicago Mercantile Exchange, September 8, 1966, p. 20:

"The earlier writers on the subject contended that the technique of selling futures contracts is circumscribed in its application to a limited number of commodities. The reasons given in support of this view were presumably derived by some process of rationalization, but their premises proved faulty. Ever since they drafted the specific list of attributes which they considered essential to qualify a commodity for entry into the futures markets, it has been discredited in actual practice. The list of qualifications that they set up can be found in many textbooks. It follows:

1. The commodity must be a basic one.
2. It must not be perishable.
3. Units of the good must be homogeneous and fungible.
4. It must be one for which the price fluctuates frequently and with wide amplitude.
5. It must be a product that can be accurately graded.
6. It must be measurable, both quantitatively and qualitatively either by weight or cubic content.
7. The supply must not be controlled by monopoly interest.
8. Nearly all manufactured articles, especially stylized ones, are unsuited for futures transactions.
9. A broad market should exist for the good, possibly a world market.
10. Finally, it should be a product that is salable at all times for liquidity."

in an extremely large economic area which had not previously enjoyed access to any substantial amount of price protection. There is no doubt that this breakthrough opened the way for the establishment of a number of other commodity futures contracts in commodities for which futures trading had previously been considered impracticable.[3]

An idea of the importance and viability of the cattle futures market can be gained from the following round numbers, all of which have been converted into figures representing an approximate number of head of cattle in the 1968–69 period:

Average open interest	1 million head
Cattle futures traded per year	25 million head
Cattle feedlot population	10 million head
Annual slaughter — beef type cattle	25 million head
Cattle and calves on farms	110 million head

Buyers and Sellers of Live Cattle Futures

The classification of users of cattle futures according to occupation is best exemplified by Exhibit VII-1, prepared at the University of Illinois in cooperation with the Chicago Mercantile Exchange, covering the open interest on that Exchange on July 28, 1967. The first three occupation groups may be assumed to include those who have a commercial interest in the cattle and beef industry but, unfortunately, these groups also include a number who may not have such commercial interests.

In spite of the difficulty with definition, it is of interest for our purpose to examine the kinds of commercial exposure to which the various traders in the first three occupational categories might be subject. We can safely combine the categories of producer and rancher as reflecting ownership of young beef cattle which are not ordinarily grown to maturity. The feeder and feedlot operator in turn may include cattlemen who specialize in the raising and/or

---

[3] Such contracts, some of which were previously relatively inactive or untested, include live hogs, fresh eggs, and iced broilers.

Exhibit VII-1. Occupation of Holders of Cattle Futures Contracts, Chicago Mercantile Exchange, July 28, 1967

Item	Occupation Groups[a]									Total
	1	2	3	4	5	6	7	8	9	
					(number)					
Total accounts	1,626	86	231	178	360	62	180	50	941	3,714
Total contracts	21,140	4,005	3,288	5,615	1,342	356	822	581	4,565	41,714
Long	9,339	853	1,455	3,731	812	255	648	142	3,003	20,238
Short	11,801	3,152	1,833	1,884	530	101	174	439	1,562	21,476
Hedge accounts	746	42	80	5	13	4	1	1	38	930
Contracts	14,996	3,302	2,134	68	226	41	1	383	524	21,675
Long	4,200	418	466	22	4	0	1	0	119	5,230
Short	10,796	2,884	1,668	46	222	41	0	383	405	16,445
Speculator accounts	868	43	149	170	342	57	179	40	901	2,749
Contracts	5,939	578	1,140	5,347	1,092	312	821	170	4,009	19,435
Long	4,966	435	976	3,551	788	252	647	117	2,852	14,584
Short	973	143	164	1,823	304	60	174	53	1,157	4,851
Other accounts	12	1	2	3	5	1	0	9	2	35
Contracts	205	125	14	173	24	3	0	28	32	604
Long	173	0	13	158	20	3	0	25	32	424
Short	32	125	1	15	4	0	0	3	0	180

(percent)

	1	2	3	4	5	6	7	8	9
Total accounts	43.8	2.3	6.2	4.8	9.7	1.7	4.9	1.3	25.3
Total contracts	50.7	9.6	7.9	13.5	3.2	0.8	2.0	1.4	10.9
Long	46.2	4.2	7.2	18.4	4.0	1.3	3.2	0.7	14.8
Short	54.9	14.7	8.5	8.8	2.5	0.5	0.8	2.0	7.3
Hedge accounts	80.3	4.5	8.6	0.5	1.4	0.4	0.1	0.1	4.1
Contracts	69.2	15.2	9.9	0.3	1.0	0.2	0	1.8	2.4
Long	80.3	8.0	8.9	0.4	0.1	0	0	0	2.3
Short	65.6	17.5	10.1	0.3	1.4	0.3	0	2.3	2.5
Speculator accounts	31.6	1.5	5.4	6.2	12.4	2.1	6.5	1.5	32.8
Contracts	30.6	3.0	5.9	27.6	5.6	1.6	4.2	0.9	20.6
Long	34.0	3.0	6.7	24.3	5.4	1.7	4.5	0.8	19.6
Short	20.1	2.9	3.4	37.6	6.3	1.2	3.6	1.1	23.8
Other accounts	34.2	2.9	5.7	8.6	14.3	2.9	0	25.7	5.7
Contracts	33.9	20.7	2.3	28.6	4.0	0.5	0	4.7	5.3

[a] 1. Farmer, feeder, producer, rancher, or feedlot operator (cattlemen).
2. Packer or employee of a packing company.
3. Commission man, livestock buyer, or livestock dealer.
4. Professional speculator, floor trader, brokerage house, or a related employee.
5. Doctor, dentist, lawyer, etc. (professional people).
6. Lending institution or a related employee.
7. Housewives and retired persons.
8. Unknown occupation.
9. All others.

SOURCE: "Users of Livestock Futures Markets," University of Illinois, Department of Agricultural Economics, Agricultural Experiment Station, AERR 94, October 1968.

finishing of beef cattle, starting with young stock (either weaners or range fed) and marketing them either as unfinished or finished beef cattle (usually steers and heifers). The classification "farmer" is obviously indefinite; it may include both farmers whose operations include beef cattle and those who have no direct interest at all in the commercial cattle industry.

Similarly, the second category, "packer or employee of a packing company," may well embrace firms which are nonslaughtering processors as well as buyers of fed beef cattle. One would assume that the word employee embraces both individuals trading for their own account and employees trading on behalf of their firm; this is another source of confusion. As will be seen later, many packers engage in cattle feeding operations and have found Live Cattle Futures useful in this connection.

The difficulty with the third category — commission man, livestock buyer, or livestock dealer — is largely the question of whether these individuals or firms have an actual commercial commitment in livestock or whether their futures trading is essentially separate from their commercial risks. An unknown portion of these trades may also represent transactions on behalf of customers, on a fee basis.

Despite the problems of definition, it can be seen that the first three occupational groups referred to accounted for 93.4% of the "hedge accounts" and for 94.3% of the hedge contracts open.[4]

---

[4] It should be noted that it is impossible to accept the classification of "hedge accounts," "speculator accounts," and "other accounts" as conforming to our definition of hedging. The Illinois report which was based upon information from 56 of the 62 clearing firms holding cattle contracts on July 28, 1967 contains the following statement:

"For the purpose of this survey, the definition of a hedger caused some difficulty. The survey instructions said: 'An account should be classified as hedge if, in your judgment, the customer used futures contracts as a regular part of his business in order to lessen risk.' This is a less-exacting definition than the one generally used of 'a position equal to and opposite his cash position.' The more-liberal definition may overemphasize the hedging aspect of these contracts."

It will be noted that the clearing members responding to the survey rather than the traders themselves were the source of this information. Their records may not always permit accurate classification, since their

At the same time these three groups accounted for 38.5% of the so-called speculator accounts and for 39.5% of the open contracts in the "speculator" category. Combining all the accounts handled by these three "commercially involved" occupational groups, we find that they held 57.6% of the open long contracts and 78.1% of the short contracts.

A more recent report, representing a survey as of May 29, 1969, has subsequently been published by the Commodity Exchange Authority.[5] This is a more comprehensive report on various aspects of the Live Cattle Futures market, but its occupational classification of traders is somewhat less conveniently presented for this particular purpose than the earlier document with which it substantially agrees. Like its predecessor, it does not specifically identify the feedlot operator or beef cattle feeder in its table showing types of trader and occupational groups. Undoubtedly, it would require a different type of survey to determine the specific cattle *operations* being hedged in the futures market, since feeding is done by farmers, meat packers and others besides specialized feedlot firms. Hence the discussions which follow must accept this limitation, which is important since feedlots are the final producers of the commodity being traded.

This same CEA report presents a semimonthly record which classifies commitments of the large (reporting) and nonreporting traders for the period from June 30, 1968 through October 31, 1969 (see Exhibit VII-2). The commitments of reporting traders are classified as to whether they are "hedging," "spreading" or "speculative" (excluding spreading). The nonreporting traders' commitments are not similarly classified. The sharp expansion of open contracts in February and March 1969 coincided with a sharp run-up of cash cattle prices. The initial growth of the open interest appeared strongest among hedgers on the short side and speculators on the long side. Later, however, spreading operations became a much larger factor. The total open interest did not fall off until September, even though commitments in the hedging and

---

nonclearing customers may in some cases include brokers who lump an assortment of traders.

[5] See USDA, CEA, *Trading in Live Beef Cattle Futures.*

EXHIBIT VII-2. LIVE BEEF CATTLE FUTURES: SEMIMONTHLY COMMIT-
MENTS OF REPORTING AND NONREPORTING TRADERS, AND TOTAL OPEN
CONTRACTS OF ALL FUTURES, CHICAGO MERCANTILE EXCHANGE,
JUNE 30, 1968–OCTOBER 31, 1969

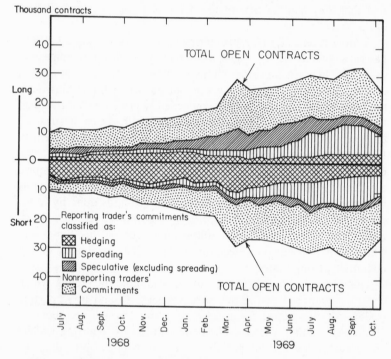

SOURCE: *Trading in Live Beef Cattle Futures*, USDA, Commodity
Exchange Authority, May 1970, p. 15.

speculative categories tapered off considerably between April and
September.[6]

The data in Exhibit VII-3 show the concurrent quotations for

---

[6] By July 1970 the total open contracts were less than half the level of
a year earlier, and trading was only about a quarter as large as in the month
of July 1969. Live Beef Cattle Futures is still one of the active markets
reported by the CEA along with wheat, corn, soybean items, and pork
bellies.

the cash price of choice steers at Chicago and the prices of various futures during the period from December 15, 1964, through October 15, 1969. In the months of March to June 1969 the more distant futures remained substantially under the level of the cash market and a very substantially inverted [7] market became evident. The price run-up in 1969 is also clearly shown in the charts prepared for the CEA report comparing cash prices with the August and the April futures (Exhibits VII-4 and VII-5). The inversion contrasts with the premium of the corresponding futures in earlier years, especially during the spring of 1967.

The price relationships shown in the charts are more diverse than the normal carrying charge relationships that exist in most futures for storable commodities.[8] However, the relationship between futures and spot prices in the cattle market does provide an important guideline, especially for the feedlot operator who is figuring the possibility of a hedged operation. He knows (and the charts bear this out) that the futures quotation will converge with the cash market as the delivery month is reached. He needs only to compare his projected costs — feeder cattle plus feed-out costs — with the futures quotation for the delivery month in which his cattle can be marketed in order to get a reasonable estimate of the profit or loss outcome if he hedges. (This assumes he is located where he can feasibly make delivery on the Exchange; if not, he has to allow for the risk of intermarket price differentials when he sells his fed cattle.) He may choose not to feed if the hedged operation shows a loss on paper; or he may go ahead and feed without hedging, gambling on a cash market price at delivery time higher than the level indicated by the present futures quotation for that delivery contract. If he hedges, of course, the profit or loss

---

[7] Discount may be a more appropriate word to describe the cattle market when futures are below spot prices. Inversion in storable commodities means the opposite of "carrying charge" premiums for the more distant futures, but this terminology is not meaningful for perishables like live cattle. For further comment upon this situation, see Haverkamp, "Potential Developments in Futures Markets of Significance to Agriculture and Related Industries."

[8] Inversions are, of course, not uncommon in grain or soybean futures relating to post-harvest delivery months — the period when new crop grains come on the market.

EXHIBIT VII-3. LIVE BEEF CATTLE: CASH PRICES FOR CHOICE STEERS AT CHICAGO UNION STOCKYARDS, CHICAGO WHOLESALE PRICES FOR CHOICE STEER CARCASSES IN CARLOT VOLUME, AND CLOSING FUTURES PRICES ON THE CHICAGO MERCANTILE EXCHANGE, BY FUTURE, MIDMONTHLY, DECEMBER 15, 1964–OCTOBER 15, 1969[1]

(In dollars per hundred pounds)

	Cash		*Future*											
	Choice		*February*		*April*		*June*		*August*		*October*		*December*	
Date	*Steers*	*Steer Carcasses*	*Odd*[2]	*Even*[3]	*Odd*	*Even*	*Odd*	*Even*	*Odd*	*Even*	*Odd*	*Even*	*Odd*	*Even*
1964					*1965*		*1965*		*1965*		*1965*			
Dec. 15	23.62	37.00			23.15		23.17[a]		23.50		23.70			
1965													*1965*	
Jan. 15	24.06	38.00			23.45		23.55		24.02		24.25		24.50	
Feb. 15	24.19	36.75			23.90		23.87		24.12		24.40		24.30	
Mar. 15	24.25	37.50			23.87		24.07		24.30		24.47		24.25[a]	
Apr. 15	25.44	39.25			25.80		25.35		25.20		24.95		24.80[a]	
May 14	27.12	41.25		*1966*			26.80		26.30		25.75		25.55	
June 15	26.62	41.38		24.85		*1966*	27.25		26.77		25.92		25.40	
July 15	26.38	41.75		24.85		25.00			26.37		25.70		25.15	
Aug. 13	27.19	41.50		24.90		24.90			27.30		26.07		25.47	
Sept. 15	27.06	41.62		24.80[b]		24.95		*1966*			26.00		25.40	
Oct. 15	26.75	40.00		24.97[a]		25.00		25.60			26.15		25.52[b]	
Nov. 15	26.50	40.12		25.22		25.60		26.25		*1966*			25.85	
Dec. 15	26.62	40.50		27.00		27.35		28.40		28.35			26.95[b]	
1966												*1966*		*1966*
Jan. 14	27.25	42.00		27.12		28.00		28.97		29.10		29.10		29.15
Feb. 15	27.88	42.00	*1967*	28.15		28.25		28.40		28.70		28.85[a]		29.27
Mar. 15	28.75	43.25	28.75			27.95		27.42		28.00		28.07[b]		28.72
Apr. 15	28.00	42.00	27.80[b]		*1967*	28.02		26.95		27.35		27.50		27.97[a]
May 13	26.81	40.50	26.95		27.10			25.65		25.87		26.20		26.95
June 15	25.25	38.75	27.10		27.30			25.60		25.57		25.85		26.42
July 15	25.19	38.50	27.80		28.50		*1967*			25.52		26.55		27.15
Aug. 15	25.69	40.50	28.22		28.90		29.40		*1967*	26.20	*1967*	26.95[b]	*1967*	27.82
Sept. 15	26.12	40.50	27.50	*1968*	27.95		28.62		28.75		29.00	26.55	29.00	27.07[b]
Oct. 14	25.44	39.25	26.60	28.65	27.00		27.55		27.90		28.40[a]	25.72	28.35	26.15
Nov. 15	24.69	38.50	26.05	28.50	27.15		28.05		28.15		28.27		28.40	25.00
Dec. 15	24.06	38.75	25.95	28.85	27.00		27.82		28.22[a]		28.40		28.57[a]	24.55

Cash and futures prices for cattle (dollars per hundredweight)[1], 1967–1969

1967

Date	Cash	Wholesale	1969	1968	1969	1968	1969	1968	1969	1968	1969	1968	1968
Jan. 13	25.25	41.00											29.10
Feb. 15	24.88	39.38		29.20b		29.35							26.97
Mar. 15	24.19	37.88		27.25		27.40					28.95		27.35
Apr. 14	24.62	39.50		27.60		27.87		27.95			26.62		27.37
May 15	25.31	40.25		27.50		27.75		27.85	28.60		26.87		28.25
June 15	25.56	41.25		28.30		28.40		28.40	26.12		26.95		27.90
July 14	25.88	42.50		28.05		28.17b	28.15	28.27a	26.50	28.40	28.00		28.15
Aug. 15	27.19	43.00		28.22		28.27	25.60	27.15	26.42a	27.70	27.85		27.90
Sept. 15	27.25	43.75		27.65	27.35	27.17	25.85	26.10	27.70	26.32	28.10		27.02
Oct. 13	27.31	42.50		26.35	25.17	26.10	25.90	25.60	27.42	25.92a	27.90		26.30
Nov. 15	26.06	41.12	26.20	25.52	25.27	25.47	26.50	25.05	27.50	25.65	27.47		25.45
Dec. 15	25.81	41.50	25.20	25.55	25.25	25.05	26.25	25.15	27.55	25.70	27.05		26.00

1968

Date	Cash	Wholesale	1969	1970	1969	1968	1969	1968	1969	1968	1969	1968	1968
Jan. 15	26.88	43.25				24.82		24.85		25.35		25.60	25.70
Feb. 15	28.12	44.00				26.15		25.82		26.02		26.15a	26.27
Mar. 15	28.19	43.00	26.25			26.90		27.27		26.07		26.20a	26.12
Apr. 15	27.81	43.75	26.15b			27.70		26.92		26.50		26.25	26.12
May 15	27.44	42.75	26.25					26.70		26.50		26.62	26.17
June 14	26.94	43.25	26.25		26.20			26.90		26.75		27.50	26.27a
July 15	27.81	44.75	26.60		26.17					27.75		26.55	27.00
Aug. 15	27.75	44.50	25.60		25.42a		26.32a			27.60		26.90	25.70
Sept. 13	28.31	43.75	25.85		25.65		25.45					27.50	26.20
Oct. 15	28.38	44.25	25.75		25.55		25.45		25.85				26.40
Nov. 15	28.62	45.50	26.60	25.75	26.20		25.90		26.02		26.05		27.35
Dec. 13	28.88		27.72	27.40	26.95		26.70		26.95		26.82		29.00

1969

Date	Cash	Wholesale	1970	1970	1970	1970	1970	1970	1970	1970	1969	1970
Jan. 15	29.25	46.00									26.62	26.60
Feb. 14	29.38	44.75									28.10	27.97
Mar. 14	30.75	46.75		29.25		29.25			26.80b		29.92	29.50
Apr. 15	30.75	47.75		28.75b		28.20		27.90	28.30		29.15	28.82
May 15	33.81	54.50		29.35		29.00	26.60	28.70	30.20	28.65	30.55b	29.85
June 13	34.44	55.00		29.35		28.90	27.92	28.70	29.55	28.60b	28.87	29.80
July 15	31.81	51.25		28.20	27.00	27.95	30.05	27.90	31.75	27.75a	28.20	28.50
Aug. 15	30.81	48.25		27.67	28.25	27.65	29.95	27.57	32.12	27.47	28.17	27.80
Sept. 15	29.38	45.75	28.00	28.25	30.50	28.12	33.10	28.10	29.87	27.92	28.95	28.25
Oct. 15	29.12	44.75	29.17	29.30	30.45	29.75	34.45	29.75	30.65	29.55		28.75

a — asked price
b — bid price
[1] When there was a range for a cash price or for the closing of a futures price, an average of the range is shown. Cash prices were for Chicago choice steers weighing 900–1100 and 1100–1300 pounds. Chicago wholesale prices were for choice steer carcasses weighing 500–600 and 600–700 pounds. When futures prices were determined by actual sales, no bid or asked prices were included in determining the average futures prices.
[2] Futures expiring during odd-numbered years.
[3] Futures expiring during even-numbered years.
SOURCE: Cash prices as reported by the USDA, Consumer and Marketing Service, Livestock Division, "Livestock Detailed Quotations" and "Wholesale Meat Quotations," December 1964–October 1969. Futures prices as reported by the Chicago Mercantile Exchange. *Trading in Live Beef Cattle Futures*, USDA, Commodity Exchange Authority, May 1970, pp. 28–29.

EXHIBIT VII-4. LIVE BEEF CATTLE: PRICES OF THE AUGUST FUTURE
AT THE CHICAGO MERCANTILE EXCHANGE, CASH PRICES AT CHICAGO
UNION STOCKYARDS, AND THE PRICE DIFFERENCE, SEMIMONTHLY,
NOVEMBER 30, 1964–OCTOBER 31, 1969[1]

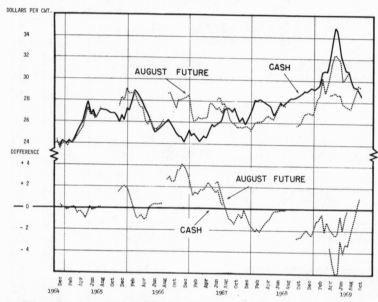

[1] When there was a range for a cash price or for the closing of a futures price, an average of the range is shown. Cash prices were for Chicago choice steers weighing 900–1100 and 1100–1300 pounds. When futures prices were determined by actual sales, no bid or ask prices were included in determining the average futures prices. Cash prices were reported by the USDA, Consumer and Marketing Service, Livestock Division, "Livestock Detailed Quotations."

SOURCE: *Trading in Live Beef Cattle Futures*, USDA, Commodity Exchange Authority, May 1970, p. 12.

EXHIBIT VII-5. LIVE BEEF CATTLE: PRICES OF THE APRIL FUTURE
AT THE CHICAGO MERCANTILE EXCHANGE, CASH PRICES AT CHICAGO
UNION STOCKYARDS, AND THE PRICE DIFFERENCE, SEMIMONTHLY,
NOVEMBER 30, 1964–OCTOBER 31, 1969[1]

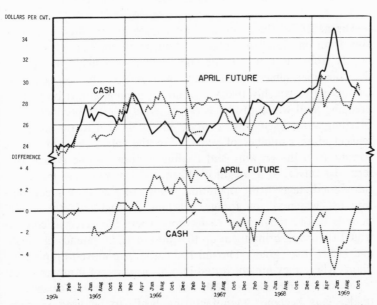

[1] When there was a range for a cash price or for the closing of a futures price,
an average of the range is shown. Cash prices were for Chicago choice steers
weighing 900–1100 and 1100–1300 pounds. When futures prices were determined
by actual sales, no bid or ask prices were included in determining the average
futures prices. Cash prices were reported by the USDA, Consumer and Marketing Service, Livestock Division, "Livestock Detailed Quotations."

SOURCE: *Trading in Live Beef Cattle Futures*, USDA, Commodity Exchange Authority, May 1970, p. 13.

on the futures will have to be entered as an adjustment of the amount realized from selling the actual cattle.[9]

Price Risks of Firms in the Cattle Business

The nature of the exposure to changing prices differs considerably from one level of the cattle industry to another. This results largely from the fact that the end product — a steak or roast on the consumer table — is a result of a long production sequence amounting to roughly two years and beginning with a beef cattle breeding herd which produces calves as its primary product. (The breeding stock itself is, of course, ultimately sent to the slaughter market after a number of years.) For the calves there are many variations in the growing and feeding pattern. In one typical pattern, the calves, at a weight of 400 to 450 pounds, are moved to the second stage of the operation. They are grazed on green pasture or "wintered" on forage, reaching a weight of 700 to 800 pounds before moving on to feedlots where they receive concentrated rations to bring them up to 1,000 to 1,200 pounds in weight and U.S. Choice grade. The finished cattle then move to processing plants where they are converted into meat; some of it moves direct to consumer markets as fresh retail cuts while some of the less tender cuts become "manufacturing beef" to be used in hamburger, sausage, canned and frozen products.

This sketchy outline identifies four stages, each of which will be discussed in turn from the viewpoint of price exposure. In addition, consideration will be given to the cattle dealers and middlemen who provide services in connection with each of the ownership transfers involved.

---

[9] The period from mid-1969 to mid-1970 offered few opportunities for profitable hedging of feedlot operations. This is no indictment of the futures market; it may instead be a distortion of the cost of feeders in the cash market relative to the prospective value of fed cattle. The industry was perhaps experiencing the inevitable repercussions from the tremendous expansion of feedlot capacities of this period which outran the available supply of feeder cattle. See "Hurt by Overcapacity, Texas Feedlots for Cattle Face Lean Earnings, Shakeout," *Wall Street Journal,* September 21, 1970, p. 10.

Operators of Cow-Calf Breeding Herds

The operator of a beef cattle herd normally takes a long-time view of his investment in livestock. His breeding herd is usually regarded as a long-time capital investment and his books are maintained accordingly. The calves which are sold do, of course, represent current output of the enterprise and the price at which they are sold is subject to wide fluctuations from period to period.

The rancher is exposed to a considerable price risk, but it is not easy to identify a specific part of that risk which can be regarded as the analogue of the value fluctuations that occur in the price of a futures contract covering Choice Beef Steers. Over any appreciable period of time, the price changes that the rancher experiences and those that occur on the commodity exchange tend to move in the same direction; but it is unsafe to assume a systematic relationship between the two. One reason for this is the difficulty of identifying and defining the price impact affecting the commercial ranch operation since this is not readily measured in statistical terms. Efforts have been made to compare the movement of Live Cattle Futures with the price of cattle from breeding herds or with the price of calves from such herds. The assumptions involved, however, are at best extremely rough approximations to the price impacts affecting the owner of the enterprise.[10] The best that can be said is that the beef cattle breeder is inevitably concerned with the changing prices of finished cattle and that he follows this market carefully, usually from day to day, even though his own marketings are infrequent and the short-time price fluctuations for his product are often far from parallel with prices on the futures market.

There is thus a rough association and a keen interest in the relationships between Live Cattle Futures and price experiences of the typical breeder herd operator. The looseness of the relationship, however, means that hedging is seldom a precise matter. It is certainly not clear, for instance, how many live cattle contracts should be entered nor which delivery months should be selected

---

[10] Interview with B. Kleberg Johnson of King Ranch, Kingsville, Texas, April 7, 1970.

to provide an approximate offset for the price impacts upon a 1,000 cow breeding herd.[11] Instead, a judgmental decision is likely to be made if the rancher is interested in the futures market as a tool to stabilize the price impacts in his business.

As far as the sale of calves is concerned there is a fairly widespread practice on the part of large ranch operators to enter into forward commercial contracts to sell their calves when they reach a given weight or growth stage. These contracts are similar to the "to arrive" purchases in the grain market. They enable the grower to fix the realization price ahead of time without resorting to a futures market. The buyer of stocker calves, in turn, can deal in actual calves with a breeder who has a good historical record of his herd and his capabilities. The buyer of stocker calves is unlikely to think of his requirements in terms of generalized specifications. (This may be one of the reasons why the Kansas City market for feeder cattle never attracted very much trading; forward commitments were possible without recourse to this market.)

Range-Grown Feeder Cattle

The production of 700 to 900 pound feeders involves a much closer relationship to the end product, fed cattle, than does the operation of the breeding herd. The young stock at 350 to 500 pounds, often called "stockers," are placed on grass or other forage feed to bring their weight up to the 700 pound level. Even as stockers they can be given at least a tentative date at which they will emerge as fully finished U.S. Choice grade cattle. In this respect it is possible to draw up a time and cost budget against which to compare the price of the fed cattle futures contract for the appropriate delivery month. However, 600 to 700 pound feeders may range all the way from a year down to three or four months before they will reach full market finish, depending on the type of feeding program they are put on. At the same time they represent a growing inventory which may have a current value amounting

---

[11] In fact, the breeding herd itself is usually regarded as a long-term (depreciable) capital asset, not a "current" inventory item.

to only 50% to 60% of that which they are expected to attain after being grown and finished.

This study did not make an intensive exploration of the range feeding stage of the cattle industry. Indirect inquiries from dealers, commission firms, consultants, and others led to the conclusion that such operators are frequent traders in the Live Cattle Futures market but that they could seldom be considered to be systematic hedgers in this market. It is our understanding that their transactions in the Live Cattle Futures market would nevertheless be classified as "hedging" under both the regulations of the Internal Revenue Service and of the Commodity Exchange Authority (see Appendix A). Be this as it may, it would be a difficult matter to define the number of contracts that would constitute a "fully-hedged position" as a matter of good business judgment. Possible uses of Live Cattle Futures by range cattle operators deserve a considerable amount of intensive study and analysis. There is undeniably a great risk in this industry, and there is little doubt that an appreciable degree of price parallelism (however imperfect) does exist between the stocker and feeder cattle industry and the futures contract. Inquiries regarding this group did not go beyond the conclusion that the relationships are highly complex, and that most futures traders from this group think in speculative terms more than in terms of any precise hedging.

Exhibit VII-6 shows a comparison between the cash market prices of slaughter steers and feeder steers monthly during the period January 1966 through July 1970. It will be seen that the prices at Kansas City for 550 to 750 pound choice feeder steers were almost always higher than the simultaneous prices for choice slaughter steers at Omaha. This is not an illogical situation in view of the fact that the cost of each 100 pounds added during the intensive feeding period may be less than the price of finished steers which fell mostly in a range from \$24 to \$30/cwt. during the period shown on the chart. A further illustration of the way in which such price spreads can vary in the cash market is shown in Exhibit VII-7 which presents monthly prices for (a) 900 to 1,100 pound choice steers at Chicago, (b) 550 to 750 pound choice feeder steers at Kansas City, and (c) choice feeder steer calves at Kansas

EXHIBIT VII-6. PRICES OF SLAUGHTER STEERS AND FEEDER STEERS,
MONTHLY 1966–1970

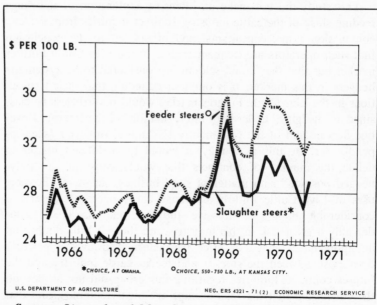

SOURCE: *Livestock and Meat Situation*, USDA, Economic Research
Service, February 1971.

City during the period January 1969 to July 1970. Comparing
an average for the first three months of this period with the last
three, the fed cattle advanced from $29.59 to $30.89, or $1.30/
cwt. Choice feeder steers moved from $29.22 to $34.82 in the
same period or an increase of $5.60/cwt., while choice feeder steer
calves rose from $32.60 to $41.11/cwt., or $8.51.

One of the consequences of these unequal price changes and of
the high relative level of feeders is inevitably to reduce the estimated
profitability of feedlot operations. The quoted prices for Live Cattle Futures at Chicago have confirmed this adverse relationship,
reaching out into the bimonthly delivery months for October and
December 1970 and February, April, June, and August 1971.
Compared with the July cash price of $31.37/cwt., the closing quo-
tations on August 21, 1970, for these futures were as follows:

October (1970) contract	29.05–.07
December contract	28.72.–70
February (1971) contract	29.20–.17
April contract	29.55
June contract	29.75
August (Omaha delivery) contract	29.40

EXHIBIT VII-7. CATTLE PRICES: CHOICE 900–1100 LB. STEERS
AT CHICAGO, CHOICE 550–750 LB. FEEDER STEERS, AND
CHOICE FEEDER STEER CALVES AT KANSAS CITY,
MONTHLY JANUARY 1969–JULY 1970

	(*Dollars per 100 pounds*)		
Year	Fed Cattle Chicago	Choice Feeder Steers Kansas City	Choice Feeder Steer Calves Kansas City
1969			
January	29.12	28.30	31.15
February	29.26	29.04	32.26
March	30.38	30.34	34.39
April	31.11	32.64	36.74
May	33.68	35.18	38.26
June	34.07	35.74	38.62
July	31.54	32.46	35.79
August	30.60	31.76	35.66
September	29.33	31.29	35.91
October	28.79	31.15	35.77
November	28.47	31.12	35.21
December	28.88	32.38	35.60
1970			
January	29.60	32.83	36.82
February	30.61	34.44	38.55
March	31.86	35.85	39.74
April	31.48	35.01	39.40
May	30.52	35.00	40.61
June	30.77	34.92	41.48
July	31.37	34.54	41.24

SOURCE: *Livestock and Meat Situation*, LMS 174, USDA, Economic
Research Service, August 1970, pp. 8–9.

If the high price of feeder calves and 550 to 750 pound feeder steers was in anticipation of higher prices for slaughter steers 5 to 12 months later, these futures quotations (all of them being well below the July cash market for fed steers at Chicago shown in Exhibits VII-6 and VII-7) certainly did not reflect such anticipations. Moreover, the variable relationship between the price of feeders and the Live Cattle Futures raises a serious question as to whether the steer futures are an advantageous hedging vehicle for a producer who will have feeder steers to sell from his range. He may be taking on more risk than he is avoiding.

Feedlot Operators

The finishing of beef cattle has been moving very strongly in the direction of large, confined feedlots handling as many as 10,000 to 50,000 head on feed at one time. It is here that huge values are involved in an individual operation with a clear relationship between the inventory price risk and the Live Cattle Futures contract which is traded in the futures market.

Our interviews suggested that the actual use of commodity futures in connection with the finishing of beef cattle is still at an early stage compared with the potential usefulness of this device.[12] The feedlot operator is already familiar with a variety of arrangements relating to his exposure to price impacts and the concept of a net position lends itself readily to his operations. He has a physical inventory for which he is responsible. He may or may not own it as a matter of legal title. He may in addition be committed to accept delivery of feeder cattle in the future either at a firm price or at a price to be determined according to a formula.[13] The feedlot operator may also engage in custom feeding of cattle owned

---

[12] For instance, one Iowa banker commented in April 1970 that he had made no loans against hedged cattle on feed. He remarked that while producers in his area would come out to a meeting arranged by the bank to discuss cattle hedging, their interest had not been followed up by action.

[13] This may be based on the Kansas City cash market for feeders on the date the feeders are shipped to him, or a formula price based upon some other market or set of indicators.

by others. He may also engage in financing some of these cattle with the animals as collateral for his loan, or he may operate on a partnership basis with respect to them. He may contract to sell his finished cattle forward on a cash-contract basis at firm prices.

After taking into account the net effect of the kinds of arrangements already enumerated, it is highly logical that he should regard the cattle futures contract as another alternative tool for managing his commercial operations. This assumes that he can with confidence anticipate the differential which will exist between the prices he can get for his own cattle and the prices likely to be realized in the markets where delivery is accepted against Live Cattle Futures.

Banks provide an important service to many feedlot operators who engage in systematic hedging operations. An example of one bank's procedure for handling hedging loans in both the "stocker" (prefeedlot) and feedlot cattle operations is a plan followed by Bank of America in California. The bank provides its managers with a set of guidelines for handling hedging in Live Cattle Futures along with its loans on stocker and feedlot cattle. This arrangement, first set up early in 1966, provides that the bank will supply the required margin deposit to the broker as a part of the total loan, and will take up the debits and credits resulting from futures price fluctuations on the short hedge position, incorporating them into the loan to its customer.

Hence, if cattle futures prices go up and the bank pays money to the broker, the loan is correspondingly increased. However, since the same price increase is usually reflected in the cash market, the value of the cattle which are pledged against the loan will have risen so that the proceeds realized when the cattle are delivered can be expected to repay the loan, plus commissions and profit to the owner. If prices of futures decline, the cash coming from the broker will reduce the amount the owner would have to repay out of the proceeds from his sale of finished cattle.

A summary of terms and conditions of this typical arrangement is presented in Appendix D, which outlines the basic guidelines as well as the procedures employed. In view of the fact that cattle feeders have historically tended to borrow near the maximum of their credit line, the availability of bank credit to assure the meeting of margin requirements is important.[14]

Various estimates were requested from commission firms and a few feedlot operators as to the percentage of operators they would classify as systematic hedgers. The answer was almost unanimous that (a) nearly all feedlot operators are very conscious of their net exposure but that (b) the degree of sophistication in their use of various tools for covering their risks or appraising those which were not covered was likely to be a matter of very rough approximations, a good deal of market savvy and intuition, and very little documented analysis and appraisal. Most of those about whom we received information directly or indirectly tended to regard the futures market as one which was still in an experimental stage and one for which they were exploring various possible uses in connection with their business. The diversity of arrangements and strategies may well be a result of the wide assortment of trade commitments and contracts that exist in the cattle feedlot industry quite apart from the formal cattle futures market.

We did not explore in depth the bookkeeping and control methods employed by feedlot operators. However, both direct and indirect inquiries verified the very widespread practice of accounting for cattle on feed by individual lots. These lots might vary from a very small number of head (25 to 40 cattle) up to large herds numbering several thousand head. In any event, the sophisticated feedlot operator usually prepared a detailed budget or estimate spelling out the expected cost of all inputs, including the cost of feeder cattle. In making this calculation it is necessary to

---

[14] In this connection, see comments by Monfort, "A Cattle Feeder Views Futures," p. 28. Mr. Monfort agreed that "since the risk is lower, the banks should be more than willing to loan additional funds." However, he suggested that many banks in fact were "not really familiar with the normal hedging operations and, particularly, with the hedging operation in the cattle business." He expected that with time the banks, which have a very important interest in financing the cattle business, would modify their attitude about hedging.

One bank which was making considerable use of futures as early as 1966 was the First National Bank, Pratt, Kansas, whose president, George T. Chandler, described his experience in the January 15, 1967, issue of *Bank News*.

estimate a number of factors such as rate of gain, feed conversion efficiency, possible veterinary costs or death losses, and the estimated assortment of finished grades which the cattle in this lot are expected to attain when ready for market. Moreover — and this is, of course, a critical consideration — the estimate must include an expected selling price for the finished product.

An illustrative sheet (Exhibit VII-8) taken from a case used for teaching purposes at the Harvard Business School[15] presents a purchase decision form which visualizes the steps involved in making the advance estimates as well as additional columns presenting performance comparisons against these estimates.

With this sort of lot-by-lot accounting it would appear that the decision maker does in effect envision a future price for his product and also that he makes a decision based upon this estimated result. It would appear to be a fairly straightforward process for him to "lock in" his price estimate if he could assume that his actual realizations would follow fairly closely the price fluctuations on the Live Beef Cattle Futures market.[16] However, it is clear that such a practice is far from universal in view of the small number of traders and contracts held, as shown in Exhibit VII-1, by operators classified in the entire group defined as "farmers, feeders, producers, ranchers, or feedlot operators."

Monfort Feed Lots, Inc. One of the country's largest cattle feeding operations is conducted by this subsidiary of the integrated cattle and beef firm, Monfort of Colorado, Inc. The total feedlot capacity was expanded in 1970 from a capacity to handle approximately 115,000 cattle at one time, with an annual feeding capability of about 275,000 cattle, to a capacity of around 215,000 head, giving an annual capability of feeding some 500,000 cattle per year.

Kenneth Monfort, president of the corporation, has stated that

---

[15] See Kern County Land Company (Inventory Management in Large-Scale Cattle Operations), Case No. AI 208, mimeo, Harvard Business School, 1962.

[16] We were informed by one feeder that private statistical studies and actual experience suggested the desirability of using the futures delivery month following the expected completion of the feeding cycle in hedging feedlot cattle which are not planned for actual delivery through the Exchange.

EXHIBIT VII-8. PURCHASE DECISION FORM, December 11, 1961

(Ideally, this analysis should be made before actual purchase, but this is very difficult and is usually done as soon as possible after placement for each lot of KCL-owned cattle. A very helpful tool in scheduling inventory flow and may indicate advantageous change in feeding pattern or sales timing. These data to determine most advantageous source area, broker, weight, timing, etc.)

2115　Head　　　　　Lot # 153　　　　　　　　　　　Broker　Cattle Commission Co — Current
12/11/61　Date In　　From　Ft. Worth, Texas

	Manage-ment Forecast	Forecast Computation		Actual Performance	Deviation			Comments on Lot
		Total Costs	Var. Costs		Actual is Better (+) or Worse (−) than Forecast		Effect on P & L (\$/hd.)	
								At Forecast 12-11-61
Purch. Price (Delv.)		\$ 24.7		\$ 24.7	— %		—	Last purchase on
Purch. Wt. (Delv.)	634 #			634 #	— %		—	major planning
Purch. Cost/Hd.		\$ 156		\$ 156				analysis # 7-61.
Feed Efficiency	10.0:1			9.7:1	+3 %		3	At Finish 5-27-62
Feed & Feeding Cost/Ton	\$50		\$ 44	\$ 48.5	+3 %		3	Good production results — fed more silage than planned.
Cost Per Lb. Prod.		25.0¢	22.0¢	23.5¢	+6 %			Price forecast fair.
Feed & Feeding Cost/Hd.		\$ 91	\$ 80	\$ 85			6	Increased profits due to increased effi-
Property Taxes/Hd.		\$ 2	\$ 2	\$ 2				ciency and higher
								sales price.
Gain (per hd. per day)	2.7 #			2.6 #	−4 %			
Head Days	135			139	−3 %			

	%	Price/cwt.	%	Price/cwt.	Grade Var.	Price Var.	%
Gain/Hd.		364 #					—
Sale Wt. (Net)		998 #		995 #			6
Cost of Sales	$ 249	$ 238		$ 243			
Sales Forecast Month of Sale May							
Choice	70	$ 25.5	55	$ 26.2	−15	+3 %	
Good & Choice	30	25.0	40	25.9	+10	+4 %	
Good			4	25.0	+ 4		
Other	—				—		
Deaths	—		1				
Average Selling Price		$ 25.4		$ 25.8		+2 %	4
Selling Price/Hd.		$ 253		$ 257			
Profit Head	$ 4	$ 15		$ 14	$ 10		10
Profit (per hd. per day)		3¢		10¢			
Break-Even Selling Price (choice)	$ 25.1	$ 24.0		$ 24.8			

Forecasted by   /s/   <u>DC</u>

\# = lbs.

SOURCE: Kern County Land Company, Case No. AI 208, mimeo, Harvard Business School, 1962.

238 *Major Commodity Complexes*

the company makes extensive use of the futures market on occasions when it is possible to anticipate a reasonable return from specific feed-out operations but that there are other times when the futures market cannot be profitably employed. If the price level of the futures contract for the delivery month in which cattle on feed will reach market grades and weights shows a satisfactory profit over the known costs that will be incurred in feeding out the cattle, a hedged operation should be given serious consideration. There may be other alternatives and other price expectations that would result in a decision not to hedge, but at least the hedge is a way of "locking in a profit."

Quoting Mr. Monfort's talk at the Livestock and Meat Futures Study Conference, sponsored by The Chicago Mercantile Exchange on November 30, 1966, we have a clear illustration of the kind of consideration that entered into a feedlot operator's decision:

> . . . For this mythical look at what a feeder is deciding, I will use Greeley, Colorado, as the site of this mythical feedlot. First of all, the feeder must figure his cost of his feeder cattle. Currently, a 700 lb. steer will cost a feeder in Greeley, Colorado, around 26¢ per pound delivered to his feedlot. This figures out at $182.00 per head. Four hundred pounds of gain will cost roughly $100.00. Death loss and interest will figure another $10.00, making a total cost in that animal at market time of $292.00.
>
> Now, that steer will be ready for market in April. The current April option, and this was yesterday, was around $27.40 delivered to Chicago. The feeder then must figure a price relationship between Chicago and his own market. It would be silly for us in Greeley, Colorado, to figure how much it would cost to market this particular animal in Chicago, since we never send him there. So, therefore, instead of this we use as a basis the historical average difference between the Chicago and the Greeley market during the month of April. We come up with a figure of $1.25 under Chicago. So, therefore, our prices, based on this $27.40 futures price, get back to a figure of $26.15 in Greeley. Figuring this out on an 1,100 pound steer, we come out with something like a figure of $288.00 which is $4.00 under our estimated cost on that steer. This is without adding the cost of our hedging operation.

Ten days ago, we had a considerably lower cost on our feeder steer and the hedge could be put on profitably. Maybe tomorrow this will again be possible. The decision the feeder faces then is a day-to-day decision. He should not only make this decision when he buys his feeder cattle, but in actuality, every day that he owns those cattle. It is very conceivable, for instance, that the cattle that we could not profitably hedge today, could profitably be hedged three months from now, after they are through their feeding period.

In short, hedging provides a tool for the feeder who wishes to minimize his market risk and assure profitability, but it can only be a workable and usable tool if the feeder is able and willing to figure his costs and relate these costs to the market on a day to day basis . . . (see Conference report, pp. 27–28).

While Monfort does not have a formal written policy regarding the use of hedging, this firm's operations make it clear that the futures market is looked upon primarily as a commercial adjunct to regular buying and selling operations, to be used when profit opportunities present themselves but not to be used as a means of operating with a fully hedged net position.

The Monfort organization values its live cattle and feed inventories on the last-in, first-out basis.[17] This has resulted in a stated inventory value in the consolidated balance sheet for August 31, 1969, of $30 million ($25.5 of it representing live cattle) instead of nearly $39 million which would have been shown on a current ("principally identified") cost basis. Hence the basic feedlot inventory is carried at a value insulated from the longer term (year-end to year-end) swings in price. However, there are sufficient changes in numbers on feed and in short-term feedout margins to leave plenty of room for use of live cattle futures contracts.

An operation as large as that represented by Monfort of Colorado undoubtedly enjoys certain advantages and disadvantages in connection with cattle futures operations. An ownership of cattle which may at times amount to one-fourth of the open interest on the cattle futures market means that it would be difficult to conduct futures trading commensurate with its total cattle holdings without

---

[17] See Monfort of Colorado, Inc., Underwriters Prospectus, January 22, 1970, p. 33.

having a distinct impact upon the price level in the futures market. At the same time, the futures trading volume is large enough to warrant a very careful following of all phases of both cash and futures markets and an alert examination of all opportunities that may arise. According to Mr. Monfort the large feeders are the ones most actively interested in considering opportunities in the futures and these may not number more than 20% of the commercial feedlot operators. The same group, however, is probably responsible for half or more of the total number of cattle on feed. It has been possible for many of the remaining feeders to enjoy the benefits of hedging by taking advantage of services offered by dealers or meatpackers willing to make firm commitments for the purchase of cattle to be delivered at a later date. This commitment can then be protected by the buyer through a matching short sale in the cattle futures market.

Since the Monfort operation is located in Colorado it would rarely be advantageous to deliver cattle against the futures contract by shipping them the distance to Omaha or Kansas City. Instead, if it is desired to make delivery, the actual cattle can be sold nearer home and a purchase of deliverable cattle arranged in the area close to the delivery points authorized in the terms of the futures contract. In fact, this procedure has been followed by the Monfort operation on a number of occasions.

One type of futures transaction that is conceivable (but not verified by this study) might occur in the case of a temporary, i.e., intrayear, divestiture of a portion of the Lifo base inventory as a result of the cash sale of finished cattle without replacement in the feedlot. This temporary liquidation of actual cattle might be covered by buying Live Cattle Futures contracts, especially if they are considered too depressed at the time to provide an acceptable feeding margin. (In such cases it may be possible to use the feedlot capacity for custom feeding for others.) Then if the Live Cattle Futures market improves, the "long hedge" will provide the needed cash to offset the possible rise in the cost of restoring inventory ownership.

Our conclusion, gained from broad but general inquiries, was that most of the feedlot operators who use futures fold the results of specific hedge operations into the cost of finished cattle delivered to customers, while *open* contracts are seldom priced or used to adjust inventory at the time of fiscal closing dates. Correspondingly, cattle on feed tend to carry a value based on cost rather than on market. Despite this generalization, which is based upon the very fragmentary information we were able to secure, there seems to be no single prescribed practice among the alternative accounting methods that are available for handling the futures position.

Livestock Middlemen and Dealers

This category of cattle merchants probably comprises the group which is closest to the cattle market and most knowledgeable regarding it. On the other hand, it includes mostly firms which act in a brokerage or commission-man capacity rather than firms which assume ownership of cattle. Most middlemen seldom trade on their own account in the cash markets for live cattle, although they may be brokers who arrange both spot and contract sales.[18]

---

[18] One example of this sort was presented by Harold J. Heinold of Heinold Commodities, Inc., Kouts, Indiana. Mr. Heinold's talk related to the feeding of hogs rather than cattle and to the use of Live Hog Futures. However his firm was providing a hedging service to farmers who wanted to hedge the pigs they had on feed. The firm provided information about hedging and possible hedging margins; it was prepared to handle the bookkeeping, the placing of hedges, the conferences with bankers, and the arrangements for deliveries or lifting of hedges when the hogs were sold to meatpackers. (See Heinold, *Proceedings of the Livestock and Meat Futures Study Conference,* pp. 55–58.)

Another example from the same seminar (see Emrich, *Proceedings,* pp. 60–64) was presented by Mr. C. O. Emrich, Manager of the Norfolk Livestock Sales Company, Norfolk, Nebraska. The primary business of his firm is the operating of a large livestock auction market. In order to be helpful to their clients, especially the smaller operators, the firm bought a seat on the Chicago Mercantile Exchange and became associate brokers, in order to provide them with "another way to offer an alternative for the smaller operator."

Mr. Emrich felt that futures trading could "apply itself to a small operation, but somehow somebody in the field needs to be the key man in the field of small operators, and this is the role we have taken in our particular area." Mr. Emrich outlined procedures for comparing the courses of action that are available to a cattle feeder through the use of futures and depicted his role as that of advisor and coordinator, studying plans, arrang-

A few operators who are primarily cattle dealers or commission firms were reported to have bought cattle to be fed out for them on a custom basis, taking advantage of favorable hedging opportunities. For their day-to-day cattle dealing operations, however, any risks they take are mostly of an extremely short-run nature and seldom involve the futures market, except as they may assist when actual cattle are in process of delivery via the Exchange machinery.

For the most part livestock dealers who trade in Live Cattle Futures do so for their own account as speculators and not as systematic users of futures as a commercial management tool. In this capacity they can make a productive contribution toward keeping the live cattle futures market in line with expectations of those possessing the best market information. Moreover, these same middlemen and dealers can perform a very useful function in facilitating deliveries by putting together deliverable lots and seeing that cattle once offered for delivery are handled in the way best suited to the needs of the person accepting the delivery.

This discussion excludes certain speculative or "investment" operations whereby investors who are not engaged in commercial cattle operations have been enabled to buy cattle through an investment or management firm and then have the operation hedged in the futures market if such protection seemed desirable. Among the firms conducting such operations in the past have been Oppenheimer Enterprises, Inc. of Kansas City, Missouri, and Clayton Investment Service of St. Louis, Missouri. In addition, there have been reports of feedlot operators soliciting investor cash in order to finance cattle for their feedyards, mostly in the West and Southwest.[19] These operations may or may not involve hedging.

---

ing financing, etc. Mr. Emrich expressed the opinion ". . . that the futures market should not be used as a guide, but actually it should be used as a tool. . . . It has been a mistake on the part of a good many people to say, well, the public thinks that in December 1967 cattle will be worth 29, and it is a mistake to assume that they are correct. . . . I think if you are going to use it [futures market] as a guide, then you'd better use it as a tool also."

[19] One such firm, Commanche Cattle Industries of Denver, Colorado, a subsidiary of Petro-Lewis Corporation, operates three feedyards with a capacity to handle up to 80,000 head. Its program contemplates investment

Meat Packers

While Exhibit VII-1, showing the occupational categories of holders of cattle futures contracts, records only 86 accounts classified as "packer or employee of a packing company," this group, representing 2.3% of all accounts, was responsible for 9.6% of the open contracts and 14.7% of the short contracts. These figures represent a very modest portion of the total trading interest in the cattle futures market. However, some of this group along with a few large feedlot operators probably comprise most of those who have made an effort to develop a methodical use of futures as a management tool.

A number of the larger meat packers such as Armour, Swift, Wilson, and Iowa Beef Processors have indeed made use of Live Cattle Futures in connection with certain of their operations. In no case were they found hedging their existing product inventories in this market. Most common use of futures was in working out specific hedged feeding operations in which a feeding program was developed to enable the company to buy feeders and pay the cost of finishing the cattle while covering the operation with a short sale in the Live Cattle Futures Market in order to lock in the feeding margin. This type of operation assured the processing plant of a supply of cattle, assuming that the short futures contracts were to be repurchased at the time the cattle were ready for market. Various arrangements have been worked out in connection with these hedged feeding operations. Sometimes the feeding is conducted on a custom basis by an outside feedlot, but sometimes the feeding is done by the processor himself. Other variations of this type of arrangement include contracts whereby the independent feedlot operator procures the young feeder animals and has a contract to deliver the finished cattle at a given date.

Wilson & Co., Inc. This company was acquired in 1967 by Ling-Temco-Vought, Inc. Sales in 1969 reached the $1 to $1.25

---

in cattle on feed extending over a period of ten years "in order to reduce the risk of the investment." Funds are supplied by investors who become limited partners, while Commanche supplies management and operating services. See *Corporate Profile,* Petro-Lewis Corporation, Denver, Colorado, July 1970.

billion level; the value of product inventories were in the $55 million range, signifying a turnover rate in the area of 22 times per year. Nevertheless, inventories at the fiscal year-end were between two and one half to three times as large as before-tax earnings in the years 1966–69, and product prices are volatile.

One of the great problems of the meatpacking industry over the years has been the handling of volatile prices, variable supplies and narrow margins. According to the American Meat Institute compilation, after-tax profits in the industry in 1969 were .92 cents per dollar of sales. The temptation to seek high volumes in order to spread the overhead costs is chronic but, because of the sensitiveness of prices, the outcome of such a course of action is almost always devastating. Wilson & Co. declared in its 1967 Annual Report:

> It is a principle simply stated and rigidly adhered to: *margin dictates volume*. If unit gross margins in our abattoirs drop below predetermined levels, we cut back on our rate of kill, instead of increasing volume to get more dollars. This action helps improve and restore adequate margins and improves the profitability of the operation.

Wilson & Co. described a program in its Annual Report for 1967 whereby the company proposed to commit itself to purchase a predetermined quantity of cattle from a producer, to be delivered at a later date, paying a price based upon the cattle futures market as quoted at the time the purchase contract was entered. The company then hedged its contracts by selling on the futures markets. (Conceivably such a contract could fix the price at some later date to be agreed upon between the seller and the company. Naturally, the latter plan would call for placing a hedge sale against the cattle at whatever date the price commitment became firm.) Then, when the cattle were ready for delivery, the company would be assured of live animals at a cost in line with the current market on the delivery date. In other words, the producer would receive the promised price, but the company's cost would be adjusted by the amount of gain or loss on the futures trade.

In order to record the company's position on all livestock procurement commitments a weekly report on Livestock Feeding,

Contract Purchases and Hedging Operations is prepared and transmitted to key officials of the company reflecting commitments for each of the major plant locations. This form appears as Exhibit VII-9. The use of forward purchases from producers on a firm-price basis varies from one time to another but appears to be very small, perhaps as little as one-tenth as great as the company's own hedging operations against cattle being fed for it on a toll basis. However, the two methods of procurement are indicative of an area in which a number of alternatives exist or can be worked out. The ones that were discussed in 1968 all related to arrangements that were timed to result in an actual procurement cost (after folding in the hedge results) approximately equivalent to the current live market at the time of delivery for slaughter.

Back of the data in the "cattle on feed" column of Exhibit VII-9 are records showing details for each lot of cattle being fed. Such records provide an estimate made in advance of the expected cost of the cattle actually being fed and a comparison of these detailed figures covering expenses, yields, cost-of-gain and similar items with the actual out-turn from the feeding operation. The form provides further details on the results of the futures market transaction relating to this particular lot of cattle. By comparing the actual totals for feedlot sales and transfers to slaughter with the earlier estimate, it is possible to summarize the results of the feeding operation on a nonhedged basis. By combining this gain or loss with the gain or loss from futures it is possible to evaluate the net outcome of the hedged operation.

For operating purposes a daily statement of the changing values of futures commitments is provided for use by those conducting the futures operations. This statement makes it possible to identify situations where there might be a profitable opportunity for making a transfer or switch and also for checking the balances in margin accounts against the amounts required. These accounts cover not only the company's own hedged cattle on feed but also the futures used to cover forward purchase commitments from other feeders.

Since the forward contract to buy and the hedged cattle feeding programs provided for fully hedged operations, the chief factors limiting the activity were the amount of capital tied up or the ab-

EXHIBIT VII-9. WILSON AND COMPANY — WEEKLY REPORT ON LIVESTOCK

	CATTLE ON FEED			
	HEAD		AMOUNT	
City of Industry			$	
Albert Lea				
Cedar Rapids				
Cherokee				
Kansas City				
Oklahoma City				
Omaha				
Other				
TOTAL			$	

Cattle Not Intended for Hedging	
Hedging Contracts and Margin Deposits As of:_____	
Under (Over) Hedged	
TOTAL	

Albert Lea	
Denver	
Ogden	
Ogden – Wool from Feeder Lamb	
TOTAL	
TOTAL	
Hedging Contracts and Margin Deposits As Of:_____	
Under (Over) Hedged	
TOTAL	
TOTAL ALL OPERATIONS	

Feeding, Contract Purchases, and Hedging Operations

FEEDER CATTLE ON CONTRACT		SLAUGHTER CATTLE ON CONTRACT		TOTALS	
HEAD	AMOUNT	HEAD	AMOUNT	HEAD	AMOUNT
	$		$		$
	$		$		$
					XXX XXX XXX
					XXX XXX XXX
					$

LAMB ON FEED		ON CONTRACT			
HEAD	AMOUNT	HEAD	AMOUNT		
	$		$		$
	$		$		$
		HOGS ON CONTRACT			XXX XXX XXX
		HEAD	AMOUNT		XXX XXX XXX
			$		$
			$		$
			$		
			XXX XXX XXX		
			$		$
					$

sence of profitable relationships between the estimated costs and realizations from feeding. Individual plant managers were involved in the actual feeding operations and it was their decision whether to go ahead with the feeding for their plant requirements. The futures trading was conducted entirely at company headquarters, although the results flowed back to the plant on whose behalf the operation was being conducted.

In connection with the contract purchase of cattle two kinds of expenses might arise before the cattle actually entered the company inventory. These are payments to the broker in case the futures market moved against the company position and actual down payments or payments on account to the producer who had contracted to sell the cattle. Such expenses were deferred in the form of miscellaneous receivables on the books and then transferred as procurement costs at the time the cattle were taken for slaughter.

Swift & Company. Swift was founded by Gustavus F. Swift who entered the meat business well over a century ago in New England. He migrated progressively from Cape Cod to Boston, to Albany, to Buffalo, then to Chicago, where the company that bears his name was established in 1885. The firm grew to become the largest meat packing firm in the world with a complete assortment of meat products. In addition, it is diversified into a number of other agribusiness lines (dairy and poultry products, fats and oils, tanning, agricultural chemicals) as well as such nonagribusiness activities as life and casualty insurance, petroleum refining and distribution, and production of various specialized chemicals for industry. Sales in fiscal 1969 exceeded $3 billion, the greater portion of which was still comprised of meat and meat products.

Price fluctuations have been an important factor in the company's operations, both because of the volatility of price movements, and because the operations are characterized by large volumes and narrow margins of profit. While inventory turnover is high (the closing inventory value has been less than one-twelfth of company sales of all products in a typical year) the actual vulnerability is better gauged by the size of inventories as compared with profits. These may well run six or more times as great as earnings before taxes.

As early as 1933 the company, acutely conscious of the impact of price change upon its annual results, adopted a policy of setting aside out of earnings in a year of rising prices a "Reserve for Inventory Price Declines." [20] This reserve was not allowed as an income tax deduction, but it did serve to affirm a principle, namely that profits reflected in the price tag that applied to basic inventories were not expendable and should be withheld from the distributable income available to pay dividends.[21] When prices fell in the 1937–38 recession, a portion of this reserve was restored to the undistributed profits category.

The problem of inventory profits and losses (or "paper profits" as they were often called) continued to receive attention, both in the meat industry and in a number of other industries during the late 1930s.[22] Various companies attempted to treat the problem. Swift's method was the reserve for inventory price declines; National Lead, International Harvester, Deere, Atlantic Refining, and other companies adopted the "base stock" method. Under this method a certain amount of basic commodity inventory (some-

---

[20] See *Swift & Company Yearbook, 1934,* balance sheet, and comment, p. 1.

[21] See Swift & Company, *50th Anniversary Year Book,* pp. 3–4.

[22] Some of the articles published during this period were:

American Institute of Accountants, "Valuation of Inventories."

Arthur, "Inventory Profits in the Business Cycle."

Arthur, "Something Business Can Do about Depressions."

Elliott, "Inventory Valuation and Profits."

Fiske, "Inventory Reserve Plans."

Harvard Law Review, June 1938, pp. 1430–1442. Discussion of base-stock inventories and federal income taxation under "Legislation."

National Association of Cost Accountants, *Yearbook 1936,* "Present-Day Problems of Inventory Valuation and Control"; papers by Maurice E. Peloubet and Ross G. Walker, pp. 164–191 and 212–216.

Nickerson, "Inventory Valuation — The Use of Price Adjustment Accounts to Segregate Inventory Losses and Gains."

Nickerson, "Inventory Reserves as an Element of Inventory Policy."

Peloubet, "Problems of Present-day Inventory Valuation."

Putnam, "The Role of Paper Profits in Industry."

Putnam, "What Shall We Do About Depressions?"

Walker, "The Base-Stock Principle of Inventory Accounting."

Walker, "Income Accounting and the Base-Stock Inventory."

times explained as that which was required to "fill the industry pipelines" or "thread the machines") was set aside as a base stock to be held at constant unit value from year to year. Finally, out of these developments emerged the last-in, first-out or Lifo method of inventory accounting which was approved under the tax laws (first, in 1939, for a few specified industries and then later made generally available). This method adopted the rationale suggested by its name, that opening inventory quantities, if they were still present in the closing inventory, could be regarded as having the same cost as they had carried at the opening of the fiscal period. Thus, increases in their market value from one year-end to the next would not be reflected in earnings, and declining markets would likewise not affect earnings so long as the "carried-in" cost (i.e., the opening inventory, whose cost might well date back several years) remained below the level of market prices at the close. This method, with all its complications of application, had the virtue of remaining within the old rule of "lower of cost or market" and of avoiding an arbitrary judgment as to how much should be "set aside" as required for the base stock or reserve for inventory price decline methods.

Against this historic background, Swift and Company, not surprisingly, adopted the Lifo inventory method for a very substantial portion of its product inventories in 1941, when the internal revenue law made it feasible. To the extent that the Lifo method is applied, it is not necessary for a company to *hedge* its basic inventories in the futures market, since there is no price impact to be matched with a futures contract.[23] One of the features of the Lifo inventory method — one which is often not recognized — is that it results in operations which approximate a replacement cost basis. Paper profits are eliminated to a considerable degree, so that reported results come much closer to realized cash results.

This excursion into inventory accounting methods is a necessary

---

[23] In some exceptional cases where market prices threaten to drop below the Lifo prices being used, a firm may want to take a futures position as a sort of insurance, but it should be remembered that this is a one-way hedge. If inventory prices at market should rise, the hedge would go against the firm but the matching inventory would still be bound at the opening inventory (Lifo) cost.

prelude to a consideration of hedging as a management tool for users of the Lifo accounting method. So long as "Lifo inventories" are not subjected to price variations, hedging is not called for. Indeed to sell futures against such inventories would be a "Texas Hedge," i.e., a speculation.[24]

This does not by any means suggest that hedging has no place for such a firm. Seasonal accumulations which are normally liquidated within the fiscal year are obviously exposed to price changes. Basis trades on specific commercial projects is another example, as are numerous instances where it is desired to balance out the long and short exposures related to unfilled orders and other commitments. Therefore, one would expect a wide assortment of hedging applications, even though the firm may be heavily committed to the Lifo accounting method for its basic inventories. This is indeed the case with Swift. Hence, we can proceed to examine some of these applications.

Swift's Hedging Policy — Live Cattle Futures. Enough has been said about Lifo inventory accounting to indicate that this method of dealing with price impacts upon the basic pipeline of inventories is a deeply imbedded company policy. Beyond this, however, are the considerations relating to seasonal accumulations, to major transactions, and to special situations in which the company has followed a policy of regarding the futures market as a part of the market structure in which it operates and one that should not be ignored when it can serve to enhance the company's commercial effectiveness.

The policy just outlined has not been stated by the company in writing. However, it is implicit in the more specific applications of hedging policy which are periodically spelled out and submitted for top executive approval by the president's office.

When a major division or subsidiary — Swift Fresh Meat Company in this instance — submits its plans for the ensuing fiscal year or season, there is included a proposal as to how large a position in the futures market is contemplated, together with an estimate of

---

[24] This operation, however, would still qualify as a "legal hedge" under the CEA Regulations. See Appendix A.

financial requirements that might be entailed and an indication of the manner in which the operation involving futures is expected to contribute to earnings.

Swift's Hedging Organization and Procedures. The types of commercial operations which have been involved in live cattle hedging activities relate almost altogether to cattle feeding or to live cattle procurement, often to a combination of both. The company conducts cattle feeding operations of its own at certain points; at others it engages the services of independent feedlots on a custom or contract basis; at still others cattle still on feed may be bought ahead for delivery at a later time when the feeding process is completed.

None of these three alternatives comprises the major procurement method of the company or the meat packing industry, which predominantly is the cash purchase in the spot market of cattle ready for slaughter. Nevertheless, the forward commitments are substantial; they represent a large dollar exposure, often carried over several months; and the price volatility to which they are exposed can have serious consequences.

Responsibility for carrying out the program, within the approved limits, rests with the appropriate headquarters commercial department at Chicago. While futures trading operations in Live Cattle Futures are all conducted from Chicago, an individual plant manager is, with few exceptions, responsible for the cattle procurement or feeding operations being hedged. Therefore, the plant manager, who may want to protect his procurement requirements, or may see an opportunity to earn a feeding profit, can initiate a request for a procurement plan to be covered by a hedge in Live Cattle Futures. More often, however, the initiative comes from headquarters, where a situation has been spotted and analyzed which looks like a favorable opportunity. This proposal may be outlined and offered to the plant manager who may accept or reject it.

Such hedged cattle feeding proposals are conducted on a lot-by-lot basis. The hedge contracts on the futures exchange may not be separately identified with each lot, but the results of hedges (in the appropriate delivery months, and covering the applicable time period) are added into the cost of the cattle when they come off the feedlot. As the cattle move to the processing plant, they are priced at the current cash market level, and a cattle-feeding gain or loss is recorded.

If the particular hedging operation relates to a forward purchase of cash cattle not owned or fed by the company, then the result of the futures contract is entered in the Cattle Buying account as an element in the procurement cost.

In the case of Swift, a key person in the handling of Live Cattle Futures hedging is the man in the Chicago office who is in charge of conducting basic economic research on cattle supplies and prices as well as the handling of actual trading in the futures market. Working closely with the Cattle Feeding and Cattle Buying Department heads, his office becomes the center for coordination of individual plant hedging operations plus a discretionary range for adjusting procurement commitments through futures transactions. Within this discretionary range, the total company hedge can be varied depending upon the existing spreads and buying opportunities in the cash market, the outlook for cattle supplies and prices, and other factors relating to the total cattle and beef positions of the company.

Hedge Accounting — Swift Live Cattle Futures. Because of the special nature of the uses of futures and their relationship to cattle operations, the method of handling the accounts is of interest. The results of closed hedges are folded into the cost of goods hedged. Such results are taken up at the time the hedge is lifted. On open hedges, the accumulated variances are carried in a special "accounts receivable" record. Neither these variances nor the cost of the goods covered by the hedge enter into results until the futures contract is closed at which time it is presumed that the goods are delivered (at current market prices).

The types of operations covered by the hedges that have been discussed have not presented any conflicts with the Lifo valuation process since (a) most of the hedges have been related to commitments rather than inventory owned, (b) some of them are seasonal or temporary in nature, and (c) the particular operations involved in the live cattle hedging are partly long positions, partly short, with a substantial offset between themselves.

Comparison of Live Cattle Hedging with Other Swift Activities in Futures Markets. Swift has employed commodity futures contracts in many of its operations from time to time. The variety of applications is wide and the objectives that are sought differ from one commodity to another and from one time to another. It is not the purpose of the present discussion to go into detail regarding each use of commodity futures by the company. However, some similarities and contrasts are worth pointing out.

The company associates the use of Live Cattle Futures with feedlot and procurement operations. It has further been pointed out that the company does not use futures as a general cover for its basic inventory pipelines. However, there are many situations where seasonal accumulations or various kinds of trade commitments make the futures market a highly valuable adjunct to commercial operations.

Most of the seasonal accumulations of beef represent "manufacturing beef," frozen boneless cuts designated for use in hamburger, sausage, and other prepared products. (It is seldom commercially feasible to freeze beef that will be sold as retail cuts.) The new Frozen Boneless Beef contract set up by the Chicago Mercantile Exchange in 1970 appears to offer a promising vehicle for use in connection with seasonal accumulations or even for imports[25] of such beef.

The new contract, after a promising initial flurry of interest, had not become firmly enough established by mid-1970 to assure the breadth of market that might be desirable for use by a large firm. The open interest in July was only 306 contracts and monthly trading that month fell to 76 contracts. At this time, therefore, the Frozen Boneless Beef contract would have to be regarded as in the experimental or developmental stage. It is not clear whether the nature of price movements or the breadth of trading interest would make it attractive enough to provide a useful vehicle. Interest regarding other possible applications of the Frozen Boneless Beef contract such as the hedging of forward sales to retailers

---

[25] The contract requires that only domestically produced beef may be delivered. However, the degree of price parallelism between domestic and imported Frozen Boneless Beef may well be close enough to validate the Mercantile Exchange contract as a hedge against imported product.

or to sausage manufacturers apparently was not large enough to provide an important use of this contract. Such application could become advantageous in the future, once the trade has become accustomed to its possibilities.

Swift also deals in large volume in hogs and pork products. Here the most active futures contract is in Frozen Pork Bellies rather than in live hogs. The seasonal requirements and the trade interest in this product have been extremely active; moreover, the volatility of price has made the contract appealing to speculators. For Swift, primary use for this contract has been in its seasonal storage operations, but the procedures for handling the pork hedging operation have been essentially similar to those applied in cattle and beef. Accumulations of the cash product have been carried at cost and the variations in the futures have been carried as deferred receivables, to be applied as an adjustment to the cash costs when the hedge is lifted. At the end of the fiscal year the handling of futures has seldom required an inventory adjustment since the product is normally liquidated before the fiscal year ends. Swift is also an important user of futures in connection with its soybean operations. These are, however, discussed elsewhere (see Chapter VI).

Processors and Retailers

In addition to the futures contracts for live cattle, subsequent contracts were developed for choice beef carcasses (fresh) and for Frozen Boneless Beef ("trimmings"). The first, at the Chicago Board of Trade, never attracted sufficient interest to test its potential usefulness and trading dried up. At the end of July 1970 there were no open contracts in choice carcass beef, a grade that would have compared in quality with that of the Live Beef Cattle contract.

The Frozen Boneless Beef contract calls for beef classified by leanness rather than by tenderness or carcass quality, since it is primarily used for grinding into processed products. The inquiries made during the course of this study did not reveal any cases where businessmen felt they could use the contracts for live cattle in conjunction with those for Frozen Boneless Beef in a manner

comparable with the employment of soybean oil futures. This is
fully understandable since the live cattle specification does not
relate to the kind of cattle most commonly used for manufacturing beef and the price similarity is limited.

This does not mean that meat packers (whether they are
slaughterers or nonslaughtering processors) have no use for the
Frozen Boneless Beef contract. There is a good deal of potential
interest, especially in connection with seasonal storage operations
for processing beef. However, the anomaly of the highly active
futures market for pork bellies, which had a July 1970 volume of
197,282 contracts against only 76 contracts for boneless beef,
is surprising. The contrast is even more striking when it is realized
that the live cattle contract in July 1970 out-traded that for live
hogs by 36,832 contracts against 6,217.

Another aspect of the markets of the beef processing and re-
tailing industries is the growth, in recent years especially, of reliance on the daily price reporting services of the National Provisioner, the leading trade journal of the meat packing industry
and publisher of the so-called "Yellow Sheet" giving wholesale
price reports for meats and meat products. This is a privately
operated market news service which canvasses the trade (buyers
and sellers in the cash market) and reports its findings on an up-
to-the-minute basis.

A very substantial share of the meat buying by retailers employs
a formula price for procurement of major beef items based on
these reports (e.g., so much over or under the Yellow Sheet).
This permits dealing on the basis of volume requirements and
services rendered with only infrequent higgling over prices. A
study of retailer meat procurement in Ohio[26] reported that none
of the retail firms covered in the study made in 1964–65 bought
beef through "unstructured competitive pricing" without the aid
or utilization of formula. The proprietary chains tended to buy
their beef by rigid formulas, while the affiliated groups (voluntary
and co-op chains) used either rigid formulas or some modification to handle temporary or local conditions. This finding is a

---

[26] Stout, Hawkins, and Marion, "Meat Procurement and Distribution by
Ohio Grocery Chains and Affiliated Wholesalers," p. 19.

striking characteristic in an industry which up to a decade or two ago insisted upon personal inspection and price higgling over such variables as quality, trim, condition and the like. What it means is that a generally accepted quoting service has been established through the Yellow Sheet, which provides a reading of changing prices of key items in a way that represents the national cash market, just as the futures quotations for Live Beef Cattle have come to provide one of the major readings and guides in the live cattle market. (The live futures, however, can and do often deviate substantially from the cash livestock market prices for comparable, par delivery quality, animals.)

This digression to bring in the Yellow Sheet price reporting service is not irrelevant to our discussion. The significance is that the price protection needs of retailers and meat dealers, who have a rapid turnover of their products (because of perishability if for no other reason), are met largely by adhering fairly consistently to the prices in the wholesale product market as reported by the National Provisioner's service. This reliance extends, we were told, to the setting of *retail* price patterns as well as wholesale.[27]

In these circumstances it was not surprising to find that Live Cattle Futures contracts were not thought of as a regular hedging instrument for retailers. At the same time the futures are carefully watched by the product buyers in the industry including non-slaughtering processors, wholesalers, retailers, institutions, and others. The futures market provides a time dimension to the market which is not elsewhere available. A few retailers have felt that there are occasionally favorable opportunities to pin down a desirable purchase. These were regarded as "special situations," not as protective hedges. The futures had been sold out without awaiting delivery since the latter would have entailed complications of cumbersome transactions, custom slaughter, and the handling of many special details.

---

[27] The study did not examine in detail this relationship, although it is pretty generally supported by the results of regular USDA reports on wholesale-retail price spreads. (See, for instance, USDA, ERS, *Livestock and Meat Situation,* various issues.)

SUMMARY

Of the efforts to develop viable futures markets for beef products and cattle, the Live Beef Cattle futures market has been outstandingly successful. Futures contracts for carcass beef, for Frozen Boneless Beef and for feeder cattle have not, as of this writing, developed a significant hedging or speculative interest on their own, nor has there appeared to be any confidence on the part of commercial operators in the beef industry that they can enter cross-hedges between these contracts. This is in contrast to the soybean complex where thriving futures markets exist for beans, oil, and meal, and where cross-hedging is frequently employed as, for example, in the case of a soybean crusher hedging beans in oil or meal.

There is a rough analogy between the use of Live Beef Cattle futures in conjunction with certain cattle feed-out operations and the basis trading that is common in the grain markets. The differential between the futures prices and the estimated cost of producing deliverable cattle is akin to a "basis." However, the term basis is not a part of the language commonly used in the meat industry. And the linkages between futures and cash markets are different in many ways from those which appear in the grains. Whereas in nonperishable products there is an upper limit on the differential "carrying costs" likely to be reached in the futures market compared with current cash quotations, the same need not be true in the live cattle market. The reason is that the upper limit for a product like grain is set by the possibility of buying cash grain and storing it until the delivery month. In the cattle industry the futures quotation can, of course, be compared with an input cost budget including feeder cattle prices, feeds and other inputs; and if a feed-out profit is assured by this calculation, the probability favors a large utilization of feedlot capacity on a hedged basis. However, the *current* price of finished cattle has practically nothing to do with this calculation since those cattle now ready for market cannot be held over for the later delivery.

One of the outcomes of this difference in relationship between cattle and grains is that cattle futures are unlikely to reflect the kind of "normal carrying charges" between the various delivery months. Inverted markets are not unusual.

The "guaranteed feeding margin" is a phenomenon in which the use of Live Cattle Futures contracts is well established. Next in importance seems to be the use of this contract for forward sales and procurement purposes, enabling both farmers and slaughterers to pin the price at which live cattle will be delivered, even though they may not be ready for some months to come. For the most part, meat packers have followed a policy of using the futures in such a way that they can assure the availability of particular lots of cattle at the time of slaughter, but at a cost or transfer price in line with the current spot market as of that date. This is in part a reflection of the fact that the vast bulk of cattle marketings are purchased on a spot basis and competitive pressures in the sale of meat products would make it highly risky to operate very far away from a current replacement cost basis.

Moving from the meat packer to the retailer, there is somewhat more leeway in the pricing of individual retail cuts and there may be a tendency over time for greater use of the futures as a vehicle for assuring a favorable level of beef costs when pricing forecasts and merchandizing opportunities promise a competitively profitable outcome.

The comparison between past practices in the meat industry and the unfolding uses of cattle futures suggests an interpretation which is supported only by judgmental perceptions based on years of experience in the meat packing business. For many years up into the 1950s it seemed reasonably clear that the meat packer occupied the role of "finding the price, at any given time, that would clear the market" in respect to the national fresh meat supply. This role has tended to move over to the mass retailer to a considerable degree in the past 15 years, and one would expect that this trend might well continue. Major retail chains and buying groups now have to make careful studies of the total market for beef and other competing products and to judge the levels at which they can profitably move the volume they, as individual firms, consider competitively acceptable under current supply conditions. The use of the National Provisioner Yellow Sheet has already become a widespread industry practice, reflecting in large part the net composite opinion of the retail trade. Packers (**not** altogether willingly) have gone along in formula-pricing their product and accepting the Yellow Sheet as the prime factor. A further conjecture would lead one to guess that large retailers may find it advantageous to apply forecasting and projection techniques to the available information, and when the occasion seems appropriate, to include in their procurement plans a forward price commitment made possible through the use of Live Cattle Futures.

CHAPTER VIII

Cocoa

COCOA is produced in the tropics and consumed mainly in temperate regions. Five countries — Ghana, Nigeria, Ivory Coast, Cameroon, and Brazil — produce about 80% of the world's output and the more developed areas of the United States, Western and Eastern Europe consume about 80% of the world's cocoa products. The cocoa bean harvest is divided into main and midcrops; the African and Brazilian main-crop is harvested from October through March, the African mid-crop from May through June, and the Brazilian mid-crop from May through September. During the main-crop period about 80% of the world's cocoa is harvested.

Exhibit VIII-1 shows recent production figures for the main producing countries in each tropical region. Note the large decreases in the Ghanaian and Nigerian crops from 1967–68 to 1968–69. These decreases largely accounted for the overall world decrease between these two crop years.

There are numerous varieties of cocoa. The two main varieties are the *Forastero* and the *Criollo*. The *Forastero* cocoas provide the bulk of the commercial crop and are the main types produced in West Africa and Brazil. The beans have a harsh, bitter taste and are known in the trade as "base" grade. The *Criollo* types are known as the "fine" or "flavor" grades due to their bland flavor and pleasant aroma. They are largely used for blending and for manufacturing quality cocoa products. The *Criollo* types are principally grown in Central and South America. Between the "base" grade *Forastero* and the "fine" grade *Criollo* is a wide assortment

EXHIBIT VIII-1. WORLD PRODUCTION[1] OF COCOA BEANS
BY COUNTRIES AND REGIONS

(In metric tons)

	1967/68	*1968/69*
Africa		
Ghana	423.5	335.7
Nigeria	235.0	186.3
Ivory Coast	146.6	144.5
Cameroon	92.0	105.0
Others	80.6	84.2
Subtotal	977.7	855.7
South America		
Brazil	147.0	156.0
Ecuador	76.0	55.0
Venezuela	24.7	25.3
Others	21.2	22.6
Subtotal	268.9	258.9
Central America & Caribbean		
Mexico	26.7	28.2
Dominican Republic	29.3	22.0
Others	26.0	26.6
Subtotal	82.0	76.8
Asia		
Philippines	4.2	4.4
Ceylon	2.2	3.0
Others	2.3	2.9
Subtotal	8.7	10.3
Oceania		
New Guinea and Papua	23.7	27.0
Others	2.6	3.9
Subtotal	26.3	30.9
World Total	1,364	1,233

[1] Production figures refer to the standard cocoa crop year: 1 October to 30 September.

SOURCE: Food and Agriculture Organization of the United Nations, Committee on Commodity Problems Study Group on Cocoa, *Committee on Statistics Report of the Twenty-Sixth Session, Rome 6–7 April 1970.* Rome: FAO, CCP:/ST 31, 8 May 1970, Appendix II.

of other growths each having unique flavor and aromatic qualities. Although the blending of cocoa beans may not be as refined a process as it is for coffee or tea, it is nevertheless an important consideration to the cocoa manufacturers.

Harvesting consists of picking cocoa pods from the trees and separating the cocoa beans from the pods. The beans are then fermented and dried, both processes together requiring from one to three weeks. The resulting dried beans are the salable product. In this condition the beans can be stored for a year or more in temperate climates but can only be stored under tropical conditions for two or three months, unless carefully warehoused.

The newer varieties of the cocoa tree generally produce a harvestable crop in the third year after planting and full production by the fifth to eighth year. High yields continue until the twentieth year when yields begin to decline. Crop hazards include weather, various diseases, and insects. In the 1965–66 crop year weather was largely responsible for reducing Ghana's crop by about 30%.[1] Black pod rot, a disease of almost universal occurrence, can cause losses of similar magnitude[2] as can the ubiquitous capsid flies.[3] Other diseases causing widespread damage are "witches broom" in the West Indies and "swollen shoot" in Africa. The world output of cocoa is thus highly uncertain. Early crop estimates are notoriously inaccurate and reliable forecasts are generally not available until well into the harvesting season.

Further processing of cocoa beans involves cleaning, roasting and hulling. Hulling separates the husk and germ of the bean from the nibs of cocoa. These nibs then go through the grinding process which produces a mass called chocolate liquor. If special products are desired, the nibs of various cocoa types are blended prior to grinding. The levels of worldwide grindings at any given time provide the standard statistics used by the trade in estimating cocoa consumption.

---

[1] New York Cocoa Exchange, Inc., *Understanding the Cocoa Market,* p. 25.

[2] Krug and Quartey-Papafio, *World Cocoa Survey,* p. 11.

[3] Weymar, *The Dynamics of the World Cocoa Market,* p. 173 (excerpt from Gill and Duffus Ltd., *Cocoa Market Report,* dated December 15, 1958).

Chocolate liquor can be used directly in making chocolate or it can be separated by a pressing technique to yield cocoa butter and cocoa powder. Cocoa butter is mainly used with chocolate liquor to produce chocolate. Some butter is also used in the pharmaceutical and cosmetic industries. Cocoa powder is used to make chocolate drinks and various flavor compounds for drinks, desserts and baking products. About 5 pounds of cocoa beans will yield 4 pounds of chocolate liquor which upon further processing will yield about 2 pounds of cocoa powder and 2 pounds of cocoa butter.

During the late 1960s the major producing countries began to establish their own cocoa grinding facilities, a step in their national industrialization plans. Most of the cocoa butter and powder produced by these countries is exported, the major importers being the United States and Western Europe. The degree to which producer countries focus on marketing processed cocoa products instead of beans has obvious ramifications for the cocoa bean market.

Cocoa Bean Prices

One writer, F. H. Weymar,[4] has found it useful to separate cocoa price movements into long, intermediate, and short-term cycles. According to this scheme, a long-term cycle is largely the result of the time lag between the initial planting and peak production of a cocoa tree. In times of poor prices many producers do not have the funds necessary to root out old and diseased trees and replace them with new plantings. This sets the stage for a future shortage of cocoa beans. When this shortage is experienced in the marketplace, prices rise and producers find themselves with the means necessary for large-scale uprooting and new planting operations. When these new trees reach peak production levels, the likely result is over-production and poor prices and the cycle is repeated.

---

[4] *Ibid.*

Intermediate-term price movements are the result of annual fluctuations in cocoa production. In Weymar's words:

> In response to (say) a weather-caused crop shortage, inventories and expectations regarding future inventories both fall, causing the price to rise. After adjustment lags, consumption and consumption expectations decline toward a level more in line with the short crop, but not before inventories have been further depleted and the price forced still higher. With the continued rise, consumption is reduced below the production rate, and the inventory decline is reversed. The price now begins to fall, but the consumption rate does not end its decline until after an adjustment lag. By this time, the inventory level is well up from its trough and increasing further, causing a continued price decline. Consumption finally begins to climb in response to the lower prices as the second half of the cycle begins.[5]

These intermediate-term price fluctuations undoubtedly prompted another writer to state that the cocoa market is characterized by extensive and relatively consistent price moves.[6]

Short-term cycles have periods of from several days to several months and are due to a variety of factors among which are speculative buying and selling, governmental interventions (in the past, certain governments have withheld cocoa stocks from the market for various time periods), transportation strikes, and inventory decisions by a few large processors (about a half dozen manufacturing firms grind about 50% of the world's cocoa production).

The business manager in the cocoa industry is, of course, most concerned with the intermediate and short-term price fluctuations as it is within the annual cycle that important transactions have to be made, while for longer swings the product price can usually be adjusted to restore normal profit margins.

Trading in cocoa bean futures contracts is conducted at the New York Cocoa Exchange and at exchanges in London, Paris and Amsterdam. The New York and London exchanges, however, ac-

---

[5] *Ibid.*, pp. 7–8.
[6] Shishko, "How to Forecast Cocoa Prices," p. 98.

count for virtually all the trading activity. Most of the trading by the firms that were interviewed can be transacted on the New York Cocoa Exchange with some use of the London market. However, there are many international firms such as Gill and Duffus which use both markets interchangeably, and the major U.S. firms carefully monitor the trading activity in London as this information is an important element in the development of trading strategies.

Par delivery specifications must be designed to accommodate the wide variety of cocoa types that may be offered for delivery. Apparently, delivery specifications have been successfully established at the New York Cocoa Exchange as under its auspices every important cocoa type has actually been delivered against cocoa futures.[7] At the New York Cocoa Exchange, the contract trading unit is 30,000 pounds of beans of good, merchantable quality in original shipping bags and delivery is authorized from warehouses licensed by the Exchange in the Port of New York District or in the Delaware River Port District. Specific discounts and premiums apply to some 31 identified cocoa types and a maximum discount of 1 cent per pound applies to all other growths which may be tendered. Prices are quoted to the hundredth of a cent per pound with minimum fluctuation being one point or 1/100 cent per pound. The trading limit is 1 cent per pound above or below the previous day's settlement price.[8] Under Exchange rules, the delivery month may be the current month or any of the ensuing eighteen months; however, trading is most active in the months of December, March, May, July, and September.

Futures trading on the New York Cocoa Exchange is not under CEA supervision. There are no speculative trading or position limits, although the Exchange has a control committee to regulate trading activity in special situations.[9] In addition, clearing members

---

[7] New York Cocoa Exchange, *op. cit.*, p. 8.

[8] After a future contract's first notice day, there is no daily limit applied to trading in that future.

[9] During the preparation of this manuscript, officers of a Swiss bank controlled by the United California Bank of Los Angeles allegedly attempted at least partially to corner the world cocoa market by trading in cocoa futures. See "Cocoa Futures Leave a Bitter Taste," *Business Week,* September 26, 1970, p. 32.

may, within prescribed limits, finance the trades of certain customers.

To sum up, it would be extremely hazardous to conduct commercial operations in the world cocoa market without some form of price protection as:

1. Reliable forecasts are not available until well into the harvest season, yet pre- and early-season decisions and commitments have to be made.
2. Recurrent intermediate-term price moves could have serious effects if one had a large, exposed commitment on the wrong side of such a move.
3. Even if one were skilled in predicting intermediate-term movements, an exposed position could lead to ruin (or riches) due to the many unpredictable short-term factors which affect cocoa and many other international commodities.

Exhibit VIII-2 shows cocoa bean availability, grindings and the rather extensive fluctuations in cocoa bean prices for the years 1947 to 1968.

Cocoa Bean Market Structure

From the producers of the beans to the ultimate consumers, cocoa passes through a number of different processing stages. Even though a complete picture of the cocoa market structure is not available, a generalized picture of the structure can be advanced as shown in Exhibit VIII-3.

Some observations regarding the symbols showing volatile or less volatile prices on this exhibit are necessary. Daily bargaining or volatile price markets are contrasted with less volatile or list-price markets. The degrees of price volatility run the gamut from high frequency, instantaneous price quotations on the major cocoa exchanges to less frequent, firm forward purchases or sale prices which may reflect a full season's supply and demand prospects. Government marketing boards may set purchase prices from farmers for a season's crop but these prices may vary from season to season. Finally, the price to the consumer is not rigid, it sim-

EXHIBIT VIII-2. COCOA: POSTWAR SUPPLY AND DEMAND

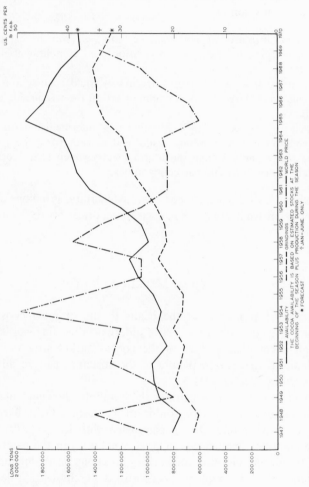

SOURCE: Gill and Duffus Limited, "Cocoa Statistics," London, October 1968, p. 4.

EXHIBIT VIII-3. MAIN ENTITIES IN COCOA MARKET STRUCTURE
AND PRODUCT FLOWS IN TERMS OF VARIABLE OR STABLE PRICE

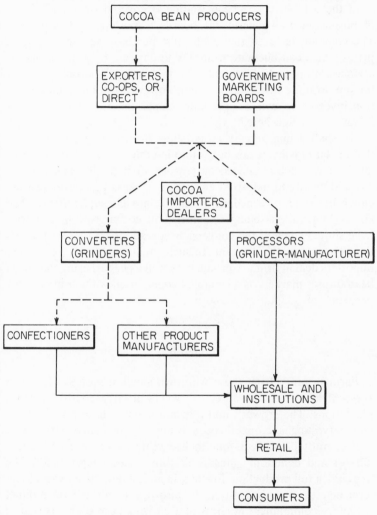

- - - - - Denotes variable price closely related to bean price.
——— Denotes stable price.

ply reflects the marketing practice of providing the consumer with stable prices.

In the exhibit, cocoa bean trading is covered by several types of businessmen — government boards, exporters, and importers. The common factor is that each must purchase and sell beans at prices which can fluctuate from day to day and hold the beans for certain time periods. There may be middlemen who only serve as brokers to unite buyers and sellers; however, insofar as this function involves no ownership commitments on the broker's part, it is not represented here.[10]

We shall define *processors* as being distinct from *converters* in that the latter convert raw beans into intermediate products (chocolate liquor, cocoa butter, cocoa powder, or bulk chocolate) which are sold mainly to industrial customers whereas processors process either beans or intermediate products into consumer items. The grinding operations being established in cocoa-growing countries have shifted some of the conversion operations up to a spot above the exporters on the diagram. In such situations, the exporters and importers deal in primary products as well as beans, using the cocoa bean futures markets as a suitable hedging tool, without major new problems of adaptation.

Farmers

Farmers range from those who own small subsistence farms in West Africa to wealthy absentee owners of large South American plantations. The grower's major commitment is in terms of raising and harvesting a crop of cocoa beans. As indicated earlier, the grower must plant trees four to five years in advance of his first harvest and commonly must wait three years longer before the trees reach full production. Further, in addition to the grower's long-term investment in cocoa trees he also has a shorter-term product inventory commitment in terms of a growing crop over a period of

---

[10] The broker may, of course, guide his customer into employing a futures contract as an adjunct to a transaction being negotiated.

six or more months. Whatever the size of a given crop, the price which he will receive for that crop is at risk from the moment the trees were planted to the date of sale. While the commitment is actually very long term, most growers think more in terms of the shorter period inventory commitment. A prediction in monetary units of the size of a grower's short-term commitment, however, is difficult to develop. Not only is it difficult to predict the amount of beans which will be harvested each year as the trees mature, this difficulty being compounded by the vagaries of weather and other growing conditions, but it is also difficult to predict the world supply of beans and episodic occurrences such as wars and political upheavals.

In short, while the growing crop is rarely considered a part of the pipeline of product flow and is seldom included in inventory statistics (since the commodity does not enter the pipeline until after the harvest) in actuality the growing crop certainly must be included as a part of the supply exposed to price risks. To make it easier for the reader to accept such inclusion, the grower's crop might more easily be thought of as inventory in gestation. The impact of the price risk exposure on this prospective supply is quite large and probably more uncertain than at any other stage in the pipeline simply because so many of the variables which affect such exposure are undefinable in quantitative terms. For this reason, it can be argued that the grower suffers the greatest risk of price exposure, and yet the small cocoa grower is typically in a very difficult position to protect himself from such price risk exposure. In cocoa countries, stabilization efforts have become a major concern of public authorities.

A form of mandatory price protection is afforded the farmer in Nigeria, Ghana, and other countries where government agencies are empowered to purchase at a fixed price the entire bean harvest. The story is quite different in the producing countries in the Western Hemisphere. In general, cocoa moves from such countries as Brazil, Ecuador, Venezuela, Mexico, and the Dominican Republic via exporters or farmer cooperatives. As the exporters must compete with the cooperatives, the net result is that the growers under either arrangement can expect to receive essentially the market price. This is not to say that such countries are free of governmental controls and subsidies. For example, in Brazil, exporters, farmer cooperatives and agencies of the government have formed the powerful Bahia Cocoa Trade Commission which sets maximum differentials for the FOB Bahia spot price under the futures prices quoted at the New York Cocoa Exchange. This incidentally is a good example of the use of commodity futures to provide bellwether price quotations.[11] However, even though there are various forms of government control and subsidies in the western producing countries, the market is less constrained than it is in the African countries. It is also true that the individual producers both in Africa and in the Western Hemisphere do not use the cocoa futures market to any great extent.

GOVERNMENT MARKETING BOARDS

Marketing boards include official or semi-official agencies empowered by law to purchase all their respective country's cocoa crop at a fixed price. Normally, the board acquires control of the beans at harvest time. Limited availability of good storage facilities means that beans have to move out of the country in the ensuing months to avoid deterioration and in order to convert them into needed cash. The price these boards receive for the crop is largely determined by market factors.

Even though a marketing board has a substantial long commitment due to its buying obligation, a board's ability to set the price paid to growers means that the probability of losing money can be minimized unless producer prices are deliberately subsidized. Rather, the board's problem becomes one of maximizing its own returns in order to build up cash necessary to finance large-scale experimentation, disease and insect control, and replanting projects. For this reason, marketing boards have typically tried to avoid being at the mercy of the market. For years the major producing countries have entered negotiations concerning the establishment of an international cocoa agreement, but as of 1970 no agreement

---

[11] See p. 46.

had been reached.[12] Some boards have tried to use the futures market to increase the overall average returns for their beans. However, there are political reasons why boards would be understandably reluctant to take positions in a market they could not control. In any event, the boards apparently have not succeeded in developing a workable plan, and in recent years marketing boards have not been active in the futures market. Firm forward sales contracts to processors or middlemen are employed. For instance, it was reported that in December 1965 Ghana had sold forward almost its entire anticipated 1965–66 main crop and Nigeria the greater part.[13] In most cases forward sales are firmly priced.

COCOA BEAN DEALERS

The market affects every act of the dealers as they move large volumes of beans and cocoa products in and out at variable prices. As pointed out earlier, it would indeed be hazardous to expose any substantial inventory position to the price swings in this market and hence a general goal appears to be the maintenance of a zero net position. Thus, although dealers coordinate or guide a substantial portion of the international cocoa pipeline, they can avoid or shift the price risks of their sizable long or short positions by effecting simultaneous offsetting trade orders or futures market commitments. As a result, most dealers view themselves as agents for both buyers and sellers, earning their profits from the services they provide (time, form and place utilities, information, paperwork facilitation) and from successful basis operations rather than from speculation.

Dealers must seek to satisfy their customers' desires for specific

---

[12] International commodity agreements typically share the main functions of futures markets, namely, to promote price stability and to provide the industries concerned with protection against price declines. Hence, establishment of an international cocoa agreement would undoubtedly have an impact on the existing uses of the cocoa futures market. What the impact would be depends, of course, on the nature of any agreement reached. However, international commodity agreements, as in sugar and coffee, need not obviate the usefulness of the futures markets.

[13] Barclays Bank, *Overseas Survey 1966,* p. 192.

bean, butter, and powder qualities. The wide variety of cocoa types in the cash market juxtaposed with the par-delivery standard grade (with its set premiums and discounts) in the futures market means there is ample room for skilled differential (basis is referred to as differential in the cocoa business) merchandising.

Types of Commercial Operations

Two firms which function in the cocoa market strictly as dealers (no grinding facilities) were interviewed. The management of the smaller of the two, General Cocoa Company, was emphatic in asserting that the nature of its business is to earn profits by providing services to both buyers and sellers and by skilled merchandising; it does not speculate, that is, it does not attempt to profit solely from price fluctuations in the futures or cash markets, nor does it take positions outside the normal net position range set by company policy. The other firm, A. C. Israel, handles somewhat more cocoa than General Cocoa Company. Its management stated that service and skilled merchandising were by far the bread and butter of their cocoa business; however, they do have policies which enable them in special circumstances to take reasonable net positions beyond their normal range.

Uses of Cocoa Futures

The policy of both dealer firms as regards their cocoa operations is to use the futures market as an aid to the conduct and profitability of their procurement, handling, and marketing operations. As one would expect in firms which provide the bridge between buyers and sellers, the procurement, custody and marketing functions are highly interrelated. For example, the procurement function may be triggered by a firm sales contract. Or procurement may be triggered by the ability to make a profit through the custody function; that is, if futures prices are at a sufficient premium over the spot price to insure the earning of carrying charges, including shipping, grading, storage, etc., and some profit, then cash beans will be purchased and hedged by selling futures. Hedging to earn the equivalent of storage can also be executed by spreading; i.e., buying·near-term futures and selling more distant futures if the premium of the latter over the former is sufficient. The near-term long futures position might then be replaced by the purchase of actual beans if spot prices become favorable, and it may later be possible to go a step farther and sell the actual beans covered by the short futures sales at prices which will earn more than would be earned by delivering the beans under the futures contract.

General Cocoa Company. General Cocoa Company follows the basic trading policy of not purchasing either actuals (beans and bean products) or bean futures contracts unless these purchases are or can be offset by sales commitments or short futures positions. This policy is not expressly written; rather the firm is small in terms of personnel and the principle is well understood. Operating strictly within this rule would keep the company's net position always near zero. It is seldom possible, however, to have exact offsets, so the net position may vary from day to day. No numerical limits on this variation have been set; however, a net position statement in terms of types, bags and lots of cocoa is developed each day and the senior trader of the firm, who is also the firm's founder and senior officer, checks these statements to insure the position is acceptable, usually no more than a few hundred tons long or short.

General Cocoa must satisfy its customers' desires for quantity, quality and timing. Profitability in meeting these requirements rests on the skill of traders. For example, to cover a sales commitment the traders must decide whether it would be more profitable to procure and store actual beans until needed, or to take a long position in futures or to execute a combination of these. To reach this decision traders must analyze a variety of factors including the supply and demand prospects for the important cocoa types, the variety of factors inherent in the differences between cash and futures prices, the availability and cost of storage, the costs of transportation, and the prospects for strikes or government actions which may impede or stop the flow of cocoa from the producing countries.

General Cocoa has no formal procedures other than the usual financial statements for systematically evaluating the results of their traders' decisions. The net position policy insures that the firm is not exposed to any significant degree to overall price risks; however, in such a closely knit firm it is largely a matter of personal judgment as to how profitably their traders have handled the residual elements in individual cases. At month's end, inventory and all commitments including open futures contracts are brought to market and a profit and loss statement is generated. This gives the firm an overall picture of how well the traders are functioning.

General Cocoa usually buys beans and bean products from the origins — the marketing boards in Africa and exporters in Brazil. In addition, it regularly deals in cocoa butter. The firm recognizes that the price of powder and butter is not strictly parallel to the price of beans but presently finds it acceptable to hedge 1 unit of butter against about 2.5 units of cocoa beans. It seems to be a general rule of thumb in the industry that the price of butter should be about 2.5 times the price of beans.

General Cocoa's business is replacement-cost oriented; that is, it buys most of its cocoa beans and products when a sale on the futures market assures the earning of carrying charges. Out of this hedged inventory cocoa is then typically sold on an immediate delivery basis (sometimes called "cash and carry") at a firm price of so many cents over the earliest delivery month's future's price, or sold via "price-to-be-fixed" contracts to be discussed below. Generally, the firm reaches its peak inventory level in March or April at the end of both the African and Brazilian main crops, and its low inventory level in October when the Africans and Brazilians start harvesting their main crops.

A. C. Israel. A. C. Israel's cocoa operation is similar to General Cocoa's in many respects. However, since the firm conducts a larger operation and trades in other commodities (e.g., rubber and coffee), A. C. Israel's net position and trading policies are necessarily more formalized. Trading policies and open limits are developed by the senior cocoa trader, who is also the firm's president, together with the chairman of the board. The senior trader is then held responsible for seeing to it that the traders he supervises operate within these policies. The world cocoa situation is constantly monitored and if major changes in policy are deemed necessary, such changes must be cleared with the chairman. Within this constraint A. C. Israel can take a very limited position based on business judgment. For example, if it appears as though actual and futures prices for cocoa have reached their low points and an upswing is imminent, the firm may authorize limits for an uncovered long position in actuals or in futures. The firm, of course, does not strive to attain this limit. The company's objective is to sell and provide services to customers; consequently, in the course of a trading day sales may keep pace with purchases and the limit may never be reached.

Cocoa dealer firms do not ordinarily take delivery of beans through the futures market since they have no control over the quality of beans which might be tendered. However, they may occasionally take delivery of beans for cash and carry purposes.[14] Dealer firms do use the futures market as a cocoa bean marketing tool as futures prices enable them to make sales on a "price-to-be-fixed" basis. To illustrate, the firms can enter an agreement whereby a customer agrees to buy a certain quantity and quality of cocoa at so many points, say 200, over the futures price for a certain delivery contract, say July — the buyer selecting the day when the price will become fixed (this type of arrangement is sometimes referred to as a buyer's call). This commitment would not be considered a part of a dealer firm's net position until the price is actually fixed. Until this time the dealer is simply short the 200 point differential. If the dealer has the specified quantity of beans in inventory, the normal procedure would be to hold this quantity hedged in July futures since the price is still to be specified. When the buyer specifies the price, the hedge would be lifted and the dealer's inventory position would be offset by the now firm-price sales contract.

A. C. Israel generates a daily position statement. The firm carefully reviews its net position to keep its exposures within acceptable limits relative to its commercial commitments and financial position. Like General Cocoa, A. C. Israel does not as a general rule like to be short. The managers feel that they can measure the downside risk of holding a long position but cannot get a good measure

---

[14] Cash and carry is a transaction in which free supplies of the cash commodity are handled with the intention to sell in the spot market or re-deliver later.

of a short position's upside risk. Also, like General Cocoa Company, A. C. Israel has no formal reports for evaluating the outcome of specific trade operations or strategies; rather the firm brings all its commitments to market once a month and develops a gross trading statement. By using a computer the firm hopes to generate this report more often than once a month as a further aid in management decision making.[15]

The New York office of A. C. Israel, which handles all the firm's domestic cocoa business, hedges cocoa butter on an approximate basis of a 2.5 to 1 ratio. A subsidiary company in Amsterdam, which also handles cocoa products, hedges butter on a variable ratio basis which seeks to reflect more accurately the butter-to-bean price ratio. Both the straight 2.5 to 1 method and the variable method have been satisfactory, although the relative merits between the methods have not been subjected to specific analysis.

In summary, the relatively minor differences between General Cocoa and A. C. Israel seem to be related to the relative sizes of the two firms. A. C. Israel turns over a greater volume of cocoa than General Cocoa handles. Hence, one would expect A. C. Israel's cocoa policies to be more formalized and its net position limits to be at times wider. In addition, A. C. Israel is diversified, whereas General Cocoa deals only in cocoa. Thus, should A. C. Israel decide to authorize an extension of its net at risk cocoa position, this strategy can be considered in the light of the full assortment of positions which the firm takes and the diversity of risks it handles.

CONVERTERS AND PROCESSORS

The procurement problems faced by both converters and processors are very similar. Surprisingly, the converters are likely to be

---

[15] Computer use in commodity trading may aid the management control function as well as the speed and logic with which trading decisions are made. It is doubtful, however, that computers will ever be able to replace the skilled commodity trader. To the quantifiable facts, which could conceivably be fed to a computer, a skilled trader adds other essentials such as bargaining ability, a personal touch, and judgment based upon intuition and years of experience.

more concerned with specific bean qualities as their industrial customers may prescribe narrow specifications as to color, consistency, and flavor, whereas the processors are in a better position to meet their needs by making a blended product from a wider selection of beans. On the sales side, however, the picture is quite different. The converter operates with significant, albeit imperfect, price parallelism between raw cocoa beans and his cocoa bean products. He also operates in an industrial market where gross margins are typically thin. On the other hand, most large processors market their consumer goods at relatively fixed prices due to a mixture of necessity (a significant volume of candy bars are sold via coin-operated vending machines) and marketing strategy. For the processor faced with relatively inflexible selling prices, the management of price risks cannot be handled in terms of the matching of parallel price changes, affecting both raw materials and finished goods, with offsetting futures market commitments. The policy of maintaining stable consumer prices does enable the commercial manager to buy his raw materials against a more or less stable sales budget. He tries, of course, to own his raw material at a favorable enough cost to protect his margins.

Most processors have some flexibility regarding product composition which gives them some margin of protection in the face of variable raw material costs. For example, they may have several formulations for their chocolate products, one of which is particularly suitable when cocoa bean prices are high and perhaps another which is suitable when other ingredients are in short supply.

A processor may find it advantageous to use the futures market as a procurement tool if quoted raw material prices appear attractive relative to known selling prices. Advantages accrue from the fact that purchasing futures contracts requires much less capital than buying and storing actual raw material that is not needed immediately, while it also enables the buyer to "shop" the cash market for a good bargain in actuals up to the time when his futures purchase would result in delivery.

In sum, the processor's inventory management policies are primarily a matter of minimizing ingredient procurement costs rather than a matter of minimizing price risk exposure.

Types of Commercial Operations

For the convenience of this discussion consumer products such as candy bars and packaged cocoa powder will be referred to as proprietary products and industrial products such as bulk chocolate, chocolate liquor, cocoa butter, and bulk cocoa powder will be referred to as bulk products.

Both converters and processors generally regard their business as that of making a profit by changing their raw materials, cocoa beans, into more useful finished goods; that is, their main emphasis is on adding quality and form utility. Three firms in the cocoa processing and converting business were interviewed in depth. All sell both bulk and proprietary products; however, the split is considerably different among the firms. General Foods is largely in the converting business. Nestle has substantial business in both areas, and Hershey sells mostly proprietary products.

Uses of Cocoa Futures

The three firms interviewed were all buyers of cocoa beans. Other firms commonly buy bulk chocolate products and their price-risk problems can be inferred from the types of transactions described below. No data are available as to the extent to which such non-grinder cocoa users engage in hedging or speculation on their own accounts, although practices are said to vary widely among the firms, some of them having large transactions in futures while others have none.

General Foods Corporation. General Foods annually purchases around 40,000 tons of cocoa beans of various types. All beans are purchased by the cocoa bean purchasing department which is a part of General Foods' Jell-O Division rather than of the general corporate purchasing department. About 35% to 40% of the company's annual requirements are purchased from the Ivory Coast on a firm-price basis. Cocoa beans purchased from the Ivory Coast are booked through independent export firms; however, the selling prices must be authorized by the government. This arrangement gives the Ivory Coast the opportunity to immediately discount the purchase contract. General Foods' remaining requirements are purchased from domestic cocoa dealers usually on a "price-to-be-fixed" basis, i.e., at so many points over the futures price for a certain delivery month, with General Foods retaining the option of naming the date (within certain prescribed limits) when the price will become fixed. An example of this type of transaction from the dealer's side was discussed earlier. Again, using July and 200 points, the buyer (G.F.) could elect to fix its actual bean costs at any time by simply notifying the seller. The cash bean costs would be determined by the price of the July futures as quoted at the time General Foods elects to fix the price, plus the 200-point differential. At this time the dealer would presumably lift his short hedge (since he no longer has a price risk on the beans) and General Foods simultaneously takes on the same or an equivalent short futures commitment to offset the price risk it has now incurred.

At times General Foods may feel that it will be able to purchase cash beans at some later time at a differential premium of spot over futures less than that which a dealer is currently willing to accept. In such a case General Foods may take a long futures position and thereby be in a position to await a more favorable differential in the cash market.

About 85% of General Foods' beans are used to make bulk products which are sold to the baking, candy, dairy, and other industries. Thin gross margins usually prevail in the industrial market and this imposes pressures on General Foods to be efficient in its conversion operations, to keep capacity fully scheduled, to give service and timely delivery, and to buy beans with high yield and quality characteristics. With these considerations, a firm cannot afford to have a transaction wrecked by price swings. In addition industrial product salesmen often find it necessary to execute firm-price sales contracts 9 to 12 months in the future and sometimes as much as 18 months ahead. A firm can ill afford to enter such sales contracts without some form of price protection. Thus, the Jell-O Division's policy is to have its bulk cocoa business operate with a zero net position. All beans in inventory, firm bean purchase contracts, and long bean futures contracts stand against firm sales contracts or sales of futures contracts.

General Foods' purchases of beans for its bulk business are based on an annual industrial marketing plan which includes a quarterly sales forecast of the types of products which the sales force has sold or anticipates selling. The production scheduling department then converts these sales needs into the quantities of bean types it will need at specific times. The company has a manager responsible for cocoa purchases and it is his responsibility to insure that the right beans are available when required.

Although it was not the purpose here to go into the actual mechanics of purchasing and hedging transactions, it should be mentioned again that for a business firm to achieve satisfactory results in its use of the futures markets, it must rely heavily on the skill of its traders. Deciding when to place and lift hedges, when to buy and store actuals, when to enter price-to-be-fixed contracts, or to take a long futures position and assume the differential risks, requires sophisticated forecasting and the judgment and intuition which are engendered by years of experience.

General Foods has developed a sophisticated accounting system which permits it to appraise the results of its bulk product business. The system features a standard bean cost which reflects the company's best estimate of what cocoa beans will cost during a fiscal cycle (April 1 to March 31), and standard conversion ratios for the bulk products. Variance accounts are used to record deviations from the standards. A hypothetical example which gives a simplified picture of how the system works follows:

> When beans are transferred from warehouses to the grinding facilities, losses due to spillage and foreign material such as sticks and stones are taken into account. Suppose the standard loss for this transfer process is 2 pounds lost per 100 pounds of warehoused beans. Let us assume that standard (or bench-mark) cost is 30¢/lb. For an actual transfer, the loss may be as much as 5 pounds, or 3 pounds more than the standard loss allowance, due to an excessive amount of foreign material. A 3-pound loss would then be applied to the transfer variance account, which in effect places the responsibility for this excess loss upon the raw bean buyer. Initially, the loss would, for convenience, be expressed in dollars at the standard bean cost of 30¢/lb. At the end of the month, however, the net of all the losses (or gains) accumulated

in the transfer variance account is adjusted to reflect the market value of the beans that were lost (or gained).

There are some 16 points in the procurement and grinding process where standard conversion ratios together with the corresponding variance accounts apply. The variance accounts provide a basis for determining at which point in the procurement-conversion process significant variations from prior budgets, standard costs, or expectations have occurred. This system also permits a very careful control of the net position. If, for example, a certain amount of beans are ground into chocolate liquor to meet a sales order, and the liquor yield is significantly below standard, this may require taking beans out of hedged inventory to make up the difference. Hedges against these additional beans would then be lifted.

When an order is sold to a customer, it is assigned a firm order number. This firm order number is applied to the variance and other accounts used to record the costs (procurement, processing, shipping, etc.) and revenue associated with this transaction. By pulling together all the entries labeled with the appropriate firm order number, the firm can examine in some detail the results of each bulk product sale.

When a firm-price sale is booked, cocoa bean hedges covering the estimated or equivalent bean content of the order are lifted. The total raw material records are then valued in two parts, consisting of:

1. The pounds and actual purchase price of beans which are still held unsold, and
2. The pounds and value (this is now a fixed value which includes the gains or losses on the lifted hedges) of beans which have been sold to customers but not yet delivered.

Monthly a computer print-out is made to check out the amounts in each of the above categories. The print-out of the undelivered order file provides General Foods with data to prepare profit forecasts by anticipated delivery period and is an important tool in the planning cycle.

Five accountants work full time on General Foods' computerized cocoa accounting system. In addition, General Foods uses the computer for cocoa price forecasting and for generating what the manager for cocoa purchases calls the "out-of-pocket" prices for various bulk products. Prices quoted on the New York futures market are adjusted for grade premiums and other differential elements which the cocoa purchasing manager feels would apply. This information is fed to a computer. The computer applies standard conversion ratios and manufacturing costs and calculates an array of "out-of-pocket" prices for bulk products by future delivery months. "Out-of-pocket" prices are calculated at least once a day and more often if the futures market is changing substantially. These prices are a valuable tool to the marketing department as they are the basis from which firm forward sales contracts are negotiated.

About 15% of General Foods' cocoa bean volume is processed as proprietary grocery items such as home cooking products, syrups, and chocolate chips. Cocoa beans purchased for this purpose need not necessarily be hedged; the decision is based on the margin built into consumer products which in turn depends upon such things as the projected demand for certain proprietary items and the competition. For proprietary needs, the manager of cocoa purchases recommends action based upon his analysis of the above factors and of the cocoa market. His recommendations must then be approved by the manager responsible for proprietary products and by senior managers within the Jell-O Division.

Nestle U.S.A. According to trade sources, Nestle U.S.A. turns over about 50,000 tons of cocoa beans annually, about half of which are used in proprietary items and the remainder are used to grind bulk products for industrial use. Unlike General Foods, Nestle U.S.A. rarely purchases beans from producing countries but relies rather on domestic dealer firms such as A. C. Israel, General Cocoa, Gill and Duffus, and others for its supplies.

Like General Foods, Nestle's (throughout this section Nestle will mean Nestle U.S.A.) policy is to have its bulk business completely covered at all times and it uses the futures market to cover commitments and to fix the price of raw materials usually through price-to-be-fixed purchase contracts with domestic cocoa dealers. Most of its bulk products are sold in advance, at times out to 18 months, on a firm contract basis. For small volume bulk sales to small companies, Nestle publishes a price list which features a 90-day guarantee of notice against price increases and declines.

Nestle's director of purchasing feels that the concept of a zero net position cannot be applied to the proprietary end of the business as the sales side is open ended and sales prices are relatively stable. The best one can do is purchase beans against anticipated proprietary product sales and handle price risks by varying the margin or by altering the processing mix or by doing both, keeping in mind, of course, constraints imposed by the firm's commercial image and the competition. Thus, the director of purchasing feels that the company is taking an exposed position when it purchases beans for use in proprietary products. Since the bulk end of the business is always covered and since all purchases of beans, either actual or through the futures market, for the proprietary business are thought of as being uncovered, the company as a whole always has a net long position in cocoa beans. The company's president approves limits on this exposure.

Nestle has one purchasing department which buys beans for both the bulk and the proprietary operations, although the accounts for each are kept separately. In contrast to General Foods' line setup, Nestle's cocoa purchasing activities are considered a staff function and the purchasing department reports to the president. Purchasing is not a direct profit center; beans are simply distributed to the three grinding facilities carrying their actual costs. The profit response to purchasing's actions eventually appears in the marketing department which may or may not get a break on costs. Evaluation of the purchasing performance is one of the functions of a weekly staff meeting with production, purchasing, financial and marketing managers represented. At these meetings the past week's activities are reviewed, future actions are discussed, and a weekly activity target is set. Purchase orders may emanate from these meetings and these orders typically instruct the purchasing department to buy so many pounds of a certain type of cocoa at a cost of so many cents per pound or better to be available at a certain future date. The cocoa purchasing agent, who reports to the director of purchasing, is then free to fill this order according to his judgments of the market, the availability of storage space, financial considerations, and other factors. He is expected to enable the company to acquire its raw material at least as advantageously as the competition.

Hershey Foods Corporation. Hershey's Chocolate and Confectionery Division is predominantly in the proprietary products business. Interviews with trade sources indicate that the company uses about 100,000 tons of cocoa beans annually and over 90% of these are used in proprietary products. Because of the proprietary nature of the business, Hershey's normal operating policy is not to hedge cocoa bean inventories in the futures market.

Hershey uses several methods to protect itself from cocoa bean price fluctuations. The Lifo method for inventory valuation protects its basic pipeline inventories (those present at both the opening and close of a fiscal period). By having a portion of its net inventory position in the form of cocoa futures, the company can preserve its physical Lifo holdings and still adjust its net exposed position. This is a special consideration affecting the user of Lifo inventory methods.[16]

By carefully monitoring the cocoa market, Hershey forecasts supply and demand and attempts to purchase its cocoa beans when forecasts indicate a favorable buying range. The firm has a policy that permits it to maintain a substantial inventory of cocoa beans so that it can buy additional beans at the best prices and not have to make forced purchases. Like Nestle, Hershey can, through price policy on finished products and through input mix flexibility, absorb some of the effects of price impacts and still maintain its margin between costs and selling prices. Finally, Hershey does make judicious use of the futures market, usually as an aid in procurement.

For procurement purposes, the firm looks upon the futures market as an aid in carrying out the simply stated objective of pur-

---

[16] Incidentally, it is not logical to apply futures contract price variances on open contracts as an adjustment of Lifo inventory values. Such variances can be treated separately as a deferred item. Closed futures, of course, enter cost of goods sold as a credit or debit.

chasing its bean requirements at the lowest possible prices. For example, the director of cocoa bean purchases, who is also a director of the corporation, may feel that he can procure his bean requirements cheaper by buying futures contracts than by entering a firm-price purchase contract with a producer or a formula pricing arrangement with a dealer. All positions in the futures market require the prior approval of four additional officers on Hersheys' Board of Directors.

The above methods for dealing with price impacts are not always entirely successful. The company's 1969 Annual Report recorded the following sales and income figures:

	Sales	*Net Income*
1968	$296,045,285	$19,898,149
1969	$315,117,453	$12,041,411

In addition the 1969 Annual Report contained the following comments:

As mentioned in our interim reports during the year, the extremely high cost of cocoa beans — the principal ingredient of our chocolate and cocoa products — depressed the earnings of the Chocolate and Confectionery Division and, hence, the Corporate earnings. These high cocoa bean prices were the result of four years of deficits in world production as compared with consumption, culminating in a very disappointing rain-damaged crop in the harvest year October 1, 1968, to September 30, 1969. While many methods to counteract increased cocoa and other ingredient costs were explored and some adopted, competition in the market place (especially from nonchocolate confections) made it impractical to preserve the margins on many of our brands.

*   *   *

At the end of 1969, we discontinued the manufacture and marketing of five-cent chocolate bars. This decision, which was reached with reluctance, was necessitated by constantly increasing costs, particularly the high price of cocoa beans. We are encouraged by the reception of this change, and we anticipate that there will be no difficulty in making the transition from five-cent bars to ten-cent bars.

SUMMARY

The international character of the cocoa bean market has several important ramifications for the United States cocoa industry. The lack of reliable forecasts of cocoa bean supplies and the ever-present possibility of unilateral actions on the part of producer (or possibly consumer) countries serve to heighten the uncertainties compared with those which exist for domestically grown commodities. As a result, each of the firms interviewed maintains an intelligence network of employees or contacts, or both, in the major producing regions and market centers. In addition these firms often subscribe to market information published by various private sources.

The contrast between the policies of bean converters and those of consumer product processors in the cocoa market serves to heighten the distinction between firms which operate with parallelism between raw materials and finished products and those whose finished product prices bear little short-term relation to raw material prices. The processor who does not have price parallelism uses the futures market mainly as a procurement tool. It gives the raw-material purchasing function an added time dimension and another device which can be used to secure the least expensive usable raw materials.

Where price parallelism does exist, the futures market offers additional benefits. Price parallelism does provide an opportunity for converters to avoid the impacts of major price swings by keeping commercial commitments fully hedged. But once a converter decides to use the futures market to reduce his net exposure to or near zero he can within this policy secure other benefits from the futures market. Free from worry about major price swings, the converter can concentrate on placing his buying and selling hedges when he thinks he can make money from changes in the spot vs. futures differential ("*the* basis") [17] and from managing his own cash transactions in light of specific hedging differentials available (the "*my* basis").[17] A trader skilled in operating on the

---

[17] See pp. 66–67.

basis may then use this expertise as a marketing tool by quoting firm prices for future product deliveries.

The main point which bears reiteration is that for firms operating under conditions of price parallelism, and this includes cocoa bean dealers as well as the converters, the idea that hedging is only a price protection device woefully understates the value of the futures market as a commercial tool.

CHAPTER IX

Frozen Concentrated Orange Juice

SEVERAL POINTS regarding raw orange production are relevant to a discussion of the Frozen Concentrated Orange Juice (FCOJ) futures market. As over 90% of the oranges used in FCOJ come from Florida groves, the focus here will be on Florida's raw orange production.

Raw oranges mature in Florida over a nine-month period commencing in October and lasting through June. Early, mid-, and late season varieties are grown; the most significant of these for processing are the mid- and late-season varieties which reach the market in December and February and are harvested through June. The internal qualities of these oranges make them highly suitable for concentrating.

From the initial planting of an orange grove, it normally takes four or five years before the trees are mature enough to produce a commercial volume of fruit. However, once the stage of maturity is reached, the trees can yield profitable volumes for several decades.

The chief hazard in raw orange production is frost. A severe freeze in December 1962 resulted in a crop of about 75 million boxes when pre-season forecasts indicated a 120 million box potential supply. The following year, 1963–64, the harvest was further reduced to about 58 million boxes largely due to wood damage caused by the 1962 freeze. However, since wood damage becomes evident in the spring following a freeze, crop forecasts for the 1963–64 season gave an anticipated output of 64.5 million boxes.[1] Thus, severe freezes can affect several seasons of production, although carry-over effects can be reasonably well predicted. Severe freezes are rare; however, cold snaps and local frost conditions can cut production in any year by 10% to 30%. The frost danger starts in December and extends through mid-February. Oranges in Florida grow best in areas where winter temperatures approach the freezing point; hence, frost is an almost inescapable risk. Other hazards include deficient or excess rainfall, diseases and pests, and storm, flood, or other damage.

FRESH ORANGE MARKET

Up until the late 1940s the major outlet for Florida oranges was the fresh market. The marketing channels were initially simple; the fruit was either consigned to an auction outlet, sold to a resident chain store buyer, or sold to a broker. Because of the fluctuations in supply, the seasonality of various strains and the limited time flexibility a grower had in marketing his perishable harvest, price risks to the growers were considerable. In an effort to partially assuage these risks, some growers joined price pooling cooperatives or participation plan marketing schemes. The attractiveness of both these arrangements stemmed from the fact that the returns to the grower were based in a prescribed way on a season's average level of fruit prices. Generally, two "seasons" were defined for a crop year, one season covering the early and mid-season orange varieties, the other season the later varieties. By joining one of these plans, the grower could avoid the risk of having his returns based solely on the spot price, date of harvest.

FCOJ MARKET

The introduction of frozen concentrated orange juice at the end of World War II profoundly affected the Florida orange industry.

---

[1] For more information on variations in supply and forecasting accuracy, see Green, "Understanding the Frozen Orange Juice Market."

Three characteristics of the product itself were largely responsible for the radical changes which occurred.

1. The internal qualities of several varieties of Florida oranges, most notably the mid-season and the Valencia oranges, make them highly suitable for concentrating purposes. The value of a crop bound for the FCOJ market began to be measured in terms of juice and pounds of dissolved sugars (referred to as "pounds of fruit solids" in the industry) rather than in terms of pounds or boxes of raw fruit. Many growers began to concentrate their production on these juicy varieties.

2. The frozen product was capable of being branded and hence was promoted on a large scale. As a result, consumer acceptance was rapid and the orange industry enjoyed a period of rapid growth. From 1950 to 1970 Florida's orange production capacity has tripled. About 65% of the recent crops have been used for FCOJ production.[2]

3. The frozen product can be readily stored for long periods in bulk form. This not only permitted year-round marketing of FCOJ but also opened new markets, namely the federal school lunch program and a small, but potentially large, export market. In addition, storability lessened the impact of freeze damage. If a frost-bitten crop is immediately processed, most of its value can be saved and a temporary market glut avoided by storing the product for sale at a future time.

The introduction of FCOJ into the Florida orange market radically altered the traditional structure of this industry. The new structure which rapidly evolved was still based upon an uncertain supply of raw oranges. Thus, during the evolutionary process, the industry sought to improve the structure by building in mechanisms which would provide some price stability. Among the mechanisms studied was the establishment of a futures market. After much debate, the Florida orange industry accorded a mixed welcome to the futures market for FCOJ. Trading began at the Citrus Associates of the New York Cotton Exchange in October 1966.

An FCOJ futures contract calls for concentrate containing about 15,000 pounds (within 3%) of orange solids (a 90-pound box of

---

[2] There is a tendency to pack larger percentages of FCOJ (which is stored) in years of large crops.

raw oranges contains about 5.7 pounds of orange solids). The delivered juice must meet specific standards including the degree of concentration, the color, and the amount of pulp.[3] It is relatively easy for concentrate processors to meet the delivery specifications. On the other hand, delivered concentrate is too concentrated for direct use as a consumer product. Delivery is authorized in Exchange licensed warehouses in Florida. Futures trading has been conducted in the December, January, March, May, July, September, and November delivery months.

In order to garner a portion of whatever oranges might be available for the rapidly expanding FCOJ market and in order to ensure efficient plant utilization, assured access to a supply of raw oranges became a prerequisite for successful processing operations. Consequently, most processors have sponsored or have become affiliated with cooperatives which are under contract to deliver their members' fruit to the processor, and some grower cooperatives have established their own processing capabilities. Another common practice is the use of participation plans whereby growers contract to deliver their fruit to a processor who will process and market the resulting FCOJ. In addition, some processors have integrated backward into grove ownership, although the usual practice is to market their own grove fruit through an affiliated cooperative. The concentrate fruit delivered through participation plans or pooling cooperatives is not priced when delivered; rather, the price ultimately paid for these oranges is tied to the processors' end product realizations through deferred formula pricing arrangements. Pricing in the FCOJ market will be discussed in more detail later.

Some of the oranges used by FCOJ processors are priced before conversion. Independent dealers, called "bird dogs," and buyers employed by various processors fan out among orange producers who have not yet committed their crops and make spot purchases or attempt to negotiate mutually acceptable purchase agreements. To avoid carrying a net position of their own, independent dealers generally do not consummate a purchase agreement until they have negotiated a sale of the oranges to a processor. Typically, purchase agreements follow two patterns: a buyer purchases a grower's en-

---

[3] Contract specifications are given in detail in an official exchange folder.

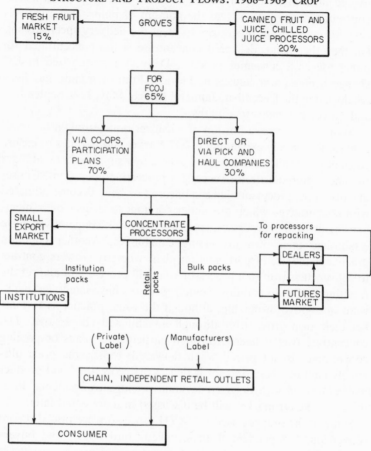

EXHIBIT IX-1. FROZEN CONCENTRATED ORANGE JUICE MARKET STRUCTURE AND PRODUCT FLOWS: 1968–1969 CROP

tire crop on the tree at a fixed price, or a fixed price per pound of orange solids delivered to the plant is arranged. In either case the buyers or independent dealers must exercise a great deal of skill in reading the market and estimating the quantity and quality of the grove fruit.

Exhibit IX-1 shows the main market entities in the FCOJ market structure and the volume flows of raw oranges for the 1968–69 orange crop. As noted in the exhibit, the information from published material and company interviews indicates that of the 65% of raw oranges bound for the FCOJ market, about 70% pass via participation plans or pooling cooperatives and are unpriced at the time of delivery and the remaining 30% are either under firm-price contracts between processors and growers, are sold at a spot price or are purchased by independent pick-and-haul brokers, including "bird-dogs." [4]

PRICING

Most retail FCOJ is sold either under a manufacturer's label such as Minute Maid or Birds Eye or under the private labels of national or local chain stores. Manufacturer's label processors strive through promotion, advertising, and quality control to market their product at premium prices. The product is sold through regional distributors or food brokers, and retailers are commonly serviced on a week-to-week basis. Private label concentrate is usually contracted for a year in advance. In a typical arrangement a retail chain will enter an agreement with a private label processor whereby the processor agrees to supply a certain annual quantity of FCOJ in monthly installments to be priced at the date of shipment. As will be shown later, the FCOJ futures market permits processors and retailers to execute either firm-priced or open-priced supply contracts. However, as of the 1968–69 season, the wholesale prices of both manufacturer's and private label concentrate were, in the majority of cases, set at or very near the date of delivery.

As mentioned earlier, about 70% of the raw oranges used for FCOJ are unpriced as they pass through the production process. The settlement prices paid to the growers of these oranges depend in a predetermined way on the prices processors receive for the processed products. Thus, instead of a situation where a price is determined by adding manufacturing costs and profits to the cost of raw materials at each successive stage in a manufacturing and

---

[4] See, for example, Goldberg, *Agribusiness Coordination,* p. 167.

marketing process, we have a situation where the price is set at the wholesale level and through a series of successive subtractions the price of the raw oranges is determined (often not finalized until the end of the marketing year).

In order to retain his raw material sources, a processor must strive to arrive at a settlement price for his raw oranges at least as good as that generated by competing processors. On the other hand, processors must offer retailers competitive pricing in order to maintain them as customers. In addition, manufacturer's label processors must try to maintain a suitable premium over the price of private label concentrate. It is through these push-pull considerations that the wholesale prices of FCOJ are determined.

In an effort to ensure fair pricing policies, an extensive price reporting system has been developed. In general, but not always, the wholesale price of private label FCOJ follows closely the "non-ad card price" of large private label processors such as Citrus Central of Florida and Lykes-Pasco Packing Co. The non-ad card price refers to one or more of the weekly price lists put out by processors who market non-advertised brands of FCOJ. This non-ad card price has emerged as a key pricing statistic in the industry. Some processors use the season's average non-ad card price as a basis for determining the settlement price to be paid for their non-priced raw orange supplies.

PRICE-RISK EXPOSURES IN THE FCOJ MARKET

Growers

The risk exposure of an owner of immature groves varies with the owner's investment, the market value of his property and the present value of the expected stream of earnings the groves will yield over several decades. The future price of oranges is a vital unknown, yet there is no mechanism within the orange market itself that such a grower can use to hedge against long-term price declines. The FCOJ futures market is not a directly useful device for such long-run protection, although the information this market makes available might be useful to him in moderating price impacts and in timing his investment decisions within a time horizon of a year or two.

The grower of a marketable orange crop has the risk of an immediate long position in the orange market long before his fruit is picked. In an effort to manage his exposure to orange price fluctuations during the orange marketing year, the producer might:

1. Contract to deliver his crop to a marketing cooperative (sometimes one which has integrated forward into processing) or directly to a processor who offers deferred formula pricing to reflect the season's average realizations for the processed product. This assures him of a market for his production; however, his dollar returns are still uncertain.

2. Sell his entire crop on the tree or enter a contract with a processor or independent dealer to deliver his crop at a firm price per pound of orange solids. Such agreements are usually executed when the crop is ready for harvesting. At that time, better estimates of crop yields can be made as well as better estimates of the industry's supply and demand variables.

3. Use the FCOJ futures market to hedge his long position in oranges by making a short sale of FCOJ futures contracts. The futures price less all the costs plus any credits that would be involved in converting his raw fruit into a deliverable state (i.e., meeting par-delivery specifications) should approximate the price per pound of orange solids which he would realize for his fruit if he has it custom processed and delivered in the futures market. It is this price which he should compare with any firm purchase offers for his fruit and with the risks and possible returns involved in holding his crop for sale at a future time. If, in view of the alternatives, the grower feels that the FCOJ futures price for the delivery month he selects reflects an attractive price for his oranges, he may consider hedging.

Although the grove owner can estimate the volume and quality of his crop prior to harvesting, if he hedges he runs the added risk that his actual volume and quality will differ from his original estimates; that is, he may turn out to be under- or over-hedged. Being over-hedged, i.e., being short on the futures market without a crop to deliver, could be financially disastrous. Such a situation may arise if a frost significantly reduces the grower's volume and quality, especially for Valencias, which will not mature until spring. Therefore, prudence dictates that a grower eying the hedging alternative should hedge no greater volume of oranges than that which he confidently expects will survive should a severe freeze develop.

The question arises as to whether a grower under contract to deliver his unpriced fruit to a cooperative or processor can sell futures contracts as a means for ensuring a satisfactory return for his oranges. By selling futures contracts against a committed crop, the grower would be under two contracts to deliver: one to the processor or cooperative, the other to the futures market. So at first glance it may appear as though the grower's risk is increased. However, the price for the delivered oranges which the grower will receive from the cooperative or processor is still uncertain; it depends either on the pool price or on the processor's deferred formula price, both of which are dependent upon or closely related to the season's average wholesale price for FCOJ. Theoretically, then, it should be possible for a grower to use the futures market to lock in an acceptable return or at least protect himself against declines in the wholesale price of FCOJ during the remainder of the pooling or processing season. Practically, the problem is to decide how to place discrete short futures sales in such a way as to offset a continuously evolving season's average price.

In one of its Hedge Guide publications, Merrill Lynch, Pierce, Fenner & Smith, Inc., presented an example of how a grower who is not a cooperative member could have successfully hedged during the 1968–69 season.[5] This example appears in Exhibit IX-2 along with a hedging example for a cooperative grower. The co-op member example suggests that at least one way for a co-op member to establish an effective hedging program is to spread the delivery months of the initial futures contract sales, and their subsequent repurchases, over a period corresponding to the period during which the, as yet unsold, FCOJ is marketed by the cooperative.

4. The grower may not choose to depart from the more traditional pattern of agricultural marketing — retaining ownership of the commodity until he is ready to deliver it, then selling it in the spot market for the best price he can get. He may move some of his crop in the fresh market and the culls to processors, or he may sell it on an unsorted basis. There are country dealers or "bird dogs" who can find a customer if he does not sell direct to processors or shippers. The grower who chooses this alternative

---

[5] "Hedge Guide to Citrus Growers," pp. 5–6.

among the several marketing methods can only be characterized as deliberately placing himself at the mercy of the harvest-time markets. He may do very well or very poorly in a particular year, but if he is a capable business manager he will at least have weighed this course of action against the other possibilities discussed above.

Processors

Although there are numerous processors in the FCOJ industry, some affiliated with a cooperative, some owned by cooperatives and some operating independently, a generalized picture of their operations can be drawn.

Typically, from 70% to 80% of a processor's raw orange supplies are not firmly priced when delivered, and from 20% to 30% are priced. On the sales side the concentrate is generally priced at or near the date of delivery. Private label concentrate is usually covered by supply contracts written in advance of the processing season which call for an overall volume of concentrate to be delivered in equal monthly shipments, priced at date of delivery. The price of manufacturer's label concentrate must be continually revised to keep margins in line with competitive constraints, and the usual practice is to issue weekly price lists. Disregarding the existence of the FCOJ futures market for the moment, the above generalized picture indicates that processors are exposed to price risks on their priced oranges; however, for their unpriced oranges they may or may not carry a price-risk exposure depending on the method they use to calculate the growers' settlement price. If this settlement price is based on the processor's realizations from selling the processed products; i.e., if the processor deducts from his revenues all costs associated with processing and marketing functions and distributes the remainder to his raw orange sources, the processor has no price risk — the grower carries this risk. If, however, the processor bases his settlement price on some sort of industry-wide pricing statistic, such as the industry's season's average non-ad card price, then there is a price risk. A processor with this type of settlement price method must ensure that his revenues at season's end are at least sufficient to pay for his raw oranges and cover all his production and marketing expenses. The risk in these

Exhibit IX-2. Grower Hedging Example and May 1969 FCOJ Futures versus "Delivered in" Prices

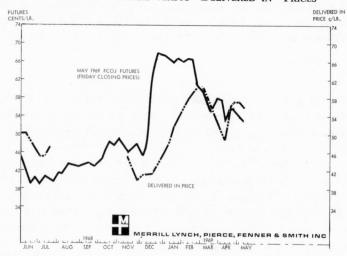

EXAMPLE OF AN INDEPENDENT GROWER HEDGING TRANSACTION – 1968/69 SEASON

Assume that you have 100 acres of round oranges and last year these trees averaged 350 boxes per acre yielding a crop of 35,000 boxes. Assume further that you averaged 6.5 pounds solids per box, or produced 227,500 pounds solids. This is equivalent to slightly more than 15 futures contracts. As a rather arbitrary rule of thumb we recommend hedging approximately one half of your potential, at least until freeze danger has passed and/or you have your oranges safely harvested. For this example then you would have sold eight contracts.

Before the freeze, the basis was not favorable, so no position would have been taken. Following the freeze price levels and basis relationship both were attractive and you sold 8 contracts on February 3 as follows:

    Sell 2 May FCOJ Futures @ 66.45
    Sell 3 July FCOJ Futures @ 66.65
    Sell 3 September FCOJ Futures @ 66.60
    Spot price for the week of February 1 was 54¢

Now let us assume you were able to sell your crop at 57¢ in the week of March 21st, catching nearly the high for the season. As soon as your crop is sold, you no longer have need for a hedge so you would have bought back (offset) your futures contracts. In this example, futures had declined (the basis narrowed) and your transaction was as follows:

    March 21   Buy 2 May FCOJ Futures @ 55.70
                    Buy 3 July FCOJ Futures @ 55.00
                    Buy 3 September FCOJ Futures @ 54.80

Exhibit IX-2. (continued)

If you had not hedged you would have received $129,675.00 for your crop – that is, 57¢ for 227,500 pounds solids.

If you had hedged you would have received $143,452, that is, 57¢ for 227,500 pounds solids plus a futures gain of $13,777. Note this important point – even though the cash market went higher after you hedged (from 54 to 57¢) you still would have made a significant net gain by hedging because of the favorable basis move

HEDGING EXAMPLE OF A CO-OP MEMBER

What if your fruit is placed in a pool and you don't know how much your return will be? We would make the same recommendation. That is, sell 2 May contracts, 3 July and 3 September on or about February 3rd.

	SOLD
February 3	2 May FCOJ Futures @ 66.45
	3 July FCOJ Futures @ 66.65
	3 September FCOJ Futures @ 66.60

Again, even though your cash return was unknown, (1) the futures levels assured a profit on your growing costs regardless of the eventual pool results and (2) the basis was favorable, suggesting a probable futures basis profit.

You would have offset these contracts during the summer corresponding with the approximate time period that your pool would be selling:

April 21	Buy 2 May FCOJ Futures @ 57.35
June 20	Buy 3 July FCOJ Futures @ 49.90
August 21	Buy 3 September FCOJ Futures @ 45.90

Last year many pools eventually returned around 50¢ a pound. In this example (227,500 pounds solids) if you had not hedged, you would have received $113,750.00 from the pool   If you had hedged, your crop income would have been $133,332, that is 113,750 from the pool and 19,582 from the futures gain. In this example, the grower marketing through the co-op benefited more proportionately than the (cash seller). This occurred because (1) cash returns were higher than the pool and (2) the co-op member was able to remain hedged for a longer time   Last year's particular situation may not prove to be typical, but it emphasizes the point that during certain periods of the year cooperative and participation members alike can and probably should effectively hedge. What if the unlikely happened and futures had not delined but instead had risen relative to spot? You would then have made delivery. Several co-ops have told us that, although a grower's specific FCOJ would not necessarily be available, as a member he could buy FCOJ from them at the prevailing cash market price to meet delivery requirements. This situation has not yet occurred in the market and we believe that is is not likely in the future.

SOURCE: Merrill Lynch, Pierce, Fenner & Smith, Inc., "Hedge Guide to Citrus Growers," Commodity Division, New York, undated, pp. 5–6.

cases can be eliminated by keeping realizations in line with or better than the industry average.

With the FCOJ futures market, the price risk on oranges owned or under firm-price purchase contract may be offset by selling FCOJ futures contracts at a price which covers, and thereby locks in, the processing costs. This is a traditional price protection hedge. For unpriced oranges and the concentrate they yield, there is little incentive to engage in price protection hedging because price changes will be in large part compensated by adjusting raw orange costs, and in cases where a risk is present it can be handled by proper marketing.

But beyond the transferring of price risks, the futures market can be used as a market extender enabling processors to move actual concentrate, that is, make or accept delivery. Accepting deliveries under the contract may, of course, require expenditures to alter the delivered product to meet customer specifications. In addition, the existence of the futures market permits astute processors to benefit from special situations such as market discrepancies or spreading opportunities and the execution of price-to-be-fixed contracts. These will be explained in the section devoted to company interviews.

Dealers

Up until the late 1960s there were almost no FCOJ "dealers" in the FCOJ market structure. By dealers we mean nonprocessor firms or individuals who buy, store, and sell concentrate as well as provide services such as bringing buyers and sellers together, arranging for transportation, and facilitating paperwork. This lack of dealers might be explained by the extensive use of supply contracts between growers and processors and between processors and retailers; hence most of the juice contained in oranges on the trees was earmarked for a specific "home." There was little if any "free supply" of orange concentrate. Moreover, processors often bought and sold bulk concentrate (concentrate in 50 or 55 gallon drums) among themselves; thus, most instances of local over- or under-supply could be smoothed out among the processors themselves.

The introduction of the FCOJ futures market enabled some business entities to profit by trading in FCOJ as a cash commodity. For instance, the spreads between future delivery contracts may permit one to take delivery of bulk concentrate and earn substantial profits by storing it for delivery against a later contract. Or a dealer might purchase bulk concentrate outright from a processor and simultaneously sell futures contracts at a price which would cover storage and a substantial profit. He could then either deliver the concentrate on the futures market or sell it outright, whichever would be most profitable. The risk in this type of operation can be closely controlled since commitments always can be paired. (This is the same as the "cash and carry" business in cocoa or the "hedging to earn storage" in grains and other products.)

Since the presence of FCOJ dealers is a recent development, their impact on the market has not yet been determined. Theoretically, any premiums of distant futures over nearby delivery month contracts should not exceed a ceiling based on the carrying charges involved in storing the commodity from a near month to a more distant month. In the past, FCOJ futures prices have reflected premiums over and above carrying charges; hence, some dealers have realized handsome profits. As more businesses assume the role of dealers, the effect should be to reduce the premiums to approximate carrying charges and thus make the FCOJ futures market more closely reflect the actual supply and demand variables in the industry.

Retailers

FCOJ is most commonly sold at retail in 6 or 12 ounce containers. Some FCOJ is reconstituted and sold single strength in cartons or bottles and some ends up as a beverage base for a variety of products. For manufacturer's label products (Minute Maid, Birds Eye, etc.), procurement is not much of a problem for the retailer as most of the initiative in getting these products placed in retail outlets rests with the manufacturer's sales representatives, and the markup is more or less automatic, without quarrel over what the level of price should be. For private label products, however, the burden is on the retailer to reach back and acquire the quality he needs at the best price. This latter procurement problem may be handled in two ways.

1. Retailers may execute contracts with processors whereby the processor provides the product under the retailer's private label in approximately equal monthly shipments to be priced at the date of shipment. This is the most widely used method. As pointed out earlier, the competitive pricing practices in the industry virtually assure the retailer that he will pay no more for his concentrate

than the bulk of his competition. Also, the price risks involved in owning inventories of FCOJ are limited, since it is industry practice to guarantee his floor stock against price decline for the stocks ordinarily on hand or in transit, ranging from 7 days' supply in Florida to 30 days' on the West Coast.

2. He may pin down the procurement cost for his concentrate prior to taking ownership. This might be accomplished by buying raw oranges or bulk FCOJ and having them converted into his desired consumer item. He might do the conversion himself or have it done on a toll basis. This method is somewhat riskier than method number 1 above, because if a retailer locks himself into a firm-price deal, he may end up paying more for his concentrate than his competitors. Of course, he hopes to end up paying less, which is the main incentive behind this method.

The FCOJ futures market offers retailers additional flexibility in using procurement method 2 by permitting them to fix the price of bulk concentrate well in advance whenever they feel the futures prices are low enough to warrant such action. The retailers may either take a long position themselves or they may arrange for their toll processor to take the position.

Normally, retailers do not hedge inventories of FCOJ since the practice in this industry, as is common in other industries as well, is to keep retail prices reasonably stable — a practice, however, which lessens the degree of parallelism between retail and futures prices. At times the futures prices may be sufficiently high to discourage retailers from ordering concentrate at costs in line with the current quotations for futures. In such a case, retailers may defer purchases in the hope that the prices will decline to more attractive levels or they may make a firm-price purchase commitment from a supplier and simultaneously hedge this commitment by selling futures. This hedge would very likely be entered in order to assure a dependable supply without locking in a cost level that is judged to be temporarily too high. In effect, the operation is the same as that of the simple hedge to protect against inventory price risks, but the purpose in this case is to shorten the exposure because of the belief that wholesale prices (and perhaps retail also) are going to decline.

Users of the Futures Market

The following presents the results of interviews with managers in the FCOJ market.

Processors

Lykes-Pasco Packing Company. Lykes-Pasco is the world's largest concentrate processor. The firm owns orange groves and is affiliated with a grower cooperative from which it receives its own as well as other growers' fruit. About 65% of its requirements are met in this way. About 20% of its requirements are obtained by supply contracts with individual growers. A total then of 85% of the company's raw material needs are secured on a formula-price basis which includes the company's own end-product realizations in the formula. The remaining 15% is typically procured by entering firm-price purchase contracts. The extent to which firm-price contracts are employed depends, of course, on whether mutually acceptable prices can be agreed to.

Lykes-Pasco sells private label concentrate and canned single-strength juice to large retail outlets and also has a substantial institutional business. Through institutional distributors, the firm sells concentrate as well as concentrate dispensers to restaurants, fast-food chains, and the like. Since the price the firm receives for its orange products determines the price it pays for about 85% of its raw orange supplies, Lykes-Pasco has a comparatively small price risk exposure. The company does not use the FCOJ futures market as it feels that it can manage the exposure it retains by other means.

H. P. Hood & Sons, Inc. Another large orange processor is H. P. Hood, long a major dairy firm and food processor in New England, and more recently active in the Florida orange business. Like Pasco, Hood markets orange concentrate under supply contracts whereby Hood processes and packages orange concentrate for large retailers and institutional customers; it also uses some for its own retail distribution. In addition, Hood does a substantial business in single-strength, chilled orange juice. Hood markets its single-strength juice under its own brand name in the New England area and also sells single-strength juice to distributors in other parts of the country. Like Pasco, Hood owns orange groves and secures most of its oranges on a supply contract basis. The remaining requirements (about 10% or 20%) are obtained at a fixed price. Unlike Pasco, however, Hood does use the futures market.

Hood has no written company policies outlining the company's permissible uses of the futures market. Two men are involved in the futures market decision processes — the manager of Hood's citrus operations in Florida and an executive vice president at the company's headquarters in Charlestown, Massachusetts. The top officers of the company together with outside consultants have engaged in numerous studies regarding the use of futures by their firm.

Hood uses the FCOJ futures market in several ways. The contract delivery specifications are such that Hood can, if prices are attractive, use the futures market as a source or an outlet for actual FCOJ. In addition, the futures market offers opportunities to hedge long ownership or firm trade commitments for oranges, to lock in a processing margin and some profit, and sometimes to receive storage margins on concentrate stocks that might otherwise have been costly to carry. Hood also can go beyond specifically matched commitments on occasion when futures contract prices offer profit opportunities which the company believes it can take advantage of without experiencing any more than "the normal businessman's risk."

One of the distinct advantages of the futures market is the flexibility it offers. For example, Hood might feel that a certain month's futures price is sufficiently high to warrant the taking of a short position at which the company could profitably deliver some of its FCOJ on the Exchange. Then later, depending on interim events, it might become even more profitable to sell cash FCOJ and lift the short position. Another alternative is simply to lift the short position and retain the actuals unhedged until sold at a still later date.

Hood's use of the futures market is tied in primarily with the FCOJ part of its business. During the orange production season, Hood builds an inventory of frozen, single-strength juice which it markets during the summer and early fall. The company feels that single-strength juice affords them a promotional advantage over reconstituted FCOJ and consequently a somewhat wider retail price policy discretion. The firm is nevertheless investigating the special implications of hedging single-strength juice inventory in the FCOJ futures market.

Citrus World. Citrus World is a federated cooperative which, through its 10 members, handles fruit from about 1,200 growers. Citrus World is integrated into processing and processes a variety of orange products (chilled juice, canned juice, salad sections) as well as FCOJ. The processing arm produces a manufacturer's label product, Donald Duck, for which it charges a premium. It also produces, under supply contracts, private label juice for grocery chains. The processing facility receives most of its raw fruit from cooperative members and pays for this fruit on the basis of its year-end realizations from all products sold. All operating and processing costs are deducted from this total realization and the remainder is distributed to the contributing members. In addition to fruit from members, the processing facility also purchases some fruit outright.

The management of Citrus World has explicit guidelines covering the permitted use of the futures market. There are four such uses:

1. Futures contracts can be sold against purchased fruit (as distinct from the unpriced fruit delivered by members) provided the futures prices permit processing costs to be locked in. Unpriced fruit is excluded from this policy because Citrus World acts essentially as a toll processor for members' fruit.
2. The futures market can be used as a source of bulk FCOJ.
3. The futures market can be used as an outlet for bulk FCOJ.
4. The futures market can be used to earn profits in an inverted market. When a premium of near months futures over more distant months exists, Citrus World may enter a spreading operation, selling near month futures and purchasing those of a distant month. Concentrate could then be delivered on the short position and the inventory reimbursed by accepting later delivery on the long position, or the spread could be canceled by reversing the positions.

308   *Major Commodity Complexes*

Coca-Cola Company Foods Division (*Minute Maid*) *and Kraftco Corporation.* Coca-Cola and Kraftco responded to our inquiry that they have limited their use of the FCOJ futures market to the procurement function. The policy of both firms is to purchase futures contracts with the intention of accepting delivery; they do not use the futures market for trading, hedging, or speculation. Both of these firms sell finished consumer products under their own brands and develop their own pricing policies. This may partially explain their particular policies. In addition, Coca-Cola uses the Lifo method of inventory valuation for certain major citrus concentrate products which, in effect, insulates the Lifo base from price change impacts at fiscal closing dates.

Retail Chains

Most retailers make little or no use of commodity futures. However, a few of the larger retail food chains (and their affiliated processing units) have developed futures trading policies for a variety of commodities, including in some cases coffee, pork bellies, sugar, cocoa, soybeans, wheat, corn, eggs, and FCOJ. These policies basically stem from viewing the commodity exchanges as alternative procurement markets, primarily for cost-determination purposes.

The Kroger Company. For instance, the Kroger Company, which is one of the largest chains, procures some of its FCOJ supplies for private label sales by means of direct supply contracts with processors, Kroger having no canning facilities of its own. If considered economically advantageous, the firm will also obtain concentrate on a firm price basis by either purchasing oranges or bulk concentrate and contracting for the necessary conversion processes. The futures market offers a means for pinning down the cost of bulk concentrate by taking a long position in FCOJ futures and either accepting delivery or using the long position to protect against adverse price impacts while shopping the cash market for a suitable supply of bulk concentrate. In addition, if raw oranges are purchased and custom processed, the futures market can be used to short-hedge the raw oranges and perhaps lock in the processing margin and some profit.

First National Stores, Inc. First National in New England is another example of a large retail food chain and processor which uses various futures markets as an aid in procurement. In the FCOJ market the firm typically enters formula-priced supply contracts with processors for about 80% of its concentrate requirements and prefers to remain flexible in securing the remaining 20%. The formula price is usually based on the "non-ad card price" on date of shipment. One of the alternatives open for procuring the remaining 20% is negotiating firm-price forward contracts with processors. In such a deal, both First National and the processing party watch the quotations in futures as a primary factor in arriving at a price. A firm price is negotiated with the understanding that the processing party may fix the cost of bulk concentrate by taking a long position in the FCOJ futures market. At the time of this survey First National did not buy and sell FCOJ futures for its own account. However, the existence of the FCOJ futures market indirectly provided a firm-price procurement alternative.

SUMMARY

The FCOJ market is not affected by many of the complexities common to other commodities. The production and processing of raw oranges takes place mainly in Florida and the market for domestically produced FCOJ has so far been almost entirely confined to the United States. In addition, unlike other commodities such as cocoa and wheat, FCOJ is not differentiated into a variety of deliverable grades which many processors may not be able to use effectively. The simplicity of the FCOJ market structure limits the variety of opportunities for making basis profits relative to commodities such as cocoa and wheat where the wide assortment of grades and especially the geographical dispersion of both producing areas and processing facilities provide ample opportunities for basis trading. Working[6] has suggested that the opportunity to make basis profits is a primary motivation behind the use of futures contracts as hedging devices.

It is significant to note that Lykes-Pasco, one of the largest concentrate processors, does not use the futures market at all, and Minute Maid, also one of the largest processors, uses the market only as an extra source of concentrate. The fact that large processors typically make little use of the orange juice futures market is reflected in Exhibits IX-3 and IX-4 which show that the total open interest on the futures market is small relative to stocks of actual FCOJ. All large traders[7] usually account for less than one-half of the open interest on either the long or short side.

A major reason why processors have not been larger users of the FCOJ futures market must surely stem from the fact that the cost of most of their raw oranges is geared by formula to either their own pricing or the season's average prices charged by private label processors. Essentially, processors have been able to coordinate their buying prices with their selling prices, generally on a season's average basis — a practice which antedated the establishment of a futures market. Since carry-over stocks are usually modest, the price risk in inventory ownership is not great despite the variations in price. Minute Maid, in fact, uses the Lifo method of inventory valuation to handle this factor.

Two additional considerations help to explain the limited degree to which orange concentrate processors use the futures market. One is the fact that, at least up to the present time, the open interest has been relatively small and large processors do not want to run the risk of making the market. Second, the FCOJ futures market is new. This condition, while temporary, compounds a

---

[6] Working, "Futures Trading and Hedging."

[7] The CEA classifies a trader as large if he holds more than 24 contracts in any one delivery month. A large trader is required to report all futures market positions and classify them as to whether they are speculations or hedges. The entire holdings of a trader who has no cash market commitments are, of course, speculative, but the futures contracts of a commercial operator which are not offset by a cash commitment (including certain anticipated production or requirement estimates) are also in the speculative category. See Appendix A.

EXHIBIT IX-3. FROZEN CONCENTRATED ORANGE JUICE —
SUPPLY AND OPEN FUTURES INTEREST,
DECEMBER 1, 1969 AND JULY 1, 1970

(Millions of lbs. of solids[1])

	Dec. 1, 1969	July 1, 1970
Supply:		
Reported stocks	107	352
Estimated production		
(65% of 140 mil. box crop[2])	519	—
Total supply	626	352
Open Interest		
Large traders position		
Speculative and spreads		
long	2.5	3.4
short	5.7	9.0
Hedges		
long	5.7	4.2
short	19.3	9.1
Small traders position		
long	44.0	27.0
short	27.1	16.5
Total:		
long	52	35
short	52	35

[1] Converted at 5.7 lbs. solids per box; .45 lbs. solids per lb. of stocks reported; 15,000 lbs. solids per futures contract.

[2] USDA crop forecast = 140 mil. boxes. Average to FCOJ = 65% of crop.
SOURCE: Based on USDA figures.

problem which has been noted throughout this study of business uses of commodity futures markets, namely, the problem of educating managers as to the benefits and drawbacks of using futures contracts.

It is clear that the major consequences of price swings in the FCOJ market are borne by the grove owners. Still, evidence indicates that few grove owners use the FCOJ futures market systematically to hedge their long commitment in oranges. Exhibits IX-3 and IX-4 show the open interest as of December 1, 1969,

EXHIBIT IX-4. FROZEN CONCENTRATED ORANGE JUICE —
SUPPLY AND OPEN FUTURES INTEREST,
DECEMBER 1, 1969 AND JULY 1, 1970

(All figures expressed as millions of lbs. of solids)

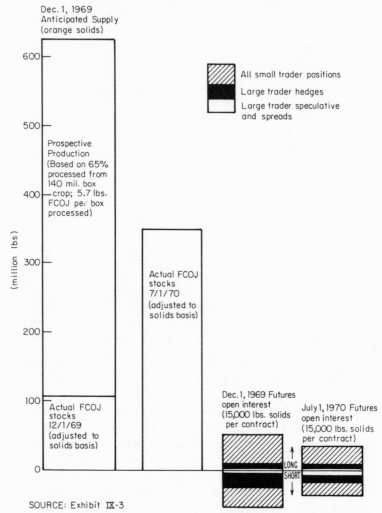

SOURCE: Exhibit IX-3

compared to the potential supply of orange concentrate implied by a harvest of 140 million boxes of oranges (a harvest predicted for the 1969–70 season). Since the short open interest is partly speculative and another part is short hedges against commitments or ownership in actual FCOJ, the amount of "hedging" against raw oranges by growers is extremely small. We have no concrete evidence as to why grove owners, who bear the lion's share of the risk, do not find the FCOJ futures market a helpful risk management tool. Perhaps it is another evidence of the traditional optimism of the agricultural producer.[8] However, several other reasons appear plausible.

1. Due to the tremendous growth of the FCOJ market, growers in Florida have, on the whole, been quite prosperous. This is in spite of volatile prices and chronic threats of glutted markets. A large processor commented that on the two occasions in the past decade when a surplus of FCOJ was anticipated, a freeze in the following season turned the potential surplus situation into a seller's market. Thus, an exposed long position in oranges has not historically been a boom or bust venture; it has been more of a boom or break-even proposition.

2. Crop damaging freezes are always a threat in the winter months and all growers face the inescapable risk that they may suffer an economic loss due to freeze damage. If a damaging freeze does occur, however, those growers who escape relatively unscathed can realize rather spectacular returns. Hence, some growers may desire to remain unhedged, thereby remaining able to fully benefit from any market booms, while those who lose much of their crop would suffer a double loss if they had to finance a short futures position without being able to deliver higher priced fruit to compensate.

3. For the grower, the common practice of belonging to a cooperative or having a sale contract for his oranges with built-in adjustments against wide seasonal price swings may well provide a better course to follow in confronting the risk of freeze damage. Beyond the sales contract and season's average pooling by cooperatives, there have been even more direct attacks upon the freeze problem (which is really a yield risk, not a price risk). This is the program for

---

[8] See, for example, articles by Haverkamp and Foote referenced in the Bibliography.

crop insurance being undertaken or considered by various groups and agencies — a matter which was not examined in detail in the present study.

The grower carries large price risks in the orange industry. He has dealt with these risks by use of a variety of stabilizing, averaging, and pooling devices. The probability is that growers will continue to be keenly interested in FCOJ futures and many of them will involve themselves in futures trading. FCOJ is a market with which growers are intimately associated, but the complexities of relationships and factors that affect them as growers defy any simple classification into the usual categories of hedging operations. The grower does have in FCOJ futures an extension of his market, and some of his use of this market may well take the form of conscious matching of offsetting risks. However, the typical grower in this industry who trades in futures can probably be best described as an "informed speculator" who also has a business risk in the cash market to judge and manage, not a risk that lends itself readily to paired transactions, zero net positions, or other conventional hedging patterns.

PART FOUR

Conclusions and Policy Applications

CHAPTER X

Futures Markets as a Tool in Corporate Strategy

WITH the wide diversity of situations and practices, of terminology and objectives, what are the common threads of rationale and the most useful rules of classification for discovering the patterns that give commodity futures their claim to serving as a vital management tool in so many industries? In the conceptual and theoretical approach of the first two chapters we have moved from the analysis of the basic economic problems of commodity price risks to the careful examination of the nature of commodity futures contracts and their relationships to cash markets. Chapter III turned to the individual firm with a discussion of industry information needs and functions in which futures operations are involved. Chapter IV considered the risks associated with price changes and various methods of dealing with them within the specialized business functions they affect. It became clear that commodity futures offer important and effective tools for dealing with price-change problems, but they are by no means the only tools available. Thus, the problem is one of defining the problems of price changes in terms of the major commercial functions and arriving at the most effective management policy mix to employ.

The ideas and concepts of the first four chapters provided a backdrop for examining the diverse experience and practices of individual firms in five major commodity complexes. Both differences and similarities abound. The purpose of the present chapter is to seek out the clues and guidelines that managements have employed or can respond to as they face risks and opportunities that beset those volatile-price industries which have access to futures markets.

IDEAS ABOUT THE ECONOMIC VALUE OF FUTURES

Economists have studied commodity futures from many points of view. Sometimes the questions they have asked are directly related to business applications, sometimes not. A good example of the broader economic questions explored by economists appears in Tomek and Gray's recent article.[1] They discuss four major questions:

1. Do futures markets help stabilize prices, or do they make them more volatile?
2. Do futures serve to improve the allocation of resources, especially by providing incentives to store commodities against later needs (or vice versa)?
3. Are futures markets a suitable instrument to be used for the implementation of public policy objectives? [2]
4. Do futures prices provide a useful forecast of later cash prices?

Most of the studies of these questions have taken the form of statistical analyses to test whether price behavior does in fact support certain hypotheses along these lines. In each instance the findings have tended on balance to support the affirmative answer to the questions as stated, but almost always with serious doubts as to the adequacy of the data and the validity of the conclusions beyond the few specific cases being analyzed. It is not our purpose here to review the economic findings and conclusions, except to point out that the studies are useful but fragmentary and that there are still many points on which economists have varied opinions. For the present study, it is important to note that the statistical tests have practically always had to rely upon statistical data and

[1] Tomek and Gray, "Temporal Relationships Among Prices on Commodity Futures Markets: Their Allocative and Stabilizing Roles."

[2] In this connection the authors refer especially to Houthakker's proposal for using futures in lieu of price support acquisitions in government price support programs. See Houthakker, "Economic Policy for the Farm Sector."

simplifying assumptions that obscure some of the important action-able requirements of a commercial business, especially as respects the cash market aspects. The businessman needs to deal with specific lots and locations, not just general averages.

Another group of statistical-economic analysts have sought to provide improved guidelines for the speculator. Some of these have employed regression or correlation analyses based on internal futures market statistics such as price movements, trading volumes, rate of change, spreads between markets, or delivery months. Others have employed published economic data using any element suspected of having supply or demand significance. The two groups are sometimes characterized as "chartists," on the one hand, and "fundamentalists," on the other. They include a good many commodity specialists or consultants who in the aggregate provide a kind of information system that gives added breadth (besides the mere trading volume itself) to the market.

A third group of questions that have given rise to economic and statistical studies of the market have been those related to regulation. The CEA has the job of seeing that the markets it regulates operate in the public interest.[3] It has made studies of trading behavior, of evidences of manipulation, of the conduct and impact of floor traders and day traders, of individual large speculative positions, and the like.[4] These are in addition to the regular assembling and reporting of market information.

In addition to the several categories of economic questions referred to above, there have been a number of studies related to business and commercial uses of commodity futures. Those which have been published have tended to be analyses relating to such things as carrying charges, cash-futures price relationships, or tests of the effectiveness of futures for risk-shifting or insurance. Many of the findings are of interest and importance to the commercial business manager; but again, they do not go all the way — they are not as exacting or as complete as the decision information required in actual hedging practice.

This is not a surprising situation. The problems of each business

---

[3] See Commodity Exchange Act, Sec. 3.
[4] See Bibliography for various CEA reports.

are unique in many respects. Intrafirm data are not generally available in published form. Moreover, the "insider" studies made by business firms are usually focused on a particular problem of the moment, a single business decision rather than a broad economic issue. Hence, it is important to recognize that the use of commodity futures as a business management tool has necessarily taken us into areas not generally covered in the available literature. What the present study has attempted has been to look at the mountain from the other side, approaching it from the viewpoint of the manager running a commercial business for whom the impacts of price changes present both problems and opportunities.

COMPARISON BETWEEN THE INDUSTRIES STUDIED AND STAGES OF THE INDUSTRIAL PROCESS

The structure of the pricing system varies from industry to industry, from one place to another, and from one stage of the industrial process to another. Among the commodity complexes selected for special attention in the present study, the one comprised of businesses using the Frozen Concentrated Orange Juice futures has a more closely articulated pricing structure[5] than the others. Here the basic element, soluble orange solids, is a common denominator, either explicitly or tacitly understood, that pervades nearly all the trading considerations from the grove owner down to the retailer. Product values, from oranges on the tree to cases of 6-ounce retail cans of frozen concentrate, are readily expressed in these units by people in the trade up and down the line. Moreover, the price of frozen concentrate, expressed in cents per pound of orange solids, has become the industry benchmark quotation in the cash market as well as in the futures.

The results of this common denominator for pricing purposes are reinforced by a number of industry practices, such as that of

---

[5] This reflects the fact that firms at all stages take explicit account in their pricing (from the beginning to the end of the product flow line) of a single common denominator (the "non-ad card price") in actual trading. In the wheat complex the pricing becomes less closely articulated at the baking or prepared mix stages.

formula pricing of raw oranges or paying the producer a return on his oranges based on the season's average realizations for the processed product. The study found businessmen taking advantage of the opportunity to use the futures market to pin down raw material costs and realization prices in anticipation of later cash transactions. Product availability could be assured ahead of time without accumulating physical inventories long before they would be needed for processing or shipment. The built-in arrangements for coordinated behavior of prices are both a cause and a result of the flexibility in the timing of commitments made possible by the existence of a futures market.

Of late there have been evidences of traders making use of the FCOJ futures market to earn storage costs. This practice has long been common in grain and some other markets when futures are at a sufficient premium compared with spot prices. This phenomenon when it occurs directs available supplies away from immediate consumption and into storage. When the premium is not sufficient to make storage profitable, the holder of cash product looks to his current marketing opportunities. Indeed, he may sell some of his current inventory holdings and buy futures to provide for his later needs. In this way the interrelationships of prices, supplies, and product-flows over time, as well as the vertical (i.e., stage-to-stage) price relationships, tend to be more orderly than they would be without the futures market.

Orange juice is picked out as an example of a highly coordinated price system in which the utilization of the futures market has, for some in the industry, become an important component. This is true in spite of the newness of the FCOJ futures market. It is reasonable to expect that more refined and sophisticated practices will continue to develop as more industry members become users.

One thing should be made clear; the factors that make orange juice prices fluctuate will still be present, whether these factors reflect supply elements, like freeze damage, or demand changes, like changing tastes or competing items. What is clear is that the industry does have the institutional arrangements in its pricing methods, and trading alternatives open to managers in both cash and futures markets, to enable each manager to manage his inventories and exposures to price impacts without having his hands tied.

Management skills become a relatively bigger factor in the handling of price impacts, and good luck a smaller one. And, if industries like wheat and flour milling are a guide, we can expect to see continuing changes in the next few years in the direction of making the FCOJ futures market an intimate working tool in the day-to-day commercial activities of more and more firms.

The cattle and beef industry offers important contrasts with the orange juice industry so far as industry pricing structures are concerned. The live and fresh products are perishable. The factors affecting spot prices may be almost independent of factors that will apply in the future; there is not the storability alternative to hold over today's abundance to meet a later shortage. There is no simple common unit for expressing prices of a breeding cow and a rib roast in comparable terms as is possible with orange solids. Once an animal is ready for slaughter, it is converted and marketed very rapidly, with very brief inventory holding.

What this situation has meant is that a much looser pricing structure exists both in terms of price parallelism between most of the major stages of the industry and in terms of orderly progressions of futures price from one delivery month to the next. The result is that except for the specialized feedlot operation, the user of Live Beef Cattle futures has to deal with only a rough kind of price correspondence between today's cash price of the products he expects to sell at a later date and the specifications being quoted in the futures market. The cattle feeder, to be sure, can and does make careful calculations and chooses between alternative courses of action in which the futures market figures prominently. Most other commercial users of Live Cattle futures have to be content with rough approximations and forecasts. It is extremely hard to see their actions in terms of matching offsetting commitments or of pinning down the price that will be realized in a later cash sale.

On the other hand, a retailer may use long futures contracts to pin down an attractive net cost for his carcass beef to be bought later and thus be protected against higher cash markets which he anticipates. If the cash market goes down instead of up, however, there is little escape from serious losses, because competitive retail markets will be closely geared to replacement costs, regardless of what the meat actually costs him (including the loss on the futures trade). The retailer whose predetermined costs are too high can be in trouble, just as he can reap a profit when they are low relative to competitors. This means that the futures do offer the retailer an option, not previously available, to use procurement judgment when he thinks futures prices will enable him to make a good buy compared with what his competitors will be paying for meat at a later date.

The contrast between orange juice and live cattle illustrates the wide range of difference that can exist from one market structure to another, both of them making effective use of commodity futures as a part of their pricing system. The other commodities given special attention in this study appear to present market structures that fall somewhere between the extremes.

The oldest, best established and most sophisticated futures operations no doubt exist in the grain and milling industries. The wheat futures markets are played like a symphony by some of the skilled operators and dealers. It is in these industries (plus soybeans) that true inventory hedging and zero net positions have come to be almost a way of life for many major businesses. The futures are a particularly keen-edged tool for firms in those stages reaching from the grain elevator through the flour mill. It is highly applicable at the farm level but direct futures trading has not been broadly employed by farmers, except in an intermittent or speculative sense. (Farmers do benefit from having a ready "to-arrive" market, which is made possible by the ability of buyers to hedge their commitments.) Beyond the flour miller, the further processors — bakers, manufacturers of cereals and prepared mixes are interested in wheat futures primarily in those cases where futures are used as a procurement, not strictly an inventory hedging, tool.

Soybeans stand out because of the existence of three futures markets instead of one. This opens up many more alternative uses and possibilities for using futures than exist in other industries and the industry has been quick to take advantage. The use of futures is practically universal. Among the managers interviewed there were some who maintained that the availability of futures had served to narrow operating margins much more than would have been the case without futures; indeed, a crusher, it was felt, would have a very hard time surviving if he did not learn to use the futures. Be this as it may, it was nevertheless clear from the relatively small sample of interviews that hedging practices and policies in this industry are much more diverse than in grain handling and flour milling.

The inclusion of cocoa in this study was in response to the desire to include an international commodity not produced in the United States, and a market not under Commodity Exchange Authority regulation. It was found that the time factor in the handling and dealing in cocoa beans and their products was often more critical than in other commodities included, but the nature of the basic factors was quite similar, and the methods of developing and carrying out policies and operating programs were in many ways alike. Perhaps the most striking differences had to do with the effects of dealing with less dependable or less adequate information, and of coping with added variable factors such as shipping, foreign exchange, and government marketing boards. These may account for the apparent volatility of the market. Nonetheless, there is a closely knit pricing structure in cocoa beans and their primary products extending from countries of origin through importers, handlers, grinders and many of the primary processors.

The cocoa producer in Africa is not much involved with the futures market; his price risks are mostly in the hands of the national marketing boards or similar agencies. At the later stages of processing, the futures are, as in the other cases examined, largely an instrument tied in with the procurement function, involving more long positions than short.

Aspects of Futures Trading Policies as Related to Business Functions

The ingredients of a systematic approach to business problems in which commodity futures can be a useful tool have required a scrutinizing look at business organization and practices that range all the way from top policy decisions to bookkeeping and tax returns.

The business manager whose activities deal with tradable commodities has in the futures market an instrument which extends, in several directions, his possibilities for managing problems related to prices and pricing. He has access to a market with more participants than the cash market alone, many of whom are eager to trade at any moment. He has an added market channel through which goods may be procured and delivered. He has a market in which the price change impacts for a carefully specified product selection can be either taken on or shifted over to others through futures contract commitments and then liquidated or resumed at will by reversing the futures contract position. He has an on-going bellwether market where competitive prices are reliably recorded and reported.

These attributes open many doors. They make it possible to engage in transactions which might otherwise have entailed unacceptable risks. They permit planning with important variables under control instead of open to unpredictable hazards. They enable the businessman to "splice in" a futures market commitment to fill in a critical gap between a purchase and sale in the cash market which could not have been matched up by simultaneous trades, either because of the time requirements for transport, conversion, and physical product handling or because of the time preferences of his suppliers or his customers. With confidence in the viability of the futures market and the prices it generates, the businessman can enter cash commitments containing a formula price contingent upon futures quotations at a later date.

No single recipe seems to apply in any phase of the problems that have been discussed. However, the following series of propositions should serve to direct the attention of a business manager to most of the critical areas that must be considered in deciding the purposes and methods most suitable for his particular situation.

(a) *Earnings motives must be recognized as the underlying guideline in decisions regarding the business use of commodity futures.*

Each function performed and each commitment undertaken must ultimately come under the criterion of contribution to earnings. Sometimes this contribution is affirmative in that it contributes to lower costs or higher realizations. At other times the contribution may be the avoidance of an uncertainty which the future enables the management to transfer to others without interrupting the carrying out of its primary commercial functions.

Planning in a firm usually means planning with earnings as a target. Planning is enhanced when the devices available include arrangements which can either pin down the price involved in a forward commitment on the one hand or leave it flexible if, in other situations, such a course is desired.

To paraphrase an old cliche, it may be said that earnings may result from buying low and selling high but the chance of accomplishing this may be considerably increased if the manager has markets where he can also buy early and sell late or vice versa.

The important distinction between most of the speculative problems relating to futures markets alone and those that involve the commercial trade as well is that the latter has to recognize futures as an adjunct to the attainment of profits from commercial operations, not as an end in themselves.

(b) *Business functions provide a handle for defining and classifying commercial requirements in which futures contracts can serve a useful purpose.*

The functions affected can be classified as procurement, processing, marketing, and custody. The performance of these functions entails commitments of ownership, contracts to buy or sell, or similar obligations which result in exposure to price-change impacts.

The manner in which these functions interact with each other, and the degree to which price changes for the particular commodity in question affects these functions, enables one to classify the ways in which futures contracts are most likely to be useful. The degree of price parallelism between a firm's raw material and its finished product will be a major factor in determining how many of the four key functions are likely to be involved in the use of futures.

(c) *The "net position" is a critical measure to be employed in the analysis and implementation of programs employing commodity futures.*

The concept of a net position is common to practically all users of commodity futures. It is a figure expressed in physical volume units to represent the net exposure to impacts from the changing

prices of a particular commodity. We have seen that this concept is
not so simple as it appears. Initially, one might assume that the
commodity in question can be expressed in terms of a single
quantity unit and the ownership and trade commitments, long and
short, would be simply balanced into a net exposure figure. However, in almost any commercial situation it is necessary to consider
many conversion factors, interpolations, and judgments before the
net position is arrived at. In addition to the clear ownership titles
and the fixed price contracts that make up this computation it is
often necessary to take into account implicit commitments which
take the form of anticipations, plans, special guarantees, and risk-
sharing arrangements, any one of which may represent an additional
exposure.

Commodity futures need not be regarded as a device limited to
the shifting of commercial price risks to others (i.e., reducing the
net exposed position). They are widely employed in the case of the
procurement function where futures are frequently employed in a
way that increases an already long net position, often represented
by so many months' anticipated requirements.

There is no special virtue in having a zero net position (often
referred to as "fully hedged"), even though this is one of the most
important patterns of business use of commodity futures markets.
Certain operations can benefit substantially from operating with a
fully hedged position and this is particularly true in the case of
dealers and simple converters where the buying prices and selling
prices have a high degree of parallelism in the cash market. Such
firms regularly conduct business in terms of "their basis," having
shifted to others the price risks that result from fluctuations in the
futures market quotations.

Where a firm has an exposure in which major processing conversions are made in the commodity, as in farm production or in
the manufacturing or marketing of packaged consumer foods, the
net position has an entirely different significance.[6] From the viewpoint of inventories as a measure of price risks it is extremely
difficult for such a firm to pin down the meaning of a zero net

---

[6] See Exhibit I-2, p. 15.

position. It is, however, important to know the amount of tradable commodity futures that will have to be sold or bought in order to provide an approximation to the likely effect of a given price change upon the results of the business. It is in this respect that a figure corresponding to the net position becomes important. For most of the industries which experience this kind of price-change impact, a statistical substitute rather than a direct inventory count is indicated as a help in judging how much of a hedge comes closest to a fully protected position.

The concept of "net position" provides only one measure or guideline for the business manager who is administering a company's hedging program. As a trader, he needs a great deal of additional detailed information for decision-making purposes, but the net position provides a summary measure which simplifies his decisions and his targets.

(d) *The use of commodity futures as a device for transferring the risk of price changes requires that the user recognize the principle of an "analogous part."*

Since the commodity futures contract carries a precise par-delivery specification, it is most convenient to use this specification as a basic benchmark. Then, all deviations or residuals between the cash commitment and these specifications represent risks which are *not*, in fact, transferred when a futures sale is made. In some commodities, particularly the grains, soybeans, cotton and the like, the trade uses the term basis as a regular part of the language. (Other commodity traders may refer to "differentials" and some traders may even speak of these residuals as "margins".) What we are emphasizing is that the cash side of a hedge position can be expressed in two parts, an "analogous part" and a set of residuals, the analogous part being the specification which is precisely complementary to the par-delivery specification of the futures contract.

The concept of an analogous part goes far to explain why many traders maintain that there is no such thing as a "perfect hedge." There is practically always some residual,[7] which can be managed

---

[7] It should be noted that, in the statistical figure described as THE BASIS, the cash side is a commodity identical with the par-delivery specifi-

as a risk like many other commercial risks in the business, in the hope of producing a profit and providing opportunities for the attainment of excellence in competitive marketing.

The manager employing commodity futures can thus regard his task in terms of the two variables, the analogous part (on which price risks can be shifted to others through a futures hedge) and the residual. There is much more to the theory of analogous parts than the simple tautological equation — [analogous parts + residuals = net cash commitment]. This statement can be expressed in total dollars or in dollars per physical unit. In these forms the equation provides a way of measuring residual risk exposure as well as aggregate positions and the amount of hedging that is indicated at a given time.

However, the matter goes farther than this. The analogous parts not only require the manager to look specifically at that portion of his net exposure which is hedgeable in futures (namely, the counterpart of the par-delivery specification of the futures market), but by the same token they require him to design a net "at risk" calculation to include conversions, yields, and commitments in a way that will clearly establish the net cash position in appropriate physical as well as monetary units. This means that he must take cognizance of each element in the residual separately.

(e) *Firms employing commodity futures, in more instances than not, operate with a loose structure for handling hedging policies.*

Even where clear-cut policies and programs exist there is seldom a written statement of overall policies and objectives which would be applicable over a long period of time. There was wide agreement in the interviews conducted for the present study that such a statement would be desirable, and in a number of cases an effort

---

cation. Hence the "analogous part" leaves almost no differentials except the values associated with the immediate or spot availability of the cash commodity and the "housekeeping" responsibilities that go with ownership pending delivery. When buyers want cash product to make nearby deliveries, there is a premium, but when abundant supplies are "looking for a home" (e.g., during harvest) there may be a discount. See Chapter II and Glossary references.

was made to develop such a statement in response to our inquiry. A written statement seems desirable, especially in view of the fact that there were a number of instances where one executive of the company indicated a policy which differed in various details from that which another executive of the same company reported.

Even though a written overall policy statement is not common, it is clear that specific operating programs and strategies do receive very high level attention in most of the firms where commodity price fluctuations have a major influence on operating results. These programs varied in the degree to which they spelled out trading guidelines, ranging all the way from a statement of extreme position limits beyond which further executive approval was required, down to precise instructions and procedures for matching every commercial transaction with a futures trade in a particular market and delivery month.

In exploring the internal organization for handling commodity futures it also became clear that the management information systems and procedures differed widely from one firm and one industry to another. Naturally, it is necessary for the person charged with commodity futures operations to have a complete record of his transactions and his status at any given time. Sometimes this individual is concerned only with the executing of transactions in the futures market; sometimes he is an intimate party to the total cash-futures complex. Among the "basis" traders in the grain market it is obvious that a futures transaction is implicitly a part of every commitment to buy or sell the cash commodity, and the trader must therefore be thoroughly familiar with all the dimensions of the paired transactions with which he is dealing. At the other extreme the futures market may be completely divorced from cash operations and regarded simply as a device for the discretionary extending or reducing of the firm's net exposure.

Naturally, the policy, the organization, and the procedural pattern must be tailored to the needs of the individual firm. Out of the present study it became clear that three major requirements ought to be met:

1. A decision structure should reach from top policy decisions down to specific implementation. This requires both a clear delegation of

responsibility and provision for appraisal of performance as well as an arrangement for the assurance of proper controls.

2. The management information system required for the making of decisions should be designed to provide the critical factors for the decision maker as well as to enable the operator down the line to plan and carry out his detailed trading activities.

3. Accounting procedures are required which will enable management to know precisely how the operations involving commodity futures contribute to the recorded results on the official operating statement and balance sheet. Strangely enough, this was one of the very difficult kinds of information to uncover in some of the firms interviewed. This difficulty was not a matter of reluctance, but rather a result of the intricacies of accounting methods. It became apparent that there are many ways of handling futures transactions for hedging. Considerable care is necessary, especially with regard to such questions as the selection of the accounts in which commodity futures operations are posted and the leads and lags involved in recording the changing status of open contracts.[8] These are discussed further below.

(f) *Accounting procedures appear to fall into three major categories.*

In interviews conducted for the present study there was no clear guideline for selecting the accounting procedure to be applied to a

---

[8] An illustration of this type of problem was presented by Rowley in his thesis, "Inventory Pricing in the Grain Industry," p. 168, which revealed the following assortment of methods of presentation of margin deposits and purchase advances in the accounts of 10 flour millers whom he interviewed:

	Number of Companies	
Method of Presentation	Margin Deposits	Purchase Advances
Account receivable	3	2
Inventory	1	4
Separate current asset	2	2
Investment	1	0
Margin deposits and purchase advances combined	1	1
Not indicated	2	1
Total companies	10	10

particular situation.[9] However, it became apparent that different methods of handling futures operations in the corporate accounts were not only justifiable but desirable where conditions differed from one type of policy to another.

For instance, in cases where futures were used primarily as a procurement instrument it would be logical to expect that the debits and credits, particularly as they applied to open futures contracts, would be deferred until actual goods are acquired for use in the business and at that time they would be applied as an adjustment to the cost of goods purchased. A somewhat analogous treatment would be expected in the case of sales of commodity futures which had the purpose of offsetting price impacts affecting a commitment that would not for special reasons show up as a simultaneous fluctuating value in the inventory account. For instance, a cattle feedlot operator may have only his input costs to record the present status of his feedlot inventory, or a farmer may be in a similar position when he has only a growing crop in the field and no inventory item in volume terms on his books. Assuming that he has sold Live Beef Cattle futures against his prospective feedlot sales, he would be expected to defer the accrued gains or losses on the futures in order to apply them to the later realization from fed cattle.

Where the futures transaction is directly matched against an item actually held in a segregated inventory account, the most common procedure for dealers and converters is to record the hedged inventory at market and to adjust this figure for the accrued debits or credits on open hedge contracts. Here, the usual formula is to apply the results of closed contracts against the cost of goods sold and the accrued results on open contracts against the market value of inventories.

A third procedure was found in a number of cases where hedging is done on a lot-by-lot basis rather than in a situation where a fully hedged position was carried as a matter of policy. In these instances the inventory was carried at identified costs and the futures contracts covering this commitment were similarly carried in a deferred account and not entered in the operating statement until the con-

---

[9] Some of the variations in accounting procedures are seen in Appendix C.

tracts were closed. This situation applied particularly where seasonal accumulations could be identified and definite dates attached to particular holdings. The accruing debits and credits from the appropriate contracts (open or closed) could be carried in a deferred account awaiting the liquidation of the commodities involved.

A considerable number of variations turned up in respect to individual company practices since managers have had to adapt their procedures to fit their specific problems. Special handling would be required in cases where basic inventories may have been valued on the last-in, first-out method. Special arrangements were also found where commodities had been purchased on a "to-arrive" basis. In some cases the product was taken into the inventory account with the first shipment on a total purchase order; in other cases title was assumed to be transferred when the first down payment was made to the supplier. In such cases the question of how to enter inventory variances on the books can become a complicated matter. It was not the purpose of the present research to examine or appraise the detailed accounting methods employed; however, some exposure to them was inescapable. By and large it was found that the decision maker was likely to be content with his reports on net positions and specific commitments since most of the questions of accounting had at most a relatively small lead or lag effect upon book results.

DIMENSIONS OF INTERNAL PRICE-RISK MANAGEMENT PROBLEMS

The exposure of a business to the impacts of changing prices is not always easy to measure. The standard inventory-hedging examples are based on a series of assumptions that are too simple to apply in most situations. For instance, the assumptions generally include such things as:

1. A high degree of price parallelism between buying and selling prices for the firm, as well as close parallelism between the cash and the futures market.
2. Virtually no ability to control buying or selling prices apart from

the general market — no room, that is, for discretionary pricing policy.
3. A substantial degree of price volatility — enough to have a serious impact on results (of the firm as a whole or at least the profit center involved).
4. Price changes that are largely unpredictable.
5. An accounting system that will reflect price changes in inventories and trade commitments (as well as in futures) on a current market basis.

To the extent that the situation confronting a particular firm differs from these assumed conditions, a careful appraisal and adaptation are important. The assumptions above would be consistent with a situation in which the hedger could be very largely guided by a single figure — *the net position.* The most naive manager might simply "cancel" his price risk with a commensurable futures position on the opposite side, and let his commercial business go on as usual, disregarding the finer points of matching individual trades or commitments.

The much more frequent procedure for the "fully hedged" operator is to apply his skills to "basis" operations, working from a continuous zero net position. This is indeed the typical grain dealer pattern, but it is greatly modified when we move to other situations where actual net exposure involves additional modifications of the simplifying assumptions. The comments which follow cannot hope to cover the problems that will arise in any particular case, but they are designed to help in identifying and handling the adaptations that are needed by a firm undertaking to develop the program that is most appropriate for itself.

After repeated attempts to classify all the factors that enter into the formulation of hedging programs and various special uses of commodity futures contracts, the diagram shown in Exhibit X-1 was selected as more complete and more useful than others. It is still suggestive rather than comprehensive, and none of the categories depicted are exclusive air-tight compartments. As the title states, it presents "points of view," recognizing that many applications involve more than one point of view. This is inevitable in view of the diversity and the interrelatedness of the many uses of commodity futures contracts by business managers. (If the diagram is not self-explanatory, the author's only defense would be to refer the reader back to the book's earlier chapters.)

Several things emerge from the broad look which Exhibit X-1 permits. The vertical shading of the first panel suggests a degree of risk-shifting through the use of futures which becomes less complete or less clear-cut as the listings progress from top to bottom. However, this aspect should not obscure the fact that the *kinds* of risk also shift as one moves from column to column. For instance, the Net Position panel assumes a manager who wants to use futures to shift to others the risk he perceives as resulting from his exposure to changes in the general market level of prices for his commodity. This approach shades off horizontally as well as vertically, since the futures market is itself a part of a total market, offering a wide assortment of elements such as internal differentials, availability, and access. By the same token, the use of futures may open the door for assuming as well as avoiding risks, and for dealing with risks such as those arising in the procurement or marketing function where price parallelism may be very imperfect and the perceived risk may be one of expected needs or budgeted sales rather than of tangible ownership or trade commitments.

The idea that there is an intrinsic virtue in a fully hedged position requires a second look. Such a policy is a most important and often useful underlying requirement and guideline (especially where price movements are volatile and unpredictable but parallel). However, as the diagram suggests, there may be reasons for aiming at a net position other than zero. The fully hedged or zero net position would be most appropriate for the basis trader (who assumes the risk as to what will happen to "his basis") whereas a business manager with highly uncertain replacement margins but reasonably predictable price levels might take a different attitude regarding the most desirable net position to assume.[10]

The net position may become a secondary, rather than the primary, guideline in working out futures market policies in many firms where prices of tradable raw materials and finished products are not highly correlated. The accuracy of net positions may lose

---

[10] Reading between the lines in most interviews was a recurrent suggestion that taking "a view of the market" was a fairly common practice (even for strict "basis" traders) over at least brief periods of time.

EXHIBIT X-1. POINTS OF VIEW IN DEVELOPING HEDGING POLICIES

Shading from protection to exposed position ⟍ *Primary Guide or → Purpose*	*Net Position Control (Inventory risk)*[1]	*Gross Position*[2] *(Total commitment factors — "a larger market")*
	1. Fully hedged (Zero net position) Large volume "basis" operators	1. Maximize turnover without net exposure
	2. Partial hedge (Constant, not zero, net position) Examples: Exclude Lifo base; hedge only seasonal accumulation	2. Spreading and arbitrage[4]
		3. Hedge excess over Lifo base
	3. Variable hedge (Planned or budgeted net position) Examples: Head-quarters managed hedge; discretionary position within limits	4. Hedge seasonal storage
		5. Use of futures to economize cash tied up in inventories, or to shorten exposure without sacrificing current throughput
	4. Variable hedge (Deliberate variances to profit from price swings) Examples: Cyclical position taking; leaning into the wind; special position taking situation	6. Disregard business needs; straight speculation

[1] This column assumes a commercial operation in which all decisions are based on cash market considerations. The net cash positions (or portions of them) are then hedged in futures.

[2] This column assumes that added cash positions will be undertaken simply because they *can* be hedged.

[4] Includes earning of storage by holding deliverable cash product against short futures. This is sometimes referred to as "cash and carry."

EXHIBIT X-1. (CONTINUED)

Procurement Tool (*Time and cost*)	Marketing Tool (*Time and price*)	Profit Margins and Incentives[3]
1. Take delivery on futures markets to get needed goods 2. Lock in margin through low-costing raw material (to cover a sale commitment) 3. Assure repurchase of temporarily liquidated Lifo base stocks 4. Anticipate storage accumulation by purchase of new crop futures 5. Use futures to attain target exposure when actuals not available 6. Pin down attractive cost for anticipated needs 7. Reach out, speculate regardless of commercial needs	1. Deliver actuals on futures market 2. Sell futures to lock in realization on goods in inventory 3. Sell futures to assure price for anticipated production 4. Cover risks on unpriced sales, requirements contracts, or "price date of delivery" 5. Liquidate unwanted risk by selling futures when cash won't move 6. Sell futures farther ahead than actuals can be booked in the market	1. Lock in margin where actuals are bought or sold on formula price to be based on later futures quotations 2. Deal in basis (This covers a wide assortment of specialized applications) 3. Use price or margin targets to determine how much business will be done, as in deciding how much to store or process 4. Pin down other half of a cash commodity trade in futures, awaiting opportunity to fulfill with actuals 5. Buy low – sell high, wherever the opportunity presents itself – all cash, all futures, or a mix including discretionary position taking

[3] The column for profit margins and incentives relates to operations in which the primary focus is not on protection from general price swings, but on earnings from residuals and differentials (basis), or even from deliberate position taking.

reliability in cases where there are numerous input cost complications, yield and conversion factors, or anticipations regarding competition or sales prospects. In such cases it may be well to work directly with cost and realization estimates as policy guides, and use net position estimates as a checkpoint observation to obtain a separate view of where the other guidelines are leading. The farmer might be in this position with his unharvested crops, or the marketer with a sales budget in which price levels (rather than price margins) may strongly influence demand.

The final entry in Exhibit X-1 may serve to call attention to the extreme that is opposite to that of using futures for routine fully hedged inventory protection. This is stated as a brash cliche, "Buy low–sell high, wherever the opportunity presents itself — all cash, all futures, or a mix including variable position taking." The automatic undiscriminating hedge may avoid risks but may vastly underachieve profitwise, whereas the full discretionary operation with futures as a wide open tool can be playing with dynamite. Both positions are useful reference points; practical applications lie mostly in between.

APPENDIXES

APPENDIX A

Note on the Meaning of Hedging

THE WORD HEDGING is used to encompass many more types of transactions and activities than can properly be incorporated into a single concise definition. Therefore, this note will not attempt to be all inclusive, but will point out some of the attributes which are most frequently present in the kind of hedging transactions discussed in this study:

1. In a hedging transaction, the hedger is normally seeking to lessen the impact that major price fluctuations would have on his business.
2. Commodity hedging ordinarily involves offsetting an actual or intended commercial commitment by using the futures market. A futures contract corresponding to a commodity actually owned or planned to be owned is sold in the futures market; likewise, a commodity which has been sold or is planned to be sold in commerce is matched by a purchase in the futures market. Some hedges may be very simple and straightforward as in the case of an owner of wheat who is able to sell contracts relating to the same commodity in the futures market. However, there are often indirect or cross-hedges wherein the commercial risk may entail one commodity or a combination, while the hedge in the futures market takes the form of a contract relating to a somewhat different commodity or set of specifications. The primary objective is usually to secure protection from price impacts by having the commercial position offset by a futures commitment that is expected to have approximately parallel price movements.
3. In general the commercial commitment, whether owned or planned, is referred to as the item being hedged; the futures contract is the hedging instrument.

4. The Commodity Exchange Authority, for purposes of defining permissible position limits in commodity futures, undertakes to spell
   out the kinds of matching transactions that can be counted as
   valid hedges — any residual balances in the futures market being
   regarded as speculative and subject to certain maximum position
   limits.

5. The U.S. Internal Revenue Service takes a distinctly different view
   of hedging from that of the CEA. The IRS is interested in defining
   "speculative" as against "ordinary" income, and it would not
   regard income from commodity futures as "speculative" so long
   as it comes from commodities regularly dealt in by the firm. Hence,
   the IRS would lump hedging with nonmatching (i.e., "speculative")
   commodity trades as producers of ordinary income so long as the
   commodity is related to the business.

   A more detailed discussion of the IRS and CEA treatment of
   speculation and hedging is presented below.

6. The word "hedging" is a term that wears a cloak of virtue, but
   like a Mother Hubbard apron it can cover a multitude of diverse
   activities and purposes. It is a "good" word. It is a mark of conservative management. So be it. But the word "hedging" (as
   distinguished from "a hedge") has been used to characterize such
   an assortment of trading activities that in the minds of some it can
   be used to describe any futures market activity by a commercial
   firm, whether there is an explicit matching of risks or not, including what most people would call speculation (but that is a
   "bad" word, unbecoming to a "legitimate" businessman).

   The present study accepts the loose common usage of the word
   "hedging" rather than attempting to assign a precise definition to
   the term. "A hedge," however, almost invariably refers to a futures contract specifically matching a commercial exposure. Where
   the word "speculation" is used, it should convey no more stigma
   than would be implied by such words as risk or uncertainty.

CEA AND IRS POSITIONS ON SPECULATION AND HEDGING

The following excerpts from the Commodity Exchange Act and
the Internal Revenue Code of 1954 together with appropriate commentary are presented as source references particularly relevant to
these agencies' use of the terms "speculation" and "hedging."

The following excerpts are from the Commodity Exchange Act:

SEC. 4a (1) Excessive speculation in any commodity under contracts of sale of such commodity for future delivery made on or subject to the rules of contract markets causing sudden or unreasonable fluctuations or unwarranted changes in the price of such commodity, is an undue and unnecessary burden on interstate commerce in such commodity. For the purpose of diminishing, eliminating, or preventing such burden, the Commission shall, from time to time, after due notice and opportunity for hearing, by order, proclaim and fix such limits on the amount of trading which may be done or positions which may be held by any person under contracts of sale of such commodity for future delivery on or subject to the rules of any contract market as the Commission finds are necessary to diminish, eliminate, or prevent such burden. . . .

(3) No order issued under paragraph (1) of this section shall apply to transactions or positions which are shown to be bona fide hedging transactions or positions. For the purposes of determining the bona fide hedging transactions or positions of any person under this paragraph (3), they shall mean sales of, or short positions in, any commodity for future delivery on or subject to the rules of any contract market made or held by such person to the extent that such sales or short positions are offset in quantity by the ownership or purchase of the same cash commodity by the same person or, conversely, purchases of, or long positions in, any commodity for future delivery on or subject to the rules of any contract market made or held by such person to the extent that such purchases or long positions are offset by sales of the same cash commodity by the same person. There shall be included in the amount of any commodity which may be hedged by any person —

(A) the amount of such commodity such person is raising, or in good faith intends or expects to raise, within the next twelve months, on land (in the United States or its Territories) which such person owns or leases;

(B) an amount of such commodity the sale of which for future delivery would be a reasonable hedge against the products or by-products of such commodity owned or purchased by such person, or the purchase of which for future delivery would be a reasonable hedge against the sale of any product or by-product of such commodity by such person.

(C) an amount of such commodity the purchase of which for future delivery shall not exceed such person's unfilled anticipated requirements for processing or manufacturing during a specified operating period not in excess of one year: *Provided,*

That such purchase is made and liquidated in an orderly manner and in accordance with sound commercial practice in con-
formity with such regulations as the Secretary of Agriculture
may prescribe.

The Internal Revenue Code of 1954 does not explicitly define
hedging and speculation in commodity futures. Rather the Code is
concerned with whether the income or losses generated by futures
transactions are capital gains or losses or ordinary gains or losses.
Capital gains and losses result from the sale or exchange of capital
assets.

The following excerpts are from the Code.[1]

PART III — GENERAL RULES FOR DETERMINING
CAPITAL GAINS AND LOSSES

SEC. 1221. CAPITAL ASSET DEFINED

For purposes of this subtitle, the term "capital asset" means property held by the taxpayer (whether or not connected with his trade
or business), but does not include —

(1) stock in trade of the taxpayer or other property of a kind
which would properly be included in the inventory of the taxpayer
if on hand at the close of the taxable year, or property held by
the taxpayer primarily for sale to customers in the ordinary course
of his trade or business;

(2) property, used in the ordinary course of his trade or business; subject to the allowance for depreciation provided in section 167, or real property used in his trade or business;

(3) a copyright, a literary, musical, or artistic composition, a
letter or memorandum, or similar property, held by —

(A) a taxpayer whose personal efforts created such property,

(B) in the case of a letter, memorandum, or similar property,
a taxpayer for whom such property was prepared or produced, or

(C) a taxpayer in whose hands the basis of such property is
determined, for purposes of determining gain from a sale or
exchange, in whole or part by reference to the basis of such
property in the hands of a taxpayer described in subparagraph
(A) or (B);

---

[1] "U.S. Internal Revenue Code of 1954," *Standard Federal Tax Reporter,*
Code Volume, Commerce Clearing House, Inc., New York, Chicago, and
Washington, D.C., 1969.

(4) accounts or notes receivable acquired in the ordinary course of trade or business for services rendered or from the sale of property described in paragraph (1); or

(5) an obligation of the United States or any of its possessions, or of a State or Territory, or any political subdivision thereof, or of the District of Columbia, issued on or after March 1, 1941, on a discount basis and payable without interest at a fixed maturity date not exceeding one year from the date of issue.

"Property" means anything owned such as inventories, fixed assets or securities and also includes rights in these things such as options to buy property. Implied in Section 1221 is the fact that a short position in a commodity futures contract is not considered a property in the hands of the holder and therefore is not considered a capital asset in the hands of the holder. On the other hand, a long position in a commodity future is considered property and may or may not be a capital asset. Section 1221(1) indicates (and this has been affirmed by various court cases) that this property [the long futures position] is not a capital asset for the taxpayer who uses the long position as an adjunct to normal commercial dealings in the commodity. If the holding of a long position is divorced from any commercial dealings in the commodity, the long position is a capital asset.

Another pertinent section of the Code is Section 1233.

SEC. 1233. GAINS AND LOSSES FROM SHORT SALES.
[Sec. 1233(a)]

(a) CAPITAL ASSETS. — For purposes of this subtitle, gain or loss from the short sale of property shall be considered as gain or loss from the sale or exchange of a capital asset to the extent that the property, including a commodity future, used to close the short sale constitutes a capital asset in the hands of the taxpayer.

Turning to hedging, the Code mentions the word in Section 1233(g).

SEC. 1233. GAINS AND LOSSES FROM SHORT SALES.
[Sec. 1233(g)]

(g) HEDGING TRANSACTIONS. — This section shall not apply in the case of a hedging transaction in commodity futures.

This means that short sales in a hedging transaction are not given capital gain or loss treatment when they are closed. Implied is the notion that the property used to offset a short position *in a hedging transaction* is not a capital asset in the hands of the holder. The Code does not, however, define what constitutes a hedging transaction, except by its reference to "stock in trade" and "property used in the ordinary course of his trade or business" in Section 1221.

The IRS deals in Sections 1221 and 1233(a) with attributes of futures operations that are in many ways analogous to the distinctions made by CEA and others under the terms hedging and speculation. The IRS draws its line in terms of the nature of the assets involved. If these assets represent a part of the "stock in trade" or "property used in the ordinary course of business" then the income derived from futures is ordinary income. This is similar to what the trade might regard as hedging income. On the other hand, the IRS treats futures that do not tie in with the "ordinary course of business," or "stock in trade" as generating capital gains or losses, which many would identify as speculative gains or losses.

Combining both the Commodity Exchange Act's and Internal Revenue Code's statements, it seems safe to conclude that hedging as defined by the CEA would be considered hedging by the IRS. The reverse, however, does not appear to hold. For example, a cattle feeder may wish to pin the cost of feed by purchasing enough corn futures to cover his feed requirement. It seems clear from Section 1221 of the Internal Revenue Code that the long position in corn futures would be considered goods in trade and hence not a capital asset in the hands of the cattle feeder. On the other hand, the feeder's long position would not be considered a legal hedge against the cattle commitment under the Commodity Exchange Act. Thus, although any gain or loss on the feeder's position would be considered ordinary income or loss, the feeder would be subject to the speculative trading limits specified by the CEA.

The confusion, ambiguities, and contradictions outlined above are apparently inescapable under present legal interpretations. The discussion in Chapter II of "The Commodity Futures Contract and the Income It Generates" would appear to offer a somewhat more consistent and rational approach.

APPENDIX B

Contract and Trading Information

CONTRACT and trading information for wheat, corn, oats, rye, and soybeans, soybean oil, and soybean meal futures illustrates the detailed specifications which represent the actual terms of a commodity futures contract.

This material, based upon Chicago Board of Trade information, was prepared by The Association of Commodity Firms, Inc. in connection with the Commodity Futures Correspondence Course. (Copyright The Association of Commodity Exchange Firms, Inc., 1970. Reprinted with permission.)

WHEAT, CORN, OATS, RYE, AND SOYBEANS

THE MARKET
   Board of Trade of the City of Chicago.
TRADING HOURS
   9:30 A.M.–1:15 (Central Time)
   Last Day: 9:30–12 noon (See Rule 252 for details)
CONTRACT UNIT
   5,000 bushels.
ACTIVE DELIVERY MONTHS
   March, May, July, Sept., and Dec. for Wheat, Corn, Oats, and Rye. January, March, May, July, August, September and November for soybeans.
QUOTATIONS
   Telequote: Wheat, W — Oats, O — Corn, C — Rye, R — Soybeans, S —
ORDER DATA
   Regulated by CEA.

COMMISSIONS (Round Turn)	Price Change	Member	Non-Member	Member Spread	Non-Member Spread	Foreign Member	Foreign Non-Member
Wheat, Corn, Rye	(One rate	$11.00	$22.00	$15.00	$30.00	$18.75	$25.00
Soybeans	for all price	$12.00	$24.00	$15.00	$30.00	$18.75	$25.00
Oats	levels)	$ 9.00	$18.00	$15.00	$30.00	$18.75	$25.00

MINIMUM PRICE FLUCTUATION
1/8¢ per bushel, $6.25 per contract.

MAXIMUM DAILY PRICE FLUCTUATIONS
Trading is prohibited during any day in futures contracts of wheat, rye, oats, corn or soybeans, at a price higher or lower than either:
1. The closing price for such grain or provisions on the previous business day, or
2. The average of the opening range or the first trade during the first day of trading in a futures contract, or
3. The price established by the Market Report Committee in an inactive future,

PLUS or MINUS, as the case may be, the following sums with respect to such commodities:

Wheat, rye and soybeans	10 cents per bushel
Corn	8 cents per bushel
Oats	6 cents per bushel

CEA SPECULATIVE POSITION AND TRADING LIMITS
CEA regulations set forth the following requirements:

Commodity	CEA Reporting Level	Customer Spec. Position Limit (CEA Rules)	CEA Reporting Form No.			
			*	**	***	****
Wheat	200,000 bu.	2,000,000 bu.	200	201	203	204
Corn	200,000 bu.	2,000,000 bu.	200	201	203	204
Oats	200,000 bu.	2,000,000 bu.	200	201	203	204
Rye	200,000 bu.	500,000 bu.	200	201	203	204
Soybeans	200,000 bu.	2,000,000 bu.	200	201	203	204

*   Clearing Members.
**   Futures Commission Merchants.
***   Futures Commission Merchants.
**** Merchants, Processors and Dealers — Series 04 reports are filed weekly by reporting merchandisers, processors, and dealers, showing positions in the cash (spot) commodity when the futures position is reportable.

DELIVERABLE GRADES
Unless otherwise specified, contracts for the sale of wheat, corn, soybeans, oats & rye shall be deemed to call for "contract" wheat, corn, soybeans, oats and rye respectively. Upon such contracts, sellers, at their option, may deliver all or part of the following grades at the following price differentials, provided that loss of grain of any one grade must conform to the minimum lot requirements of Rule 290:

Wheat Differentials

No. 1   Soft Red
No. 1   Dark Hard Winter
No. 1   Hard Winter   at 1¢ premium
No. 1   Yellow Hard Winter
No. 1   Dark Northern Spring

(No. 1 Heavy grades at 1/2¢ additional premium)

No. 2   Soft Red
No. 2   Dark Hard Winter
No. 2   Hard Winter   at contract price
No. 2   Yellow Hard Winter
No. 2   Dark Northern Spring
No. 1   Northern Spring

(No. 1 Heavy Northern Spring at 1/2¢ premium)
(No. 2 Heavy grades at 1¢ premium)

* No. 3   Soft Red   at 1¢ discount
* No. 3   Dark Hard Winter

DELIVERABLE GRADES (Cont'd)

* No. 3   Hard Winter ⎫
* No. 3   Yellow Hard Winter ⎬   at 1¢ discount
* No. 3   Dark Northern Spring ⎪
  No. 2   Northern Spring ⎭

    (No. 2 Heavy Northern Spring at contract price)
    (* No. 3 Heavy grades at contract price)

  * All factors equal to No. 2 grade or better (including test weight, heat damage, total damage, shrunken and broken and contrasting classes) except foreign material (maximum 2%), total defects (maximum 8%) and total wheats of other classes (Maximum 10%).

Corn Differentials

No. 1	Yellow Corn	at 1/2¢ per bushel over contract price
No. 2	Yellow Corn	at contract prices
No. 3	Yellow Corn	at 2-1/2¢ per bushel under contract price
(maximum 15-1/2% moisture)		

Oats Differentials

No. 1	Extra Heavy White Oats	at 2¢ per bushel over contract price
No. 2	Extra Heavy White Oats	at 1¢ per bushel over contract price
No. 1	Heavy White Oats	at 1¢ per bushel over contract price
No. 3	Extra Heavy White Oats	at contract price
No. 2	Heavy White Oats	at contract price
No. 1	White Oats	at contract price
No. 3	Heavy White Oats	at 1¢ per bushel under contract price
No. 2	White Oats	at 4¢ per bushel under contract price
No. 3	White Oats	at 4¢ per bushel under contract price

Bright Oats shall carry no additional premium or discount.

Rye Differentials

No. 1	Plump Rye	at 5¢ over contract price
No. 2	Plump Rye	at 2-1/2¢ over contract price
No. 1	Rye	at 1¢ over contract price
No. 2	Rye	at contract price

Soybean Differentials

U.S. No. 1	Yellow Soybeans	at 3¢ per bushel over contract price
U.S. No. 2	Yellow Soybeans	at contract price
U.S. No. 3	Yellow Soybeans	at 3¢ per bushel under contract price
(14% or less moisture)		

DELIVERY POINTS

    In store in a regular warehouse in the Chicago Switching District.

ISSUANCE OF NOTICES

    Last Trading Day: No trading in last 7 business days of delivery month.

    First Notice Day: Last business day of the month preceding the delivery month.

    Last Notice Day: Next to the last business day of the delivery month.

    Time and where issued: Notice of delivery of grain and memorandum of sales, together with statement of final position in the current month, must be delivered to the Clearing House by 2:00 p.m. on the business day preceding the day of delivery. The Clearing House shall pass such notices to buyers, who must take delivery and make payment before 1:00 p.m. on the business day following, except on Saturdays or banking holidays when such delivery must be taken and such payment made before 9:30 o'clock a.m. the next banking business day.

TRANSFER OF NOTICES

    Prior to the cessation of trading in the current delivery month, a buyer of grain futures who receives a notice of intention to deliver may, on the same day, sell the grain specified therein and deliver the identical notice, together with the name of his buyer, to the Clearing House not later than 2:00 p.m., except that on the last day of trading in the delivery month, if such

TRANSFER OF NOTICES (Cont'd)
    last day is other than Saturday, the time for delivery of the above shall be extended until
    3:00 o'clock p.m., and if the last day of trading is on Saturday, such time shall be extended
    until 1:45 p.m. The Clearing House shall then, on the same day, pass the notice to the buyer
    obligated by the oldest contract to take delivery.
WHEN PAPERS CONCERNING DELIVERY ARE DUE
    See information in Issuance and Transfer of Notices.
ALLOWANCES ON INVOICE
    Refer to the Rules and Regulations of the Chicago Board of Trade for full details.

CRUDE SOYBEAN OIL

THE MARKET
    Board of Trade of the City of Chicago.
TRADING HOURS
    9:30 a.m.–1:15 p.m. (Central Time)
    last day — 9:30 a.m.–12 noon (See Rule 252 for details)
CONTRACT UNIT
    60,000 pounds (tank car)
ACTIVE DELIVERY MONTHS
    January, March, May, July, August, September, October and December.
QUOTATIONS
    Telequote Symbol — BO —
ORDER DATA
    CEA regulated.
COMMISSIONS
(Round Turn)

Price Range	Member	Non-Member	Member Spread	Non-Member Spread	Foreign Member	Foreign Non-Member
One Rate	$15.00	$30.00	$20.00	$40.00	Same as domestic rates.	

MINIMUM PRICE FLUCTUATION
    1/100th of one cent per pound — $6.00 per contract.
MAXIMUM DAILY PRICE FLUCTUATIONS
    1 cent per pound above or below the Clearing House settlement prices for such Crude Soybean
    Oil on the previous business day. These provisions shall not apply to trading in the current
    month on and after the first notice day thereof.
CUSTOMER SPECULATIVE POSITION LIMIT
    None.
CUSTOMER SPECULATIVE DAILY TRADING LIMIT
    None.
REPORTS TO CEA
    The CEA requires that a person who holds or controls 25 or more open contracts in any one
    future on any contract market file a report relative thereto on Form 1003.
DELIVERABLE GRADES
    It shall be one of the following types: Expeller pressed, expeller pressed degummed, solvent
    extracted, or solvent extracted degummed. Mixtures of one type with any other type shall not
    be deliverable.
    It shall contain not more than 0.3 % moisture and volatile content.
    It shall be lighter in green color than Standard "A" and when refined and bleached shall
    produce a refined and bleached oil of not deeper color than 3.5 red on the Lovibond scale.
    It shall refine with a loss not exceeding 7 % as determined by the "closed cup" method or 5 %
    as determined by the "neutral oil" method.
    It shall have a flash point not below 250 degrees Fahrenheit, closed cup method.

DELIVERABLE GRADES (Cont'd)

No lower grade shall be delivered in satisfaction of contracts for future delivery. A higher grade may be delivered at contract price except that where the refining loss is less than 7% as determined by the "closed cup" method, a premium of three-fourths of one percent of the cash market price at time of loading shall be paid for each one percent under the 7% refining loss, and where the refining loss is less than 5% as determined by the "neutral oil" method, a premium of one percent of the cash market price at the time of loading shall be paid for each one percent under the 5% loss (fractions figured throughout) with a maximum credit of 4-1/2%.

DELIVERY POINTS

Warehouses shall be within the limitation of an area not east of the Indiana-Ohio boundary; nor south of Louisville, Ky.

All prices of Crude Soybean Oil shall be basis Decatur, Illinois, with freight adjustment to New York, N.Y. When delivery is made at a point other than Decatur, Illinois, the Seller shall make an adjustment to Buyer by decreasing or increasing the amount due on delivery notice by the difference between carload freight from point of delivery to New York, N.Y., as compared with Decatur, Illinois, to New York.

Transit billing may be applied to shipments at warehouseman's option with warehouseman to get any advantage of such transit application; however, warehouseman must protect the lowest lawful local carload rate from point of loading stated in warehouse receipt or demand certificate to destination indicated in shipping instructions, and such transit billing must allow at least one additional transit beyond delivery point.

ISSUANCE OF NOTICES

Last trading day — No trading in last 7 business days of delivery month.

First notice day — Last business day of the month preceding the delivery month.

Last notice day — Next to the last business day of the delivery month.

Time and where issued. Notice of delivery must be delivered to the Clearing House by 2:00 p.m. on the day preceding the day of delivery, except on Saturday when such notices must be delivered before 12:30 p.m. provided the Crude Soybean Oil futures market is open that Saturday; further except that on the last day of trading in a delivery month the time for delivery of a delivery notice shall be extended until 3:00 o'clock p.m., and if the last day of trading of a delivery month is on Saturday, such time is extended until 1:15 o'clock, p.m. The Clearing House shall, the same day, pass such notice to buyers who must take delivery and make payment, before 1:00 o'clock p.m., on the business day following, except that on Saturdays or banking holidays such deliveries must be taken and payment made before 9:30 o'clock a.m., the next banking business day. Payment is to be made by certified check on a Chicago bank. Except as otherwise provided, all charges for storage, car rental, etc., shall remain the responsibility of the Seller until payment is made.

TRANSFER OF NOTICES

Prior to the cessation of trading in the current delivery month, a buyer of Crude Soybean Oil futures, who receives a notice of intention to deliver, may sell the oil on the same day provided the sale is reported to the Clearing House. He shall deliver the same notice together with the name of his buyer to the Clearing House by 2:00 p.m. except on Saturday when such notices must be delivered before 12:30 p.m., provided the Crude Soybean Oil market is open on that Saturday; further, except that on the last day of trading in a delivery month the time for delivery of a delivery notice shall be extended until 3:00 o'clock p.m. and if the last day of trading is on Saturday such time is extended until 1:15 o'clock p.m. The Clearing House the same day shall then pass the notice to the buyer who is obligated by the oldest contract to take delivery.

WHEN PAPERS CONCERNING DELIVERY ARE DUE

See information in Issuance and Transfer of Notices.

ALLOWANCES ON INVOICE

Refer to the Rules and Regulations of the Chicago Board of Trade for full details.

SOYBEAN MEAL

THE MARKET
Board of Trade of the City of Chicago.
TRADING HOURS
9:30 a.m.–1:15 p.m. (Central Time)
Last day: 9:30 a.m.–12:00 noon (See Rule 252 for details)
CONTRACT UNIT
100 tons (2,000 pounds per ton)
ACTIVE DELIVERY MONTHS
Trading may be conducted in the current month and any subsequent months. January, March, May, July, August, September, October and December.
QUOTATIONS
Telequote Symbol SM —
ORDER DATA
CEA Regulated.
COMMISSIONS
(Round Turn)

Price Range	Member	Non-Member	Member Spread	Non-Member Spread	Foreign Member	Foreign Non-Member
One Rate	$15.00	$30.00	$20.00	$40.00	Same as domestic	

MINIMUM PRICE FLUCTUATION
5¢ per ton — $5.00 per contract.
MAXIMUM DAILY PRICE FLUCTUATIONS
Five dollars per ton above or below the Clearing House settlement prices for such Soybean Meal on the previous business day.
Price basis for daily trading limits for inactive futures may be determined by the Crude Soybean Oil and Soybean Meal Committee. These provisions shall not apply to trading in the current month on and after the first notice day thereof.
CUSTOMER SPECULATIVE POSITION LIMIT
The limit on the maximum net long or net short position which any person may hold or control in soybean meal, either alone or in conjunction with any other person, is 480 contracts of 100 tons each in any one future or in all futures combined.
The foregoing limit on position shall not be construed to apply:
(1) to bona fide hedging transactions, as defined in Section 4a (3) of the Commodity Exchange Act; nor (2) to positions commonly known in the trade as "crush" or "reverse crush" spreading positions; nor (3) to transactions or positions in soybean meal futures by a processor or merchandiser of or dealer in feed ingredients other than soybean meal, to the extent that the bona fide purpose and the reasonable effect of such transactions or positions are to offset the price risk incident to the ownership, purchase, or sale of such feed ingredients, provided such risk is not otherwise off-set; nor (4) to sales or short positions by a processor of soybeans, to the extent that such sales or short positions are off-set in quantity by the meal content of such soybeans owned or purchased by such processor, provided the price risk incident to such ownership or purchase is not otherwise off-set.
A position of 25 or more contracts of 100 tons each, long or short, in any one future whether owned or controlled or carried for any person, either alone or in conjunction with any other person, shall be a reportable position. Every member, or partnership or corporation for which a membership is registered under Rule 226, shall report each and every reportable position to the Office of Investigations and Audits at such times and in such form and manner as shall be prescribed by the Business Conduct Committee.
The word "person" shall be construed to import the plural or singular, and shall include individuals, associations, partnerships, corporations, and trusts.
REPORTS TO CEA
CEA requires a person to file reports on Form 1103 when he holds or controls 25 open contracts in any one future on any one contract market.

DELIVERABLE GRADES

All prices of Soybean Meal shall be basis free on board cars Decatur, Illinois, in multiples of 5 cents per ton. Contracts shall not be made on any other price basis. The contract grade for delivery on future contracts shall be Soybean Meal in bulk which conforms to the following specifications:

44% Protein Soybean Meal, produced by conditioning ground soybeans and reducing the oil[1] content of the conditioned product by the use of hexane or homologous hydrocarbon solvents to 1% or less on a commercial basis. Standard specifications are:

Protein................................minimum 44.0%
Fat....................................minimum 0.5%
Fiber..................................maximum 7.0%
Moisture (when shipped by Processor)......maximum 12.0%

It may contain a non-nutritive inert, non-toxic conditioning agent to reduce caking and improve flow-ability, in an amount not to exceed that necessary to accomplish its intended effect, but in no case exceed 0.5%. The name of the conditioning agent must be shown as an added ingredient.

Testing methods shall be those approved by the Association of Official Analytical Chemists and American Oil Chemists Society.

(1) All loading of soybean meal against Soybean Meal Shipping Certificates shall be in bulk free on board cars basis Decatur, Illinois. Shipment shall be via railroad and shipper shall prepay freight.

(2) Payment for Shipping Certificates designated as either "ETL Basis Territory"; "Semi-Unrestricted Territory" will be at delivery price.

(3) The seller may at the time of delivery furnish Shipping Certificates designated as either "ETL Basis Territory" or "Semi-Unrestricted Territory" subject to the following terms and conditions:

(a) When the Shipping Certificate is designated "ETL Basis Territory" the owner shall specify a destination in the "ETL Basis Territory" (viz.: Destinations in the United States east of a north-south line from Madison, Indiana, through Muncie to Howe, Indiana, thence due north to the Canadian border: and on and north of the main line of the Norfolk & Western R.R., to Norfolk, Virginia, including the Virginia Cities Gateways), which may include routing via the Detroit Gateway when requested:

(1) When shipment is ordered on "mileage rates" (rates published TL-CTR-E-772-E, ICC C-638, supplements thereto or re-issues thereof), shipper shall prepay freight, charging owner the lowest lawful rate, applicable to the quantity shipped, on bulk soybean meal from Decatur, Illinois, to owner's destination.

(2) When shipment is ordered on the "McGraham Rates" (rates published in TL-CTR-C/TN 245-I, ICC C-375, supplements thereto or re-issues thereof), shipper shall prepay freight, charging owner the lowest lawful rate less a refund of $2.00 per ton to the owner, applicable to the quantity shipped, on bulk soybean meal from Decatur, Illinois, to Boston or Baltimore, whichever is designated by the owner, and make an adjustment equal to the difference, if any, in the prepaid transportation charges had the shipment been made to Boston or Baltimore, based on the billing applied, if any, against the shipment.

The requirement that the owner specify a destination is to permit the determination of the freight adjustments to be made. Thereafter, owner may divert loaded cars off shipper's track to any destination he chooses, including destinations outside "ETL Basis Territory," paying direct to railroads any additional freight costs resulting from such diversion.

(b) When the Shipping Certificate is designated "Semi-Unrestricted Territory" the owner may specify shipment to any destination in the Continental United States (excluding the State of Alaska) except Decatur, Illinois and destinations within a thirty-mile radius of Decatur, Illinois, but including destinations in Canada east of Windsor, Ontario and the shipper shall prepay freight, charging owner the lowest lawful milling in transit carload freight rate, applicable to the quantity shipped, on bulk soybean meal from Decatur, Illinois to the specified destination. Owner may designate whether shipment is to be made at "transit rates" or at "mileage rates" as named in Trunk-Line-Central Territory Railroads Tariff Bureau Freight Tariff E-772-E, ICC C-638, supplements thereto and re-issues thereof. If shipment is made at

DELIVERABLE GRADES (Cont'd)

"mileage rates" (as described above) shipper shall charge a premium of $1.00 per ton and shipper shall prepay freight charging the owner the lowest lawful domestic mileage carload rate (applicable to the quantity ordered) from Decatur, Illinois to named destination.

DELIVERY POINTS

Warehouses	Location	Daily Shipping Requirements (Tons)
Archer Daniels Midland Co.	Decatur, Ill.	1,000
Cargill, Inc.	Chicago, Ill.	454
Cargill, Inc.	Cedar Rapids, Ia. (East)	400
Central Soya Co., Inc.	Chicago, Ill.	150
Central Soya Co., Inc.	Decatur, Indiana	875
Central Soya Co., Inc.	Delphos, Ohio	200
Central Soya Co., Inc.	Gibson City, Ill.	250
Central Soya Co., Inc.	Marion, Ohio	150
Central Soya Co., Inc.	Indianapolis, Ind.	200
Central Soya Co., Inc.	Bellevue, Ohio	250
Lauhoff Grain Co.	Danville, Ill.	400
Ralston Purina Co.	Bloomington, Ill.	350
Ralston Purina Co.	Iowa Falls, Iowa	450
Ralston Purina Co.	Lafayette, Ind.	325
Ralston Purina Co.	Louisville, Ky.	350
A. E. Staley Mfg. Co.	Decatur, Ill.	600
Swift & Company	Champaign, Ill.	400
Swift & Company	Frankfort, Ind.	400

ISSUANCE OF NOTICES

Last trading day: No trading in the last 7 business days of the delivery month.

First notice day: Last business day of the month preceding the delivery month.

Last notice day: The business day immediately preceding the last day for delivery. Delivery must be made no later than the second business day following the last day for trading.

Time and where issued: Notice of delivery must be delivered to the Clearing House not later than 2:00 p.m. on the day preceding the day of delivery of Soybean Meal Shipping Certificate, except that no notices shall be delivered on Saturday if the soybean meal futures market is not open that Saturday; further, except that on the last day of trading in a delivery month the time for delivery of a delivery notice shall be not later than 3:00 o'clock p.m. The Clearing House shall pass such notice to buyer who must take delivery and make payment before 1:00 o'clock p.m. on the business day following the stopping of the delivery notice except that on Saturdays or banking holidays such deliveries must be taken and payment made before 9:30 o'clock a.m. the next banking business day.

TRANSFER OF NOTICES

Prior to the cessation of trading in the current delivery month, a buyer of Soybean Meal Futures, who receives a notice of intention to deliver, may sell the soybean meal on the same day provided the sale is reported to the Clearing House. He shall deliver the same notice together with the name of his buyer to the Clearing House by 2:00 p.m. except on Saturday when such notices must be delivered before 12:30 p.m., provided the Soybean Meal market is open on that Saturday; further, except that on the last day of trading in a delivery month the time for delivery of a delivery notice shall be extended until 3:00 o'clock p.m., and if the last day of trading is on Saturday such time is extended until 1:15 o'clock p.m. The Clearing House the same day shall then pass the notice to the buyer who is obligated by the oldest contract to take delivery.

WHEN PAPERS CONCERNING DELIVERY ARE DUE

See information in Issuance and Transfer of Notices.

ALLOWANCES ON INVOICE

Refer to the rules and regulations of the Chicago Board of Trade for full details.

APPENDIX C

Inventory Pricing and Valuation Methods

THIS appendix contains selected items from the available balance sheets of firms that were involved in the present study. In addition, three tables are presented based upon a series of research studies conducted by the American Institute of Certified Public Accountants and titled *Accounting Trends and Techniques*. The tables were assembled by C. Stevenson Rowley, Jr., in his Ph.D. thesis, "Inventory Pricing in the Grain Industry: A Study of Current Practices," University of Wisconsin, 1970 (reproduced with the author's permission).

WHEAT

(Taken from 1969 Annual Reports unless otherwise specified)

Company	Net Sales	Net Income After Taxes	Inventories	Accountants
Allied Mills, Inc.	$ 266,157,561	$ 6,402,323	$ 33,660,702[1]	Lybrand, Ross Bros. & Montgomery
Bay State Milling Co.	Private			
CPC International	$1,218,029,293	$55,296,577	$221,331,550[2]	Main Lafrentz & Co.
Cargill	Private			
Continental Baking Co.*	$ 621,037,640	$14,665,652	$ 31,880,153[3]	Arthur Young & Co.
Continental Grain	Private			
Dixie Portland Flour Mills	Private			
General Foods (in thousands)	$ 1,893,760	$ 132,886	$ 311,444[4]	Price Waterhouse & Co.
General Mills (in thousands)	$ 885,242	$ 37,547	$ 106,653[5]	Peat, Marwick, Mitchell
International Milling	$ 338,962,132	$ 4,914,119	$ 50,877,594[6]	Peat, Marwick, Mitchell
Kellogg	$ 542,198,955	$44,632,861	$ 59,252,451[7]	Price Waterhouse & Co.
National Biscuit Co.	$ 726,227,000	$30,839,000	$ 88,837,000[8]	Lybrand, Ross Bros. & Montgomery
Pillsbury Co.**	$ 569,233,572	$14,440,771	$ 76,079,744[9]	Touche, Ross, Bailey & Smart
Quaker Oats Co. (in thousands)	$ 553,879	$ 24,614	$ 57,851[10]	Haskins & Sells
Nebraska Consolidated Mills	$ 191,937,157	$ 5,096,090	$ 22,511,494[11]	Peat, Marwick, Mitchell

* 1967 Annual Report, effective Sept. 13, 1968, acquired by ITT.
** 1968 Annual Report.

¹ (Allied Mills, Inc.): Valued at lower of average cost or market.

² (CPC International): At lower of cost or market.

³ (Continental Baking Co.): At lower of cost (principally first-in, first-out) or market.

⁴ (General Foods): At lower of cost (primarily average) or market.

⁵ (General Mills): Package foods, toys and games, chemical

products, etc., at lower of cost or market	$ 80,872,000
Grain for processing and flour at market, after appropriate adjustments for open cash trades, unfilled orders, etc.	13,045,000
Containers, supplies, etc. at cost	10,301,000
	$104,218,000
Advances on grain and other commodities	2,435,000
	$106,653,000

⁶ (International Milling): United States and Canadian inventories of grain (including wheat held for account of The Canadian Wheat Board), flour and millfeeds are valued on the basis of replacement market prices of grain and feed prevailing at February 28, adjustment of open grain and flour contracts also being made to market. All other inventories of any significance are stated at the lower of cost (first-in, first-out) or replacement market.

⁷ (Kellogg): At lower of cost (average) or market.

⁸ (National Biscuit Co.): At the lower of average cost or market.

⁹ (Pillsbury Co.): Grain is stated on the basis of market prices at May 31, including adjustment to market of open contracts for purchases and sales. The company follows a policy of hedging grain and certain other inventories to the extent considered practicable to minimize risk due to market price fluctuations. Other inventories have been stated at cost (first-in, first-out) or market, which ever is lower.

	May 31, 1969
Grain	$21,065,776
Other raw materials	22,604,256
Finished products	26,870,797
Containers and supplies	5,538,915
	$76,079,744

¹⁰ (Quaker Oats Co.): At lower of cost or market.

¹¹ (Nebraska Consolidated Mills): Wheat and flour inventories are generally hedged to the extent practicable and are stated at market including adjustment to market of open contracts for purchases and sales. Inventories not hedged are priced at the lower of average cost or market.

	June 29, 1969
Wheat and flour	$ 7,724,407
Mixed feed, ingredients and coarse grain	7,452,252
Containers, etc.	1,502,854
Livestock, poultry and related inventories	4,652,339
	$21,331,852
Advance on commodity purchases	1,179,642
	$22,511,494

SOYBEANS

(Taken from 1969 Annual Reports unless otherwise specified)

Company	Net Sales	Net Income After Taxes	Inventories	Accountants
Cargill	Private			
Central Soya	$ 556,691,398	$ 11,055,556	$ 37,704,469[1]	Arthur Young & Co.
Anderson Clayton	$ 503,821,000	$ 6,434,000	$ 62,386,000[2]	Peat, Marwick, Mitchell
Archer Daniels Midland	$ 320,787,250	$ 3,393,566	$ 44,589,637[3]	Ernst & Ernst
Farmers Union Grain Terminal Association	$ 28,982,254	(loss) ($1,345,202)	$ 21,011,335[4]	Touche Ross & Co.
General Foods (in thousands)	$ 1,893,760	$ 132,886	$ 311,444[5]	Price Waterhouse & Co.
Procter & Gamble	$2,707,553,000	$187,447,000	$348,588,000[6]	Haskins & Sells
A. E. Staley	$ 297,582,000	$ 8,254,000	$ 31,805,000[7]	Haskins & Sells
Swift & Co.	$3,107,600,000	$ 21,921,000	$197,439,000[8]	Arthur Young & Co.

[1] (Central Soya):

August 31, 1969

Grain, soybeans, soybean oil and soybean meal valued at market adjusted for hedges and undelivered contracts	$12,055,490
Feed, special soybean products and poultry at processed cost	16,366,508
Ingredients, containers, supplies and other merchandise at lower of cost, on a first-in, first-out basis, or market	9,282,471
	$37,704,469

[2] (Anderson Clayton): Commodity inventories of $30,573,000 are valued at quoted market prices less selling costs and other items; all other inventories of $31,813,000 are valued at the lower of average cost or replacement market.

[3] (Archer Daniels Midland):

At lower of cost (first-in, first-out method) or market:	
Soybeans and other raw materials	$11,859,533
Sundry products	3,810,138
Materials and supplies	914,064
Total	$16,583,735

At market:	
Wheat and other grains, flour and meal	$19,071,397

At lower of cost (last-in, first-out method) or market:	
Soybean oil, linseed oil, sperm oil, crude fish oil and certain grains	$ 8,934,505
Total	$44,589,637

Inventories at market have been priced on the basis of market prices for grain at June 30, including adjustments of open purchase and sale contracts to market at that date. The company generally follows a policy of hedging its transactions in these and certain other commodities to the extent practicable to minimize risk due to market fluctuations.

Inventories at lower of cost (last-in, first-out method) or market have a current cost in excess of the inventory basis used in the financial statement of $1,985,000 at June 30, 1969, and $2,550,000 at June 30, 1968.

[4] (Farmers Union Grain Terminal Association, *1970 Annual Report*): Grain at market, including appropriate adjustment of open purchase and sales contracts where applicable, except that flax is stated essentially at average cost; processed grain products and farm supplies, at the lower of cost (first-in, first out) or market.

The Association follows the general policy of hedging its grain inventories and unfilled orders for grain products to the extent considered practicable for minimizing risk from market price fluctuations. However, the inventories are not completely hedged, due in part of the absence of satisfactory hedging facilities for certain grains and geographical areas and in part to the Association's appraisal of its exposure from expected price fluctuations.

[5] (General Foods): At lower of cost (primarily average) or market.

[6] (Procter & Gamble): At lower of cost (partly Lifo) or market.

[7] (A. E. Staley): Corn and soybeans for domestic operations are costed on the last-in, first-out method and for foreign operations are at the lower of average cost or market. All other inventories are at the lower of first-out, first-out cost or market.

A summary of inventories at year-end, in thousands of dollars, is set forth below:

Sept. 30, 1969

Corn and soybeans	
Domestic operations	$ 3,218
Foreign operations	3,433
Finished and in-process products	16,598
Ingredients and supplies	8,556
Total	$31,805

[8] (Swift & Company): Product inventories of $182,303,000 (1968 — $182,378,-000) include a substantial portion valued at cost under the last-in, first-out (Lifo) method. Other product inventories are valued at current cost or approximate market, less cost to sell. Ingredients and supplies of $15,136,000 (1968 — $16,858,000) are valued at the lower of current cost or market.

BEEF

(Taken from 1969 Annual Reports unless otherwise specified)

Company	Net Sales	Net Income After Taxes	Inventories	Accountants
Armour & Co. (in thousands)	$ 2,153,357	$ 18,093	$ 181,360	Price Water-house & Co.
Colonial Provision Co.	Private			
Iowa Beef Packers	$ 675,065,000	$ 3,312,000	$ 10,911,000[1]	Touche, Ross, Bailey & Smart
Kern County Land Co.*	$ 138,965,272	$22,710,309	$ 45,950,782	Haskins & Sells
Monfort of Colorado, Inc.**	$ 161,859,122	$ 4,273,475	$ 30,167,209[2]	Ernst & Ernst
Swift & Co.	$3,107,600,000	$21,921,000	$197,439,000[3]	Arthur Young & Co.
Wilson & Co.*** (in thousands)	$ 1,024,567	$ 10,202	$ 57,558[4]	Price Water-house & Co.

* 1966 Annual Report, acquired by Tenneco.
** Information taken from Prospectus dated January 22, 1970.
*** 1968 Annual Report.

[1] (Iowa Beef Packers, Inc.):

	November 1, 1969
Lower of cost (first-in, first-out method) or market:	
Cattle on feed and feeding ingredients	$ 5,399,000
Carcasses	2,147,000
Operating Supplies	993,000
Approximate market less allowance for selling expenses:	
By-products	1,843,000
Processed cuts	529,000
	$10,911,000

[2] (Monfort): The inventories have been consistently valued as follows: live cattle and the feed inventory on the basis of the lower of cost (under the last-in, first-out method) or market; dressed meat and by-products, on the basis of market, less allowance for distribution and selling expenses; and the live sheep and supplies, at the lower of cost (first-in, first-out method) or market.

The major classes and amounts of inventories at August 31, 1969, are as follows:

Live cattle	$25,501,948
Live sheep	763,143
Feed	1,827,848
Dressed meat	1,392,466
By-products	300,835
Supplies	380,969
	$30,167,209

Inventories included in the calculation of cost of products sold are as follows:

August 31, 1966	$17,936,315
August 31, 1967	20,246,254
August 31, 1968	22,551,483
August 31, 1969	30,167,209

Had the cattle and feed inventories been stated at principally identified cost rather than at lower of cost (last-in, first-out method) or market, total inventories used in the calculation of cost of products sold would have been as follows:

August 31, 1966	$22,276,329
August 31, 1967	24,622,259
August 31, 1968	27,477,710
August 31, 1969	38,959,741

[3] (Swift & Company): Product inventories of $182,303,000 (1968 — $182,378,-000) include a substantial portion valued at cost under the last-in, first-out method. Other product inventories are valued at current cost or approximate market, less cost to sell. Ingredients and supplies of $15,136,000 (1968 — $16,858,000) are valued at the lower of current cost or market.

[4] (Wilson & Co.[8]: Inventories are stated as follows: certain products at cost on the basis of last-in, first-out, other products, where costs were not ascertainable, at market, less allowance for selling and distribution expenses, and the balance of products and supplies at the lower of first-in, first-out cost or market.

The practice of pricing certain products at market, less allowance for selling and distribution expenses, may have the effect of including unrealized profits or losses in the financial statements; however, these amounts are not significant and have not been eliminated.

Appendix C

COCOA

(Taken from 1969 Annual Reports unless otherwise specified)

Company	Net Sales	Net Income After Taxes	Inventories	Accountants
General Cocoa Co.	Private			
General Foods (in thousands)	$ 1,893,760	$ 132,886	$ 311,444[1]	Price Waterhouse & Co.
Hershey Foods	$315,117,453	$12,041,411	$64,231,839[2]	Arthur Andersen & Co.
Adrian C. Israel	Private			
Mars, Inc.	Private			
National Biscuit Co.	$726,227,000	$30,839,000	$88,837,000[3]	Lybrand, Ross Bros. & Montgomery
Nestle Company	Private			

[1] At lower of cost (primarily average) or market.

[2] Inventories of cocoa beans, almonds, peanuts, and milk, together with such material and wage costs included in finished goods and goods in process are substantially all stated at cost, under the last-in, first-out method. The remaining inventories are stated at lower of cost or market under the first-in, first-out or average cost method.

[3] At the lower of average cost or market

STATISTICAL SUMMARY OF INVENTORY
VALUATION METHODS

Following is a summary of findings from studies made by the American Institute of Certified Public Accountants, covering the period from 1964 to 1968.

TABLE C-1. FREQUENCY OF OCCURRENCE AMONG 600 COMPANIES OF VARIOUS INVENTORY PRICING METHODS, 1964–1968
(Total in each year exceeds 600 because some companies used more than one method)

Pricing Method	1964	1965	1966	1967	1968
Lower-of-cost-or-market	410	416	431	433	495
Lower-of-cost-or-market; and cost	63	67	52	51	22
Cost not in excess of market	41	41	49	53	26
Cost	37	33	34	33	60
Cost; less than market	24	33	42	44	29
Cost or less than cost	19	21	23	22	12
Lower-of-cost-or-market; and one or more other bases	15	8	8	9	2
Cost or less than cost, not in excess of market	6	6	6	6	7
Market	3	5	4	3	14
Other	24	16	16	15	5
Total	642	646	665	669	673

SOURCE: American Institute of Certified Public Accountants, *Accounting Trends and Techniques* (New York: AICPA, 1964–1968). (Data assembled by C. Stevenson Rowley, Jr., for Ph.D. thesis, University of Wisconsin, 1970.)

TABLE C-2. FREQUENCY OF OCCURRENCE AMONG 600 COMPANIES
OF VARIOUS COST DETERMINATION METHODS, 1964–1968
(Total in each year exceeds 600 because some
companies used more than one method)

Cost Determination Method	1964	1965	1966	1967	1968
First-in, first-out	188	199	213	231	240
Last-in, first-out	193	190	191	184	179
Average cost	159	163	176	187	177
Standard cost	32	30	28	28	26
Retail cost	16	15	17	18	19
Actual cost	14	14	13	13	23
Replacement or current cost	7	10	12	13	13
Production cost	10	7	5	4	8
Accumulated cost	0	6	6	9	7
Approximate cost	5	5	5	4	0
Other	11	9	10	17	12
Total	635	648	676	708	704

SOURCE: American Institute of Certified Public Accountants, *Accounting Trends and Techniques* (New York: AICPA, 1964–1968). (Data assembled by C. Stevenson Rowley, Jr., for Ph.D. thesis, University of Wisconsin, 1970.)

TABLE C-3. FREQUENCY OF OCCURRENCE AMONG 600 COMPANIES
OF VARIOUS MARKET DETERMINATION METHODS, 1964–1968

Market Determination Method	1964	1965	1966	1967	1968
Current replacement values (by purchase or reproduction)	45	41	41	39	36
Net realizable value (recoverable cost)	22	20	31	24	22
Selling price	10	7	5	8	10
Purchase price	6	4	3	0	0
Hedging procedure values	3	5	7	7	7
Other	3	0	0	10	2
Total	89	85	87	88	77

SOURCE: American Institute of Certified Public Accountants, *Accounting Trends and Techniques* (New York: AICPA, 1964–1968). (Data assembled by C. Stevenson Rowley, Jr., for Ph.D. thesis, University of Wisconsin, 1970.)

APPENDIX D

Bank of America Guidelines for Live Beef Cattle Hedging Loans

March 29, 1967   LIVE BEEF CATTLE FUTURES   484.3
                              CONTRACTS

1. GENERAL   Cattlemen can obtain a measure of price insurance
               by hedging their inventories of live beef cattle in
the commodity markets.

B of A will finance the needed margin required in live beef cattle futures contracts subject to the conditions outlined below. Margin is the money a commodity trader deposits with his broker as evidence of his good faith.

Live beef cattle futures contracts are presently being traded by the Chicago Mercantile Exchange and the Chicago Board of Trade. Delivery of beef cattle, while expected to be infrequent, must be made at either Omaha, Nebraska, or Chicago, Illinois, if a midwestern contract is being filled for delivery, or at Artesia, California, if a western contract is being filled. The specifications for cattle which are acceptable for delivery are available from a representative of any commodity broker.

Every borrower wishing to hedge inventory with cattle futures must arrange to open a commodity account with a licensed broker of his own choice.

2. REQUIREMENTS   The margin money deposit required of
                    traders in live beef cattle futures contracts
may be financed if the following are met.

(a) The purpose of the sale of the futures contract must be to hedge an inventory of cattle owned by the applicant.
(b) The inventory must consist of cattle being fed in a feedlot or "stocker" cattle on grass pasture.
(c) The cattle inventory is to be financed by B of A and must be in the custody and care of an experienced feeder or cattleman.

(d)   Provision must be made for the necessary cattle feed.
(e)   The borrower's interest in his commodity account must be assigned to the bank.
(f)   Borrower must furnish B of A with a monthly position report showing his schedule of open contracts.

3.   APPLICATION   Include borrower's request for funds to finance his margin requirements as a "facility" within (or in addition to) his usual line of credit. Initial margin requirements may be $300 to $800 per contract, depending on the policy of the broker. The bank agrees to make further advances if borrower is called upon for additional funds to maintain his margin.

If a borrower requests funds to finance margin requirements after he has been granted a line of credit, submit Cr-115 (Branch Loan Credit Report).

4.   LOAN AMOUNT   The loan amount may be 100% of the margin required, either initial or for maintenance, by the borrower's brokerage firm.

5.   DOCUMENTATION   In addition to the usual documentation, observe the following requirements.

(a)   Include the words "Accounts and Contract Rights" under item 7 on the N-285 (Financing Statement).
(b)   Prepare a security agreement "Assignment of Hedging Account." Have it executed by the bank and borrower and acknowledged by the commodity broker. Obtain this security agreement from Loan Supervision.

6.   REPORTS   Request the borrower's broker to furnish copies of the following:

(a)   confirmation of all borrower's buy and sell orders;
(b)   monthly reconciliation of the borrower's commodity trading account;
(c)   settlement reports when contracts are closed out;
(d)   notice of margin calls.

7.   CLOSING OUT OPEN CONTRACTS   Physical delivery of live cattle to fulfill the requirements of a contract is expensive. For this reason, commodity brokers will normally encourage clients to close out open contracts.

The bank has the right to liquidate a borrower's position. An order to close out the borrower's position may be telephoned to the broker; however, borrower's broker is not required to act until he receives written notice from the bank.

SECURITY AGREEMENT

ASSIGNMENT OF HEDGING ACCOUNT

WHEREAS, the undersigned, _____,
hereinafter called the Debtor, whose address is _____,
carries an account (No. _____) with the firm of _____,
as brokers, hereinafter called the Broker, whose address is _____

for trading in beef, cattle (live) futures contracts and/or dressed beef (steer carcasses) futures contracts; and

Debtor is now indebted to BANK OF AMERICA NATIONAL TRUST AND SAVINGS ASSOCIATION, _____

_____ Branch/Office, hereinafter called the Secured Party, at_____
California, and expects to incur additional indebtedness with the Secured Party for the purpose of financing further transactions in
said contracts;

NOW, THEREFORE, it is agreed by and between the parties hereto as follows:

1. As additional security for the obligation of the Debtor to the Secured Party, and for the payment of all monies which the Secured Party may hereafter loan or advance to the Debtor, the Debtor hereby grants a security interest in and assigns and transfers to the Secured Party all funds which may hereafter accumulate or become withdrawable from or paid out of the account of the Debtor with the Broker, including any balance which may remain to the credit of said account upon the closing thereof; subject, however, to the prior payment of all indebtedness of the Debtor to the Broker, as such may exist from time to time, including fees and commissions, which may have been incurred in connection with Debtor's transactions with Broker, and to the Broker's lien, and the right of foreclosure thereof in connection with any indebtedness of Debtor to Broker (including any right of the Broker to close out open positions without prior demand for additional margin and without prior notice).

2. The Broker is hereby authorized and directed to pay to the Secured Party upon its demand all funds that may hereafter be withdrawable or payable out of said account of the Debtor with the Broker, and the Debtor agrees that he will not withdraw or attempt to withdraw any funds or other property from said account except as permitted by this Agreement. The Secured Party is hereby authorized and fully empowered without further authority from the Debtor to request the Broker to remit to the Secured Party any funds that may be due to the Debtor, and the Broker is hereby authorized and directed to pay to the Secured Party such sums as it shall so request or demand without the consent of or notice to the Debtor.

3. The Debtor hereby constitutes and appoints the Secured Party its true, lawful and irrevocable attorney to demand, receive and enforce payments and to give receipts, releases, satisfactions for, and to sue for all monies payable to the Debtor and this may be done in the name of the Secured Party with the same force and effect as the Debtor could do had this Security Agreement not been made. Any and all monies or payments which may be received by the Debtor, to which the Secured Party is entitled under and by reason of this Security Agreement, will be received by the Debtor as trustee for the Secured Party, and will be immediately delivered in kind to the Secured Party without commingling.

4. Nothing herein contained shall be construed so as to prevent the Debtor from remaining the owner, subject to the interest of the Secured Party as it may appear, of the account with the Broker. Until the Secured Party elects to the contrary and delivers notice of such election in writing to the Broker, the Debtor may make such additional transactions in his said account with the Broker as the Broker shall be willing to accept for execution. In the event the Secured Party does make such election and does deliver such notice to the Broker, the Debtor shall not thereafter execute any transactions in the said account and the Broker shall not accept for execution any such transactions without the concurrence of the Secured Party, except transactions in liquidation of any then outstanding commodity or commodity futures positions.

5. Whenever the Secured Party deems it necessary for its protection, it shall be entitled, without the consent or concurrence of, or prior notice to, the Debtor, to direct the Broker to liquidate any or all then outstanding open positions in the Debtor's said commodity account and to direct the said Broker to pay to it, the lender, the credit balance as shall exist in the said account after such liquidation and after the payment to the Broker of all the indebtedness of the Debtor to the Broker in connection with transactions in this account.

6. Any sums paid by the Broker from the account of the Debtor to the Secured Party under this Agreement shall be applied by the Secured Party to the payment of any indebtedness owing by the Debtor to the Secured Party. The balance remaining after the payment of said indebtedness shall be paid by the Secured Party to the Debtor. The receipt or receipts of the Secured Party for such funds so paid to it by the Broker shall as to the Broker operate as the receipt of the Debtor as fully and as completely as if funds had been paid to the Debtor in person and receipted for by the Debtor.

7. If at any time during the continuance of any such contract or contracts, the Broker may require additional margin in order to protect such contract or contracts, the Secured Party may advance to said Broker on behalf of the Debtor such amounts as may be required to protect such contracts, provided, however, that the Debtor shall in all respects remain liable to the Secured Party for any amounts so advanced pursuant to the terms of any agreement entered into between the Secured Party and the Debtor in connection with the transactions covered by this Agreement and Assignment.

8. The Secured Party is hereby authorized and empowered to receive from the Broker, and the Broker is authorized and directed to deliver to the Secured Party, copies of confirmations on all contracts executed for the account of the Debtor, copies of the monthly position and ledger account of the Debtor, and copies of any and all matters pertaining to said account of the Debtor with the Broker.

9. As between the Debtor and the Secured Party, this instrument shall remain in full force and effect until cancelled in writing by the Secured Party, or by the Debtor when and if the Debtor no longer is indebted to the Secured Party. Any cancellation of this instrument shall be without effect as to the Broker until the Broker is notified in writing by the Secured Party.

10. The Debtor hereby represents and warrants to the Secured Party that the account or accounts above assigned have not heretofore been alienated or assigned.

11. This Agreement shall be binding upon the Debtor, and upon his executors, administrators or assigns, and it shall be binding upon and inure to the benefit of any successors of the Secured Party and the Broker.

Dated this _____ day of _____, 19 _____.

Bank of America
NATIONAL TRUST AND SAVINGS ASSOCIATION

By _____

(Title) _____

By _____

(Title) _____

Acknowledgment

To: BANK OF AMERICA NATIONAL TRUST AND
SAVINGS ASSOCIATION

_____, California

The undersigned, _____, whose address is _____

_____, hereby acknowledges receipt of a copy of the above mentioned
Security Agreement and Assignment, and agrees to abide by the provisions thereof. No previous assignment or claims against the
above described account or accounts have been received by the undersigned.

This copy received _____, 19 _____.

Broker _____

By _____

(Title) _____

3333-1

APPENDIX E

List of Cooperating Firms

THE sampling procedure for the present study presented questions of selection and classification which were resolved on the pragmatic basis that information and knowledge were to be found among the knowledgeable people and practitioners rather than in a statistical sampling process.

The assortment of firms interviewed reflects this selection process. No effort has been made to distinguish between those firms whose officials were interviewed in depth and those who were consulted for information on specific questions or practices. In all instances the attitude was one of full cooperation, often involving information regarded as highly confidential. The study is indebted to these firms as well as to many other firms and individuals not specifically mentioned here.

Allied Mills, Inc., Chicago, Ill.
American Institute of Certified Public Accountants, New York, N.Y.
Anderson, Clayton & Co., Houston, Texas
Anheuser-Busch, Inc., St. Louis, Mo.
Archer Daniels Midland Company, Decatur, Ill.
Armour and Company, Chicago, Ill.
Arthur Andersen & Co., Chicago, Ill.
Arthur Young and Co., New York, N.Y.
Association of Commodity Exchange Firms, Inc., New York, N.Y.

Bache and Co., New York, N.Y.
Bank of America, San Francisco, Calif.
Bay State Milling Company, Boston, Mass.
Board of Trade of the City of Chicago, Chicago, Ill.

Cadbury Brothers, Ltd., Birmingham, England
Cargill, Incorporated, Minneapolis, Minn.
Central Soya Company, Inc., Fort Wayne, Ind.
Chase Manhattan Bank, New York, N.Y.
Chicago Mercantile Exchange, Chicago, Ill.
Citrus Associates of the N.Y. Cotton Exchange, New York, N.Y.
Citrus World, Lake Wales, Fla.
Colonial Provision Co., Inc., Boston, Mass.
Commodity Exchange Authority, Washington, D.C.
Continental Baking Co., Rye, N.Y.
Continental Grain Company, New York, N.Y.
CPC International, Inc., Englewood Cliffs, N.J.

Dixie Portland Flour Mills, Inc., Memphis, Tenn.
Doane Agricultural Services, Inc., St. Louis, Mo.

H. Elkan and Co., Chicago, Ill.
Engelhard Minerals & Chemicals Corp., New York, N.Y.
Ernst and Ernst, Cleveland, Ohio
Evans Packing Company, Dade City, Fla.
Experience, Incorporated, Minneapolis, Minn.

Farmers Union Grain Terminal Association, St. Paul, Minn.
First National Stores, Inc., Somerville, Mass.
Flour Mills of America, Inc., Fort Worth, Texas

General Cocoa Company, New York, N.Y.
General Foods Corporation, White Plains, N.Y.
General Mills, Inc., Minneapolis, Minn.
W. R. Grace & Company, New York, N.Y.
Grain and Feed Dealers National Association, Washington, D.C.

Hayden Stone, Inc., New York, N.Y.
H. Hentz and Co., Chicago, Ill.
Hershey Foods Corporation, Hershey, Pa.
H. P. Hood & Sons, Inc., Charlestown, Mass. and Dunedin, Fla.

International Multi-Foods, Minneapolis, Minn.
Iowa Beef Processors, Inc., Dakota City, Neb.
A. C. Israel Commodity Co., Inc., New York, N.Y.

Kellogg Company, Battle Creek, Mich.
Kern County Land Co., Bakersfield, Cal.
King Ranch, Kingsville, Texas
H. S. Kipnis and Co., Chicago, Ill.
Koelsch Grain and Feed Co., Inc., Boston, Mass.

Kohlmeyer and Co., New Orleans, La.
Kraftco Corporation, New York, N.Y.
The Kroger Company, Cincinnati, Ohio

Longstreet-Abbott and Company, St. Louis, Mo.
Lowry and Co., Inc., New York, N.Y.
Lykes-Pasco Packing Company, Dade City, Fla.

Mars, Inc., McLean, Va.
Merrill Lynch, Pierce, Fenner and Smith, Inc., New York, N.Y.
Mid-America Foods, Inc., Humboldt, Iowa
Minneapolis Grain Exchange, Minneapolis, Minn.
The Minute Maid Division of the Coca-Cola Company, Houston,
    Texas
Monfort of Colorado, Inc., Greeley, Colo.
Multiponics Incorporated, New Orleans, La.

National Biscuit Company, New York, N.Y.
Nebraska Consolidated Mills Co., Omaha, Neb.
The Nestle Company, Inc., White Plains, N.Y.
New York Coffee and Sugar Exchange, Inc., New York, N.Y.
New York Cocoa Exchange, Inc., New York, N.Y.

Peat, Marwick, Mitchell & Co., New York, N.Y.
The Pillsbury Company, Minneapolis, Minn.
Procter & Gamble Co., Cincinnati, Ohio

Quaker Oats Company, Chicago, Ill.

Ralston Purina Company, St. Louis, Mo.
Revere Sugar Refinery, Charlestown, Mass.

A. E. Staley Mfg. Co., Decatur, Ill.
Standard Brands, Inc., New York, N.Y.
Supermarkets General Corp., Woodbridge, N.J.
Swift Edible Oil Company, Chicago, Ill.
Swift & Company, Chicago, Ill.

Touche, Ross, Bailey and Smart, New York, N.Y.

U.S. Department of Agriculture, Washington, D.C.

Wilson & Co., Inc., Chicago, Ill.
Winnipeg Grain Exchange, Winnipeg, Manitoba

GLOSSARY

THE following definitions are drawn from a variety of sources and in some cases represent the author's own interpretations.

ACTUALS — The physical commodities, as distinguished especially from futures contracts. See CASH COMMODITY.

ANALOGOUS PART — The holder of a cash commodity or commitment can express the specifications for that commitment in two parts: one, the "analogous part" which corresponds precisely to the set of specifications (including the storage and delivery service) of a designated futures contract, and the other part representing all of the "residual components" by which his own commodity deviates from that specification (including premiums or discount factors resulting from quality, location, availability or even processing required to meet the futures contract specifications). The ANALOGOUS PART (a) and the "residual components" (b) are expressed in terms of itemized specifications or attributes.

> NOTE: For actual trading purposes the trader usually has a simple dollar-per-unit summary figure, HIS BASIS, which includes not only the price differences between the futures and the cash market quotations for an identical specification (i.e., "analogous part"), but also the price reflections resulting from all specification differences between the futures and the cash transaction actually entered. It is the comparison between (1) the personal appraisal or valuation of these residual components, and (2) the simple price spread in the market (that is, by subtracting the futures price of the short hedge from the long cash commitment price), that can guide the basis trader in deciding the commercial attractiveness of a particular hedged trade (see Chapter II, pp. 51–69).

ARBITRAGE — Simultaneous purchase of cash commodities or futures in one market against the sale of cash commodities or futures in the same or a different market to profit from a discrepancy in prices. Also includes some aspects of hedging. See SPREAD.

BASIS — The difference between the price of an "actual" and a futures contract. The variety of meanings of "basis" is discussed in Chapter II, pp. 64–69, including THE BASIS, MY (YOUR, HIS) BASIS, MY OPPORTUNITY, or CLOSE OUT BASIS.

BASIS GRADE — Standard contract grade or grades, designated by an Exchange, on which contract deliveries are based. Alternative grades may be designated at price differentials as defined by an Exchange. See PAR-DELIVERY SPECIFICATION.

BUYER'S CALL — Purchase of a specified quantity of a specific grade of a commodity at a fixed number of points above or below a specified future, with the buyer being allowed a certain period of time within which to fix the price by either purchasing a future for the account of the seller, or indicating to the seller when he wishes to fix the price. See PRICE-TO-BE-FIXED.

BUYING HEDGE — Buying futures to hedge a firm or intended cash sales commitment. See HEDGING.

CARRYING CHARGE — The expense, such as storage charges, insurance, interest charge, and other incidental costs involved in ownership of stored physical commodities over a period of time. May be reflected in futures contracts by successively higher prices for each succeeding future in so-called "normal carrying-charge markets."

CASH AND CARRY — Taking delivery of the actual commodity in warehouse and hedging it by selling higher quoted futures contracts. For a storable commodity it is possible to keep switching the hedge forward until premium disappears.

CASH COMMODITY — Actual physical commodities as distinguished from futures contracts.

CASH MARKET — Any market where trading in a cash commodity occurs.

CASH POSITION, or Net Cash Position — This represents the net commitments in the cash market without taking into account commodity futures commitments (cf. NET POSITION).

CEA — The Commodity Exchange Authority.

CERTIFICATED STOCKS — Quantities of commodities designated and certificated for delivery by an exchange under its grading and testing regulations at delivery points and/or warehouses specified and approved by the exchange.

CLEARING HOUSE OR ASSOCIATION — A central agency (generally a separate corporation) set up or authorized by an exchange through which transactions of members of the exchange are cleared and financial settlements effected. The Clearing House declares a clearing or settlement price at the close of each trading day. Each clearing member then receives or pays, depending on his net position, a sum equal to the net sum of all price changes which have occurred that day on his open position. Without the Clearing House operation, the substitution of contracting parties one for another would be impracticable.

CLEARING MEMBER — An exchange member who is also a member of the Clearing House or association of such exchange and entitled to clear the trades in his own name.

CLEARING PRICE — See SETTLEMENT PRICE.

CONTRACT — (1) The bilateral obligations of buyer and seller in a transaction. More precisely, the contract becomes a commitment between each party and the Clearing House.

(2) A unit of the commodity being traded. Orders must also specify the number of bushels or other quantity units to be bought and sold.

CONTRACT GRADES — The grades of a commodity listed in the rules of an exchange as those that can be used to deliver against a futures contract, including a scale of premiums and discounts. See PAR-DELIVERY SPECIFICATION.

CONTROLLED COMMODITIES — More properly "regulated commodities." Those commodities named in the Commodity Exchange Act over which the Commodity Exchange Authority has regulatory supervision for the broad purpose of seeing that commodity futures trading is conducted in the public interest. The term has nothing to do with the control of prices.

COVER — (1) The cancellation of a short position in any future by the purchase of an equal quantity of the same future. See LIQUIDATION.

(2) The use of futures contracts to offset firm or intended commitments in the cash commodity.

CROSS-HEDGING — A futures position in a commodity other than (but considered to be related to) the commodity being hedged. Selling soybean oil futures against soybean inventories is an example of a cross hedge. Cross-hedging between various feed grains is also possible.

CROSSING AGAINST ACTUALS — When a commodity covered by a short futures hedge is sold, it is possible, under the rules of most exchanges, to transfer to the buyer not only the commodity itself, but also the short futures position covering the commodity.

The transfer of the short futures position from seller to buyer is called "crossing against actuals."

DELIVERABLE GRADES — See CONTRACT GRADES.

DELIVERY MONTH — The calendar month during which a futures contract matures.

DELIVERY NOTICE — The notification of intent to deliver the actual commodity in accordance with a futures contract, issued by the seller of the future to the Clearing House.

DELIVERY POINTS — Those locations designated by commodity exchanges at which a commodity covered by a futures contract may be delivered in fulfillment of the contract.

DELIVERY PRICE — The settlement price fixed by the Clearing House at which deliveries on futures are to be executed, assuming par delivery specifications are met.

DIFFERENTIALS — (1) The discounts or premiums applicable when specifications and delivery points differ from par delivery terms of a futures contract. The rules of many exchanges prescribe the scale of differentials which must be allowed.

(2) In some commodity markets, the term "differential" is commonly used as a synonym for "basis." See BASIS.

EQUITY — The current asset balance ("receivable from broker") in a futures trading account with all open contracts posted at the going prices of the markets involved.

FORMULA PRICE — A price not initially determined, but one which is to be based in a specified way on information which will become known in the future, such as a commodity futures price at some later date, a government price report, a season's average price, etc.

FREE SUPPLY — The quantity of a commodity available for immediate sale.

FULL CARRYING CHARGE — (1) In market parlance, the cost involved in owning storable cash commodities over a period of time; includes storage, insurance and interest charges on borrowed working capital.

(2) In futures, the cost, including all charges, of taking actual delivery in a given month, storing the commodity and redelivering against a later delivery month contract.

FUTURES CONTRACT — See discussion, Chapter II, pp. 27–31. A

"future" (singular) means the contract for a particular delivery month.

FUTURES MARKET — A market organized for the trading of futures contracts.

HEDGING — The word "hedging" is used in such a variety of ways that a simple inclusive definition is difficult to develop. Appendix A focuses on the use of the word hedging by two government authorities, the Commodity Exchange Act and the Internal Revenue Code. Both documents use the word in connection with futures markets. Since hedging is broadly used by economists to cover the concept of executing offsetting commitments of any kind for purposes of reducing risks, neither of the above documents is broad enough to be considered inclusive. We have accepted "hedging" in its broad, if imprecise, usage as including nearly all commercial uses of futures markets. (See index for numerous references under "Hedging, definition problems.")

INITIAL MARGIN — See MARGIN.

INVERTED MARKET — A price structure, existing at a given point in time, in which the prices of futures contracts are lower for delivery dates progressively more distant into the future. This may occur because of an immediate need for the commodity, because of the anticipation of new supplies being made available in the future, or a variety of other reasons.

IRS — United States Internal Revenue Service.

LIQUIDATION — The cancellation of a long position in any future by the sale of an equal quantity of the same future. See COVER.

LONG — (1) The buying side of an open futures contract.

(2) A trader or firm whose net position shows an excess of purchases over sales. See NET POSITION.

LONG THE BASIS — This is said of one who has bought cash or spot goods and has hedged them with sales of the futures. He has therefore bought in the cash market at a certain basis, or differential, above or below the futures and hopes that when he sells the cash commodity, this basis will have moved in his favor, yielding a "basis profit." See HEDGING. Also, refer to Note on BASIS, Chapter II, pp. 64–69.

MAINTENANCE MARGIN — See MARGIN.

MARGIN — The amount of money or collateral deposited by a client with his broker, or by a broker with the Clearing House, for the purpose of insuring the broker or Clearing House against loss on open futures contracts. The margin is not a part payment on a purchase.

(1) Initial margin is the total amount of margin per contract required by the broker when a futures position is opened, and will be the same regardless of whether a long or short position is assumed.

(2) Maintenance margin is a sum, usually smaller than, but a part of, the original margin, which must be maintained on deposit at all times. If a customer's equity (see EQUITY) in any futures position drops to or under the maintenance margin level because of adverse price action, the broker must issue a margin call for the amount of money required to restore the customer's equity in the account to the initial margin level. This is compulsory under exchange rules in most cases. See Chapter II, footnote 3, p. 28.

MINIMUM FLUCTUATION — The minimum unit (in quoted points or fractions) by which futures prices may change. Often expressed also in terms of dollars and cents per contract.

NET POSITION — (1) For the individual or firm, net position is the difference at any given time between: (a) owned inventory of a commodity either in raw, semi-, or finished form and firm-price purchase obligations for the commodity including long futures contracts held, and (b) firm-price sales obligations for the same commodity including short futures contracts held. In both (a) and (b) the commodity must be expressed in the same physical units, i.e., bushels, bags, pounds, etc. Net position expresses the volume of the commodity which is at risk in terms of price level changes. See discussion, Chapter III, pp. 77–80.

(2) For an industry as a whole, see discussion, Chapter I, pp. 14–24.

OPEN CONTRACTS — Contracts in the futures market which have been bought or sold without the transaction having been completed by subsequent sale or re-purchase, or actual delivery or receipt of commodity. In any futures market, at any given time, the number of futures contracts bought by all customers exactly equals the number sold by the same or other customers. Thus, published figures representing OPEN INTEREST always mean either the total of LONG contracts or the total number of SHORT contracts, never the sum of the two.

ORIGINAL MARGIN — Same as initial margin. See MARGIN.

PAR-DELIVERY SPECIFICATION — The bench-mark grade, deliverable without a premium or discount. Futures price quotations relate to this particular set of specifications. See CONTRACT GRADES, BASIS GRADE.

POINT — The unit in which changes in futures prices are quoted in trading and market reports.

PRICE LIMIT — The maximum fluctuation in price of a futures contract permitted during one trading session, as fixed by the rules of an Exchange. See Chapter II, footnote 4, pp. 29–30.

PRICE-TO-BE-FIXED — Term applied to a purchase or sale agreement whereby the exact price of a commodity is to be based on a specific number of points over or under a specified futures contract price. See BUYER'S CALL and SELLER'S CALL.

ROLL FORWARD — Shifting a futures market position forward (from one delivery month to a later one) as, for instance, by buying back the futures contract that protects your cash position (i.e., inventory) and simultaneously selling another futures contract for a later delivery month. Rolling *backward* involves the *opposite* transaction, and moves the delivery month nearer.

SELLER'S CALL — The same as BUYER'S CALL with the difference that the seller has the right of determining the time to fix the price. See PRICE-TO-BE-FIXED.

SETTLEMENT PRICE — The daily price at which the Clearing House clears or updates all the day's open contracts; also a price which may be established by the Exchange to settle contracts unliquidated because of Acts of God, strikes, war, floods, market congestion, or other such causes. See DELIVERY PRICE.

SHORT — (1) The selling side of an open futures contract.

(2) A trader or firm whose net position shows an excess of sales over purchases. See NET POSITION.

SHORT THE BASIS — A person or firm who has sold the cash commodity which he does not then own but which sale he has hedged with a purchase of futures is said to be short the basis. In all likelihood he has sold the commodity at a certain "basis" but expects to buy the commodity later for delivery to his customer at a more favorable "basis." His long hedge in futures is expected to protect him against any adverse price changes in the meantime.

SPECULATION — (1) In the context of commodity futures trading, the buying or selling of futures contracts for the purpose of making a profit from price moves of the futures alone, without respect to commitments in the cash commodity.

(2) Any price-risk exposure not matched as a hedge. See TEXAS HEDGE.

SPOT COMMODITY — The actual or cash commodity (as distinguished from futures) available for immediate delivery. See TO ARRIVE.

SPOT PRICE — The price at which a physical commodity is selling at a given time and place for immediate delivery.

SPREAD (or) STRADDLE — These terms mean the same thing, but in practice the grain trade uses the term "spread" whereas other commodity interests use the term "straddle." A spread may be defined as the purchase of one future against the sale of another future of the same commodity or a different commodity in the same or different markets. CEA defines spreading only in terms of the same commodity, whereas exchanges define it to include different but related commodities. See ARBITRAGE.

STRADDLE — See SPREAD.

SWITCH — See ROLL FORWARD.

TENDER — Notice of intention to deliver, transmitted through the Clearing House to a selected holder of a long position. See DELIVERY NOTICE.

TEXAS HEDGE — A commitment in commodity futures which, either consciously or inadvertently, increases rather than decreases exposure to the impacts of price changes. See SPECULATION.

TO ARRIVE — A cash transaction (usually referring to a purchase) contracted at a firm price but not yet delivered.

BIBLIOGRAPHY

American Institute of Accountants, Special Committee on Inventories, "Valuation of Inventories," *Journal of Accountancy*, August 1936, pp. 122–132.

Arthur, Henry B., "Economic Risk, Uncertainty and the Futures Market," in *Futures Trading Seminar, Vol. III*. Madison, Wisc.: Mimir Publishers, Inc., 1966.

———. "Impact of Agricultural Programs upon Market Structures and Functions," in *Futures Trading Seminar, Vol. II*. Madison, Wisc.: Mimir Publishers, Inc., 1963.

———. "Inventory Profits in the Business Cycle," *American Economic Review*, Vol. XXVIII, No. 1, March 1938.

———. "Something Businesses Can Do About Depressions," *The Journal of Accountancy*, Vol. LXVII, No. 1, January 1939.

———, James P. Houck, and George L. Beckford, *Tropical Agribusiness Structures and Adjustments — Bananas*. Boston: Division of Research, Harvard University Graduate School of Business Administration, 1968.

American Institute of Certified Public Accountants, *Case Studies in Auditing Procedure — A Grain Company*, New York, 1949.

Bailey, Fred, Jr., "What Every Banker Should Know About Commodity Futures Markets," reprint of the following articles from *Banking*:

"What a Futures Market Is and How It Works," October 1967.

"Hedging for Country Grain Elevators," November 1967.

"How Farmers Can Use the Futures Market," December 1967.

"The Cattle Feeder and the Futures Market," January 1968.

Bakken, Henry H., remarks concerning "Adaptation of Futures Trading to Live Cattle," *Proceedings of the Live Cattle Futures Study Conference*, Public Relations Committee, Chicago Mercantile Exchange, mimeo, September 8, 1966.

Barclay's Bank, *Overseas Survey, 1966*, William Lea & Co. Ltd., London, 1966.

"Base Stock Inventories and Federal Income Taxation" (under legislation), *Harvard Law Review*, Vol. 51, No. 8, June 1938.

Belveal, L. Dee, *Commodity Speculation With Profits in Mind.* Wil-
mette, Illinois: Commodity Press, 1967.

Board of Trade of the City of Chicago, *Commodity Trading Manual,*
1966.

————, *Training Manual,* mimeo., undated.

Board of Trade Clearing Corporation, *Party to Every Trade,* Chicago,
undated.

Briloff, A. J., "Income Tax Aspects of Commodity Futures Transactions," in *Guide to Commodity Price Forecasting,* Henry
Jiler, editor. New York: Commodity Research Bureau, 1965.

Central Soya Company, Inc., Case No. AI 268R. Boston: Harvard
Business School, 1968.

Chandler, George T., "Hedging Cattle Works for Us," *Bank News,*
Kansas City, Mo., January 15, 1967, pp. 25–26.

"Cocoa Futures Leave a Bitter Taste," *Business Week,* No. 2143,
September 26, 1970.

Cocoa Statistics. London, England: Gill and Duffus Limited, October 1968.

Cootner, Paul H., "Common Elements in Futures Markets for Commodities and Bonds," *American Economic Review,* Vol. 51, No.
2, May 1961.

————, "Returns to Speculators: Telser versus Keynes," *Journal of
Political Economy,* Vol. 68, No. 4, August 1960.

Ehrich, R. L., "Development of Livestock and Meat Futures," *Livestock and Meat Futures Study Conference,* Chicago Mercantile
Exchange, November 30, 1966.

Elliott, V. L., "Inventory Valuation and Profits," *Executive Service
Bulletin,* Metropolitan Life Insurance Company, November
1935.

Emrich, C. O., remarks concerning "Financing and Risk Transfer
Through Livestock and Meat Futures," *Livestock and Meat Futures Study Conference,* Chicago Mercantile Exchange, November 30, 1966.

Fiske, Wyman P., "Inventory Reserve Plans," *National Association
of Cost Accountants Bulletin,* July 15, 1938.

Food and Agriculture Organization of the United Nations, Committee on Commodity Problems, Study Group on Cocoa, *Committee on Statistics Report of the Twenty-Sixth Session, Rome,
April 6–7, 1970.* Rome: FAO, CCP:ST 31, 8 May 1970.

Food Research Institute, Stanford University, *Proceedings of a Symposium on Price Effects of Speculation in Organized Commodity*

Markets, Food Research Institute Studies, Supplement to Vol. VII, 1967.

Foote, R. J., "Changing Role of the Futures Markets as Viewed by a Commercial User and Price Analyst," paper given at Annual Meeting of American Agricultural Economics Association, University of Missouri, August 11, 1970.

Geiger, H. Dwight, "The Grain Futures and Cash Markets (and Some of Their Accounting Implications)," *The Arthur Young Journal,* Winter 1969.

Gill and Duffus Ltd., "Cocoa Market Report," London: December 15, 1958.

————, "Cocoa Statistics." London: October 1968.

Gold, Gerald, *Modern Commodity Futures Trading.* New York: Commodity Research Bureau, Inc. (1961 edition).

Goldberg, Ray A., *Agribusiness Coordination: A Systems Approach to the Wheat, Soybean, and Florida Orange Economies.* Division of Research, Harvard University, Graduate School of Business Administration, Boston, 1968.

Goldfein, Lawrence, and Lester Hochberg, "Use of Commodity Straddles Can Effect Impressive Tax Savings," *The Journal of Taxation,* Vol. 29, No. 6, December 1968.

Grain and Feed Dealers National Association, *Management Accounting Manual,* Washington, 1968.

Gray, Roger W., "The Characteristic Bias in Some Thin Futures Markets," *Food Research Institute Studies,* Vol. 1, No. 1, November, 1960.

Green, Leslie, "Understanding the Frozen Orange Juice Market," in *Commodity Year Book 1968,* Harry Jiler, editor. New York: Commodity Research Bureau, 1968.

Gunnelson, J. A., "A Study of the Impact of Organizational Changes in Agricultural Commodity Markets on Futures Markets," Purdue University (unpublished thesis), January 1970.

Haverkamp, L. J., "Potential Developments in Futures Markets of Significance to Agriculture and Related Industries," paper given at Annual Meeting of American Agricultural Economics Association, University of Missouri, August 11, 1970.

Hayden, Stone Inc., "Commodity Trading Has Numerous Advantages Over Trading in Stocks," *Commodity Commentary,* February 2, 1970.

Heinold, Harold J., remarks concerning "Financing and Risk Transfer Through Livestock and Meat Futures," *Proceedings of the Live-*

stock and Meat Futures Study Conference, Chicago Mercantile
Exchange, November 30, 1966.

Heironymus, T. A., *Uses of Grain Futures Markets in the Farm Business.* University of Illinois Agricultural Experiment Station Bulletin 696, Urbana, Illinois, September 1963.

Hershey Foods Corporation Annual Report, 1969.

Hicks, J. R., *Value and Capital.* Oxford, England: Clarendon Press,
2nd edition, 1946.

Houthakker, H. S., "Can Speculators Forecast Prices?" *The Review of
Economics and Statistics,* Vol. 39, No. 2, May 1957.

———, *Economic Policy for the Farm Sector.* Washington: American
Enterprise Institute for Public Policy Research, November 1967.

———, "Systematic and Random Elements in Short-term Price Movements," *American Economic Review,* Vol. 51, No. 2, May 1961.

*Kern County Land Company (Inventory Management in Large-Scale
Cattle Operations),* Case No. AI 208, mimeo. Boston: Harvard
Business School, 1962.

Keynes, J. M., *A Treatise on Money.* New York: Harcourt, Brace
and Company, 1930.

Knight, Frank H., *Risk, Uncertainty and Profit.* Houghton Mifflin Co.,
1921 [1957].

Krug, C. A., and E. Quartey-Papafio, *World Cocoa Survey.* Rome:
Food and Agriculture Organization of the United Nations, 1964.

Kuznets, Simon, "Changing Inventory Valuations and Their Effect on
Business Savings and National Income Produced," *Studies in
Income and Wealth, Vol. I.* New York: National Bureau of Eco-
nomic Research, 1937.

Logue, Robert P., "Matching Costs with Revenues in the Flour Milling
Industry," *The Accounting Review,* Vol. XVI, No. 2, June 1941.

Management Accounting Manual. Washington: Grain and Feed Dealers National Association, 1968.

Merrill Lynch, Pierce, Fenner & Smith, Inc., "Hedge Guide to
Citrus Growers," New York: Commodity Division, undated.

Monfort, Kenneth, "A Cattle Feeder Views Futures," *Proceedings of
the Livestock and Meat Futures Study Conference,* Chicago Mercantile Exchange, November 30, 1966.

Monfort of Colorado, Inc., Underwriter's Prospectus, January 22,
1970.

Moore, Allan Q., "Hedging Commodities in International Trade,"
paper delivered at International Commodities Conference, New
York, September 30, 1970.

National Commission on Food Marketing, Technical Study No. 5, *Organization and Competition in the Milling and Baking Industries,* Washington, 1966.

New York Cocoa Exchange, Inc., *Understanding the Cocoa Market.* New York: Commodity Research Bureau Publications Corporation, 1968.

Nickerson, Clarence B., "Inventory Reserves as an Element of Inventory Policy." *The Accounting Review,* Vol. XII, No. 4, December 1937.

————, "Inventory Valuation—The Use of Price Adjustments Accounts to Segregate Inventory Losses and Gains," *National Association of Cost Accountants Bulletin,* Sec. 1, October 1, 1937.

Paul, Allen B., "The Pricing of Binspace — A Contribution to the Theory of Storage," *American Journal of Agricultural Economics,* Vol. 52, No. 1, February 1970, p. 1.

Peloubet, Maurice E., "Problems of Present-Day Inventory Valuation," *National Association of Cost Accountants Bulletin,* Sec. 1, March 1, 1937.

Petro-Lewis Corporation, *Corporate Profile,* Denver, July 1970.

Putnam, G. E., "The Role of Paper Profits in Industry," *Harvard Business Review,* Vol. IV, No. 2, January 1926.

————, "What Shall We Do About Depressions?" *Journal of Business,* Vol. XI, No. 2, April 1938.

Raclin, Robert L., "Futures Market in Soybeans and Their Products," speech delivered at the Congress of the International Association of Seed Crushers in Amsterdam, the Netherlands, June 3–7, 1963.

Rowley, C. S., Jr., "Inventory Pricing in the Grain Industry: A Study of Current Practice," University of Wisconsin (unpublished thesis), 1970.

Schonberg, James S., *The Grain Trade: How It Works.* New York: Exposition Press, 1956.

Shishko, Irwin, "How To Forecast Cocoa Prices," in *Guide to Commodity Price Forecasting,* Harry Jiler, editor. New York, Commodity Research Bureau, 1965.

Stout, Thomas T., Murray H. Hawkins, and Bruce W. Marion, "Meat Procurement and Distribution by Ohio Grocery Chains and Affiliated Wholesalers," *Research Bulletin 1014,* Ohio Agricultural Research Development Center, Wooster, October 1968.

Swift & Company, 50th Anniversary Year Book, Covering Activities for the Year 1934.

Technical Note on Commodity Hedging, ICH 13G233 AI 269R. Boston: Harvard Business School, 1968.

Telser, Lester G., "Futures Trading and the Storage of Cotton and Wheat," *The Journal of Political Economy*, Vol. 66, No. 3, June 1958.

Tomek, W. G., and Roger W. Gray, "Temporal Relationships Among Prices on Commodity Futures Markets: Their Allocative and Stabilizing Roles," *American Journal of Agricultural Economics*, Vol. 52, No. 3, August 1970.

Understanding the Cocoa Market, New York Cocoa Exchange, Inc. New York: Commodity Research Bureau Publications Corporation, 1968.

"U.S. Internal Revenue Code of 1954," *Standard Federal Tax Reporter, Code Volume*. New York, Chicago, and Washington: Commerce Clearing House, Inc., 1969.

"Users of Livestock Futures Markets," University of Illinois, Department of Agricultural Economics, Agricultural Experiment Station, AERR 94, October 1968.

U.S. Department of Agriculture
  Commodity Exchange Authority
    Commitments of Traders in Commodity Futures, Cotton — Frozen Concentrated Orange Juice — Potatoes — Wool, monthly, New York Regional Office.
    Commodity Exchange Act As Amended, revised February 1970.
    Commodity Futures Statistics, July 1969–June 1970, Statistical Bulletin No. 464, March 1971.
    Trading in Live Beef Cattle Futures, May 1970.
    Trading in Wheat Futures, May–November 1967, March 1968.
  Economic Research Service
    Agricultural Markets in Change, Agricultural Economic Report No. 95, July 1966.
    Fats and Oils Situation, FOS 254, January 1970.
    Livestock and Meat Situation, LMS 174, August 1970.
    Wheat Situation, National Agricultural Conference, Washington, February 16–19, 1970, WS 211, February 1970.
  Foreign Agricultural Service, *Foreign Agriculture Circular*, "Fats, Oils, and Oilseeds," FFO 6–70, July 1970.

Venkataramanan, L. S., *The Theory of Futures Trading*. New York: Asian Publishing House, 1965.

Walker, Ross G., "Income Accounting and the Base-Stock Inventory," *Credit and Financial Management*, May and June 1938.

————, "Some Financial Questions in Inventory Valuation," in *National Association of Cost Accountants Year Book,* 1936.

————, "The Base-Stock Principle in Income Accounting," *Harvard Business Review,* Vol. XII, 1936.

Weymar, F. H., *The Dynamics of the World Cocoa Market.* Cambridge: The M.I.T. Press, 1968.

Working, Holbrook, "Futures Trading and Hedging," *American Economic Review,* Vol. XLIII, No. 3, June 1953.

————, "Hedging Reconsidered," *Journal of Farm Economics,* Vol. 35, November 1953.

————, "New Concepts Concerning Futures Markets and Prices," *American Economic Review,* Vol. 51, No. 2, May 1961.

Index